War, Capital, and the Dutch State
(1588–1795)

Historical Materialism Book Series

The Historical Materialism Book Series is a major publishing initiative of the radical left. The capitalist crisis of the twenty-first century has been met by a resurgence of interest in critical Marxist theory. At the same time, the publishing institutions committed to Marxism have contracted markedly since the high point of the 1970s. The Historical Materialism Book Series is dedicated to addressing this situation by making available important works of Marxist theory. The aim of the series is to publish important theoretical contributions as the basis for vigorous intellectual debate and exchange on the left.

The peer-reviewed series publishes original monographs, translated texts, and reprints of classics across the bounds of academic disciplinary agendas and across the divisions of the left. The series is particularly concerned to encourage the internationalization of Marxist debate and aims to translate significant studies from beyond the English-speaking world.

For a full list of titles in the Historical Materialism Book Series
available in paperback from Haymarket Books, visit:
www.haymarketbooks.org/category/hm-series

War, Capital, and the Dutch State (1588–1795)

by
Pepijn Brandon

Haymarket Books
Chicago, IL

First published in 2015 by Brill Academic Publishers, The Netherlands
© 2015 Koninklijke Brill NV, Leiden, The Netherlands

Published in paperback in 2016 by
Haymarket Books
P.O. Box 180165
Chicago, IL 60618
773-583-7884
www.haymarketbooks.org

ISBN: 978-1-60846-691-7

Trade distribution:
In the US, Consortium Book Sales, www.cbsd.com
In Canada, Publishers Group Canada, www.pgcbooks.ca
In the UK, Turnaround Publisher Services, www.turnaround-uk.com
In all other countries, Publishers Group Worldwide, www.pgw.com

Cover design by Jamie Kerry of Belle Étoile Studios and Ragina Johnson.

This book was published with the generous support of Lannan Foundation
and the Wallace Action Fund.

Printed in Canada by union labor.

10 9 8 7 6 5 4 3 2 1

Library of Congress Cataloging-in-Publication data is available.

For my great-grandfather
Herman (Hersch) Ohringer (1899–1995)

a lifelong courageous fighter
who refused to go into the trenches
for someone else's war

:.

In 't midden van den twist, en 't woeden nimmer moê,
Verheft uw stad haar kroon tot aan den hemel toe,
En gaat door vuur en ijs eene andre wereld vinden,
En dondert met geschut op alle vier de winden.

(In the midst of all strife, never tired of raging,
Your city [Amsterdam] heaves its crown unto the very heavens,
And goes through fire and ice to find another world,
Guns thundering in all four directions of the wind.)

JOOST VAN DEN VONDEL, Gijsbrecht van Aemstel (1637) Act 5.8

• • •

Then every thing includes itself in power,
Power into will, will into appetite,
And appetite (an universal wolf,
So doubly seconded with will, and power)
Must make perforce and universal prey,
And last, eat up himself.

WILLIAM SHAKESPEARE, Troylus and Cressida (1609) Act 1.3

• • •

And I hope that you die and your death'll come soon
I will follow your casket in the pale afternoon
And I'll watch while you're lowered down to your deathbed
And I'll stand o'er your grave 'til I'm sure that you're dead.

BOB DYLAN, Masters of War (1963)

•••

Contents

List of Charts and Tables

Translations of Frequently Used Dutch Terms

Admiraal-generaal	Admiral general
Admiraliteitscollege	Admiralty Board
Bewindhebber (van de VOC, WIC)	Director
Burgemeester	Burgomaster
Commies	Clerk
Convooien en licenten	Customs
Directie (van de Levantse handel, etc)	Directorate
Equipagemeester	Master of Equipment
Advocaat-fiscaal	Fiscal advocate
Gecommitteerde Raden	(Members of) Provincial Government
Generaliteit	Generalty
Gouverneur-generaal	Governor general
Kapitein-generaal	Captain general
Last en veilgeld	Extraordinary customs
Ontvanger-generaal	Receiver general
Raad van State	Council of State
Raadspensionaris	Grand pensionary
Rekenkamer	Audit Office
Schepen	Alderman
Stadhouder	Stadtholder
Staten (van Holland, Zeeland, etc.)	Provincial States
Staten Generaal	States General
Vroedschap	Magistrate

Note on Currency

The main currency used in the Dutch Republic was the guilder (f). One guilder was divided in 20 *stuyvers* (st) or 240 *penningen* or *deniers* (d). In this study, for larger amounts sums have been rounded off to guilders, or otherwise to round decimals of a guilder. In the Province of Zeeland, the main currency used was the Flemish pound. One Flemish pound exchanged for 6 guilders.

Acknowledgements

Like the Duke of York in *Henry VI*, in order to 'pry into the secrets of the state' one has to 'wake when others be asleep'. Nevertheless, there were many times when writing this book truly was a collective engagement. The number of people who assisted me with their critical remarks and observations, searching questions, or inspiring example is too large to sum up. Let me therefore simply state here that I found myself lucky to be part of a community of kindred spirits, inside the academy and outside. Most of all, I was pleasantly surprised by the number of my activist friends who, while fully emerged in the daily chore of fighting the powers that be, understood the merits of spending years researching the powers that were. Many of them were even willing to consider this part of a common endeavour to throw light on present conditions, and I hope this book will not disappoint them in that respect.

However, there are some people who need to be mentioned by name. First and foremost among those is Marjolein 't Hart. As my daily supervisor in writing the dissertation that was then, with only minor adjustments, turned into this book, she accompanied me at every step of my research. The end result has been incomparably better for this than it would have been without her theoretical insight, her advice – on the text itself as well as on how to survive writing – and, on very rare occasions, her active disagreement. Leo Noordegraaf, my principal supervisor, could not be actively involved in this process, but I am grateful for his presence at a distance. I hope I managed at least in part to do justice to his adage of steering 'between positivism and hermeneutics'. Marcel van der Linden was kind enough to step in at the last moment to act as the second principal supervisor, after making many useful suggestions along the way. I was more than happy to re-encounter Marti Huetink of Brill when first starting to think of this project as a book-to-be. His enthusiasm as well as that of his colleagues at Brill who skillfully worked on the production of this volume has been encouraging throughout. Sebastian Budgen, Peter Thomas, David Broder, and Danny Hayward of the HM team have from early on shown great trust, and have continued to be very supportive throughout the book's rather long period of gestation.

I embarked on this journey as part of a Flemish-Dutch research group, funded by NWO and FWO. The result of this project has been two dissertations, an international conference, various articles, and a collective volume published by Brill. Thomas Goossens, Griet Vermeesch, and Jeffrey Fynn-Paul have provided the perfect research team. During the process of writing, I could also profit from participation in various inspiring communities of working historians: the

Posthumus Graduate School, Henk van Nierop's 'Aio-club' for PhD researchers working on the 'Golden Age' at the UvA, the reading group for critical history hosted by Marcel van der Linden, and the international Contractor State Group. Thanks to financial contributions from the Dutch Council for Scientific Research (NWO) and the Bendikson Fund, I was able to spend two short periods of research and writing at the Huntington Library in San Marino, California. As a Bendikson Fellow I had to divide my time between finishing this book and starting my follow-up research. My stay in San Marino in the summer of 2012 provided me with the ideal context for making the transition between the two. Steve Hindle, Juan Gomez, Carolyn Powell, and Jaeda Snow of the Huntington Library helped to make this stay productive. Apart from the scientific results, this was also a highly pleasant period, and no one has to be thanked for this more than Eli, Mollie, and Jack, an intellectual dog if ever you could find one.

Karwan Fatah-Black and Matthias van Rossum started writing their PhDs approximately at the same time as me, and from the outset found themselves in equally rotten conditions. We overcame our sorrows in hours of nightly discussions, occasional rants at the injustices of this most ghastly of all tasks, and conspicuous consumption of alcohol. Their camaraderie pulled me through more than one moment of mild despair. So did the unconditional support of Maina van der Zwan, who read and commented on the entire manuscript, but most of all proved to be the truest of friends throughout. I could not have finished this project without his encouragement and help. Apart from anything else, my parents Desi and Sander and my grandparents Mirjam, Maup, and Floor from my earliest age have created an environment that regarded learning as the pinnacle of self-improvement, while teaching me that knowledge is only useful if it is geared towards improving society. The thanks I owe them for this cannot be summed up in such a text, but I hope they accept the book itself as a small show of gratitude.

Visits to the archive are seldom life-changing, let alone visits by others. But that one visit made by Willemijn Wilgenhof on a beautiful summer's day in April 2011 was. Ever since, she has been my love, my muse, my coach, my editor, my sparring partner, and my greatest joy. In a very real sense, this book is the result of her labours as well as mine.

Introduction

In his 2010 novel *The Thousand Autumns of Jacob de Zoet*, David Mitchell captures the interaction between two societies, both seemingly suspended outside time but on the brink of being overtaken by modernity.[1] The year is 1799, the location Deshima, the small artificial island in the Nagasaki Bay that served as the single point of entry for European traders into Edo Japan. Since the 1640s it was controlled by the Dutch East India Company (*Vereenigde Oostindische Compagnie* or VOC), both for running the profitable Japanese copper trade and for representing the Dutch state at the Japanese court. The VOC servants that figure in Mitchell's novel still fulfil this classical double role of merchants and diplomats, agents of a Company that in Asia functioned as a state in its own right, and in the Dutch Republic as a state within a state. But they do so under conditions of desperate uncertainty. The Company they worked for has been nationalised in 1796 by a single decree of the revolutionary National Assembly now ruling the newly established 'Batavian Republic'. Their mode of operation is rapidly becoming obsolete, a remnant of the times in which states left substantial parts of their activities abroad to private or semi-private 'brokers' rather than their own bureaucrats. The arrival of a single British man-of-war reconnects the small community of Deshima with the global stream of time, forcing their self-enclosed world to come crashing down.

Deshima at the turn of the nineteenth century might have been the last refuge of the particular state form that characterised the Dutch Republic from its birth in 1588 to its demise in 1795. All early modern empires relied heavily on brokers like the VOC in the organisation of warfare – merchants, speculators, capitalists, all of whom ran important swathes of state activity on their own right and for a profit. Warfare on land was dominated by mercenary armies in which officers maintained a more or less independent position as directors of their own 'company economy', only integrated into the state's logistics through the intermediation of scores of private suppliers and financiers.[2] Warfare at sea was brought under state control at an earlier date, but still involved armed merchant-men, privateers, colonial companies, as well as far-reaching integration between naval bureaucracies and local economic elites.[3]

---

1 Mitchell 2010.
2 Redlich 1964 and 1965.
3 Bromley 1987 and Bruijn 2000.

Privatised warfare was the hallmark of capitalism in its infancy, putting into perspective the sprawl of private military contracting in our own age, symbolised by the ignominious Blackwater Inc.[4] Understanding its – always partial – subjugation to the operation of centralised, bureaucratic states is an important key to the major transformations of the relations between profit, power, and the use of arms that occurred over the half millennium of capitalism's existence as a formative element of the world-system.[5] In the Dutch Republic the independent involvement of entrepreneurs in the organisation of warfare reached extraordinary proportions, and remained a key characteristic of state organisation at a time when other European states made considerable headway in integrating these 'brokers' into processes of bureaucratic centralisation. Explaining the resilience of brokerage structures in warfare and the impact this had on the interaction between state formation and capitalist development during the 'Dutch cycle of accumulation' is the main aim of this book.

The fundamental proposition of the literature on early-modern state formation is Tilly's much cited aphorism that 'war makes states, and states make war'.[6] In his magisterial overview of this process *Coercion, Capital, and European States*, Tilly argues that while different societies followed divergent paths in their adaptation to the pressures of warfare, the overriding demands of European power-struggle forced these paths to converge into major transitions in the nature of the state. For Europe in the medieval and early modern periods, he singles out two key transformations. The first was the transformation from 'patrimonial states', in which rulers extracted the resources necessary for warfare as tribute or rent from their vassals and subjects, to 'brokerage states', which relied heavily on parcelling out the organisation of warfare to independent capitalists. Tilly situates this transition for the main power-contesters in Europe during the late middle ages around 1400. The second transition was that between the brokerage form of state organisation and nationalisation, a process that reached a tipping point roughly around 1700.[7]

The typology of states developed by Tilly was underwritten by the renewed popularity of the 'military revolution thesis'.[8] According to this thesis, the

---

4   Scahill 2007.

5   Wallerstein 1974, 1980, 1989, and 2011.

6   The expression is so well known that it almost attained a life of its own, but it was first introduced in Tilly 1975a, p. 42.

7   Tilly 1992, p. 29. Also see the powerful restatement of this idea of successive stages of state formation by Glete 2002, p. 56.

8   Michael Roberts first introduced the concept in his 1956 inaugural lecture 'The military revolution in Europe, 1560–1660', reproduced in Rogers 1995. Geoffrey Parker was the key

introduction of gun-powder, the growing importance of siege-warfare as a result of the development of the *trace italienne*, and the transformation of military discipline resulting from Maurits's and Gustav's army reforms changed the rules of the game for states in the organisation of warfare. This led to a redefinition of the very role of the state. Unable to rely on feudal levies to supply them with the kind of professional soldiers necessary to fight their wars, rulers became increasingly dependent on trained mercenaries. War to a large extent became 'monetarised'.[9] While disagreeing on important questions such as the prime causes of the changes in warfare, the chronology, and whether a long, drawn-out period of successive renewals can properly be described as a 'revolution' at all, military historians generally agree that the large-scale warfare that developed in the course of the seventeenth century could only be carried out by heavily centralised states.[10] But it is exactly this assumption that the case of the Dutch Republic challenges. Historians of the Dutch state are left with a riddle: how could a state that for all appearances was so unlike the ideal of a powerful state play such a central role in the early modern state system? Or, posed from the opposite end, why did sustained involvement in warfare not lead to a fundamental transformation in the Dutch state form?

Dutch War-Making and State-Making: Three Solutions to a Riddle

Violence and war were the perpetual condition of Dutch early modernity. 'Has there ever been an age', one political pamphleteer rhetorically asked in 1650, 'in which there were born greater alterations, perturbations, changes, ascendancies, downfalls, than in ours?'

> The great have become small, the small have become great. War has turned into peace for some, peace into war for others. Friends have become foes, and foes have become friends. All foundations have been dissolved, that which seemed impossible has become possible, what was

---

figure in the revival of Robert's thesis, presenting his own version of the concept in Parker 1988. Also see the other essays collected in Rogers 1995.

9   E.g., Lucassen and Zürcher 1998, and Meinhardt and Meumann forthcoming. Already in the *Grundrisse*, Marx noted that many of the essential categories of capitalism, including the dependence on wage labour, came to fruition earlier in the army than 'within bourgeois society' itself. Marx 1953, p. 29.

10   See the essays in Rogers 1995.

below has come out on top, and what was on top has sunk below, one lays to ruin the other, and these ruins remain ruins, sickness exists without cure, wounds without healing.[11]

The Republic itself was born from a long and ultimately victorious struggle against the Spanish Habsburg Empire.[12] During the seventeenth century it fought every major competing power in a 'war without end'.[13] In the nearly two centuries between 1600 and 1795, the Dutch Republic was at war for 52 years with Spain, 44 years with France, and 15 years with England. There were six decades of intermittent military confrontations with the Portuguese Empire starting at the beginning of the seventeenth century – mainly concentrated on the East Indies, the West-African coast and Brazil but occasionally spilling over into open warfare in Europe, including a naval blockade of Lisbon in 1657. Troops of the Republic intervened in the Thirty Years' War on a massive scale. During the 1650s the Dutch navy repeatedly operated as the decisive force in power struggles between Denmark and Sweden and appeared before Danzig to ensure Dutch supremacy in Baltic trade. In all, the Dutch Republic was directly involved in European great-power struggle for 74 years during the seventeenth century. The Dutch state of the eighteenth century was a warring state like that of the seventeenth, albeit at a lower level of direct engagement. At the mid-eighteenth century, it still maintained one of the largest armies and navies of Europe, and continued to rank among the leading global empires.[14] It counted 35 years of European warfare between 1700 and 1795 (28 when discounting the period of lukewarm engagement in the War of the Austrian Succession before the French invasion of 1747) – not that much less than the belligerent French state.[15] War was decisive for the international and financial position of the Dutch Republic at the start of the eighteenth century, and a crucial factor in internal political changes in 1618, 1650, 1672, 1747, the 1780s, and again in the 1790s. Alongside formal inter-state conflicts in the 'centre' of the world-system the Dutch engaged in almost continuous low-intensity warfare in the 'periphery', sometimes spilling over into

---

11   Teelinck 1650, p. 3. All translations from Dutch and other languages to English in the text and in footnotes are my own, unless quoted directly from an English-language edition.

12   't Hart 2014.

13   Prak 2005, pp. 27 ff.

14   Dunthorne 1986, p. 113.

15   Félix and Tallett 2009, p. 148 gives the number of 50 war years for France in the period 1672–1783, as against 40 for the Dutch Republic.

full scale war. On the island of Java alone the voc was engaged in twenty-one years of warfare accompanying three crises of succession during the first half of the eighteenth century. The Dutch engagement in trans-Atlantic slavery demanded permanent military support. Corsairs and pirates, merchant companies, and local rulers never ceased to fight each other over the spoils of the Dutch commercial empire. Yet the state underpinning these efforts was the exact opposite of centralised and bureaucratic. It was a federation of provinces, heavily dependent on the autonomous powers of its plethora of cities, a republic governed by its internally divided commercial elites. The civil servants at the national or 'generalty' (*generaliteits-*) level were outnumbered by those of Holland, the most prosperous province.[16] Seen from the military revolutions thesis or Tilly's account of the transition from brokerage to nationalisation, the Dutch Republic was an anomaly.

Roughly three solutions exist to the riddle of early modern Dutch power: one centred on the international balance of forces, a second on the economy, and a third – which will be followed in this book – on the social relations underpinning the state. The first of these, perhaps providing the easiest way out of the problem that the Dutch Republic poses to the standard story of European state formation, is to argue that it could only be successful by default. As Geoffrey Parker insisted, against the grain of most pre-1970s Dutch historiography, the rebellious provinces of the Netherlands could only emerge from their struggle against Europe's most powerful state of the day because they never received the undivided attention of the Spanish crown. Successive diversions of funds from warfare in the Netherlands to the – ultimately more important – Mediterranean engagements allowed the Dutch to regain strength at crucial turning points in the Revolt.[17] Similarly, the civil and religious wars that ripped apart France and England in the mid-seventeenth century provided the space in which a tiny state could emerge from the 1648 Peace of Westphalia as Europe's dominant nation. The shift of fates that sounded the death-knell for Dutch success according to this line of reasoning was inaugurated by the adoption of aggressively anti-Dutch Mercantilist policies by France and England in the 1650s and was fully consummated with the joint invasion by France, England, and the bishoprics of Munster and Cologne of the Dutch Republic in 1672. Once faced by the full might of its more centralised competitors, the federal Dutch Republic had to go under, even if it managed to hold out against the onslaught for a few more decades.

---

16   't Hart 1993a, p. 207.
17   Parker 1970 and Parker 1972.

But the argument that the Dutch Republic only managed to hold its adversaries at bay by default concedes too little to the actions of the Dutch state itself. First, although it is certainly true that the financial and political problems faced by its competitors provided the Dutch Republic with important military opportunities, only a relatively strong state could take advantage of these opportunities to the extent that it did. As Jan Glete noted in his comparative study of European powers, far from being successful by default, '[t]he small republic was in fact Europe's most concentrated area of modern military competence and armed forces'.[18] Second, the most formidable achievements of this state did not occur in the period when its competitors were weakest, but precisely in the second half of the seventeenth century when the Republic was faced with sustained military and naval challenges. The highpoint of its supremacy at sea falls between the 1650s and the 1670s, when the Dutch navy was the main arbiter in the Baltic as well as the Mediterranean.[19] In the history of armed diplomacy, there are few moments comparable to William III's 1688–9 invasion of the British isles at the head of 15,000 troops, effecting 'regime change' with one of the Netherlands' major international competitors.[20] On land, the army reached its apex only around the turn of the eighteenth century in the course of the 'forty years' war' against France. Third, a strong case can be made that the success of the Dutch Republic did not occur despite it being a federal state with strong features of bourgeois self-government, but because of it.[21] The military and naval reforms of the seventeenth century gave the central state considerable control over its armed forces on land and at sea.[22] But as this book will show, they did so for most of this period while not only preserving, but strengthening the federal features of the Dutch state and the independent or semi-independent role of brokers. What is most surprising is not the penultimate failure of the Dutch Republic in the struggle against its main European adversaries, but its success in withstanding them for almost all of the seventeenth century. This success raises the important question of whether it is really true that centralised and national states were always bound to overtake non-centralised and brokerage states in the organisation of warfare – as it were forming the implicit aim of the process of state formation merely waiting to be fulfilled.

A second, less teleological line of reasoning focuses on the interaction between economic growth and decline and the 'institutional incapacities' of

---

18   Glete 2002, p. 141.

19   Israel 1989, pp. 217 ff.

20   Israel 1991 and Troost 2005, pp. 195 ff.

21   Glete 2002, p. 167, and Prak and Van Zanden 2009.

22   Van Nimwegen 2010 and Bruijn 1993, pp. 75 ff.

the Dutch eighteenth-century state. The core of this argument is that it was
the extraordinary wealth associated with the Dutch 'Golden Age' that carried
the Dutch state's success in warfare, but that a dramatic turn of fate occurred
around the time of the 1713 Peace of Utrecht.[23] A combination of classical
'imperial overstretch' as a result of four decades of warfare with Louis XIV's
France, economic decline that spelled the end of the Dutch 'Golden Age', the
limitations put on Dutch military capacities by the limited size of the population, and an involution of the Dutch state elites often described as 'aristocratisation' and declining interest in trade, forced the Dutch Republic out of international great-power competition.[24] Following Tilly's dictum that wars make
states, the outcome was predictable. Freed in large part from the pressures
of warfare, the eighteenth-century Dutch state apparently remained stuck in
its seventeenth-century brokerage form. Conservative in their approach to the
world, Dutch state elites became passive in their attitudes towards their own
society and institutions.[25]

The links between the economic success and martial achievements of the
Dutch Republic were strongly asserted by contemporaries. A rather extreme,
but in its underlying assumptions not unrepresentative statement to this effect
could be found in a pamphlet from 1650, directed against the moves of the
Province of Holland to reduce the size of the military in the aftermath of the
Peace of Westphalia:

> What certainty has peace brought you? War has made you great, peace
> makes you small. War has brought you splendor, authority, deference from
> all potentates. Peace makes you suspicious to all, including the least, even
> Portugal. War has expanded your boundaries to the East and West, peace
> leads to their loss. War, impoverishing all other nations and Empires, has

---

23   Throughout this study, I will use the term 'Golden Age' only in inverted commas. While
       the expression is so ubiquitous in Dutch historiography and so central to arguments on
       Dutch prosperity and decline that it is impossible to avoid, the Age was never 'golden'
       for the large majority of the inhabitants of the Dutch Republic, and it certainly was not
       for those who sailed its ships, fought its wars, worked the plantations of the East and the
       West as enslaved labourers, or harvested the nutmeg that made fortunes for the VOC.

24   The 'aristocratisation thesis' was developed by Roorda 1964, and expanded by Van Dijk
       and Roorda 1976.

25   The continued influence of this argument can be seen from its reappearance in successive
       'generations' of handbooks of Dutch history. Hovy 1980, Van Deursen 2006, pp. 163–6.
       Hovy's notion of 'institutional incapacity' was already forcefully criticised in Fritschy
       1988b.

made you rich, has flooded your country with silver and gold, peace makes you poor. War has made all industries and traffics grow and prosper, peace makes them disappear and decay. War has been a bond of union and accord, peace of strife and discord.[26]

Foreign contemporaries often shared this view. The Italian observer Bentivoglio argued that war had made Amsterdam into the commercial centre of the world.[27] On the eve of the Second Anglo-Dutch War an English pamphleteer could write of the Dutch: 'Of all the World they are the people that thrive and grow rich by Warre, which is the Worlds ruine, and their support'.[28] While underrepresented in studies of Dutch early modern political theory, the idea of a close and positive correlation between war and economic growth formed a strong current in contemporary political economy.[29] However, during the War of the Spanish Succession and its aftermath, the destructive impact of war on the financial health of the state came to dominate political debate.[30] As Holland's most perceptive statesman of the time, Simon van Slingelandt, noted:

The finances of the state are so depleted by the last war, that the state would find itself in utter perplexity if it would suffer the misfortune to be involved in a new war before its finances have been saved to a certain extent, which will at best be a task of many years.[31]

---

26   ΦΙΛΑΛΕΘΙΥΜ 1650, pp. 4–5.

27   Bentivoglio 1983, p. 33: 'La guerra hà gatto diminuir sommamente in Anuersa il traffico, & hà data occasione a'popoli dell'Ollanda, e della Zelanda d'aprirsi quello dell'Indie; onde per questi due rispetti principalmente è venuto a crescer poi tanto in Amsterdam. Ne'tempi passati Anuersa era il magazine delle mercantile, che fuol distribuire l'Europa; e Lisbona la piazza di quelle, che vengon dall'Indie. Hora dopo la guerra si vede, ch'Amsterdam hà tirato a se quasi tutte le mercantile dell'Europa, e dell'Indie; e che n'hà spogliato quasi intiernamente Anuersa, e Lisbona'.

28   Anonymous 1664, p. 42.

29   Van Tijn 1992. Of course, the moral denunciation of war as destructive for life, liberty, trade, and religion was equally widespread. One of the interesting aspects of the seventeenth-century representation of war is how these two contradictory strands could exist side by side, apparently without friction. This is particularly clear from the works of the most important poet of the Dutch 'Golden Age', Vondel. Cf. Duits 1998, and Schama 1991, pp. 221 ff.

30   Nijenhuis 2002, p. 126.

31   'Consideratiën over de defensive alliantiën welke jeegenwoordig aangebooden worden aan den Staat in conjunctie met Groot-Brittanniën, opgesteld in het laatst van novemb. 1715', in Van Rappart 1978, p. 307.

During the second half of the eighteenth century oppositional writers harked back to the glorious days of naval prowess and Dutch great-power aspirations they associated with the seventeenth century. They restored the ideal of assertive international action combined with commercial growth, but only to counterpoise this ideal to the lack of such a positive combination in their own time.[32]

The idea that the rise and decline of Dutch commercial hegemony went hand in hand with the ability of the Dutch state to operate as a European great power seems so self-evident that it has become something of a trope in the literature on the history of international relations. In his standard work, Paul Kennedy could take the Dutch case as one of the main examples of the 'very significant correlation *over the longer term* between productive and revenue-raising capacities on the one hand and military strength on the other'.[33] However, his justified warning that this correlation can only be established 'over the longer term' has not always been heeded. Many writers have assumed the same direct relation between 'imperial overstretch' in the War of the Spanish Succession and the eclipse of the Dutch Republic that was already suggested in eighteenth-century debates.[34] Such a view does not sufficiently take into account the thorough re-evaluation in Dutch historiography of the contrasts between the 'golden' seventeenth century and its 'barren' eighteenth century counterpart. Already from the late 1950s onwards, for example, Dutch economic historians have argued that the loss of economic hegemony was a much more uneven and gradual process than had traditionally been assumed. The Dutch remained very strong in international carrying trade, colonial trade, and especially finance until the middle of the eighteenth century. Economic decline was absolute in a number of important sectors of manufacture, but only relative to the international competition in many other areas. The Dutch Republic remained one of the richest – per capita perhaps the richest – societies in Europe.[35] The evocation of the image of absolute and overall decline was a political tool in eighteenth-century debates, not a factual description of the

---

32 Leonard Leeb 1973, pp. 86 ff., and Velema 2007, pp. 77 ff.

33 Kennedy 1988, p. xvi.

34 E.g. Aalbers 1980, p. 1, which opens with the assertion: 'In fact the Republic of the Seven United Netherlands after 1713 politically is a second rate power. This political decline was caused by the growth in influence of other powers, most notably Great Britain, and the financial deprivation of the Republic'.

35 This much more nuanced view of Dutch 'decline' was first argued by De Vries 1959, and by now is generally accepted. For a relatively recent overview, see De Vries and Van der Woude 1997.

state of the country. It is true that as a result of changing economic conditions a top-layer of the capitalist class transformed itself from successful merchants and merchant-industrialists into successful internationally-oriented merchant-financiers and investors.[36] But however significant in the long run, there is no inherent reason why such a shift in economic centrality from the field of production to that of trade and ultimately finance would lead to an immediate loss of military strength. It certainly did not substantially undercut the ability of the Dutch state to raise funds for warfare – after all, if everyone else could borrow on the Amsterdam capital market to finance their armies, why not the Dutch state?[37] While the long-term connections between 'economic decline' and loss of great-power status are not put into question, these historiographic reconsiderations suggest that the actual mechanisms operating between the two were much more mediated, complex, and equivocal than has traditionally been suggested.[38]

Both solutions to the enigma of the Dutch state outlined here – the first the suggestion that the power of the Dutch state emanated from the weakness of others, the second that its base was purely dependent on a relatively short bout

---

36   A transformation that for example can be seen from the figures on regent investments in Prak 1985, p. 117.

37   On the continued ability of especially Holland to borrow for war, see Fritschy 1995, and Dormans 1991, pp. 97–102.

38   The same goes, *a fortiori*, for two other factors that keep on surfacing in the margins of the debates on the connections between economic decline and military strength: population and geography. Olaf van Nimwegen rightly points out that during the eighteenth century creditworthiness to pay for professional armies, not size of the population, was still the dominant determinant of military strength, Van Nimwegen 2002, p. 12. There is no inherent reason why a population of less than two million could sustain the Dutch Wars against France with its population of 20 million during the seventeenth but not during the eighteenth century, or why this factor was so important for the Dutch Republic but not for Prussia with its 2.35 million inhabitants at the time of Frederick the Great (for the size of the Prussian population: Wilson 2009, p. 116). Already at the end of the eighteenth century, the leading Dutch statesman Laurens Pieter van de Spiegel dealt with this line of reasoning: 'One has to consider the population of the Republic not only as consisting of so many heads, but as so many heads of wealthy people, who all more or less have possessions, or can gather possessions by their labour. Their welfare continuously attracts strangers to come and share in it. And because of these riches, the Dutch can employ other people in their service ... and thereby bring their population at all times at the height they judge necessary considering the circumstances. The examples of this are visible in navigation, the militia, at certain times in agriculture, in dike-building, and most of all in the plantations'. De Vries 1958, p. 89. On the analogous argument over the size of the territory of the Dutch Republic, see Lachmann 2002, p. 167.

of economic success – must assume that the eventual loss of great-power status was only the natural course of events. But both approaches encounter serious problems of chronology and causation, which prevent them from accounting for the complex, often partial, and long drawn-out nature of the decline of Dutch hegemony within the world-system. A third solution manages to avoid both problems by focusing on the strengths rather than the weaknesses of the Dutch state. This solution rests on Tilly's notion that there was a specific 'city-states' or 'capital-intensive' path of state formation that the Dutch Republic followed. The close connections between capitalists and bureaucrats characteristic of this path allowed state makers to draw much more successfully on the resources of their subjects than their more centralised counterparts, giving them a marked advantage in the era of brokerage-warfare. However, once nationalised warfare gathered steam, the extraordinary influence of urban elites over policy decisions in those states prevented rulers from raising the level of taxation and state intervention in the economy to a degree matching the requirements of international great-power competition.[39] This solution carries strong overtones of what the Dutch historian Jan Romein – with the Dutch eighteenth century in mind – once called 'the law of the handicap of a head-start'.[40] Romein developed his 'law' as a counterpart to Trotsky's much more familiar 'law of uneven and combined development', popularised in the Gerschenkronian version as the 'advantages of backwardness'.[41] In analogy to these, Romein tried to show why former 'front-runners' in the world economy tend to cling to the institutions that once gave them an advantage over their competitors, even if these become outdated – citing reasons of convenience, the excessive costs of replacement of functioning but old-fashioned techniques, or ideological conservatism.[42]

---

39   Tilly 1992, p. 160.

40   Romein 1948.

41   Leon Trotsky first coined this notion in the wake of the 1905 revolution to explain the apparent contradiction of one of Europe's least developed countries experiencing highly advanced forms of working-class upheaval, and later elaborated it as part of his critique of the Stalinist concept of 'socialism in one country'. Key texts in Trotsky 2010. Gerschenkron's version of this idea, much indebted to Trotsky's theories but less elaborated, can be found in Gerschenkron 1962. Theories of uneven and combined development have recently experienced a minor comeback in the literature on international relations, as can be seen from the debates in recent issues of the *Cambridge Review of International Affairs*, e.g., Callinicos 2007 and Callinicos and Rosenberg 2008.

42   Van der Linden 2007.

A problem with Tilly's description of a city-state path that 'bit itself in the tail' is that it rests on the assumption that the advantages of the brokerage-model of state formation came to a sharp and sudden end around 1700, returning in a less teleological fashion to the idea that there is an all-overriding tendency in early modern warfare to strengthen the national state. Though acknowledging that differences in 'state physiology' played an important role in determining the line of march, in Tilly's view this did not influence the general trend towards nationalisation, for

> the increasing scale of war and the knitting together of the European state system through commercial, military, and diplomatic interaction eventually gave the warmaking advantage to those states that could field great standing armies; states having access to a combination of large rural populations, capitalists, and relatively commercialized economies won out. They set the terms of war, and their form of state became the predominant one in Europe. Eventually European states converged on that form: the national state.[43]

This notion has come under sustained criticism. As Frank Tallett pointed out, what deserves our attention 'is not so much the bureaucratic centralization engendered by the demands of war, but rather the *decentralization* which they entailed'.[44] Recent works on the British, French, and Spanish states during the 'long eighteenth century' all affirm the continued role of independent entrepreneurs in the organisation of warfare in those countries, as well as the continued ineffectiveness of national states.[45] Brokerage seems to have been a central tool for state-makers across the board, and to have remained so well into the eighteenth century. The difference between the Dutch Republic and its competitors appears to lie more in the way in which brokerage structures were integrated into the overall framework of the state, than in whether or not they were fully replaced. To push the point, it might be more useful to envision the Dutch Republic as one extreme of the norm of European state formation than as the great early modern exception, the last successful representative of the city-state path.

Despite this important proviso, the great strength of the third, social relations oriented solution outlined here is that it does not assign the state a passive

---

43   Tilly 1992, p. 58.
44   Tallett 1992, p. 200.
45   See the next section for references.

role as a mere receptor of the 'external' pressures of warfare or the 'internal' pressures of economic development. Instead, it envisions the state as a mediating structure within a complex of conflicting social forces. States make war, but they do so, to paraphrase Marx, not in conditions of their own choosing and often not with the results that state-makers had in mind before launching themselves onto the battlefield. And wars do not only make states, but can unmake them as well – pushing for the preservation of once successful models of organisation, strengthening class factions with access to arms, giving economic beneficiaries of warfare an interest in the defence of the status-quo. To understand the specific mixture of 'making' and 'unmaking' characterising each path of state formation, it is necessary to examine concretely how this process of mediation functions. This can only be done by examining the social networks, forms of interaction, and political and ideological conflicts behind institutional developments. Such a concrete examination for three key sectors of the organisation of warfare in the Dutch Republic forms the empirical core of this book.

Typologies of the Early Modern State Form

As might be clear by now, the enterprise undertaken here rests on a hive of historiographic debates. The emphasis on the impact of warfare on state formation stimulated a large and ever growing literature on the question of how early modern European states in their institutional arrangements accommodated the pressures of military and naval competition.[46] For no other period has the inner working of military-industrial and military-financial complexes been subjected to so much thorough empirical research as for the years between 1550 and 1815.[47] This book does not intend to present a comparative study in the

---

46   Literature on war and state formation in non-European states is still more limited, with the important exception of the Ottoman Empire, which of course straddled European and Asian theatres of war. See Murphey 1999, Aksan 2002, Ágoston 2009, and Karaman and Pamuk 2010. For other non-European Empires, see e.g., Richards 1981 and Roy 2005.

47   A very summary survey of the most recent Anglophone literature suffices to underline this point. For Britain, there is Bannermann 2008 and Knight and Wilcox 2010, for France Parrott 2001 and Rowlands 2002, for the Dutch Republic Van Nimwegen 2010 and 't Hart 2014. Apart from these monographs, there are major syntheses such as Jan Glete 2002 and David Parrott 2012, and collaborative volumes such as Contamine 2000, Tallett and Trimm 2009, Bowen and González Enciso 2006, and Stephen Conway and Torres Sanchez 2011.

sense of systematically tracing the similarities and differences in the administrative structures employed by Dutch state-makers and their foreign counterparts. But as the remarks on Tilly in the last section suggest, highlighting the peculiarities of the Dutch trajectory of state formation in and of itself begs the question whether there was a main pattern of which this particular case was either a variant with its own characteristics or a deviation. Therefore, considerations arising from direct comparison will be latently – and sometimes explicitly – present throughout this investigation.

This study will employ the terminology commonly used in the literature on early modern state formation – Tilly's lineage of 'brokerage' and 'nationalised' states, the concept of the 'fiscal-military' state, and the more recent notion of an eighteenth-century 'contractor state'. Rather than forming rival explanations, these terminologies focus on different but interrelated aspects of a single process. The first centres on the question of why certain areas of military and naval organisation were drawn into the realm of the state and others were not. The second focuses on states' financial capacities and the specific institutions designed for the enhancement of its revenue-raising capacities in the context of war. The third gives priority to the interaction between states and markets in areas such as military production and supply. All three models are perfectly well applicable to the Dutch case. The Dutch Republic was a brokerage state in its continuous involvement of economic elites in the execution of its warring tasks, a fiscal-military state in its methods of and aims in raising money, and a contractor state in its persistent reliance on the market for its military and naval logistics. Apart from these general terms, the frequency of references to the organisational structure of the Dutch state in this book gave rise to the need for a shorthand description of the state-form of the Dutch Republic. To stress the two most characteristic features of Dutch institutional arrangements, the – perhaps somewhat cumbersome – term 'federal-brokerage state' was chosen for this aim.

Each of these terms requires some further explanation, for each comes with a heavy load of theoretical baggage. Despite problems of chronology and hidden teleology, the brokerage-nationalisation dichotomy still forms the most generic approach to the institutional forms of interaction between capitalists and the state in the early modern period. Both in its strengths and in its weaknesses, Tilly's choice of categories was heavily indebted to the German sociological tradition.[48] Three thinkers warrant special attention: Werner Sombart, Otto

---

[48]   For a broader critical evaluation of Tilly's theoretical development, see Van der Linden 2009, especially pp. 245–9.

Hintze and Max Weber. In his 1913 *Krieg und Kapitalismus*, Sombart posited in stark terms the correlation of the three large-scale processes central to Tilly's contribution – the rise of capitalism, the genesis of the modern state, and the transformation of the nature of warfare. Starting from the image of war as 'the great destroyer', Sombart quickly turned towards its opposite characteristic:

> Der Krieg hat kapitalistisches Wesen nicht nur zerstört, der Krieg hat die kapitalistische Entwicklung nicht nur gehemmt: er hat sie ebenso gefördert, ja – er hat sie erst möglich gemacht, weil wichtige Bedingungen, an die aller Kapitalismus geknüpft ist, erst im Kampfe sich erfüllen mußten. Ich denke vor allem an die Staatenbildung, wie sie zwischen dem 16. und 18. Jahrhundert in Europa vor sich geht, die eine Voraussetzung war für die eigenartige Entfaltung des kapitalistische Wirtschaftssystems. Die modernen Staaten aber, das wird man nicht erst zu belegen brauchen, sind allein das Werk der Waffen ...[49]

The remainder of the book, however, was not focused on this 'indirect' contribution of warfare to capitalist development through state formation, but on the ways in which capitalists themselves were directly involved in the organisation of warfare. For Sombart, this typical 'brokerage' involvement functioned as a motor for capitalist development – leading to the amassing of wealth, the spreading of the 'capitalist spirit', and the expansion of commodity markets.[50]

Sombart's idiosyncratic reading of early modern history, heavily influenced by the mechanical materialism then current in German Social Democracy, made him prioritise the directly economic benefits of warfare. The influence of war on the development of bureaucratic rationalism was examined more thoroughly by Weber and Hintze. In what must be read as a direct reply to Sombart's thesis, Weber argued that war should not be seen as the origin of capitalist development, but rather as one of the catalysts of a process already underway.

---

49   'War has not only disrupted the capitalist essence, war has not only put a break on capitalist development: it has also furthered it, yes, it has even made it possible. For the important circumstances to which all capitalism is tied, must first fulfil themselves in struggle. I think in the first place of state building, as it took place in Europe between the sixteenth and the eighteenth centuries, which was a precondition for the distinctive trajectory of the capitalist economic system. However, one hardly has to prove that the modern states are only the product of armed might' (Sombart 1913, p. 11).

50   Sombart 1913, p. 14.

Er ist allerdings, und nicht nur in Europa, Träger des Kapitalismus gewesen; aber dieses Moment war nicht entscheidend für dessen Entwicklung. Sonst hätte mit zunehmender Deckung des Heeresbedarfes durch Eigenregie des Staates der Kapitalismus wieder zurückgehen müssen, eine Entwicklung, die aber nicht eingetreten ist.[51]

The counterfactual is important. For Weber the very process by which much of the direct practical organisation of warfare was taken out of the hands of individual capitalists and thus out of the realm of profit and the market – analogous to Tilly's transition from brokerage to nationalisation – was at the same time the process of the creation of a 'rational state bureaucracy' that is indispensable for the functioning of modern industrial society.[52] A second theme in Tilly's lineage of brokerage and nationalist forms can also be directly inferred from its Weberian precursor: the historic necessity of the replacement of independent city-states as the main carriers of capitalist development by national states that more effectively combined the requirements of accumulation and coercion.[53]

While Weber emphasised the rational aspects of bureaucratic development, Otto Hintze provided the idea of the totalising logic of this state. For Hintze, the rise of Prussia was at one and the same time the victory of the 'Gesamtstaat', and Friedrich Wilhelm I owed his success as a military commander directly to his role as the creator of a 'militärisch-bureaukratischer Absolutismus'.[54] Much of the implicit teleology towards the national state present in the 'military-revolution thesis' derives from this privileging of the military-bureaucratic total state as the superior organisational framework for warfare. A full generation later, Fritz Redlich sketched the pre-history of this victory as the rise and fall of the 'military enterpriser'. Locating the heydays of this particular type of entrepreneur during the Thirty Years' War with the operation of mercenary armies such as Wallenstein's, Redlich posited that the history of military organisation was that of the integration of the independent 'company economy' under control of the captain-entrepreneur into larger regimental economies,

---

51   'It [privatised war] has truly, and not only in Europe, been a carrier of capitalism; but this was not the decisive moment of its development. Otherwise, the growing control over military requirements by the state itself should have meant a regression of capitalism – a development which did not take place' (Weber 1924, p. 266).

52   Weber 1947, pp. 331–2. Also see Allen 2004, p. 135.

53   Tilly 1992, pp. 190–1.

54   Hintze 1927a, p. 180.

and ultimately into the confines of the totalising bureaucratic organisation.[55] Tilly's notion of the 'brokerage' state centrally rested on this gradually disappearing type of entrepreneurship singled out by Redlich. His overemphasis on the extent to which brokerage forms disappeared, and his neglect of the many forms in which independent capitalists continued to be crucial to the organisation of warfare, is thus firmly embedded in the theoretical lineage of his argument.

Tilly's general assumptions on the nature of state formation remain highly influential, but most later research focused on the working of state institutions on a more concrete level.[56] Following the famous dictum of Cicero that 'money forms the sinew of all wars', John Brewer introduced the term 'fiscal-military state' to capture the overbearing role of the monetary factor in the development of state bureaucracies.[57] In his account, the creation of strong fiscal institutions did much more than allow states to raise increasing amounts of revenue. In the process, bureaucratic bodies restructured the very relation between the state and capital markets, the connections between large-scale financiers and other economic interest groups, and the nature of the political interaction between economic elites and state bureaucrats. In his conclusion, Brewer explained how

> [t]hese interests struggled to understand, subjugate or exploit the fiscal-military juggernaut that emerged, through the collision of conflicting forces ... They tried to do so by one of two, somewhat contradictory, processes: on the one hand, by circumscribing the state's power; on the other, by colonizing the state in order to gain control of its resources.[58]

Brewer's influential book on the eighteenth-century British state was followed by more general examinations of the nature of fiscal-military states.[59] Apart from providing a more concrete way to envision the links between warfare and the development of financial bureaucracies, this terminology opened a bridge to adjacent debates on the 'financial revolutions' in the relations between states and capital markets.[60] Applying the concept to other states than eighteenth-

---

55   Redlich 1965, p. 16.
56   Partly reflecting the influence of military historians with their strong empiricist bent. Black 1999, p. 671.
57   Brewer 1988, p. 88.
58   Brewer 1988, p. 251.
59   Thompson 1995, Bonney 1995, Lindegren 2000, and Storrs 2009.
60   The 'financial revolutions' thesis was first posited by Dickson 1967. For more recent

century Britain led to a recognition of the many different forms taken by the process of 'circumscribing and colonising' of the state by economic elites that Brewer had described. It also turned attention to the ways in which the state-makers themselves used those attempts for their own ends. As Jan Glete pointed out, states had to find new ways to gain access to the economic resources of their subjects, and the two combined led to far-reaching interpenetration that moulded the boundaries between the two:

> The basic features of the market and the hierarchy are important to keep in mind when studying the development of early modern states. They tied both systems in a more or less conscious search process for optimal solutions to difficult problems, but in practice it was seldom a question of a choice between two clear-cut alternatives: an atomistic market and a strict formal hierarchy. *Networks of contacts* also mattered.[61]

Networks of contacts play an increasingly important role in the most recent historiographic developments, most notably the shift from the question of the raising of revenues to that of their actual employment in areas like recruitment, military production, and supply. Of course, these aspects were never really absent. Indeed they already had been prominently present in Sombart's research project. They were central to the development of the 'war and society' school that arose in the 1960s and 1970s. In Martin van Creveld's formulation:

> [B]efore a commander can even start thinking of manoeuvring or giving battle, of marching this way and that, of penetrating, enveloping, encircling, of annihilating or wearing down, in short of putting into practice the whole rigmarole of strategy, he has – or ought – to make sure of his ability to supply his soldiers with those 3,000 calories a day without which they will very soon cease to be of any use as soldiers; that roads to carry them to the right place at the right time are available, and that movement along these roads will not be impeded by either a shortage or a superabundance of transport.[62]

---

overviews of the debates that also include the case of the Netherlands, see 't Hart 1997 and Gelderblom and Jonker 2011.

61   Glete 2002, p. 58.
62   Van Creveld 1977, p. 1.

Nevertheless, it seems fair to say that for a while the impact of war on structures for taxation and loans drew attention away from the equally momentous changes in the organisational relations between states and capitalists in
production and supply. The recent introduction of the idea of the eighteenth-
century 'contractor state' helps to once again bring to the fore this particular
side of state formation.[63] It highlights the continued, often central role of capitalists after the arrival of standing armies and navies during the second half
of the seventeenth century, thereby extending the reach of Tilly's concept of
brokerage from its original narrow confines.

The arrival of yet another descriptive term for seventeenth- and eighteenth-
century state formation, however, raises a broader question about the heuristic
status of the terminology. Do 'brokerage'-, 'fiscal-military'-, and 'contractor'-
elements really signify specific types of state, or do they simply capture different forms of activities that all early modern states – as well as states over a far
wider historical timeframe – engage in? Weber was adamant that ancient Rome
possessed a powerful class of 'rational' capitalist financiers that backed up its
wars.[64] Were their activities indicative of the existence of a fiscal-military state
in classical antiquity? Travelling in the opposite direction, a recent increase in
the activities of poor Somalians pushed into piracy by the ravages of global
industrialised fishing led to debates in Dutch parliament about whether the
protection of freight-carriers should be carried out by the state navy, or left to
heavily armed employees of security firms.[65] Is this a return to brokerage forms
of warfare? If not, what about the much more extensive use of private soldiers
by the American army from Iraq to disaster-stricken New Orleans and Haiti?[66]
If all modern capitalist states possess some vestiges of a military-industrial
complex channelling orders and funds to selected suppliers, does that mean
the eighteenth-century 'contractor state' never ceased to exist?

The meaning of these rhetorical questions is to show that rather than being
the characteristic features of a particular phase of state formation, brokerage,
fiscal-military, and contractor arrangements are some of the means employed
within a long historic timeframe by very different states to solve similar types

---

63   The first monograph to explicitly use this concept is Knight and Wilcox 2010. A session
      around this theme took place at the 2010 World Economic History Conference in Utrecht,
      the proceedings of which have been published as Conway and Torres Sánchez 2011, and a
      further collection of essays appeared in 2012 as Harding and Solbes Ferri 2012.

64   Weber 1924, pp. 286–7.

65   'Kamer steunt uitbreiding missie tegen piraten', *De Volkskrant*, 12 June 2012.

66   Silverstein 2000, Scahill 2007, and Scahill, 'us mercenaries set sights on Haiti', *The Nation*,
      19 January 2010.

of problems. This realisation affects some of the core evolutionary claims in the literature on state formation. Tilly's 'convergence' of paths seems not to consist of series of long transitions between sharply delineated phases, but rather a series of restructurings of the state, producing changes in the balance between brokerage and national institutions, tributary and fiscal-military arrangements for revenue raising, and between solutions to logistical problems based on requisitioning, buying, and making. Throughout the seventeenth and eighteenth centuries, rulers and bureaucrats experimented with ways to combine direct state intervention and far-reaching reliance on capitalist self-organisation to the greatest effect. For all, the ability to implement state-centred, bureaucratic solutions in a modern sense was limited by the fact that neither politics, nor civil society, nor even the market had yet attained the 'impersonal' character that enables the state bureaucracy to appear as the social repository of an imagined non-particularistic, totalising rationality, the guardian of the combined interests of the nation.[67] In one of those sweeping generalisations of which only the nineteenth-century social sciences were truly capable, Marx identified the central role of middlemen in this historic period:

> In the economic domain, e.g., financiers, stock-exchange speculators, merchants, shopkeepers skim the cream; in civil matters, the lawyer fleeces his clients; in politics the representative is of more importance than the voters, the minister than the sovereign; in religion, God is pushed into the background by the 'Mediator', and the latter again is shoved back by the priests, the inevitable middlemen between the good shepherd and his sheep.[68]

Clearly, the preponderance of (proto-)nationalised solutions was stronger in absolute monarchies than in bourgeois city-states. Both for the French and the Spanish monarchy, to take the two obvious examples, the literature clearly shows a great reluctance of the crown to give too much leeway to the commercial classes. Dynastic interests often took precedence over economic considerations. This does not mean, however, that the Habsburg and Bourbon state did

---

67   Gerstenberger 2007. For Marx's own (during his lifetime unpublished) treatment of the
        logic of bureaucracy in a number of condensed passages highly reminiscent of Weber's
        later development of the notion of bureaucratic rationality, see his 1843 'Kritik des Hegel-
        schen Staatsrechts (§§ 261–313)', Marx 1961a.
68   Marx 1961b, pp. 772–3. English translation available at: http://www.marxists.org/archive/
        marx/works/1867-c1/ch29.htm, accessed 26-11-2014.

not rely heavily on capitalist middlemen. It primarily meant that in the inter-action between the state and its entrepreneurs, decision-making power tilted more towards the former than the latter.[69] In contrast, both in bourgeois repub-lics like Venice and the Dutch Republic and in the British constitutional mon-archy, bureaucrats and capitalists engaged on a much more equal footing.[70] In all cases the same ingredients were present: emerging markets, developing bur-eaucracies, cities vying for influence, commercial interests and interests of state overlapping and conflicting in ever more complex patterns. But the outcome of this mixture depended both on the proportions in which these ingredients were available, and on the historic conditions of their recombination. Compar-ing the Northern and Southern Netherlands powerfully underlines this point. Both geographic areas were characterised by high levels of urbanisation, com-mercialisation, and the presence of strong capitalist elites. But the launching of an independent state in the course of the Dutch Revolt allowed the Northern Netherlands to mobilise these factors for warfare with great success, while sub-jection to foreign monarchies for a long time transformed the urban landscape of the Southern Netherlands quite literally into the pastures on which other powers could graze.[71]

As scholars have tentatively started to suggest, the idea that war produced an all-overriding advantage for one particular combination of bureaucratic centralisation and reliance on the market could in fact be a projection from the nineteenth and twentieth century into early modernity.[72] This shifts the meaning of the central question posed at the start of the introduction. The persistence of federal-brokerage structures for warfare in the Dutch Repub-lic seems less of an exception, a holding out against the inevitable march of history, and more as one side of the continuum of early modern state forms. If there was a single moment of convergence when state-makers across the board, even in the Dutch Republic, became proponents of tipping the balance definitively towards national solutions, it only came with the French Revolu-

69 E.g. Parrott 2001, and Rowlands 2002. One of the classic studies of the interrelation between the French crown and entrepreneurs that forcefully brings out this point is Bam-ford 1956. For the Spanish state, see Glete 2002, and for practical examples Torres Sánchez 2009, and Torres Sánchez 2012.

70 For summary comparisons that stress this aspect, see 't Hart 2000, Lachmann 2003, and O'Brien 2006.

71 See the dissertation of Thomas Goossens that was written in conjunction with this book as part of the VNC-research project 'Networks of state and capital' (Goossens 2012). Also De Schryver 2002.

72 Parrott 2012, pp. 3–4.

tion, and it did so as much for political as for purely military reasons. Until the arrival of the *levée en masse*, war created pressures in the direction of nationalisation as well as pressures leading to the continued reliance on brokerage structures. Rather than supposing the superiority of national over brokerage forms, research should lay bare the structural conditions and types of interaction between states and ruling classes that produced the particular outcomes of these conflicting pressures.

Finally, the term 'federal-brokerage state' that is employed in this study should be read in the same vein. Rather than capturing an 'essence' of the Dutch state, signifying a particular 'stage' in which the Dutch Republic remained stuck and emphasising its 'failure' to become national, the term is primarily descriptive. It concentrates on two dominant elements of the solutions that were persistently favoured by Dutch state-makers when faced with concrete problems in the organisation of warfare – their tendency to devolve power downwards towards local and provincial institutions rather than to create national administrative bodies, and to favour brokerage over bureaucracy. Of course, no descriptive term is ever completely void of deeper ontological meanings – meanings pertaining to what the state *was* rather than what it *did*. The remainder of this introduction will suggest that a continued preference for federal-brokerage solutions reflected certain fundamental features of Dutch state-society relations. But nonetheless, they remained solutions rather than fixed properties, and the fact that these solutions were singled out and not others ought to be explained, not assumed.

The Dutch Cycle of Accumulation

The general background and historic timeframe for the argument presented here is provided by what the economist Giovanni Arrighi in his major synthesis of capitalism's *longue durée* described as the 'Dutch cycle of accumulation'.[73] The basic supposition behind this choice of words, of course, is that the economy of the Dutch Republic can indeed be characterised as capitalist. There has been a huge debate among Marxist and non-Marxist scholars alike on whether this is the case. Distinguished historians such as Eric Hobsbawm and more recently Ellen Meiksins Wood have argued, in the words of the latter, that 'the Dutch Republic enjoyed its Golden Age not as a capitalist economy but as the last and most highly developed non-capitalist commercial

---

73   Arrighi 2002, pp. 127 ff.

society'.[74] Marx himself famously described the Netherlands as 'the head capitalistic nation of the 17th century' in the section on 'original accumulation' in the first volume of *Capital*.[75] But this seems to be contradicted by the passages in the third volume of *Capital*, where he stresses the limits to capitalist development in societies dominated by merchant capital.[76] Exegesis of sacred texts thus does not provide any answers here, as unfortunately it seldom does for anyone but the true believer. Only serious historical enquiry can show to what extent capitalist forms of production took root in early modern Dutch society.[77] This study examines the question 'at one remove', through the prism of the state and its warring activities. Time and again, it will show how the proficiency of the Dutch state in waging war in the famous 'last instance' rested on its ability to draw on the advanced nature of the Dutch economy: an enormous tax-base generated by the far-reaching commodification of the economy, the availability of diverse networks of suppliers of military and naval goods that could be tapped through market methods, a large 'reserve-army' of wage labourers to man the quays and dockyards, the warships and the battlefields, a managerial mindset of state-administrators acquired in business and then applied to every aspect of social life.

But what kind of capitalism was this? Following Braudel and Wallerstein, Arrighi posited that international capitalism developed through a number of phases marked by the consecutive hegemonies of core states. The aim of his concept of systemic cycles was 'to describe and elucidate the formation, consolidation, and disintegration of the successive regimes through which the capitalist world economy has expanded from its late medieval sub-systemic embryo to its present global dimension'.[78] Focusing explicitly on the interplay between capitalist expansion and the shifts in power within the international state system, this notion provides a theoretical framework that connects the main themes of the book. According to Arrighi, the Dutch cycle formed a crucial turning point in the development of the capitalist world-system, transferring the logic of capital accumulation from the primarily regional scale it had

---

74 Wood 2002, p. 94. Cf. Hobsbawm 1967, pp. 44–5.

75 Marx [1867], p. 704. Interestingly enough, he does so in a passage that focusses specifically on the role of the state, taxation, and colonialism in the development of capitalism.

76 Marx 1991, p. 448.

77 An extensive overview of historiographic debates, showing among other things the extent to which capitalist relations went beyond the 'superficial' realms of trade and finance and were connected to capitalist production in agriculture and manufacture, is provided in Brandon 2011b.

78 Arrighi 2002, pp. 9–10.

still had with the Italian city states to the world at large. Doing so required a coupling of the needs of profit and of power at a much higher rate of intensity than had characterised earlier social formations, something that was not consciously sought after but nevertheless achieved in the Northern Netherlands in the course of the Dutch Revolt. In Arrighi's reading of the history of Dutch capitalism, this fusion of profit and power reached its highpoint around the 1650s, then to dissolve under pressure of 'economic decline' during the downward phase of the cycle that stretched from the second half of the seventeenth century to the second half of the eighteenth. Again following Braudel and Wallerstein, Arrighi argued that the hallmark of capitalist hegemony was the ability to combine economic leadership in the key sectors of manufacture, trade, and finance. 'Decline' from this position was a gradual process, starting in manufacture, slowly enveloping certain areas of trade, and arriving only late in the day in finance – explaining how a loss of hegemony could go hand in hand with an assertive role for Dutch investors on the world market.[79]

New in Arrighi's approach is the centrality he accords to the organisational character of relations between capitalists and the state in creating the possibilities and limits of each successive cycle. In *The Long Twentieth Century*, he envisions the succession of the different systemic cycles as a series of historic shifts from 'cosmopolitan finance' forms of capitalism to 'state monopoly' forms and back. The Dutch Republic, in his view, came to supersede Genoa as the international centre of capital accumulation by reconstituting a form of 'state capitalism', based on the 'continuing internalization of protection costs by the Dutch capitalist class organized in the Dutch state'.[80] But if this internalisation of the costs of warfare signified a form of state capitalism, it certainly was not state capitalism of the modern type, where the state takes control over large swathes of the economy out of the hands of private capital. On the contrary, it was an extreme example of Brewer's 'colonisation of the state by the economic elites', where the state itself was run directly as an extension of the process of accumulation by sections of the capitalist class.[81] In an argument heavily dependent on Jonathan Israel's account of the rise and fall of 'Dutch primacy in world

---

79   Arrighi 2002, pp. 127 ff.
80   Arrighi 2002, p. 151. Arrighi took the important notion of 'protection costs' (signifying the part of surplus value destined to cover the costs of the armed defence of future profits), and 'protection rents' (a redistribution of surplus value regulated by the surplus-profits gained from more efficient armed protection), from the eminent writer on Venice's prime, Frederic C. Lane. See Lane 1958, p. 411.
81   Brewer 1988, p. 251.

trade', Arrighi held that the 'Dutch cycle' found its limits in two self-induced processes.[82] First, the very success of the Dutch model stimulated its emulation by competitors, leading to mercantilist challenges to Dutch hegemony in the core areas of European trade. Secondly, the intensification of international competition this engendered, with its ensuing increase in government spending, stimulated the international merchants at the helm of the Dutch state to divert their investments towards the international market for state bonds, leading to de-investment in trade and industry at home.[83] The state, firmly under control of those same investors, did not challenge the flow of investments that caused the loss of hegemony in production and trade, ultimately undermining the ability of Amsterdam to function as the financial centre of the world. In this way, both in its success and in its demise, the course of the Dutch cycle was bound to the specific configuration of relations between state and capital that characterised the Dutch state.[84]

Arrighi's insistence on a strong relationship between the development of the international state system and the capitalist world economy has been criticised from different theoretical directions.[85] However, its great strength remains that

---

82   Israel 1989. For a more recent comparative study of the nature of Dutch commercial hegemony, which is much more in tune with the current debates in Dutch economic history, see Ormrod 2003.

83   Arrighi 2002, pp. 142–4, and pp. 156–8.

84   Cf. the characterisation of the Dutch state in Lachmann 2002, Lachmann 2003, pp. 360–4, and Adams 2005.

85   The most prominent critics sharing Arrighi's Marxist starting point write from within Robert Brenner's approach to the rise of capitalism. Most of them reject that any society in early modern Europe can be described as capitalist before seventeenth-century England, and tend to see the Dutch Republic as a representative of older, non-capitalist forms of commercial societies. See Meiksins Wood 2002, p. 94, and Teschke 2003, p. 208. Incidentally, Brenner himself did see the Dutch Republic as capitalist, albeit a form of capitalism that never escaped the primordial A-phase of development. See Brenner 2001. For a forceful rejection of the Brenner approach to the rise of capitalism, see Banaji 2010. Also see the thoughtful discussion on the notion of the international employed by Wood and Teschke in Callinicos 2009, pp. 75 ff. Of course, non-Marxist authors would also contest major features of Arrighi's narrative. Nevertheless, many working within the framework of the currently influential New Institutional Economics (NIE) would agree about the positive interaction between the peculiar state form of the Dutch Republic, including its proficiency in war, and its extraordinary success as a motor of early modern capitalist development. This certainly was the assumption of the founding work of this school, North and Thomas 1973, pp. 132 ff., although its stress was more on the influence of the Dutch state form on the evolution of a specific set of property rights and the lowering of transaction costs than on its efficiency in facing challengers abroad. More recently,

it allows for a reintroduction into the debates on state formation of one of
the key insights of Marx's original theoretical enterprise from the standpoint
of global history: its insistence on the inherently international nature of the
birth of capitalism as a social system, captured in the famous remark in *Capital* Volume I that 'the different momenta of primitive accumulation distrib-
ute themselves ... more or less in chronological order, particularly over Spain,
Portugal, Holland, France, and England'.[86] The level of centrality accorded by
Arrighi to the role of warfare and the state in this process of international 'distribution' also makes his approach less vulnerable to the general criticisms of
historical materialism developed in the 1970s and 1980s by historical sociolo-
gists such as Theda Skocpol, Michael Mann, and Anthony Giddens, who saw
an alleged under-theorisation of the question of power as 'the origin of some of
the chief limitations of his [i.e., Marx's] scheme of historical analysis'.[87]

Examining these theoretical issues more closely would require a different
type of book. However, four concrete criticisms can be made of Arrighi's view
of the 'Dutch cycle' that relate directly to the subject of this research. First, his
insistence on a binary opposition between 'state (monopoly)' and 'cosmopolitan (financial)' forms of organisation as different moments (temporarily and
geographically) of the cycle of accumulation can distract from the very real
ways in which these were competing aspects of the same moment. Even in
the case of the Dutch Republic, capitalists worked both through and around
the state. This research, for example, will show how the VOC – understandably
presented by Arrighi as the clearest case of the merging of state and capital –
at the high point of its activities managed to combine reliance on the state in
European waters with keeping at bay the state beyond Cape Hope. More generally, the level of state-capital integration differed over time and for different
groups of merchants.

---

authors working within the framework of NIE have turned more explicitly to the question of the role of warfare, e.g. North, Wallis, and Weingast 2009, and Gennaioli and Voth
2011. There are important points of convergence between those writings and the approach
followed here, especially in the insistence that markets do not function in a political and
institutional void. However, the lack of class-specificity accorded to the functioning of
institutions by NIE, as well as its tendency to approach the production of power as essentially an extension of a fetishised market logic through the notion of 'public goods', are
strong reasons to prefer the reading of the state and warfare developed by Arrighi et al.

86   Marx s.d., p. 703. A statement that, for the purposes of completeness – and also to cleanse it
of the vestiges of euro-centrism – should be further widened to include at least the Islamic
trading system and the Yangtze Delta during the mid-to-late Ming period.

87   For the original formulations of this critique, see Skocpol 1979, Giddens 1981, Mann 1986
and Mann 1993. The quotation is taken from Giddens 1981, p. 3.

Second, while insisting on the geographic dimensions of capital accumulation and the uneven division of power on the international field, Arrighi tends to underestimate the internal spatial dimensions that crucially influenced the position of the state.[88] The federal element within the federal-brokerage make-up of the Dutch state, as well as the impact of this federalism on the development of the Dutch cycle, are almost absent from his description. This reflects the tendency in Anglophone literature to reduce the Dutch state to its most influential component, the Province of Holland. As Jonathan Israel concludes:

> The notion that the United Provinces was, in any sense, political or economic, the city-state of Amsterdam, implying that Amsterdam ruled the rest as Venice and Genoa ruled their subject territories, is a total misconception. Nowhere else in the early modern world was the close economic collaboration of a network of maritime towns, inland manufacturing towns, fishing ports, and inland specialized agriculture anything like so intricately organized and federated as in the Dutch Republic during the seventeenth century.[89]

Hollando-centrism was a political reality as well as an ideological strand of the Dutch 'Golden Age', but one that was always contested.[90] As this study purports to show, the organisation of state-capital relations worked out very differently for the Amsterdam or the Zeeland Admiralty Board, and for financiers based in The Hague or Groningen. These differences had long-term effects on the ability of the state to overcome the limits of the Dutch cycle.

A third, and closely connected, problem is the tendency to define the social character of the Dutch state merely by the influence of – primarily Holland-based – international merchants. However real this influence was, it certainly was not the only feature of Dutch politics. Most non-Marxist literature with equal justification stresses another basic characteristic of the Dutch state: its persistent 'particularism', providing each often highly localised corporate body with its own island of influence.[91] Stuck in the notion of a 'pure' merchant state, Marxist writers have often missed the more complex and elaborate ways in

---

88 An attempt to include these spatial dimensions of capital accumulation in the theoretical framework provided by Marx was undertaken by Harvey 2006a [originally 1982], Chapters 12 and 13. For a recent summary, see Harvey 2006b.

89 Israel 1989, p. 415.

90 See for one important example Prokhovnik 2004, pp. 162–7.

91 Price 1994, and Van Nierop 2007, p. 65.

which the state tried – with varying success – to connect the interests of the major long-distant merchants that built their luxurious houses along the Amsterdam canals with those of sections of the nobility as well as the urban middle classes throughout the Seven Provinces.

The fourth and perhaps most fundamental problem is a rather caricatured view of Dutch early modern capitalism as a pure 'merchant capitalism'. This concept is deeply flawed. The idea that Dutch hegemony was driven by dominance of the rich trades, instead of this dominance being the result of the measure of development of its home economy, is by now almost universally rejected.[92] In the words of Immanuel Wallerstein, '[s]o much ink has been spilled to explain why Holland did not industrialize that we tend to overlook the fact that it did do so'.[93] As will be shown in more detail in a chapter on the naval shipyards, the Dutch state not only acted as a promulgator of trade but also of capitalist production.

Thus, while Arrighi's theoretical framework highlights important aspects of the interplay between state and capital that this book examines further, his actual description of the 'Dutch cycle of accumulation' is much weakened by an overtly traditionalist and in some respects outdated rendering of the main lines of Dutch history. In explaining the Dutch 'rise and decline', Arrighi all too often has to fall back on the unsatisfactory notion that the root-causes of Dutch strength and weakness lay outside the Netherlands. Among others, this can be seen from his acceptance of the idea that

> as soon as the territorialist states themselves [i.e., France and England] followed the Dutch path of development by becoming more capitalist in structure and orientation and by throwing their lot in overseas commercial expansion, as they did from the late seventeenth century onwards, the exceedingly lean structure of the Dutch state was transformed from a decisive competitive advantage into an insurmountable handicap.[94]

A more nuanced approach to the development of the Dutch state requires a thorough re-examination of its role in the cycle of accumulation that will differ from Arrighi's original approach in important respects.

---

92   For a more extensive survey of the literature, as well as a criticism of the idea of Dutch capitalism as 'merchant capitalism' rather than an important stage in the development of capitalism proper, see Brandon 2011b.

93   Wallerstein 1980, p. 100. Despite this salient observation, Wallerstein did treat Dutch capitalism primarily as a function of its success in long-distance trade.

94   Arrighi 2002, p. 208.

The Federal-Brokerage State and its 'Historic Bloc'

Based on the four points of criticism outlined in the previous section, the role of the state in the Dutch cycle of accumulation can be pictured in a more dynamic way than was done in Arrighi's original description. Each stage of the cycle was accompanied as well as shaped by a reconfiguration of the relation between state and society. A short overview of this process is necessary to understand the concrete examination of these relations at the practical, institutional level pursued in this book.

Arrighi's choice to start his description of the cycle with the onset of dominance over Baltic trade in the decades preceding the Dutch Revolt against the Habsburg Empire logically follows from the view that it was merchant capital that drove Dutch expansion. But most economic historians today recognise that the roots of success already went back to the late middle ages. A highly effective symbiosis between urban trade and production and the rise of capitalist agriculture in parts of the late medieval Netherlands predated Dutch dominance in Baltic trade by several centuries.[95] The real first phase of the Dutch cycle thus fell in the period before the formation of an independent Dutch state. At that point, the Northern and Southern Low Countries were still divided among a splattering of feuding mini-states, highly divergent both in their political structures and their economic make-up. Unification of these territories started from above, by their subjection first under the Burgundian and then under the Habsburg crown. Individual provinces could assert themselves on the international terrain, as was done by the Province of Holland in its rivalry with the Hanseatic towns over access to the Baltic Sea.[96] But in general, it was the lack of a strong overbearing state and the peripheral position of especially the Northern provinces to the composite states that gained control over them that allowed their towns and capitalists to develop relatively unhindered.[97]

The Dutch Revolt that started in 1566 and flared up in full force in 1572 dramatically changed both the socioeconomic conditions and the political setting in which capital accumulation could take place, thus launching the second, hegemonic phase of the cycle. Three results of the Revolt are of significance

---

95 For the different trajectories of the transition to capitalist agriculture in the different regions of the Low Countries, see especially the work of Bas van Bavel, e.g., Van Bavel 1999, Van Bavel 2010a, and Van Bavel 2010b, as well as Blockmans 1993. For the interplay between urban and rural development, see, e.g., Van Zanden 1993, and Mielants 2001.

96 Sicking 2004.

97 Tilly 1992, pp. 52–3.

here, all unintended but therefore no less portentous. Freed from the centralising aims of the Habsburg crown and the essentially feudal world-outlook of
the factions of large nobles that stood behind it, the seven northern provinces
in which the revolt was successful became the territory of a new state that concentrated political and economic power to an extraordinary extent in the hands
of a coalition of large-scale international merchants and smaller-scale urban
and rural oligarchs.[98] It was clear even to most contemporary observers that
the attitudes of this new ruling coalition to the exigencies of commercial development were completely different from those of most other states of the day.
As the English diplomat William Temple poignantly observed:

> The Government manag'd either by men that trade, or whose Families
> have risen by it, or who have themselves some Interest going in other
> men's Traffique, or who are born and bred in Towns, The soul and being
> whereof consists wholly in Trade, Which makes sure of all favour that
> from time to time grows necessary, and can be given it by the Govern-
> ment.[99]

The continuing struggle against the Habsburg Empire launched this new-born
state onto the world stage. After the defeat of the Spanish Armada in 1588,
Dutch fleets were free to challenge Habsburg power far from the sandy shores
of Holland and Zeeland. The main theatres of war on land shifted to the
peripheral provinces of the Dutch Republic, where the struggle retained its
violent, civil-war-like features.[100] But it was on sea that Dutch superiority to the
former Habsburg overlords became most apparent, and the foundation of the
East and West India Companies in the first decades of the seventeenth century
allowed the state to transform an essentially defensive 'war of liberation' into a
war of conquest and empire-building.[101]

Internally, the formation of a unitary state grafted capital accumulation
onto a much larger geographic grid. Territorial unification created new links
between urban centres and agriculture, enhanced internal transportation, and
integrated the Amsterdam entrepôt more thoroughly with its economic hinterland.[102] However, there were real limits to economic integration. There

---

98   't Hart 1993a.
99   Temple 1673, p. 226.
100   Adriaenssen 2007.
101   Israel 1989, pp. 38 ff.
102   De Vries 1974, p. 120, Lesger 1993, and Lesger 2006.

always remained a large gap between the key sectors of capitalist production connected to international trade – such as shipbuilding, textiles, or arms
production with their developed economies of scale connected to the main
centres of export – and the mass of commodity production that was small
scale and locally oriented.[103] Numerically, Dutch industry was still dominated
by small businesses, creating a capitalist class that was divided between a top
layer of international merchant-industrialists and merchant-financiers whose
interests were primarily supra-national, and a large mass of small 'masters'
whose interests were equally integrated into a socioeconomic structure geared
towards the production and sale of commodities, but for whom the field of
activity did not stretch far beyond the borders of their town or region.[104] Politically, this created an enormous support-base for the kind of localist particularism that became entrenched in the federal make-up of the state. While international politics were in principle relegated to the 'generalty' level, economic
policy was mainly decided at the urban and provincial level, strengthening the
uneven development between the various regions instead of enabling the state
to challenge it.[105]

The federal-brokerage character of the state cemented these divisions in
a dual way. Formally, political power rested on a three-tiered system of geographic representation. At the local level, urban magistrates were chosen from
the upper-middle and upper classes by a system of co-optation. These magistrates, together with the numerically weaker representatives of the rural nobility, delegated members to the Provincial States. At the top of this pyramid was
the States General (*Staten Generaal*) that was composed of delegations from
all seven provinces, each holding a single vote. The most distinctive feature of
this system of government, compared to other early modern states, was the
great weight that it gave to representatives of the towns. The urban dominance in the Provincial States and delegations to the States General was most
pronounced in the seaborne provinces Holland and Zeeland, but even in most
other provinces urban and rural representation were at least equal, if not directly in favour of the towns.[106] Because voting rights in the Provincial States
and the States General were not weighed, the formal structure of decision-
making strengthened the influence of smaller voting towns. To compensate

---

103   Van Dillen 1970, p. 197.
104   Cf. Lis and Soly 1997.
105   't Hart 1993b, pp. 115–18 and Noordegraaf 2009a. For a case study for regional dynamics in
      one industry, see Yntema 2009.
106   Fockema Andreae 1961, p. 40.

for this, the larger towns – Amsterdam in particular, housing over ten percent of the population of the Republic, and representing an even greater share in its wealth – ensured they had a stronger position within the executive bodies. Both in the Council of State (*Raad van State*), the main executive board of the States General, and the daily government of the Provincial States (*Gecommitteerde Raden*), the wealthier towns managed to ensure greater weight. Jealously guarding the federal nature of the state, equity between the provinces more than administrative efficiency was the guiding principle in composing bureaucratic institutions from the Generalty Audit Office to the Admiralty Boards.[107] The same was true for the various commissions preparing resolutions on foreign policy questions.[108]

Parallel to this political structure, power in the Dutch Republic was further divided among various corporatist interest groups executing state-like functions and connected to the state in a much looser, sometimes only informal way. The federal structure of politics allowed those inhabiting these islands of brokerage organisation to consolidate their influence, playing local, provincial, and national structures against each other to maintain leverage over the activities of the state.[109] Most relevant to the subject of this book are the forms of brokerage power that stretched the realms of politics and the market for the organisation of warfare, such as the chartered trading companies with their extensive prerogatives for taking military action. But the dependence of the state on semi-private institutions went much further than that. The House of Orange, the most prominent example, formally attained its great influence over Dutch republican politics and the army through the election of its head to the position of stadtholder (*stadhouder*) of each of the seven provinces. But this influence was bolstered by it being the informal centre of an elaborate structure of patronage networks.[110] Even during the two long 'stadtholderless periods' (1651–72 and 1702–47) when the House of Orange was stripped of its executive

---

107   Federalism was so much thought to be the defining element of the Dutch political organ-
         isation that grand pensionary Johan de Witt could even contest the widespread use of the
         name 'Dutch Republic' in foreign publications, 'which is judged to be not appropriate for
         it, while these provinces do not form *una respublica*, but each province *separately* forms a
         sovereign respublica. And for this reason the United Provinces should not be called *respub-*
         lica (in singulari numero), but rather *respublicae foederatae* or *unitae*, in plurali numero'.
         Letter to Gerrit Pietersz Schaep, 10 May 1652, Fruin 1906, pp. 61–2.
108   Grever 1973, p. 43.
109   Groenveld and Wagenaar 2011.
110   Mörke 1997 and Janssen 2008.

functions, its members retained great influence through their local clients and their ability to operate as a 'party' with an international as well as a regional presence.[111] In a similar way, the Calvinist church functioned as a political platform but outside the state proper.[112] This position could turn it into a powerful framework for the mobilisation of lower-class opposition against regent rule, in the same way the Orangist party could at moments of crisis. But its leading bodies in fact tied the church closely to the ruling families and cemented their coherence as a social group.[113]

This combination of formal and informal roots of political power is perhaps best understood through the theoretical work of the Italian Marxist philosopher Antonio Gramsci. Borrowing a notion from Georges Sorel, Gramsci introduced the concept of the 'historic bloc' to understand the nexus of social relations, political institutions, and ideas that enable ruling classes to rule.[114] For Gramsci, a historic bloc ties the economic ruling classes – numerically too weak to dominate society in their own right – to parts of the middle and subaltern classes. In order to have any weight, the historic bloc must be rooted in the deep (economic) structures of society, but it can only be so in complex and contradictory ways. Political institutions and ideologies do not simply reflect social relations. They form the terrain on which conflicting classes and class-factions fight for 'hegemony', successfully integrating some sections of the population while excluding others. State power is the ultimate focus of these conflicts, but the state itself is redefined by Gramsci. In his notion, the state includes not only the formal trappings of politics, defined by him as the 'political state', or a collection of bureaucratic institutions, designated the 'state apparatus', but all institutions – formal as well as informal – that anchor class power.[115] Using those intellectual tools, Gramsci assembled the materials for rewriting the history of Italian politics as the long development of the modern bureaucratic state (in its totalitarian form, at the time of his writing) out of its medieval 'corporate' predecessors.

Gramsci's concept is helpful for the study of the early modern Netherlands because it goes beyond two simplistic but widespread notions of the state structure of the Dutch Republic: on the one hand, its conceptualisation as the purest of pure forms of merchant capitalism, ruled exclusively

---

111   Bruggeman 2007 and Onnekink 2011, esp. pp. 143–4.
112   Frijhoff 2008, pp. 105–7.
113   Schilling 1991, pp. 102–3 and p. 130.
114   Hoare and Smith 1978, p. 366.
115   Thomas 2009, pp. 68–71, pp. 141–3, and pp. 170–3.

by its merchant elites, and, on the other hand, its visualisation as a form of proto-democracy, based on representative structures and popular participation. Rather, the federal-brokerage structure of the Dutch state allowed it to mediate between a powerful merchant class oriented toward the world market, and social relations in production that remained predominantly small scale and local. The middle and upper strata of the urban small producers could feel represented by the state as long as its federal make-up provided easy access to career opportunities, contracts, and local economic protection, extending in turn their willingness to accept its rule and pay taxes. At the same time, extensive influence over the 'informal state' of powerful brokerage institutions gave the large international merchants, financial oligarchs, and the highly commercialised nobility disproportionate leverage over the ultimate deployment of state resources.

The coalition created by this state was inherently unstable. Instead of helping to overcome regional divisions and corporate particularism, federal-brokerage institutions locked those contradictions inside the state apparatus itself. Dutch politics turned into a constant haggling over influence. Furthermore, the lower classes were weakly integrated into this framework, and therefore easily mobilised by factions of the ruling class that temporarily found themselves ousted from power. Even at the level of the towns, as Van Nierop notes, '[t]here were no institutional or formal means through which the citizenry could express its opinions or criticize the magistrates'.[116] Therefore, almost every major external shock to the Dutch Republic was accompanied by revolutionary situations of sorts.[117] Finally, and perhaps most fatally for Dutch economic development in the long run, while loosely tying the interests of international trade to those of small-scale local manufacture, the Dutch state did not greatly stimulate their mutual integration and structurally privileged the former over the latter. This formed a major difference with its main competitor, England, as David Ormrod suggests in his study of the two commercial empires:

> Compared to their Dutch counterparts, English statesmen were, in the long term, driven to give equal attention to the protection of manufacturing, agricultural and commercial interests. For the Dutch of course, the last-mentioned remained of paramount importance.[118]

---

116   Van Nierop 1997, p. 161.
117   Cf. table 1.4.
118   Ormrod 2003, p. 49.

But the impact of these divisions and weaknesses was dampened by the extraordinary success of the Dutch 'Golden Age'. Around 1650 the Dutch cycle reached its zenith, expressed in but not caused by the combination of dominance over the two main axes of early modern trade: that between the Baltic and the Mediterranean, and that between the East Indies and the Atlantic. Agriculture and industry experienced new bouts of export-oriented growth, while the Amsterdam bourse became the financial centre of the world. Unity between the different elements of Dutch hegemony seemed to emerge spontaneously, underwriting the outward power of the States General while enabling them to retain their non-interventionist attitude towards the home economy.

The transition from the second, hegemonic phase of the cycle to the third – in which the Dutch Republic lost first its lead in manufactures, then in trade, and finally in finance, as well as its position as a European great power – can be seen as a second restructuring of the relations between state and society. But this restructuring should not be seen as a sudden break resulting from military or financial incapacity, nor as a turning away from commercial interests of the Dutch political elites. Its most important feature was the slow disintegration of the historic bloc that had supported the international power of the state. While manufacture, the motor of the urban economies, started to falter, leading to impoverishment of sections of the lower classes as well as sharpening political dissatisfaction among parts of the middle classes, the wealthy investors – often with great success – continued to search for ways to make profits by strengthening their connections to the global markets. The result was what Jan de Vries and Ad van der Woude described in their major overview of Dutch early modern economic development as a break-down of the connections between the various sectors of the Dutch economy.[119] The state, tied too closely to the conflicting sections of the elites through its federal-brokerage structures to mount a strong challenge to these trends, began to reinforce them. Attempts to reorganise the core institutions of the state along centralising lines practically came to nothing.[120]

Not the incapacity of its individual institutions, but the continuing success of these institutions in translating the pressures of their capitalist backers was what paralysed the Dutch state in the face of the loss of hegemony. In international power projection, as much as in the home economy, the results of

---

119   De Vries and Van der Woude 1997, pp. 681 ff.

120   That does not mean that in subordinated areas no steps towards centralisation were taken, but these steps left the overall federal-brokerage framework firmly in place. Cf. Groenveld, Wagenaar, and Van der Meer 2010.

this were geographically spread unevenly. While forced to cede their position as main power-brokers in the Baltic and Mediterranean regions, the Dutch long remained among the leading bulk-carriers in these regions, even if their share in total trade gradually declined. And an absolute decrease in the value of European trade was at least partially compensated by the growing weight of East and West India trade.[121] Meanwhile, Dutch finance lived its halcyon days. Only during the second half of the eighteenth century did the consequences of the loss of hegemony become fully visible, leading to a period of intense political and ideological crisis for the Dutch *ancien régime*, and eventually the revolutionary overthrow of the federal-brokerage state.

Content and Structure of the Book

After this historical-theoretical overview, the key theoretical presumptions of this book can now be summarised as follows. Private arrangements for warfare were an essential feature of inter-state competition during capitalism's infancy. These forms of brokerage did not so much belong to a clearly delineated stage in state formation, but were one among the various options that all early modern rulers had to choose from in their attempts to meet the pressures of international military and naval competition. The great preference of Dutch rulers for this particular option reflected structural features of Dutch society: the extent of capitalist development, the way the federal state responded to the geographic and sectional imbalances of its early economic breakthrough, and the nature of the 'historic bloc' underlying the state. The relation of this state to the economic elites in general, as well as in specific areas of bureaucratic organisation, changed with and in turn influenced the course of the Dutch cycle of accumulation.

Based on these considerations, three central hypotheses can be formulated to answer the main question outlined at the start of this introduction: why brokerage structures for the organisation of warfare had such perseverance in the Dutch Republic and how this in turn effected the development of Dutch capitalism and the state – or, reformulated along the lines of the theoretical explorations presented here, why the successive restructurings of the relations between state and society accompanying the Dutch cycle of accumulation did not lead to a shedding of the federal-brokerage model. The first hypothesis is that the persistence of brokerage structures was not necessar-

---

121   Israel 1989, pp. 377 ff., De Vries and Van der Woude 1997, p. 499, and Ormrod 2003, pp. 56–7.

ily a mark of the failure of the state, but could also be the result of success. The long-lasting ability of this particular type of organisation in mobilising the economic resources of society for the production of power allowed war to foster brokerage structures as much as it challenged them. The second hypothesis is that the survival of federal-brokerage structures does not underwrite the 'aristocratisation thesis' on the eighteenth-century state. Federal-brokerage structures could well continue to provide a framework for positive stimulation of capitalist development in the individual aspects of the state's activities, and remain responsive to the demands of capitalist economic elites. The third hypothesis is that eighteenth-century 'decline' in the effectiveness of the Dutch state should not be envisioned as the wholesale collapse of bureaucratic efficiency in individual areas of organisation, nor of overall institutional failure. The political crisis that enveloped the Dutch state rather consisted of a 'growing apart' of the different sections of the state, articulated through the sharpening of regional divisions and through the inability to recombine the various strands of institutional development into an overall programme for state reform matching the demands of late eighteenth-century power struggle.

These hypotheses will be tested by following the development of the Dutch federal-brokerage state from its revolutionary birth in the initial stages of its Eighty Years' War against the Spanish Habsburg monarchy to its equally tumultuous demise in the course of the Atlantic wave of revolutions from the 1770s to the turn of the nineteenth century. Three main areas of interaction between the state and capitalists in the organisation of warfare were singled out for this investigation: the joint activities of Admiralty Boards and commercial companies in the armed protection and expansion of trade; the interaction between Admiralty Boards and home markets in the production and supply of war fleets; and the operation of financial intermediaries between the provincial treasuries and the capital market in troop payments. Together, these three cases reflect the major strategic terrains of Dutch warfare: the struggle for dominance over European waters, the conquest of an overseas commercial empire, and the quest for security through engagement in continental wars. Each of these sectors was responsible for a major part of military expenditure. Troop payments formed by far the largest component of army expenditure, naval construction and supply the bulk of naval outlays, while the VOC and the WIC remained the most significant institutions for privatised warfare. By including these three sectors, this study encompasses branches of the Dutch state's armed activity that usually are treated separately: the navy, the warring merchant companies, and the army. This allows for an examination of the overall tendencies in the development of the Dutch state form in a way that would not have been feas-

ible by examining one of these sectors in isolation. The three sectors that are
investigated also encompass the relations between the state and very different
types of capitalist entrepreneurs, from the international merchants who sat on
the Admiralty Boards to the local small-producers who played a role in naval
supply and the large and small financiers who put up their credit for troop payment.

All selection is contentious, and more had to be left out than could be
included. The arms trade, for which the Dutch Republic became a major international hub during the first half of the seventeenth century, is only touched
on in passing.[122] This choice also leads to a strange omission of characters.
The Trip family – who dominated the Dutch-Swedish cannon trade in the
mid-seventeenth century and built a giant house along one of the Amsterdam
canals larded with cannon balls and olive branches to ensure that their achievement was noticed – will hardly appear in these pages.[123] The evolution of the
command structure and regimental organisation of the Dutch army is barely
touched on.[124] The same is true for the ways the Dutch Republic organised
the defence of its borders and garrisoned its soldiers.[125] This study leaves out
much of the important debates within the state on 'grand strategy', and – perhaps disappointing the military aficionado – will say very little about the actual
course of the wars in which the Dutch Republic fought. Even after leaving out
all of these potential areas of investigation, the amount of source material available remained daunting. The study charges freely across two centuries, and
three major aspects of warfare. Each of these would probably have warranted
a separate monograph, and taken individually would perhaps have been better
served. But the advantages of their combination hopefully outweigh the disadvantages of the more summary treatment necessitated by the scope of this
project. Given the fragmented nature of Dutch political administration and the
high-level involvement of non-bureaucratic actors, the sources are scattered
over many different archives. With the navy governed by five different Admiralty Boards and supervised by the States General, the army paid from seven
different provincial treasuries, and the merchant companies administrated by
chambers in different towns in the Dutch Republic, sharp and sometimes pain-
ful choices had to be made in the use of archival collections. In the case of the
Admiralty Boards, these choices were further aggravated by the burning down

---

122 De Jong 2005. Also see Westera 1999.
123 Klein 1965.
124 For more on this subject, see Zwitzer 1991, Swart 2006, and Van Nimwegen 2010.
125 Vermeesch 2006 and Vermeesch 2009.

of the then newly centralised marine archive in the mid-nineteenth century. As far as the limits of a single book permit, breadth of sources has been attempted where focus was lacking in the sources and vice versa.

The structure of the book flows from the theoretical framework outlined in this introduction. The first chapter puts the creation of federal-brokerage arrangements in the three areas under investigation in the context of the emergence and consolidation of the state from the Dutch Revolt to the mid-seventeenth century. It explains how merchant companies, Admiralty Boards, and financial intermediation in troop payment represented very different types of organisation, but all in their own way reflected the fundamental charac-teristics of the federal-brokerage state. Chapters Two to Four then trace the developments of these forms of organisation in each individual sector from the zenith of the Dutch cycle around 1650 to its third phase of financialisation and relative decline in the mid-eighteenth century. Each of these chapters will search for the particular combination of the pressures of warfare, internal insti-tutional dynamics, and wider economic context that led to the partial or total preservation of federal-brokerage arrangements. The fifth and final chapter will examine the crisis of the Dutch *ancien régime* as, among other things, a crisis of the federal-brokerage state form. It will show how each of the three sectors of state-organisation central to the book became subject to political debate, reform attempts, and ultimately revolutionary challenges. In doing so, this chapter will show the historic limits of the federal-brokerage state model.

The subject of this book is a particular state form, rather than the individu-als that inhabited this state or placed demands on it. But a careful attempt has been made to avoid writing a book on structures without seeing these struc-tures as the outcome and backdrop of human agency, the real substance of history. As far as possible, this study has striven to give names and faces to the bureaucrats and capitalists involved in making war, money, and the state. It has tried to keep an eye on their opinions as well as the content of their purses and portfolios, in the firm belief that culture and ideology do not reflect interests in a simple and straightforward way, and that perceptions are moulded by social action as well as shaping and motivating it. Concentrating on those running the state and the economy makes this a history from above. But where appropriate, acknowledgement has been given to the fact that even the most belligerent merchants did not carry sharp and shrapnel into the bellies of their ships, that generals usually did not lift one finger to move so much as a single cannon, and that, for all their proficiency in administration, the honourable members of the Admiralty Boards did not build men-of-war. War, as well as economic success, was made by the perennial others of the capitalist world-system. At the very best, these outsiders 'profited' from performing their parts by receiving a daily wage or soldiers' pay. At worst they found themselves on the receiving end, as the maimed, murdered, impoverished, subjected, or enslaved. However, on the rare occasions when they managed to violently break into the process of state formation – as they did at the end of the eighteenth century – they reshuffled the playing deck of their rulers in fundamental and often unexpected ways.

The Making of the Federal-Brokerage State

Merely a few years after the end of the Eighty Years' War that established the Dutch state as a European power, an extensive discussion of the fundamentals of the constitution riveted Dutch politics. This debate perhaps forms the best starting point for an examination of the rise and consolidation of the federal-brokerage state, the unique political structure that emerged from the Dutch Revolt. On 18 January 1651 some 300 delegates from the seven provinces of the Dutch Republic gathered in The Hague at the invitation of the States of Holland. This 'Great Assembly' came together at a momentous time. Only three years after the Peace of Westphalia, the young Republic found itself at the height of its economic expansion and international influence. To emphasise that this was a meeting of victors, the meeting hall was decorated with banners that had been captured from Spanish adversaries on land and at sea. The bellicose adornment had caused some controversy in commercial circles due to the extensive free trade agreement that the Dutch Republic and the Spanish king had concluded barely a month earlier.[1] Internally, the country had moved along the abyss of civil war when Stadtholder William II in July 1650 had brought his troops before the walls of Amsterdam in an attempt to forcefully end a long conflict over military finances and command. But the sudden death of William II that same year had averted this danger.[2] For the adversaries of the stadtholderate, the Great Assembly presented an opportunity to solidify a new stadtholderless status quo.

But the regent-rulers gathering in The Hague were also presented with grave challenges. The most pressing was the question of how to hold together a federal state containing so many conflicting claims for power without an 'eminent head'. In essence, this was the question asked by the Zeeland delegation at the start of the Great Assembly:

> ... [I]t is not likely, Highly Esteemed Gentlemen, that this *unity* will be observed as it should be, when the members of this body would collide because of internal *disagreements* and misunderstandings, and it is practically unthinkable that there would never arise differences within

---

1   Van Aitzema 1669c, p. 498.
2   Poelhekke 1973b, and Israel 1998, pp. 700 ff.

a government which, as ours, is composed of *seven free and sovereign provinces*, each in turn consisting of diverse members and cities ... and those themselves in turn represented by persons of various moods and interests, and regulated according to various laws, constitutions and customs.[3]

The speech of the Zeeland delegation echoed a popular theme in contemporary debates. As one pamphleteer summarised, pointing to the all too recent experience of war with Spain:

Inwardly we have *perpetuum discordia fomitem* [endless fuel for discord], outwardly we have a very powerful neighbour and extremely hostile enemy, who will never shrink from employing all possible means to recuperate what he has had to abandon against his will ...[4]

Given the precarious international situation and the recent clash between Amsterdam and William II, it is no surprise that one of the main sources of discord singled out in these debates was the question of control over the States army. Together with the question of the political constitution of the Union and the place of religion in politics, this was one of the three main items on the agenda proposed by the States of Holland. There was general agreement on the proposition made by the Friesland delegates that military affairs demanded a structure for decision-making that was more centralised and efficient than the one offered by the regular meetings of the States General. The delegates defended this point of view by referring to two maxims that belonged to the general repertoire of seventeenth-century statecraft:

... [T]hat in times of peace, one has to count on war, and that the nature of war brings with it, *quod ratio ejus non aliter bene constet quamsi uni reddatur* [that its rationale does not sit well with anything but unity]. [This unity is needed] both in order to maintain secret intelligence, without which one cannot be on guard and which can only remain secret among a small number of persons ... and in order to ... make sure one is ready and prepared ... for all eventualities ...[5]

---

3   Van Aitzema 1669c, p. 503. All italics are in the original, unless otherwise stated.
4   Rivo Ursino 1651, p. 13.
5   Van Aitzema 1669c, p. 510.

But how to guarantee such unity? Holland and most other provinces straightforwardly rejected the call to install a new stadtholder as captain general of the Dutch troops. Instead they successfully pushed for a strengthening of the Council of State, the main executive organ of the States General, composed of representatives of the seven sovereign provinces.[6] At the same time, however, they made sure that individual provinces received far-reaching authority over the companies and regiments on their provincial payroll. This was a dual victory for the Province of Holland. More than half the Dutch troops were paid out of its treasury, so more direct provincial control over the army directly strengthened its position within the state. Furthermore, Holland held the largest vote within the Council of State, which in its composition reflected 'the unequal contribution and interest that [the different provinces] have in the conservation of the common state'.[7] But other provinces stood to gain as well. In return for continued financing of the soldiers, yet more power was devolved from the generality to the provincial level, neatly divided according to the size of their purse. A further strengthening of provincial control over the troops enabled local authorities to redirect potential spin-offs of deployment – in the form of lucrative officer posts, supply contracts or loans for troop payments – to the paying provinces.[8]

This solution to an important internal conflict was characteristic for the Dutch state as it emerged from its eight decades of war against the Spanish Habsburg Empire. It reflected both the federal character of the political institutions and their brokerage nature, combining extensive local and provincial autonomy with structures that favoured the close involvement of capitalist elites in the execution of state tasks. The mixture of federalist and brokerage elements was particularly clear in the institutions created for the organisation of warfare. At first sight, these institutions formed a highly irregular pattern of ad hoc solutions, resulting from endless negotiations between politicians and members of various elite groups at the local, provincial and national level such as took place during the Great Assembly. Their establishment did not follow a pre-ordained plan, but was the result of a long series of contingencies. Nevertheless they proved enduring, suggesting there was more to their establishment than a series of more or less random responses to a prolonged state of emergency.

---

6   Zwitzer 1991, pp. 29–30.
7   The formulation is taken from the 'Deduction of Holland to the Great Assembly', Van Aitzema 1669c, p. 517.
8   't Hart 2014.

This chapter will examine the interplay between contingency and structure in the emergence of the Dutch federal-brokerage state. Section 1.1 surveys how in the course of the Dutch Revolt the federal-brokerage 'scenario' gained precedence over three alternative directions of state formation. The three sections that follow analyse the rise of federal-brokerage solutions on a more concrete level. Each focuses on one of the three main areas of the organisation of warfare that will be examined throughout the rest of this book. Section 1.2 deals with the warring function of merchant companies, section 1.3 with the way Admiralty Boards interacted with local capitalist elites in naval production and supply, and section 1.4 with the strong independent position of financial intermediaries in troop payment. The final section of this chapter looks at the ideological and political underpinnings of the Dutch state. These combined pragmatic coalition-building with powerful integrative notions that provided the language in which Dutch Republican rulers tried to overcome the divisions inherent in the federal-brokerage structure of the state. Together, these sections form an answer to the question posed by the Zeeland delegation at the start of the Great Assembly: the question of how unity could be maintained in an internally fragmented state, thus helping to explain how this uniquely formed state could emerge from its long war of independence as the dominant force within the expanding capitalist world-system.

1.1   The Dutch Revolt and the Establishment of the State

The state that successfully challenged Habsburg power in Europe and bey-ond had strong antecedents. Economically, the Dutch Republic emerged as the leading commercial power of Europe on the heels of a long surge of devel-opment that had already started in the medieval period. The course of this phase of the Dutch cycle of accumulation had left its imprint of sharply uneven regional development between the highly urbanised seaborne provinces as centres of production and long-distance trade in the West, and the heart-lands of capitalist agriculture and small-scale production in the East.[9] In fin-ance, developed urban and provincial structures for taxation and state loans were already in place before the start of the Revolt, forcing both the Habsburg authorities and their opponents into constant negotiation with local elites to

---

9   Blockmans 1993, Van Zanden 2001, Van Bavel 2010a, Van Bavel 2010b. For some additional
     considerations on the medieval roots of Dutch capitalism, as well as a more comprehensive
     survey of the historiography, see Brandon 2011b.

fund their struggles.[10] All seaborne provinces employed their own rudimentary navies for the protection of trade and fisheries, and Holland had already shown itself to be a force to be reckoned with in North European waters by intervening assertively in the Lübeck wars of the first decades of the sixteenth century.[11] Members of the urban bourgeoisie had already been involved to a high degree in military logistics.[12] Both federalism and strong interaction of – provincial – state authorities with local economic elites thus were well rooted in the Northern Netherlands' past.

Yet in 1550, it had by no means been inevitable that out of these medieval roots would grow the particular constellation of institutional arrangements that eventually became the Dutch Republic. The basic features of the new state only took shape during the long war against the Spanish Habsburg Empire, and were consolidated in the internal and external convulsions that accompanied it. The federal-brokerage state was one of the 'scenarios' implicit in these confrontations, but only became the dominant scenario with the defeat of three alternative directions for state formation that had been on the table during the first decades of the Revolt: centralisation under (restored) Habsburg control, a union of the Dutch provinces with one of the Habsburg Empire's European rivals, or a devolution of the loose alliance of provinces into its provincial component parts. During the initial stages of the Revolt, each of these scenarios seemed as likely, if not more likely, than the course towards independent statehood that was eventually taken. The first scenario, further centralisation under the Spanish crown, had been well underway at the time of the outbreak of the Revolt, and formed one of the main reasons for the rise of opposition movements among the higher and lower nobility.[13] But the nobles who in 1566 rallied at the Brussels court to demand greater leniency in religious persecution and respect for their local prerogatives were far from advocating independence.[14] Opposition to Habsburg centralisation hardened only in the course of the Revolt. Whereas in the 1570s differences over religious toleration had still been the main cause for the foundering of peace talks, by 1588 the acceptance of far-reaching autonomy for the States General and the individual provinces had become central to negotiations between rebels

---

10   Tracy 1985, pp. 57 ff., 't Hart 1993a, pp. 18–19, Tracy 2001, Fritschy 2003, Van der Heijden 2006, pp. 62 ff., Tracy 2008, Zuijderduijn 2009, Zuijderduijn 2010.
11   Bijl 1951, pp. 21 ff., and Sicking 2004, pp. 31 ff., and pp. 209–12.
12   Gunn, Grummitt, and Cools 2007, pp. 56 ff.
13   Parker 1979, pp. 47 ff., and Van Nierop 2001a, pp. 29–47, pp. 37–8.
14   Van Nierop 2001b, pp. 58–62.

and rulers.[15] In that year the Union of Utrecht, a treaty concluded in 1579 between the seven Northern provinces, was transformed from a temporary alliance into the political foundation of the Dutch Republic. The document came to be seen as a substitute constitution, and guaranteed a large measure of autonomy to each of the seven provinces. It transferred to the Generalty level only those issues that had a direct bearing on the interests of all the provinces combined, primarily defence against 'external and internal lords, kings, or princes, lands, provinces, towns or members' that would wage war against the United Provinces.[16] Defending their autonomy in revolution and war bound the core of the provincial elites to the principles set out in 1579. Unless forced upon them by military defeat, a settlement with the Spanish crown that would overthrow this state of affairs and restore the centralisation-scenario was by that time no longer feasible.[17]

The establishment of the independent Republic also meant the final collapse of the second scenario, a closer union with one of Philip II's European rivals. This option had been tried and tested for ten years, and had been the strong preference of the leader of the Revolt, William of Orange, up to his murder by a fanatic follower of the king of Spain in 1584.[18] However, both candidates selected to administer the Netherlands at the behest of a foreign crown, the Duke of Anjou and the Earl of Leicester, failed miserably in their attempts to rein in provincial particularism. The experience of the Leicester years – when the foreign governor had tried to mobilise his troops, militant Calvinism, and the urban lower classes to challenge the power of the provincial states and the States of Holland in particular – strengthened the ruling classes of the latter province in their determination to secure their own influence by the establishment of a fully independent Dutch state.[19] The strengthening of this conviction not only occurred as the result of internal struggles, but also because of the external developments of the war. The fall of Antwerp in 1585 assisted in the rise of Amsterdam as the centre of European bulk-carrying trade, while the defeat of the Spanish Armada in 1588 allowed the Dutch to take competition with the Habsburg Empire into the East and the West Indies.[20] The Dutch had become major contestants for leadership within the capitalist world-system, thereby

---

15   Hibben 1983, pp. 228–39.
16   Clause three of the Union treaty, reprinted in Groenveld 2009, p. 62.
17   For the long-lasting impact this had on notions of sovereignty in the Dutch Republic, see Baena 2011, pp. 133 ff.
18   Swart 1994, pp. 214–21, and 247–50.
19   Oosterhoff 1988, pp. 178– 9.
20   Israel 1989, pp. 37–42.

decreasing the likelihood of a permanent union with any of their European competitors.

At the same time, consciousness of the challenges and opportunities encountered by the new-born state on the international terrain also formed a permanent barrier to the third option: provincial devolution. This option had never presented itself as acutely as the others, but the strength of Holland's particularism did form a constant threat to the unity of the seven provinces. Nevertheless, the danger was counteracted by other, more powerful forces. Politically and militarily, the mutual dependence of Holland and the other provinces was too strong to risk a break-up. The economic superiority of Holland over the other provinces was so great that it always remained the financial lynchpin of Dutch military efforts. On the other hand, without the protecting ring of the inland provinces 'Holland's garden' would be too exposed to foreign intrusion to bloom.[21] Though there might not have been a lot of love, unity between the seven provinces therefore was more than just a marriage of convenience. This was true for economic reasons too. While circuits of commodity production and trade overall remained highly localised and connected to the world market only through the nodes of individual trading cities, the Habsburg period and the ensuing Revolt did set off some measure of intra-provincial economic integration. Burghers of Holland's towns became major land-investors in the other provinces, a process enhanced by land reclamations and the sale of former church property.[22] An impressive network of water transportation connected the various rural and urban trading zones.[23] In a real sense, successful engagement in international trade became tied to an economic hinterland that stretched across most of the Republic, albeit in highly uneven ways. Without producing anything approaching a 'national' ruling class, the local groups of ruling families were connected by more than expediency alone.

In this way, from the least likely option, the creation of an independent state had become the preferred option for the core of the Dutch bourgeoisie. By the turn of the seventeenth century the basic contours of the federal-brokerage state were drawn. Its political apparatus was made up of a three-tiered system of local governments, the sovereign Provincial States, and the States General, assisted by a relatively small bureaucracy. The federal arrangements of the 'political' state allowed for almost unmediated access of the ruling class – both

21 Tracy 2008, chapters III.7 and IV.10.

22 De Vries 1974, pp. 192 ff., and De Vries and Van der Woude 1997, p. 39.

23 De Vries 1978, p. 56.

large landowners and the urban bourgeoisie – to the process of policy-making. On the other hand, a powerful set of 'semi-formal' and 'informal' institutions reserved substantial political influence for particular interest groups within the ruling class, such as the nobility (through the stadtholderly court and military entrepreneurship), the long-distance merchants (through the merchant companies), or the powerful Amsterdam merchant community (through the special role of the Amsterdam burgomasters in the making of foreign policy, as well as through the city's great financial weight, enshrined in the foundation of the Amsterdam Bank of Exchange). The fact that the alternative trajectories of state formation were turned aside in the course of the Revolt can be seen as the result of a series of contingencies, the political outcome of a decades-long struggle whose result was in no way pre-ordained. But at the same time, the federal-brokerage model reflected deep-seated features of Dutch society that in hindsight help explain why this and not the other three scenarios came out on top. Cumbersome though it might seem, this state form integrated the main sections of the Dutch ruling class, those directed towards long-distance trade and those more strongly rooted in localised circuits of production and exchange, as well as creating a framework for coalition-building between the ruling class and sections of the urban middle classes. At the same time, the combination of formal, semi-formal, and informal political institutions enabled the Dutch state to tap society's economic resources for warfare at a scale sufficient to defeat the mighty Spanish Habsburg crown. Summing up this result of the process of state formation during the Dutch Revolt, Charles Tilly wrote:

> They [the seven provinces] made up a surprising state: an archipelago of bourgeois republics, each with its own militia, fiercely defending local privileges against the demands of the Stadhouder and even of their own creature, the States General. Nevertheless, the provinces and the States worked out a remarkably efficient division of labour, the provinces taxing and administering, the States waging war.[24]

How complete the victory of this particular model was can be gauged from the way in which around 1650 all three alternative scenarios briefly resurfaced, only to be dispelled as ghosts from a distant past. The attack of William II on Amsterdam in 1650 ushered in a pamphlet war that lasted for a year.[25] In the eyes of the most militant adversaries of the House of Orange, the conduct of the

---

24   Tilly 1993, p. 67.
25   Poelhekke 1973a.

stadtholder had raised the danger of a return to semi-monarchical authoritarianism only two years after the claims of the Spanish crown on the Dutch provinces had been destroyed for good.[26] But, as historian Poelhekke noted, the tone within the mainstream of debate was much more conciliatory. Making very liberal use of the notion of sovereignty, the function of the stadtholder as 'upper-sovereign' envisioned by his supporters was not one of an absolute monarch, but merely that of a unifying element among the provinces that would, in the words of one pamphlet writer, remain 'sovereign and free as a prince in taking their own state-wise resolutions without anyone being able to command them in anything'.[27] From the opposite side, the court-historian of the anti-stadtholderly party Lieuwe van Aitzema confirmed the unwillingness of the States of Holland to upset the general framework of the state in the wake of the death of William II:

> They could have said: we are sovereigns over our province, and over our purse. If we have given some authority to our stadtholder and captain general in the past, that is over now, and we take it back. Because of his death (*quae omnia solvit*) we have inherited it, God Almighty has returned it to us. And if the Danish master of court Ulefelt in 1649 in The Hague had reason to say: if our King is dead, we cannot only choose whomever we want, but also have the power to choose none and remain masters ourselves, Holland could speak in the same vein with even more justification. But they have never employed this language. Instead, they have contented themselves to maintain the old and prior style of government of this nation.[28]

As this remark signals, the opposite scenario to royal centralisation – provincial devolution – was equally off the cards. Practically the only serious proponent of Holland separatism was Pieter de la Court, the influential political economist behind Holland's grand pensionary during the First Stadtholderless Period, Johan de Witt. In his famous *True Interests of Holland*, he argued that this province alone was capable of maintaining a *Pax Neerlandica* at sea, while a desirable cutting back on military expenses was only forestalled by the harmful union with the other provinces:

---

26   Rowen 1988.
27   Cited in Poelhekke 1973a, p. 38.
28   Van Aitzema 1669c, p. 516.

This is the Condition of *Holland* in a time of perfect Peace; what will it be then when we consider, that the *Hollanders* must not only scour, or clear the Sea from Enemys, and defend their Towns and Country against all Foreign Force, but that they have also charged themselves with much more than the Union of *Utrecht* obliged them to, with the keeping of many conquered Citys, and circumjacent Provinces, which bring in no Profit to *Holland*, but are a certain Charge, being supply'd by that Province with Fortifications, Ammunition-houses, Victuals, Arms, Cannon, Pay for the Soldiers, yea, and which is a shameful thing to mention, with Guard-houses, and Money for quartering of Soldiers?[29]

In the polemic that followed the publication of the *True Interests*, this aspect of De la Court's argument was most vehemently rejected. As one of his critics wrote:

After he [De la Court] has well defended the interest of the merchants, he starts complaining about the other provinces, which make Holland carry the sole burden of the sea. It seems to me that this complaint has some reason, but when he speaks of leaving those provinces, he puts Holland on a dangerous road. Truly, the King of Spain would have spent many millions if he would have found a way to separate us ... When we are united, we are invincible, but separated, everyone can defeat us. The merchandise of Holland is trafficked to the other provinces and that of them into ours, and therefore we cannot be separated from them and they cannot be separated from us.[30]

Both in its geopolitical, and in its economic dimensions, this argument perfectly summed up why even among the Holland merchants De la Court's secessionism did not find real support.

Perhaps the most curious return to the arguments on state form of the 1580s was the 1651 proposal of Cromwell to form a 'closer union' between England and the Dutch Republic. The English ambassador, invited to speak at the Great Assembly in The Hague, argued for something that went farther than a normal diplomatic agreement between states, though falling short of a merger of the two republics. The delegation emphasised that the two young republics shared their protestant faith, conceptions of individual liberty against royal usurpa-

---

29   [De la Court] 1702, p. 23. For the political background of his ideas, see Weststeijn 2010.
30   Parival 1662, pp. 14–15.

tion, and trading interests against all the crowns of Europe, giving them an interest in joining defences.[31] The ambassadors, who in the streets and in front of their lodgings were met by hostile Orangist crowds, were hardly received more gently in the Assembly itself. Alluding to the Mercantilist economic idea that the profit of one state could only be the loss of another, the reply to Cromwell's embassy made perfectly clear why the Dutch Republic preferred to follow its own interests, and its own interests alone, in deciding its foreign policy:

> Commerce and traffic are often most plausibly mixed with great jealousy, especially between neighboring republics. As two twins, they constantly fight and wrestle with each other over their primogeniture, that is, profit. Therefore it can also be compared to connected waters, where the growth at one place is the erosion at another. For this, many wise and far-sighted persons have judged that commerce would be handled with more profit and security by this state if England would remain a kingdom, than if it is turned into a republic ...[32]

The resoluteness with which the pamphleteers of the 1650s could respond to these proposals makes clear how much had changed since the 1580s. The real scenarios for the future of the Dutch state of that time now appeared as theoretical excursions with only a faint bearing on the realities of the day.

1.2   Types of Brokerage 1: Merchant Warriors

In the course of the Eighty Years' War, the main features of the Dutch state had congealed around the federal-brokerage model. But this model left great room for practical variations at the level of individual institutions. The brokerage solutions that the rulers of the Dutch Republic employed in the organisation of warfare can be divided into three fundamental types. At one end of the spectrum, there was the situation in which merchants or other types of capitalist entrepreneurs bore full responsibility for the execution of war-related tasks, and governed them as their own private undertakings. The merchant companies, especially the VOC and WIC that held far-reaching prerogatives for possessing and administrating colonial territories and waging war, were the

---

31   Van Aitzema 1669c, p. 657.

32   Anonymous 1651, pp. 6–7.

clearest example of this form. On the other end of the spectrum stood those cases in which capitalists themselves were appointed and remunerated as state officials, handling contracts in the name of governmental bodies, managing state enterprises, and introducing market-derived practices in the execution of state tasks. As will be clear when examining the Admiralty Boards, the involvement of members of the leading commercial families in naval administration was structured in such a way that it inhibited the rise of large permanent bureaucracies, instead preserving the personal ties between officials and the market characteristic for brokerage institutions. A third type of brokerage, situated between the two extremes, put state officials in nominal control but left the execution of their tasks almost entirely to capitalist entrepreneurs, who did so within confines that were determined and regulated by the state. The large-scale involvement of private financiers in the payment of troops will be examined as an example of such 'institutionalised brokerage'.

Clearly, the first type of brokerage gave capitalists most room for manoeuvre and the greatest possibilities to push the state into adopting their priorities. The Dutch East India Company was one of the most powerful brokerage institutions of the early modern age. The root of this power lay in its ability to draw on a larger capital than any of the competing foreign institutions, and in the extensive autonomy it had received from the state in its overseas operations. Whereas its first major competitor, the Portuguese *Estado da India*, always remained the commercial branch of the crown's territorial ambitions, the VOC was from its inception primarily a commercial enterprise, employing violence to protect its profits. The significance of this shift was already emphasised by Niels Steensgaard:

> Simplifying greatly, one might say that here the relationship between 'profit' and 'power' is reversed. The Estado da India was a redistributive enterprise, which traded in order itself to obtain the full benefit of its use of violence, whereas the [Dutch and English East India] Companies were associations of merchants, which themselves used violence and thereby internalized the protection costs.[33]

---

33   Steensgaard 1973, p. 114. A very similar point was made already by Van der Oudermeulen in his famous 1785 memorandum: 'The Portuguese and even more so the Spaniards have come to East India not so much by perseverance to set up a simple trade with the inlanders, but to gain strongholds there, expand them, and govern them as kings and victors ... Our intention was to gain large windfalls by expeditions to far countries' (Van Hogendorp 1801, pp. 64–5).

The first charter of the VOC, drawn up by the States General in 1602, was explicit about the extent to which the company was free to engage in military activities in its own right. Article 35 of the charter established:

> ... [T]hat those of aforesaid Company, East of Cape Bonne Esperance as well as in and beyond the strait of Magelhaes, are entitled to make alliances as well as contracts with princes and potentates in the name of the States General of the United Netherlands, i.e., of the high authorities themselves. They are also entitled to build fortresses and strongholds there, summon and employ governors, soldiers, and public prosecutors ...

The next article gave the Company the right to act 'by any means that it can employ' against encroachments on its commercial activities. Further emphasising the autonomy of the Company from the state, article 39 decreed '... [t]hat it is not allowed to take ships, cannons, nor ammunition from said Company to serve the nation, other than with the Company's consent'.[34]

The willingness of the States General to grant the VOC far-reaching autonomy in the area of colonial warfare was connected to the ambition to carry the war against the Spanish Habsburg crown into the East Indies, and the belief that private interests would commit East India traders to take this task upon themselves voluntarily.[35] The argument was put in so many words in a meeting of the States General of 1 November 1603, little over a year after it had issued the charter to the Company. Representatives of the VOC were sternly admonished to make sure that Company ships would be well equipped and received instructions to engage 'the enemy's ships and goods',

> by which they will enlarge their reputation, not only to maintain, but to continue and expand their trade, which they would otherwise ... be bound to lose. And this has been the principal reason why the Gentlemen States General have procured the unification of the companies, and granted the charter and authorisation to do damage to the enemy.[36]

---

34 'Octroy, by de Hoogh Mog. Heeren Staten Generael der Vereenighde Nederlanden verleendt aen de Oost-Indische Compagnie' (Staten Generaal 1701, pp. 12–13).

35 Van Dam 1929, p. 484.

36 Rijperman 1950, p. 630. The companies referred to are the 'pre-companies' for Asia, united in the VOC in 1602.

While the VOC was a private enterprise, the States General ensured its influence over company policy in a number of ways. It had the power to withdraw or
renew the charter on which the VOC's monopoly position in Asian trade rested,
although in practice this charter became fixed for increasingly long periods of
time. The company directors (*bewindhebbers*) also had an obligation to hand
over yearly reports on their trading results to the States General. Local governments exerted influence over the governing boards of the VOC chambers. Strong
mutual ties between company and state were consciously fostered. Especially
during the first twenty-five years, when the VOC's presence in Asia was still
insecure and in Europe the Republic repeatedly had to fight for its survival, privateering, conquest, and assistance in war often took precedence over trade. At
this time, the relationship between state and company was at its most symbiotic and mutual financial or military aid was frequently given.[37]

This symbiotic relationship sometimes led to vehement arguments among
VOC investors about whether too much attention was given to military activities
at the cost of trade, and whether the state benefited more than shareholders
from the investments made in the Company.[38] These were intersected by the
sometimes diverging interests of investors in the Republic and the Company's
representatives in Asia. Later in the seventeenth and eighteenth centuries, such
arguments were reproduced in light of the growing relative weight of the costs
of colonial administration produced by the territorial gains of the VOC. In 1685
the leading Dutch diplomat and Company director Coenraad van Beuningen
famously summed up this dilemma by stating that the VOC was 'a company
of commerce but also of state'.[39] However, even a coloniser as ruthless as Jan
Pietersz Coen was never in doubt that the ultimate aim of warfare for the
Company was profit. This acknowledgement was the foundation stone of the
division of labour between the VOC and the state, which, if maintained, would
benefit both:

> ... [T]he General Company [i.e., the VOC] wages war for the United Neth-
> erlands in East India. If someone would say that it should abstain from
> this, and that the common country in its turn has its hands full of its own
> defence, the answer to this is that without the might of arms the trade
> with East India cannot be maintained, nor can the state of the United

---

37   Enthoven 2002, p. 39.
38   The latter argument was forcefully advanced in an anonymous pamphlet from 1644,
      reproduced in Van Dam 1929, pp. 514 ff.
39   Quoted Gaastra 2003, p. 57.

Netherlands be maintained without the trade with East India ... Send us yearly (we ask you once again, in the interest of our common welfare) a large quantity of ships, men, and money, and Your Honours will in time become masters of the most important trade of the entire world ...[40]

One of the most remarkable features of the organisation of the VOC is how its internal structure mirrored that of the Dutch state. Six 'chambers', situated in Amsterdam, Middelburg, Delft, Rotterdam, Hoorn, and Enkhuizen, organised the sending out of merchant fleets and the trade in East Indian products. At the head of the Company stood a college of 17 directors elected from the chambers. Five out of six cities with a VOC chamber also housed an Admiralty Board, and the important committee meetings of the 17 directors were styled after the Admiralty Boards' joint meetings in The Hague, the *Haagse Besognes*.[41] The VOC thus copied the federal structure of the state, enabling it to develop close links to the 'political state' at the local, regional and generalty level.[42] An important difference with the regular representative organs of the state, however, was that the commercial character of the VOC allowed it to select its leading cadres even more thoroughly on the basis of class and wealth. The rules for appointing directors strongly favoured large shareholders over small shareholders, the rich Amsterdam chamber over the five other chambers and members from the ruling oligarchic families over outsiders.[43]

While the other merchant companies were very much like the VOC in the way they replicated the federal structure of the Dutch state, the balance between trade and power was different for each. Erected in 1621 to gain a commercial foothold in the Americas, where Spanish territorial control was much more firmly rooted than in the East Indies, the West India Company or WIC in practice became a military extension of the Dutch state first, and a merchant company second.[44] Its charter granted the WIC prerogatives for warfare and the conclusion of treaties in terms that were almost literally copied from the VOC charter. But it is significant that in the WIC charter these conditions were put almost at the beginning of the text, rather than towards the end. Furthermore, extra clauses were added that were absent from the VOC charter,

40   Missive to the directors of the VOC, 22 January 1620, Colenbrander and Coolhaas 1919, p. 531.
41   Gelderblom, De Jong, and Jonker 2011.
42   Van Brakel 1908, pp. 81–2, Enthoven 2002, p. 39.
43   Gaastra 2003, p. 32.
44   Den Heijer 1994, pp. 33–4.

promising the WIC extensive state support in the form of soldiers and fortresses.[45] The strong emphasis on war and privateering, coupled with the long
drawn-out and ultimately unsuccessful attempt to take over Portuguese Brazil,
formed a lasting barrier to the creation of a stable investor base for the first
WIC. In 1674 it was replaced by the second West India Company. The debts
accumulated by the first WIC were cleared, and a new charter and slimmed-
down administrative structure guaranteed that from then on trade would take
precedence over war. The ambitions of the Company were tempered accordingly. The WIC operated from a smaller colonial base than its Asian counterpart,
and was forced to accept the partial abolition of its monopoly status in the
West Indies.[46] Nevertheless, thanks not in small part to direct military support
from the Dutch state, the first and second WIC did provide the groundwork for
the profitable role of Dutch capitalists in the transatlantic trade in enslaved
Africans, and for the eighteenth-century economic success of the Caribbean
plantation economy that would become one of the major expansion areas of
Dutch trade.[47]

The European context again produced a different kind of institution. There,
the intensity of inter-state competition and the tightly woven pattern of diplomatic relations left no room for merchant companies to wage war or make
treaties with foreign states at their own calling. But the widespread use of forms
of irregular warfare such as privateering and piracy did force the Baltic, Norwe-
gian, French, Mediterranean, and Levantine merchants to pay serious attention
to trade protection. In the early years of the seventeenth century some trading companies were erected using the model of the VOC, but within those
companies the regulation of the market soon gained precedence over military functions.[48] The monopolistic tendencies inherent in the structure of the
colonial companies did not sit well with the extent and accessibility of most
European trade. Therefore a different model of cooperation arose in the form
of merchant directorates. Basically these were self-regulatory bodies consisting
of a number of the leading members of a merchant community.[49] The director-

---

45   Conditions ii–vii of the charter. Staten Generaal 1637.
46   Den Heijer 1994, pp. 111 ff.
47   Nimako and Willemsen 2011.
48   This for example was the case with the Nordic Company, erected in 1614 mainly to limit
      competition in the whale trade and share the losses from English attacks on the whaling
      fleet. Van Brakel 1908, pp. 27–9.
49   These directorates should not be confused with the *Directies*, which were urban bodies
      that organised convoys on important trade routes next to the Admiralty Boards until the
      mid-1650s. See Chapter Two.

ates attained the right to enforce protective measures for all merchants of this community, such as sailing in convoy, carrying cannons, or manning ships with soldiers. The directorates also functioned as lobbying groups, advising Admiralty Boards in the organisation of cruising and convoying, protesting custom raises or suggesting protective measures for their trade, and fulfilling limited diplomatic functions. The first and probably most successful example was the Directorate of Levantine Trade, which was erected in 1625 at the request of 37 merchants to organise protection against 'the robberies up to the Davis Strait by those of Algiers, Tunis and others'.[50] Much later, directorates for the Eastern and Moscovian trade were erected along similar lines.

Despite differences in the balance between trade and warfare, monopolistic or free trade policies, internal organisation, wealth, and influence, these merchant companies and directorates shared important characteristics as brokerage institutions. All were private or semi-private institutions, engaging in warfare or armed protection as extensions of their commercial activities. Where warfare seemed to overtake commerce in prominence, as was the case in the first WIC, it directly threatened the vitality of the institutions themselves. State and merchants thus had a mutual interest in maintaining the independence of these brokerage institutions. The federal structure of the state also made it harder for authorities to encroach upon this independence, since every move by a regional group of rulers to try and gain greater control over sections of the merchant companies could be counteracted by rulers and merchants from other regions. In this way, particularly the colonial companies could gain and maintain their exceptional influence as states within the state.

1.3   Types of Brokerage 2: Merchants as Administrators

Forms of brokerage in the organisation of state navies differed substantially from those centring on the activities of merchant companies. Nevertheless, while more bureaucratic in nature than their commercial counterparts, capitalists were still employed at every level of naval organisation and often in ways that gave them decisive influence on planning and decision-making. Until the rise of the modern factory, the building and equipment of a fully armed warship remained the largest, most concentrated form of investment in material goods that either the state or private entrepreneurs could undertake.[51] As bur-

---

50   Heeringa 1910, p. 968.
51   As estimated by Brewer 1988, p. 34.

eaucratic institutions, naval administrations had to develop strong links to the market to be able to execute their tasks. The way in which this was done differed from country to country, varying between cases in which the state firmly controlled most stages of production and supply to cases in which much initiative was left to private capital.[52] The Dutch Republic was an example of the latter. In his comparative study of early modern navies, Jan Glete noted that '... [t]he connection between the interest base and the composition and operations of the state navy is unusually clear in the Dutch case'.[53] To a great extent this was due to the organisational structure of Dutch naval administration, in which five independent Admiralty Boards – located in the main ports of Holland, Zeeland and Friesland – were governed by colleges consisting of delegates from the different towns and provinces. The States General, which supervised the Admiralty Boards, consisted of delegates from the same towns and provinces. The main permanent source of funding for the navy was provided by custom incomes, and thus directly linked to trade. A strong social bias in the selection of delegates to the colleges further strengthened the ties between naval administration and local merchant communities.[54]

The division of naval administration into five separate institutions was a child of the Dutch Revolt. During the 1570s, the motley crews of the disorganised Sea-Beggar fleet were transformed into a rudimentary navy. Initially, this was done on a purely local basis. It was the establishment of a 'Closer Union' between the two core rebel provinces Holland and Zeeland in 1576 that led to the formation of a joint navy under the leadership of William of Orange. Since Amsterdam at this time was still loyal to the Habsburg rulers the then insignificant port city of Rotterdam became the location of the Admiralty Board. This could have worked in favour of the creation of a centralised naval administration, since Rotterdam had little political weight of its own and was located near Delft, the seat of the Prince of Orange, and The Hague, the bureaucratic centre of the Republic.[55] However, Zeeland administrators rejected what they perceived as Holland's domination over the new naval institutions. Before the

---

52   Good examples of the former are Sweden, Spain and France. Glete 2010, p. 28, Torres
      Sánchez 2009, p. 162, Mémain 1936, pp. 295–6, and Symcox 1974, pp. 40–1. A good example
      of the latter is the English navy, especially after the reforms of the mid-seventeenth
      century. Rodger 2004, pp. 44 ff.
53   Glete 1993, p. 154.
54   For general descriptions of the functioning of naval administration, see Bruijn 1970,
      pp. 40 ff., and Bruijn 1993.
55   Koopmans 1990, pp. 27–8.

Revolt, the Zeeland town Veere had housed the principal institutions of the Habsburg navy, and now the province refused to give up its position so easily.[56]

Tensions between centralising and particularist tendencies became even more pronounced after the murder of William of Orange in 1584, during the troubled governorship of the Earl of Leicester. Leicester strove to bring naval direction under the supervision of the Council of State. In order to placate those who opposed the centralisation of power, he agreed that executive power would be divided over three Admiralty Boards. Next to a Rotterdam Admiralty Board, he proposed one in Zeeland and one in the Northern Quarter of Holland, which would reside in the important Zuiderzee port-city Hoorn. However, Hoorn had its own reasons to refuse at this point, and Amsterdam – which by now had joined the revolt – managed to manoeuvre itself into position to claim the third Admiralty seat. When Leicester left, fragmentation went even further. Central authority over the navy shifted from the Council of State to the States General, in which provincial and local interests were reflected even more strongly than in the former institution. Meanwhile, the Northern Quarter of Holland protested against the usurpation of its seat by Amsterdam. A fourth Admiralty Board was established that was shared between the two Northern Quarter towns Hoorn and Enkhuizen. Finally, in 1596 the two northernmost provinces Friesland and Groningen managed to enforce the establishment of a fifth Admiralty Board, located first in the Friesland port Dokkum and later in Harlingen. The naval instruction issued by the States General in 1597 affirmed this division into five independent Admiralty Boards, allowing each far-reaching administrative autonomy; the choice of naval officers, including their own admirals; and the right to fit out convoying expeditions as long as this was done 'in good correspondence' with the other Admiralty Boards and the States General.[57]

The manner of allocating funds was another factor strengthening the federal and brokerage character of the navy. The Admiralty Boards drew their income from two principal sources. The first, permanent source of revenue was formed by customs (*convooien* and *licenten*).[58] The Admiralty Boards themselves were responsible for the collection of these taxes in the cities where they were located and in a series of offices along administrative borders (the *buytencomptoren* or outside offices). The costs of administering the collection

---

56   Sicking 2004, p. 407.

57   'Instructie voor de Collegien ter Admiraliteyt', 13 August 1597, Staten Generaal 1689, p. 11.

58   't Hart 1993a, pp. 100 ff.

of these taxes were high, and the efficiency of the Admiralty Boards in fulfilling their duties in this respect was often questioned. Furthermore, given the great variations in economic strength within the Republic, financing naval power through a tax on trade tended to emphasise the existing inequalities in the weight of the different Admiralty Boards. However, direct control over the raising of customs gave the towns in which the Admiralty Boards were situated leverage over an important instrument of economic policy. This advantage to the local elites far outweighed any potential disadvantage arising from the inefficiencies of localised collection, and they henceforward defended the privilege of housing their own Admiralty Boards tooth and nail. The system of funding also strengthened the sway of merchants over the employment of the navy, since they could argue that paying for the upkeep of the fleet entitled them to the benefit of naval protection. The fact that the Dutch name chosen for the ordinary customs was 'convoy' affirmed this direct link.

The second source of income for the Admiralty Boards equally strengthened local control. This was formed by subsidies decided on by the States General, earmarked for particular purposes such as the building or fitting out of a number of warships. As was the case with all other funds allocated by the States General, the actual collection of these subsidies was distributed over the different provinces through a quota system. Each individual subsidy or 'petition' had to be approved by every single province in an often painstaking process of negotiation. Even when approval was granted, provinces could forestall payment for many years, or sometimes forever. Especially during times of war, these subsidies could far outstrip the income from customs, and non-compliance of individual provinces could seriously harm naval performance. Again, this provided a political route for merchants to pressure the Admiralty Boards by using their influence over the Provincial States.[59]

Of course, the rulers of the Dutch Republic were not blind to the need for cooperation between the five Admiralty Boards. Soon after the establishment of the federal navy, attempts were made to increase the level of coordination, sometimes going as far as proposing full administrative centralisation. Already in 1589 stadtholder Maurits of Nassau tried to establish a 'College of Supervision' (*College van Superintendentie*), but failed in the teeth of opposition from the more peripheral provinces Zeeland and Friesland, which feared Holland control over the new institution. Significantly, in the run up to the instruction of 1597 formalising the federal nature of naval institutions, centralised alternat-

---

59   Bruijn 1993, pp. 6–9.

ives were seriously contemplated once again. Just preceding the acceptance of the final version of the new instruction, a resolution noted that there had been thorough discussion:

> how and in what way the administration of customs and the policy of the affairs of the Admiralty Boards, with their appurtenances, could be accounted for to the greatest advantage of the Generalty and contentment of the United Provinces; either by the introduction of a general college, with deputies thereof in the respective quarters, or by the erection of several colleges ...[60]

This discussion in the run up to the instruction of 1597 was certainly not the last time that centralisation was contemplated. In the 1630s stadtholder and admiral general Fredrick Henry of Orange made several attempts at administrative unification. He proposed to separate convoying, which he intended to remain in the hands of the five Admiralty Boards, from the fitting out of the blockading fleet for Flanders, which he tried to organise through one directorate operating from Hellevoetsluys.[61] This directorate would be supervised by

> a *permanent college* with its necessary officers, which would reside in The Hague, for which the most able and experienced Gentlemen Councillors from the respective Admiralty Boards would be employed, or some other pious, experienced, and able persons that will be selected for this task ...[62]

However, the proposal suffered the same fate as its predecessors, this time because of opposition from the Amsterdam burgomasters.[63]

The structure of naval administration ensured strong influence of local elites. At the head of each of the five Admiralty Boards was a college made up of representatives from towns and provinces. As was the case in all sections of the Dutch state, an intricate system of cross-representation had to ensure that all major towns and regions could take part in decision-making (see table 1.1). However, in each case the province in which the Admiralty Board was located was assigned the biggest delegation, containing half or more of the seats. With dominance over three out of five Admiralty Boards, and two-fifths of the total

---

60   Japikse 1926, p. 516.

61   Bruijn 1993, pp. 27–8.

62   Quoted from the original document in Van Aitzema 1669b, p. 594.

63   Van Aitzema 1996b, pp. 595–7, and Bruijn 1993, p. 28.

TABLE 1.1   *Number of representatives of each province in the five Admiralty Boards*

	Holland	Zeeland	Guelders	Utrecht	Friesland	Overijssel	Groningen	Total
Rotterdam Admiralty Board	7 *	1	1	1	1	1	–	12 (1644–1795)
Amsterdam Admiralty Board	6 **	1	1	1	1	1	1	12 (1606–1795)
Zeeland Admiralty Board	2 ***	6/7	–	1	–	–	–	9/10
Northern Quarter Admiralty Board	6 ****	1	1	1	1	1	–	11 (1606–1795)
Friesland Admiralty Board	1	–	1	1	4	1	2	10 (first half 17th century–1795)
Total number of representatives	22	9/10	4	5	7	4	3	54/55

* Nobility, Dordrecht, Delft, Rotterdam, Gorinchem, Schiedam, Den Briel
** Nobility, Haarlem, Leiden, Amsterdam, Gouda, Edam
*** Permanent: Amsterdam / on turn: Dordrecht, Delft, Rotterdam
**** Amsterdam, Gorinchem, Alkmaar, Hoorn / Enkhuizen, Monickendam, Medemblik
SOURCE: 'REPERTORIUM VAN AMBTSDRAGERS EN AMBTENAREN 1428–1861',
HTTP://WWW.HISTORICI.NL/RESOURCES/REPERTORIUM-VAN-AMBTSDRAGERS-EN-AMBTENAREN-1428
-1861, ACCESSED 26-11-2014

number of seats in all Admiralty Boards, Holland's share of control over naval administration exceeded that of the other provinces. Permanent seats in three out of the five Admiralty Boards gave Amsterdam an institutional advantage over the other Dutch towns. Besides the advantages in the distribution of seats, delegates from the home province of each Admiralty Board also benefited from closer proximity. In Amsterdam, for example, the representatives of Groningen, Friesland and Overijssel were mostly absent from important meetings, so that Holland's representatives could easily carry the vote.[64]

Prosopographic research confirms the ways in which the system of selection of personnel tightened the links of Admiralty Boards to the leading merchant

---

64   Bruijn 1970, p. 41.

TABLE 1.2   *Political ties of members of the Admiralty Boards*

Years	Number of councillors	Average years in in function	Function in local government	Function in provincial government	Function in national government
Representatives from Holland on the Amsterdam Admiralty Board					
1586–1699	170	5.1	151 (89%)	66 (40%)	29 (17%)
1700–95	116	5.8	107 (92%)	43 (37%)	26 (22%)
Representatives from Zeeland on the Zeeland Admiralty Board					
1584–1699	56	15.0	45 (80%)	55 (98%)	13 (23%)
1700–95	37	15.1	36 (97%)	37 (100%)	4 (11%)

SOURCES: SEE ANNEX ONE AND TWO

families. Annex One and Two contain two lists of Admiralty councillors: that of the representatives from Holland on the Amsterdam Admiralty Board, and of the Zeeland representatives in the Zeeland Admiralty Board. Table 1.2 sums up the extent to which Admiralty councillors engaged in political careers at the local, provincial and national levels of the Dutch state. The table affirms in particular how well integrated the Admiralty councillors were into the world of urban politics. Not only did almost all representatives of the towns gain their position on the Admiralty Boards through local office, often they had been or later became aldermen or burgomasters, the highest functions in urban politics. In Zeeland, strong local representation and strong integration into provincial politics went hand in hand.[65] With fifteen years, the average length of service to the institution was quite long. In contrast, Holland councillors on the Amsterdam board only served for periods of five to six years and were, by nature of the system of appointment, less tied to provincial politics than their Zeeland counterparts. Quick replacement helped to ensure that naval administrators remained true to the interests of their hometowns, therefore inhibiting the emergence of a strong bureaucratic culture focused on the institution they served.

The two lists also affirm a second point. Members of the Admiralty Boards were not only selected for their ties to local and regional politics. Their collect-

---

65   This had an administrative reason: in Zeeland, membership of the Provincial Government (the college of *Gecommitteerde Raden*) was coupled directly with the position of Admiralty councillor, also explaining the long tenureship of positions within the Admiralty Board.

ive biography reads like a *Who's Who* of Dutch Republican commercial elites. Out of the 287 Holland councillors, 54 also served as directors of the VOC, WIC, or the Society of Suriname. Among the Zeeland representatives ties with colonial trade were weaker, with eleven out of ninety-three councillors holding positions as directors of the local chambers of the VOC or WIC. But as Annex Two shows, many had strong family ties that connected them to one of the two companies. Perhaps more important is that, at least in Amsterdam, from the last quarter of the seventeenth century onwards the position of Admiralty councillor and VOC director were often combined. This ensured that at most times the VOC had at least one and sometimes more than one direct representative in naval administration. The connections between the Admiralty Boards and the colonial companies did not end there. Personal and family connections bound these two sections of the brokerage state even closer together. During the first half of the seventeenth century, the Amsterdam Admiralty Board contained three sons of founding traders of the VOC: Andries Bicker, Pieter Pietersz Hasselaar and Jacob Poppen. Jacob Cornelisz van Neck, known as one of the most influential Amsterdam Admiralty councillors of this period, had been admiral and investor in the 1598 East India fleet.[66]

Thanks to Elias's major study of the Amsterdam elite, much is known about the economic background of the Amsterdam Admiralty councillors. Table 1.3 gives an overview of the extraordinary wealth and connections of this group. Members of the Amsterdam Admiralty Board did not simply represent the largest merchant houses. They were part and parcel of them. In fact, their estimated wealth places them at the highest rungs of the economic elite.[67] Though more sparse, the data on wealth and income of the other councillors included in Annex One and Two affirm this image. Of the fifteen Leiden representatives for whom such figures are available, seven bequeathed an inheritance of over ƒ100,000, putting them among the richest of their town.[68]

Close ties to the merchant community at large were not only characteristic for the Admiralty councillors, but also for the small bureaucratic staff that served the Admiralty Boards. In Amsterdam, from 1641 until 1795 the position of secretary of the Admiralty Board was held by only two families, De Wildt and Backer. David de Wildt, who was secretary from 1641 to 1671, was the son of Haarlem representative and magistrate Gillis de Wildt.[69] In all likelihood

---

66   Terpstra 1950, pp. 152–3.
67   Burke 1974, pp. 55–6.
68   Prak 1985, p. 115.
69   Elias 1903, p. 392 and p. 468, and Elias 1905, pp. 876–7.

TABLE 1.3   *Wealth and connections of Amsterdam Admiralty councillors*

Period	Nr. of councillor	Director of VOC or WIC	Active merchant (Elias)	Son or son in law of active merchant (Elias)	Estimated wealth * (in guilders)	Estimated yearly income * (in guilders)
1586–1650	14	3	12	12	329,000 (6)	
1651–1700	15	12	5	15	245,000 (8)	
1701–50	10	5	2	9	1,795,000 (2)	22,000 (5)
1751–95	15	10	6	8	448,000 (5)	13,000 (7)
Total	54	30	25	44	465,000 (21)	17,000 (12)

* Average, number of councillors on which the figure is based within parentheses.
SOURCES: ELIAS 1903 AND ELIAS 1905

his father was not of extraordinary wealth. But in 1674 David de Wildt's widow bequeathed a sum of ƒ200,000. Two of David's daughters married merchants who were involved in trade with the Admiralty Board, the rich rope makers Hendrik and Jan Lijnslager.[70] His son Hiob de Wildt took over the position of secretary, which he held until 1704.[71] He married twice, first to Susanna Reael, daughter of Governor General of East India Laurens Reael, and after her death to Barbara de Neufville, daughter of the head of one of the leading Amsterdam merchant houses. Hiob de Wildt himself took to the ox trade, a profession that was closely related to victualing the VOC and the navy. His estate amounted to ƒ170,000. His son David was secretary until 1729.[72] Two of his daughters were married into leading merchant and banker families, that of Bicker and Pels. His son Job did not become secretary of the Amsterdam Admiralty Board, but receiver general of the same institution.[73] In 1742 his yearly income was estimated at twelve to fourteen thousand guilders. The post of secretary was

---

70   In 1691, Anna de Wildt, in the capacity of Hendrik Lijnslager's widow, supplied the Amsterdam Admiralty Board with ƒ197,812.8 worth of rope, thereby acting as by far the largest single supplier to the Admiralty that year. National Archive (henceforth NA), Archief Admiraliteitscolleges, no. 1930. 'Register ordonnantien Admiraliteit van Amsterdam, 1691'.
71   Elias 1903, pp. 392–3, and Elias 1905, p. 851.
72   Elias 1903, p. 109, p. 393, p. 447, and Elias 1905, p. 640, p. 705, p. 814.
73   Elias 1903, pp. 393–4, and Elias 1905, p. 807 and p. 899.

taken over by the then treasurer of the Admiralty Board, Cornelis Backer, and after him by his son Cornelis Cornelisz, who married the daughter of leading Amsterdam merchant banker Pieter Clifford.[74]

Although office holders everywhere in Europe were selected from the upper-middle classes and the rich, the strength of political and economic ties of Dutch naval councillors to the urban ruling classes was exceptional. In countries like Sweden, France and England a professional naval administration developed much earlier, selected respectively through aristocratic background, patronage of the crown, or service as naval officer.[75] Even though the Dutch navy formally became a state navy relatively early, the high level of integration between naval administration and the leading merchant families signified the continuation of brokerage, albeit in a form that was more state-centred than that practised by the commercial companies.

1.4   Types of Brokerage 3: Financial Intermediaries in Troop Payments

The third type of brokerage solution was one in which a task that nominally remained in the hands of state officials was in practice executed by private contractors and intermediaries, operating on their own capital and initiative but within confines that were determined by state regulation. This was the case with military solicitors (*solliciteurs militair*), financial agents who were responsible for the regular payment of troops. Military solicitors were financial middlemen, who often handled large sums of money which they drew on their own account on the credit market to cover for the arrears of the provincial treasuries that issued the payment ordinances for the States army.

In 1650 the *Political and Military Handbook* of M.Z. Boxhorn gave a concise description of the by then well-established practice of military soliciting. The most important challenge for the state in paying the troops, he argued, was 'to pay all of the soldiers their salaries every week or at most month, even though the payment office is almost depleted or becomes impoverished'.[76] Military solicitors helped to solve this problem. The term 'solicitor' in the early modern Netherlands had a wider use than in modern English and could be applied to brokers in politics and trade. The services of professional solicitors were used, for example, for sending requests to the Provincial States or the States General.

---

74   Elias 1903, p. 362, and Elias 1905, pp. 680–1, p. 757, p. 894, and p. 913.
75   Glete 2010, pp. 297 ff., Pritchard 1987, pp. 37–8, and Rodger 2004, p. 187.
76   Boxhorn 1674, p. 63.

In exchange for a fee, a solicitor would make sure all the required formalities were attended to, and a well-connected solicitor could also function as a sort of early modern lobbyist, using his contacts to open the right doors or make sure that a request landed at the right desk.[77]

Military solicitors did fulfil such general brokerage functions, handing in requests and filing complaints for the captains or colonels they served. But as Boxhorn's description makes clear, by the 1650s their primary function was financial. During the first half of the seventeenth century, military solicitors became the crucial link between the provincial treasury and the troops in the field. The process of troop payment started with the issuing of an ordinance by the Provincial States. The task of military solicitors was to collect the money from the provincial treasury (*comptoir*) and transfer it to the company captains, who were responsible for paying the soldiers. If the state ran out of funds (as happened more often than not), the solicitor guaranteed the continuation of payment 'either by his own means or by money received from others on interest'. In executing these tasks, Boxhorn acknowledged, 'those solicitors are driven by the hope for a large and secure profit'.[78] The solicitors received a salary out of the money they received from the States, and above this sum the solicitors could obtain an interest over the money they advanced. Especially in times of war, the earnings from interest payments could far surpass the salaries paid to the agent.

When and how this system of 'military soliciting' started remains unclear. According to Zwitzer's authoritative study of the States army, the first mention of military solicitors in the resolutions of the States General and the States of Holland dates from the years 1610–11.[79] However, military solicitors already appear sporadically in resolutions from a much earlier date. In 1578 the States General gave orders for the mustering of the artillery train of General Querecques. The results of the muster would be used as the basis for paying the soldiers through

> quelque solliciteur ou agent, pour retirer des Estatz lettres de décharge de leur trésorier general, chascun sur sa province respectivement, pour recepvoir paiement, qui sera ausdictes provinces défalcqué sur leur moyens généraulx ...[80]

77   Knevel 2001, p. 167.
78   Boxhorn 1674, pp. 63–4.
79   Zwitzer 1978, p. 78.
80   '[S]ome solicitors or agents, for drawing bills of payment from their treasurer-general on

The earlier date of origin of 'military soliciting' is of some significance. It suggests that this practice arose 'from the ranks' as one of many possible solutions to the chaos in army finances prevailing in the first decades of the Dutch Revolt, not as some well-thought-out strategy implemented from above. The resolutions of the States General of the early 1590s still mention frequent cases in which companies were not paid at all for many months, sometimes resulting in mutiny.[81] Similar problems continued to plague the Dutch Republic throughout the Eighty Years' War.[82] Various emergency solutions were put into practice, from asking the rich States of Holland to advance the money for poorer provinces, to levying forced contributions in the Dutch countryside, or drawing on the personal credit of high officials.[83] Considering this administrative chaos, the need for a broker presenting their case to the States General and helping to solve the immediate problems arising from non-payment might have been greatest for companies operating far away from home. It is likely that the commanders of foreign troops did not have the same range of local political and economic contacts that were available to indigenous officers. In the 1580s Leicester continuously complained that the States General were not forthcoming with the necessary funds to pay the English companies, and in order 'to keep the men from starving' he had to take credit from English merchants who lived in the Netherlands.[84] For this early period military solicitors are mainly mentioned in connection with foreign companies. The German companies of Hohenlohe already employed a 'solicitor or servant' in the late 1580s, who made requests for payment to the States General.[85] In the first decade of the seventeenth century, the French regiments were served by the solicitors Esaias Châtelain and Pieter Parret.[86] The English companies employed several solicitors as well, who, apart from assisting in paying the troops, also played a role in finding accommodation.[87]

---

the States, everyone on that of his respective province, for receiving payment, covered by said provinces out of their general means' (Japikse 1917, p. 248).

81   Japikse 1923, pp. 154–8.

82   De Cauwer 2008, pp. 149–51 and pp. 206–9.

83   For loans on the Province of Holland: Japikse 1923, p. 156; for levying the countryside: Japikse 1923, p. 166, and Adriaenssen 2007, pp. 202–4; for drawing on personal credit: Japikse 1923, p. 169.

84   Neale 1930, p. 384.

85   Japikse 1922, pp. 123–4 and p. 129.

86   Rijperman 1957, p. 143, p. 145, p. 392, p. 393, p. 705, and Rijperman 1970, p. 193 and p. 521.

87   Rijperman 1957, p. 682, and Van Deursen 1971, p. 72, p. 145, and p. 432.

During the first decades of the seventeenth century more and more companies employed military solicitors, and the practice also spread to non-foreign
regiments. This process went hand in hand with the first steps towards form-
alisation of soliciting practices. In 1606 a number of solicitors, among whom
the solicitor of the French regiments Châtelain, were summoned by the States
General to take an oath promising to observe the existing regulation for troop
payments.[88] And in 1608 the members of the Provincial Government of Holland
(*Gecommitteerde Raden*), the functionaries responsible for the daily management of the affairs of the Provincial States, issued their first general order for the
payment of soldiers through the intermediation of 'the solicitors of the companies in The Hague'.[89] It would be wrong to assume that in those early years
the business of military solicitors much resembled the relatively well-ordered
system described by Boxhorn for the 1650s. The terms on which soliciting took
place seem to have been negotiated per case. In 1615 the merchants Caspar
van Uffelen, Johan Baptista Colpin, and Guido de la Maire offered to handle
the payment of the garrisons in the Lands of Gulik, demanding 1.5 percent
interest per month, and a mere one month term for repayment.[90] The Council
of State did not agree to those conditions, considering them exorbitant.[91] To the
complaint about the high interest rate it added fears of a profiteering scheme,
suggesting that the three merchants wanted to speculate on the differences
in the exchange rate between The Hague and the provinces the money had
to be transferred to. However, handling money transfers over larger distances
could be a source of loss as well as gain, and high interest rates might well have
been considered a compensation for great risks. A serious matter for debate
during those early years of soliciting was the question of who would carry the
risks of sending large amounts of money through insecure lands. In one case,
French regiments garrisoned in a border area were withheld their wages after
the Province of Holland had supplied the funds, since neither the solicitors nor
the captains were willing to share the risks of transport.[92]

---

88   Rijperman 1957, p. 673.
89   NA, Archief van de Gecommitteerde Raden van de Staten van Holland en Westfriesland,
     no. 3291, Indices op de Resoluties 1624–59.
90   Van Deursen 1984, p. 430.
91   In the Republic, army payment did not take place monthly but once every *Heeremaand*
     or pay month of 42 days, dividing the year in eight full pay months and one '*korte
     Heeremaand*' or short pay month of 29 days. At 1.5 percent per pay month, the yearly
     interest rate in this case would have amounted to 13 percent.
92   Van Deursen 1984, p. 329.

Military soliciting only became applied across the board during the relative quiet of the Twelve Years' Truce with Spain (1609–21). Resolutions dealing not with individual financiers but introducing regulation for military soliciting in general followed in the 1620s and 1630s, when the war resumed in full force. A resolution by the Provincial Government of Holland from 1622 strengthened the position of military solicitors vis-à-vis the captains who employed them. It gave them the right to redeem any outstanding debts when a captain died by selling the arms in possession of the company involved. Furthermore, it prohibited captains from firing their solicitors without the consent of the Provincial Government.[93] And in 1632 it resolved 'to free and secure [the solicitors] from all accidents, whether through capture by the enemy or otherwise', promising to repay any money that was stolen or lost on the way to the frontlines.[94] The introduction of such regulations transformed military soliciting from one of many temporary solutions to the problem of non-payment into the preferred way to organise the payment of troops. At one and the same time, this enabled the state to draw funds on the credit markets more easily, and strengthened the position of private intermediaries within the system of military financing.

1.5   Political and Ideological Foundations of the Federal-Brokerage State

As the example of military soliciting shows, the formation of federal-brokerage practices could occur through a long series of more or less ad hoc decisions, aimed at solving immediate crises in military organisation. However, the persistency with which such solutions came to the fore suggests a deeper underlying consensus on the desirability of structures that maintained both the federal character of the Republic and strong interaction between state and entrepreneurs in the organisation of warfare. To understand the foundations of this consensus, it is necessary to take a look at the political and ideological sources for unity within the state more generally.

All states rule through a mixture of coercion and consent, and the Dutch Republic was no exception. The idea that the strength of the state emanates from harmony between citizens, and that the aim of politics was to overcome

---

93   NA, Archief van de Gecommitteerde Raden van de Staten van Holland en Westfriesland, no. 3000. 'Resoluties 1621–1624', and Zwitzer, *Militie van den staat*, p. 94.

94   NA, Archief van de Gecommitteerde Raden van de Staten van Holland en Westfriesland, no. 3000B. 'Resoluties 1630–1635', fol. 132 vso.

the sources of division, was deeply ingrained in Dutch political theory.[95] But how could a state consisting of so many conflicting and overlapping institutions maintain the adherence of the competing sections of the ruling class, let alone of the population at large? Simon Stevin, the theorist and mathematician behind Maurits's army reforms at the end of the sixteenth century, neatly summed up the problem:

> In civic questions, one favours war and the other peace, this person considers it necessary to engage in taxation and making public costs and that opposes it; meaning that whichever side the ruler chooses, he receives the ingratitude and hatred of a large crowd. Yes, even when he is God-fearing, loyal and just, they will still call him a blasphemer, traitor and thief of the common means ...[96]

The federal-brokerage character of the Dutch state represented an elaborate compromise between strongly institutionalised interest groups. The price of this compromise was a state that was internally cartelised, and therefore politically unstable. War brought internal tensions to the fore, and revolutionary crises accompanied every major shift in the international situation (for an overview of such crises, see table 1.4). However, given the volatile nature of early modern politics in general, the most surprising fact perhaps is the ease with which the Dutch Republic overcame these moments of contention. Despite violent shifts between stadtholderly and stadtholderless regimes in the two centuries between the 1590s and the 1780s, the Dutch ruling class managed to avoid the sort of long-term paralysis that plunged both the English and the French into civil war. Until the end of the eighteenth century, revolts at least at the leadership level were aimed at shifting the balance of power within the

---

95   E.g., Burgersdijck 1649, p. 35: 'Finis doctrinae Politicae est, felicitas universae Reip. quae in eo sita est, ut omnes pie probeque vivant: deinde ut omnia iis, quatenus fieri potest, suppetant, quae ad vitam commode degendam necessaria sunt, & ad res communes, & communia jura civitatis adversus vim externam, defendenda. Ex hisce duabus rebus tranquillitas oritur & concordia civium, quod est maximum Reipub. robur.' [The aim of political learning is the happiness of the entire state. This happiness consists of all people living piously and justly. Furthermore that the people receive all things, as far as possible, which are necessary to live a comfortable life, and which serve to defend the common interest and the common rights of society against force from outside. From these two conditions arise tranquillity and harmony between the citizens, which is the most powerful strength of the state.] Thanks to Dirk van Miert for the translation from Latin to English.

96   Stevin 2001, p. 62.

TABLE 1.4   *Revolutionary crises in the Dutch Republic*

Year	Nature of the crisis	International context
1617–18	Power struggle between Maurits and Oldenbarnevelt, accompanied by religiously inspired urban revolts	End of the Twelve Years' Truce (1609–21)
1650–3	William II's attack on Amsterdam, beginning of First Stadtholderless Period in the midst of rioting	Peace of Westphalia (1648) and First Anglo-Dutch War (1652–4)
1672–3	Orangist uprisings in many cities lead to fall of the De Witt regime and installation of William III as stadtholder	Combined attack on the Dutch Republic by France and England (1672)
1703–6	Death of William III leads to widespread rioting against client regents in Guelders, Overijssel and Zeeland, beginning of the Second Stadtholderless Period	War of the Spanish Succession (1701–13)
1747–50	Orangist revolution installs William IV as stadtholder with extended powers	French invasion leads to intensification of the War of the Austrian Succession (1747)
1785–7	Patriot Revolution, ended in failure and restoration of William V's regime by Prussian troops	Major defeat in the Fourth Anglo-Dutch War (1780–4)
1795–1801	Batavian Revolution, end of the old republic	French Revolutionary Wars (1793–5)

SOURCE: 'T HART 2011, P. 109

framework of the federal-brokerage compromise, not at overthrowing it. The stability of the central institutions of the state in the face of recurrent political conflict points towards the strength of their socio-political underpinnings, or, in Gramscian terms, their underlying 'historic bloc'.

One source of stability was the organisation of political life beneath the level of party conflict. Because of the central role of the House of Orange in all major turning points, traditional historiography emphasised the importance of the political divisions between the adherents and opponents of the stadtholderate within the Dutch state. In his 1961 dissertation D.J. Roorda criticised this view by arguing that regionally or locally oriented 'factions' formed the real core of political life. Not fundamental ideological differences over issues of domestic and foreign policy, but climbing the social ladder by strengthening one's local connections was the main motivator behind these networks of regent families.[97] Even though successive stadtholders tried to gain greater influence over the system of appointing functionaries at the local or regional level, they only managed to do so for the long term in the peripheral provinces.[98] Thus, factions remained more important in deciding who was in and who was out than the two vying parties. And although every major shift of power between Orangists and anti-Orangists had consequences for individual adherents of the losing factions, the core networks behind these factions proved highly adaptable to changing political conditions. Surely, the factions did not annul the impact of violent temporal clashes over general policies, sharp political and personal divisions, or popular mobilisation behind one of the two major parties. But they did provide a lasting framework for the reintegration of the top layers of both contending parties into the local, regional and national power structure.

The lists of Admiralty councillors in Annex One and Two provide a good illustration of the basic continuity among the ruling families throughout periods of political crisis. After the constitutional crisis of 1618 two out of five Holland councillors in the Amsterdam Admiralty Board were replaced because of their party adherence, but the others remained in position. In 1672 Cornelis de Vlaming van Outshoorn lost his seat, but only to re-enter the political establishment as burgomaster of Amsterdam a few years later. It was not until the 1747 revolution that brought to power stadtholder William IV that a full half of the Holland Admiralty councillors were replaced for political reasons. In Zeeland, none of the councillors from the province itself were removed due to party struggle in those three crises. Only in 1703 did the inception of the Second Stadtholderless Period lead to political shifts within the Admiralty Board, when some of the administrators most closely associated with the old regime became the bud of popular rioting over upper-class corruption.[99]

The factions provided a lasting mechanism for the distribution of jobs among the leading families within the Dutch elite and a way to ensure long-term continuity of power within a strongly divided constituency. But they do not suffice to explain how a state that institutionally cemented the sectional

---

97   Roorda 1961, Chapter One, Roorda 1964, and S. Groenveld 1990, pp. 75 ff. Also see Adams
       2005, on the role of family networks as an aspect of factional politics.
98   On the limits of the stadtholderly patronage system during the seventeenth century, see
       Janssen 2008, p. 107 and pp. 170 ff., and Wilders 2010, pp. 140 ff.
99   Bijl 1981, pp. 49 ff.

interests of each of its component parts managed to overcome these divisions to such an extent that it could play the role of a hegemonic power. Two other sources of stability must be briefly examined. The first is the special position of the Province of Holland, and within Holland the special position of Amsterdam, as economic lynchpins of Dutch power. The second is the availability of a number of powerful ideological notions that helped to present the strong class-biases and local particularism entrenched in the Dutch state as a reflection of the interests of the nation as a whole, thereby providing an ideological basis for consent.

The special position of Holland and Amsterdam in Dutch Republican politics needs little elaboration. It has left such an imprint that the name of the province still functions as *pars pro toto* for the Netherlands at large. As the richest province, and, within this province, the richest town, these two entities held great sway over public finance and the determination of state policy. Demographically, Holland was by far the most dynamic part of the country until the end of the seventeenth century. Its population more than tripled between 1514 and 1680, when this province alone housed 883,000 people, or almost half the less than two million inhabitants of the Republic. In the course of the century between 1550 and 1650, the population of Amsterdam quadrupled. The city was home to around 220,000 inhabitants at its high-point of urban expansion. With an overall urbanisation rate of 40 percent, the Republic was an anomaly in the pre-modern world. But within this anomaly, Holland itself was the exceptional case, with its urbanisation rate of over 60 percent.[100] The economic weight of the province was even greater. Formally, Holland paid 57.7–58.3 percent of ordinary war budgets during most of the seventeenth century, but the actual share paid by this province often was even larger.[101] Politically, the grand pensionary (*raadspensionaris*) of Holland acted as a substitute prime minister to the Republic as a whole, especially during the two Stadtholderless periods. Amsterdam always loomed large in their considerations. Grand pensionary Johan de Witt acknowledged as much when contemplating Dutch policy in the Baltic region in 1657, writing in a letter to an Amsterdam burgomaster:

> ... and your honour can rest assured that I, in this case as well as in any other of weight and importance, will always ... have my eyes singularly directed at the city of Amsterdam and the sentiments of those governing this

---

100   De Vries and Van der Woude 1997, p. 52, p. 61, and pp. 64–5.
101   '␣t Hart 1993a, pp. 80–1.

city, since their considerable interest in the state means that it deserves to be held in high consideration above all others.[102]

Holland and Amsterdam particularism could be the cause of great friction within the state, slowing down decision-making processes over proposals that were not directly to the benefit of the sea-provinces. In the same year that De Witt wrote the above letter, he also complained bitterly about the unwillingness of Amsterdam to consider intervention in the affairs of the bishop of Munster, strongly favoured by the inland provinces:

> Deliberations in the current extraordinary meeting of the Gentlemen States about the Munster affair have unexpectedly turned sour and uneasy, since the Gentlemen deputies of the city of Amsterdam have with great seriousness opposed the general inclination of said meeting on aforementioned subject. And since this essentially hurts the interest of the inland provinces, that I feel are greatly annoyed by the slowness of the Province of Holland in a matter of their interest ... it has to be feared that if the Province of Holland will maintain this retardation, the other provinces will in turn hold back their support in cases most harmful for the interests of the trading provinces ...[103]

Dutch Republican politics thus often took the form of pragmatic haggling. But it was haggling between partners that were mutually dependent – as was shown painfully during the 1672 invasion, when Holland only survived the joint Anglo-French-Germanic attack by using the Southern and Eastern provinces as a buffer zone – and haggling between partners that at the same time were fundamentally unequal. Characteristically for the federal-brokerage nature of the state, the States of Holland could operate at one and the same time as the core constituent element of the States General, and as a pressure group for the interests of Holland or Amsterdam merchants.[104] This dual position

---

102   Johan de Witt to Cornelis de Graeff van Zuidpolsbroek, 2 February 1657, in Fruin 1906, p. 468.

103   Johan de Witt to Cornelis de Graeff van Zuidpolsbroek, 18 October 1657, in Fruin 1906, p. 514.

104   For example, while decisions over convoying were formally taken by the Admiralty Boards in concordance with the States General, the States of Holland often discussed and acted upon requests by merchants to pressure these institutions for increased protection. See section 2.5.

helps to explain why Holland politicians jealously guarded the independence of action granted to them within the federal-brokerage structure of the state but were willing to act as financial guarantors to the Republic whenever this became imperative for the survival of the state. And given the imbalance in wealth, the other provinces could try to counterbalance the central role of Holland, but never to unsettle it completely. In a polemical pamphlet directed against the Hollando-centrism of Pieter de la Court's *True Interest of Holland*, Constantijn Huygens pointed out that the interests of Holland could never again be threatened the way William II had done in 1650,

> ... since the States of Holland have now become so powerful and well established, that not only lickspittles and slavish people, but even the stadtholder will be careful not to try anything tending to this, not to cause general ruin ...[105]

Much of the negotiations between the different power groups within the Dutch state rested on the case-to-case balancing of particular interests, pushing ideology into the background in favour of sometimes astonishing candour in political affairs. Pragmatism is a luxury that is affordable to the successful. The theorisation of the spectacular rise of Dutch power was an obsession among those that wanted to follow the same trail.[106]

That does not mean, however, that the political haggling behind the making of Dutch foreign policy was completely void of theoretical principles. Dutch seventeenth-century political theory developed a number of powerful theoretical notions that helped to provide ideological coherence to an internally divided state. Next to mutual economic benefits distributed through the faction networks of elite families and the institutionalised power-negotiations through the 'political state', these notions formed a third source of stability cementing the historic bloc between large international traders, urban oligarchs and their middle-class constituencies. These were the sources of 'hegemony' behind the Dutch state. A full examination of such notions goes beyond the confines of this study, and should at least include the dual role of Calvinism in creating a shared sense of purpose among the elites as well as channelling lower-class dissent; seventeenth-century Republicanism and theories of the mixed constitution as sources of legitimisation of the state's constitution; and the role of the family in mediating the space between public and private life. But a particularly

---

105   Huygens 1663, pp. 93–4.
106   Nijenhuis 2002, and Reinert 2009.

powerful set of notions arose to justify the role of the state in Dutch commercial expansion, and for the purposes of the present study an examination of these suffices to illustrate the ideological components of the Dutch historic bloc.

The most famous of these integrative notions is Grotius's development of international law, shaped directly to fit the requirements of Dutch expansion in the East Indies.[107] Grotius's concept of *Mare Liberum* was an 'operative fiction' par excellence, reflecting real interests in mystifying ways that served to uphold an existing power structure. As many contemporary and later observers have noted, the Dutch were interested in free seas for themselves, not for the English East India Company, the Portuguese Empire, or for Asian coastline traders. They operated on the basis of 'mare liberum' when dealing from a position of strength, as was the case with a whole string of trade agreements concluded immediately following the Peace of Westphalia.[108] But they were willing to 'close the seas' whenever it fitted their interests better, as they did with the Flanders coast after the fall of Antwerp. Nevertheless, Grotius's theory provided more than just an ideological prop. As Grotius himself explained, the general freedom provided to the trading communities in the Dutch Republic gave them a superior justification for commercial warfare over their competitors, especially the Portuguese, 'since their profit is mixed with the profit of the whole human race, which the Portuguese try to spoil'.[109] By thus universalising Dutch trading interests, the fiction of 'mare liberum' provided Dutch foreign policy both with a source of justification and with a moral economy of conquest.

Equally, Dutch development of political economy was not as empty of theoretical assumptions as is often assumed.[110] It has long been debated whether or not Dutch Republican rulers were Mercantilists in their economic thinking. If the concept is narrowly defined as a specific set of policies to ensure a positive balance of trade, increase the quantity of precious metal within national borders and stimulate national industry by state intervention, Dutch rulers at

---

107   Recently, the political background behind the formulation of Grotius's theories has come under close scrutiny in a whole string of publications. See Van Ittersum 2006, Wilson 2008, and Weindl 2010.

108   E.g., Anonymous 1650, opening with the establishment of the right of free trade with all countries with which the Republic was not at war: 'Premierement les Subjects & Habitants des Provinces Unies du Pays Bas, pourront en toute seureté & liberté naviger & trafiquer dans touts les Royaumes, Estates & Pays, qui sont, ou seront, en paix, Amitié, ou Neutralité avec l'Estat desdites Provinces Unies' (2vso).

109   De Groot 1614, p. 77.

110   E.g. Kossmann 1987b.

most acted – in the words of the economic historian Voorthuijsen – as 'occasional Mercantilists'.[111] Increases in trade tariffs were particularly unpopular among the elites for their perceived negative effects for the large overseas merchants. Protection of industry was generally seen as a task for provincial or urban politics.[112] However, as Van Tijn has shown in a study of four seventeenth-century economic thinkers, rejection of these practical proposals associated with Mercantilism often went hand in hand with the acceptance of all or most of its core theoretical propositions. Non-Mercantilist Dutch writers agreed with their foreign counterparts on three fundamental points: first, that the power and wealth of a state depend on the number of economically active inhabitants, especially the proportion of the population engaged in manufacture and trade; second, that foreign trade is the source of wealth, especially when it is connected to home manufactures; and third, that the total volume of world trade is constant, so that the economic gain of one country of necessity is the loss of another.[113] Together these theoretical principles, repeated and elaborated in popular debates, political literature, and moral tracts, helped to explain how the expansion of trade was not only the well-understood self-interest of the merchant class, but in fact served the interests of the nation as a whole. They provided a theoretical foundation for the extraordinarily strong identification of interests of trade with interests of state, so characteristic for the Dutch Republic.[114]

The third theoretical position mentioned by Van Tijn also provided a framework to think about the interrelation between war and commerce. If all trading nations could only advance directly at the cost of their neighbours, war became not just an important instrument for economic development, but its necessary corollary. Understanding war as an economic factor, a subject pushed to the background by the development of free-trade ideologies in the nineteenth century, was central to the intellectual project of seventeenth-century political economists. For them, the choice between war and peace always remained one of expediency and preference, not of principle. Global competition by neces-

---

111   Voorthuijsen 1965, p. 130.

112   The important though idiosyncratic economic and political thinker Dirk Graswinckel argued that daily policy in matters concerning industry should be the prerogative of towns and provinces, and that only in cases where manufacturing interests clearly exceeded provincial borders should it be brought before the States General. Graswinkel 1667, p. 725.

113   Van Tijn 1992, pp. 7–8.

114   A fairly typical example of this can be found in the Anonymous 1675, p. 4, where the author argues '[t]hat everybody knows ... that on the growth and protection of commerce alone is built the wealth of this state'.

sity resulted in global trade wars. The reason for this was summed up in an unpublished memorandum by Gerrit Schaep to the reputedly peace-minded magistrates of Amsterdam:

> Because everyone knows as clearly as the light of day, that the prosperity and welfare of all people is envied, discussed, and fought over by their friends and neighbours as well as by their enemies and strangers ...[115]

The same basic position was also accepted by the advocate of peace and free trade Pieter de la Court, who argued that although peace was the 'true interest' of Holland, it was simply unattainable given the competitive nature of international relations:

> If we consider the uncertainty of this World, especially in Europe, and that we by Traffick and Navigation have occasion to deal with all Nations, we ought to hold for a firm and general Maxim, that an assured Peace is, in relation to Holland, a mere Chimera, a Dream, a Fiction, used only by those, who like Syrens or Mermaids, endeavour by their melodious singing of a pleasant and firm Peace, to delude the credulous Hollanders, till they split upon the Rocks.[116]

Based on the demonstrable preponderance of such 'realism' in Dutch Republican political literature, modern writers who see Mercantilism primarily as a theory linking the international employment of state power and commercial expansion have little hesitation including the Republic among early modern Mercantilist states.[117]

Combined, the faction- and family-networks at the base of Dutch politics, the special role of Holland and Amsterdam as power-brokers in all fundamental questions of foreign policy, and the existence of a number of powerful shared notions providing this policy with a universalising rational and moral calling helped to overcome the structural division within the federal-brokerage state. But their cohesive capacity was not limitless. A historic bloc is characterised by those it leaves out, as much as those it manages to include. The structural inequalities in political access between sea-provinces and inland-provinces, between Amsterdam and the other trading towns, between the wealthy inter-

---

115 Kernkamp 1895, p. 343.
116 [De la Court] 1702, p. 242.
117 E.g., Irwin 1991, O'Brien 2000, and Rommelse 2010.

national merchant-industrialist or merchant-financiers and the urban small traders – let alone the day-labourers, soldiers, sailors – never ceased to haunt the rulers of the Dutch Republic. Nevertheless, the federal-brokerage state provided a framework in which such divisions could be temporarily resolved, even if this sometimes happened only after violent crises. Secondly, and perhaps more importantly, there were long-term economic limits to the integrative capacity of the state. Above all, it rested on the continued positive interplay between overseas commercial expansion and a flowering of the main productive sectors at home that created a real, if temporary convergence of interests between the urban middle classes and large international merchants and financiers. Under the pressure of the gradual uncoupling of trade and finance on the one hand and home-production on the other that characterised the later phase of the Dutch cycle of accumulation, the disintegrative aspects of the structure of the Dutch state became more apparent. However, as long as the Dutch Republic moved from strength to strength, economically and militarily, these centrifugal tendencies did not undercut the hegemony of the federal-brokerage state. Rather, success tended to solidify the essential features of the Dutch state as it emerged from its long war against the Habsburg Empire.

Conclusions

This chapter has shown how the federal-brokerage institutions of the Dutch state arose from a series of historical contingencies, connected to the direct requirements of the rebellious forces fighting the Spanish Habsburg crown, and reflecting the strong particularistic pressures among the different components of the Revolt's power base. In 1550 three scenarios of state formation had seemed feasible that each differed fundamentally from the one that was reaffirmed so triumphantly in the Great Assembly of 1651. Until the establishment of the Republic in 1588, monarchical centralisation under the Habsburg crown, a close political alliance between the seven rebellious provinces and one of Spain's European rivals, or an even more far-reaching devolution of power to the separate provinces had each been on the table. Their defeat in favour of the creation of an independent federal state was one of the many unforeseen outcomes of the revolutionary upheaval.

The same can be said of the formation of the individual institutions that formed the backbone of the federal-brokerage state. Each of the specific institutions examined here arose after a period of political haggling, experimenting, and sometimes intense competition for influence between towns, provinces, merchants, the stadtholder, and various other contenders. In the case of the

Admiralty Boards, attempts to form a unified navy under the direct command of the central state were actively blocked by trading ports hustling for influence over naval employment and customs collection. The VOC and WIC, supported financially, militarily, and politically by the States General for their ability to challenge the Habsburg Empire in its farthest corners, had conflicts over priorities between war and profit built in to their very structures. And in troop payment, systems of financial intermediation between state and market were only slowly regulated as the most pragmatic solution for otherwise almost insurmountable financial problems.

Nevertheless, this apparently chaotic combination of improvised institutions exhibited a pattern that reflected some of the essential features of Dutch society. The way in which every new arrangement for the organisation of warfare was designed to match the highly localised structure of political power, as well as to involve substantial sections of the capitalist economic elites, allowed for the integration into the state of two different but connected interest bases: the leading merchants oriented towards international trade, and the top and middle layers of the urban small producers. These connections could be organised in three very different ways. In the case of the commercial companies, especially the VOC and WIC, the tasks of war were relegated to commercial institutions wholesale. The Admiralty Boards exhibited an opposite pattern, in which the top layers of the ruling class were directly integrated into the running of state institutions. A third form was presented by the military solicitors, who acted as financial middlemen at the behest of the state and within the confines of bureaucratic regulation, but still managed to secure for themselves substantial independence in order to run state functions as their own private business. Each solution in its own way reproduced the federal-brokerage nature of the state at large. Taken together, these institutions enabled the state to tap into the great wealth generated by the early expansion of capitalism in the Netherlands, and to enlarge the geographic base for accumulation internally as well as externally. In doing so, the Dutch state proved uniquely capable of transforming the rudimentary beginnings of capitalist development, created in the medieval phase of the cycle of accumulation, into a launch pad for hegemony within the world-system.

Consisting of a complex network of overlapping and sometimes conflicting institutions and constituencies, the Dutch Republic became subject to frequent and violent internal divisions. However, these divisions could be overcome by the strength of the 'historic bloc' underlying the state, cemented by the real political and personal connections between the ruling families through their faction networks, constant political coalition-building and haggling centred on the unevenly divided powers of provinces and towns, as well as a number of

powerful integrative political and economic notions shared among the different sections of the ruling class and large parts of the middle class. Only under
the pressure of the sustained economic and military setbacks of the late eighteenth century would the basis for this consensus finally dissipate. But in 1651,
gathered in their meeting hall in The Hague under the banners of their defeated
adversaries, the rulers of this state could well imagine themselves standing at
the centre of the world.

Merchant Companies, Naval Power, and Trade Protection

The early modern period was the age of the merchant-warrior, when global commodity chains were welded together by lead and iron. In the words of Braudel, 'Holland in the Golden Age was already living on a world scale, engaged in a process of constant partition and exploitation of the globe'.[1] This chapter deals with the organised interaction between merchants, commercial companies, trade directorates, and Admiralty Boards behind this 'living on a world scale'. Naval warfare and trade protection involved two sets of institutions, both tied to the commercial classes in their own specific way. The Admiralty Boards were part of the formal 'state apparatus', supervised by the States General. Their directive bodies were composed through a complex system of cross-representation, tying the five separate boards to local political elites while at the same time ensuring the involvement of the leading merchant families. Parallel to these Admiralty Boards there were the merchant companies and directorates, some of which were little more than commercial lobbying groups, while others – first and foremost the voc and wic – acted as 'informal' state or semi-state institutions. Merchant companies had a stake in the organised use of violence to back up their commercial interests, and to varying degrees entertained the right to exercise such violence on their own behalf. The previous chapter sketched the emergence of these parallel sets of federal-brokerage institutions in the context of the Dutch Wars of Independence against the Habsburg Empire. This chapter will trace their evolution from the mid-seventeenth to the mid-eighteenth century, i.e., from the highpoint of hegemony to the post-hegemonic phase of the Dutch cycle.

The direct cooperation between states and the commercial classes in naval warfare forms one of the clearest examples of brokerage practices during the early modern period. The creation of a capitalist world market was a deeply violent process. Historians have often focused on the activities of the chartered colonial companies, but these by no means provide the sole model for the armed expansion of trade in the early modern period. The independent role of entrepreneurs in war at sea took many forms, from armed struggle for control

---

1 Braudel 1992, p. 220.

over the main venues of trade, to piracy and privateering, to full-scale armed interventions. The 'naval revolution' of the 1650s and 1660s, in which war fleets consisting mainly of hired merchant vessels were partially replaced by state navies of purpose-built ships of the line, influenced the balance between the state and merchants, but did not do away with privatised warfare.[2] It merely changed the parameters within which Admiralty Boards and merchant companies negotiated, cooperated, and competed for authority over the use of force. Shifts between market-provided and state-provided violence were by no means one-directional. Under Colbert, the French state embarked on a major programme of shipbuilding, briefly handing the French crown control over the largest war fleet in Europe. But financial duress and maritime failures forced Louis XIV to abandon his ambitions in this area during the Nine Years' War, and base his entire naval strategy on a return to brokerage warfare through the privateering ventures of the *guerre de course*.[3] Overall, however, the naval revolution gave priority to bureaucratic institutions in the organisation of direct inter-state conflict at sea, while still allowing plenty of room to merchant-organised violence in areas more directly linked to commercial competition.

Strategically, war fleets served at one and the same time to protect important trading routes and as instruments of power projection. The two were not always easily combined, as was noted by Pieter de la Court in his *True interest of Holland*:

> And then it also commonly happens, that our Enemys either by whole Fleets do entirely obstruct our Trade by Sea, or by Privateers may make incredible Depredations upon us. For by reason that our Fishery and Foreign Trade are so greatly dispersed, *Holland* is not able to defend them in all places, and be Masters at Sea at one and the same time ...[4]

Even though the ultimate aim of mastery of the sea envisioned by all major political economists at the time was the protection of fishery and foreign trade, the difference between the spatially restricted strategic geography of naval rivalry and the potentially global demands of trade protection in the short term could create intense conflict over priorities of employment. Warfare at sea

---

2 On the transformation of naval warfare during the 1650s and 1660s, see Glete 1993, pp. 173 ff., Palmer 1997, and Bruijn 2000.

3 Symcox 1974.

4 [De la Court] 1702, p. 231.

could cause temporary disruptions in international trade. Moreover, different groups of merchants competed for the use of state resources in support of their own sectional interests. All of this created the need for organised forms of interaction between merchant capitalists and Admiralty Boards as the main state agents for trade protection.

This chapter will focus on the institutional structures through which different sections of the commercial classes worked to influence naval policies.[5] Section 2.1 examines the influence of the 'naval revolution' of the mid-seventeenth century on the general organisation of violence at sea. Sections 2.2–2.5 will take a closer look at the variety of brokerage, semi-brokerage, and state forms of warmaking that emerged as a response to the naval revolution in the three main geographic areas of Dutch trade: the East Indies, the African West coast and the West Indies, and Europe. In each area merchants responded to a different constellation of geographic, military, and political forces, with very different outcomes for the dynamics between trade and protection and between state power and merchant-organised violence. Finally, section 2.6 will investigate how, in the long run, these structures influenced the strategic geography of naval intervention.

Overall, this chapter will challenge a long-cherished myth in Dutch naval history: the idea that a combination of declining financial resources and a loss of influence of merchants over the direction of naval affairs led to a secular decline of Dutch naval power from its summit at the time of the first three Anglo-Dutch Wars to its abysmal failure in the Fourth Anglo-Dutch War. It is true that during the final half of the eighteenth century there developed an unbridgeable gap between the Dutch navy and the main battle-fleets of Europe. However, this chapter will show that this was not caused by financial decline but by conscious choices prioritising trade protection over power projection. Furthermore, rather than signifying a loss of control of merchant elites over naval spending, these choices affirmed their continued weight in the making

---

5   There is of course a long line of literature touching on the role of economic factors and merchant interventions in Dutch Republican foreign policy. General overviews are provided by Boxer 1965, Franken 1968, Rietbergen 1988, Israel 1989, and Blom 1997. Specific episodes of such interaction are treated (among others) in Elias 1920, Israel 1982, Groenveld 1984, Rietbergen 1997, and Antunes 2004, pp. 141ff. The structural relations between trading communities and the state have mostly been studied from an economic, not a politico-military point of view. For a recent overview, see Gelderblom 2009a. An outstanding study of the role of competition among capitalists for political influence over naval priorities across the channel around the same period is Brenner 2003.

of naval policy – and thereby an important way in which the federal-brokerage state form that guaranteed this influence affected the long-term chances for Dutch commercial hegemony.

2.1   The Naval Revolution and the Challenge to Dutch Trade

The 1650s formed a watershed in European states' attitudes to naval warfare. Naval policies, the tactics employed in battles at sea, the make-up of war fleets, and the structure of naval bureaucracies all changed in significant ways in the short space of time between the English Civil Wars of the 1640s and the Second Anglo-Dutch War of 1665–7. English and French challenges to Dutch supremacy in the carrying trade, epitomised by the English Naviga-tion Acts and Colbert's reforms in France, led to an intensification of both economic and military competition at sea. Simultaneously, line-ahead tactics – the practice of sailing and firing follies in a strictly regulated order developed during the English Civil Wars, and then employed with great success against the Dutch during the First Anglo-Dutch War of 1652–4 – gave standardised warships or ships-of-the-line a decisive edge over the hired merchant-men that previously had formed the bulk of war fleets. The building and main-tenance of permanent purpose-built war fleets required much more soph-isticated naval institutions than had previously existed, such as specialised shipyards, dry and wet docks, large-scale storage facilities, and a bureau-cracy capable of administrating such facilities in a relatively economic fash-ion. It has been argued that this rapid transformation of the nature of naval warfare warrants the title of a 'military revolution' much more than the centuries-long evolution of warfare on land to which this concept is usually applied.[6]

In his classic study of the long-term consequences of war on the develop-ment of Dutch trade, Frits Snapper tried to establish a direct link between the shift away from the use of merchant ships for naval warfare and a marked loss of influence of merchant elites over Dutch foreign policy during the second half of the seventeenth and most of the eighteenth century.[7] He even sug-gested that 'the change of technique making it impossible that a merchant ship could easily be transformed into a warship ... brought a different kind of

---

6   Palmer 1997, pp. 123–4.
7   Snapper 1959, pp. 160–1.

TABLE 2.1   *Strength and composition of the Dutch fleet, 1653*

	14–18 pieces	22–8 pieces	30–8 pieces	40–6 pieces	54 pieces	Total
Ships owned by Admiralty Boards	3	25	24	13	1	66
Ships hired by Admiralty Boards	2	35	8	1	–	46
Ships hired by *Directies*	–	32	10	–	–	42
Total	5	92	42	14	1	154

SOURCE: DE JONGE 1858, PP. 762–3

people to the head of the Republic'.[8] After Snapper, no author proposed such a straight line from the abolition of one particular type of brokerage warfare at sea to changes in the nature of the Dutch political elites.[9] A closer look at the circumstances and course of naval reorganisation during the 1650s and 1660s reveals how much this was a continuation of the interaction between merchant bodies and Admiralty Boards, rather than a sharp break. What did change, however, was how this cooperation was organised. The existing plethora of ad hoc brokerage solutions, often costly and inefficient, was replaced by a slimmed-down version of federal-brokerage arrangements in which the respective roles of merchant bodies and Admiralty Boards became more clearly demarcated.

The transformation of the Dutch war fleet only took place after the limits of a mostly hired fleet had been shown in battle. As table 2.1 shows, hired merchant-men were still the dominant factor in the Dutch fleet that confronted the English during the First Anglo-Dutch War. Naval expenditure had declined in the run up to the war, reflecting Holland's turn against heavy war expenditures after the Peace of Westphalia. This had increased the dependence on hired ships in case of emergency. The majority of these ships were not suited to carry more than 28 guns, and, being built for storage capacity, they were often bulky and relatively slow. They faced an English fleet that had been expanded by a major building programme of heavy, well-equipped and purpose-built men of war, suited for carrying 42, 56, or 60 guns.[10]

---

8   Snapper 1959, p. 262.
9   E.g., Israel 1989, which does not make any mention of this factor.
10   Bruijn 1993, pp. 69 ff.

Almost half the hired merchant-men employed in 1653 were provided by so-called *Directies*.[11] These institutions were typical for the kind of ad hoc brokerage solutions favoured by the state before the naval revolution of the 1650s. In 1631 the States General had accepted the creation of separate naval institutions by a number of the major trading towns (Amsterdam, Hoorn, Enkhuizen, Edam, Medemblik, and Harlingen) that functioned parallel to the Admiralty Boards, as an answer to an increase in the privateering hazard faced by Dutch merchants. The *Directies* were run by burgomasters and merchants in the same way as was also done by colleges erected for the protection of the Dutch fishing fleets, levying a special tax on the merchants who benefited from the extra convoys. The ships of the *Directies* operated under the command of the Admiralty Boards, and at times of war were incorporated into the Dutch navy. The creation of these institutions allowed for an extension of armed convoying and the potential size of the fleet without an unpopular increase of taxation for the population as a whole.[12] However, a stream of complaints about the *Directie* ships during the First Anglo-Dutch War showed the incapacity of these institutions to provide both ships and trained captains that were up to the tasks created by the English advance in military technique. In one case, the crew of a ship provided by the Amsterdam *Directie* sent a petition signed by fifty-seven men, stating:

> We, the undersigned officers, sailors and soldiers, are not planning on taking sea with the ship *Den Witte Engel*, nor planning to do so with the captain ... because the ship is not suited for war. For as soon as there is only a slight wind, the gun-ports are below the water-line. Or do the gentlemen [directors] plan to kill so many souls as there are on this ship *Den Witte Engel*?

The crew subsequently asked for the removal of the captain, stating that he was drunk the entire period the ship had been at sea. Finally, they asserted that their refusal to sail was no desertion, since they were willing 'to serve the fatherland till the last drop of blood', provided that they could do so on a suitable ship under proper command.[13] In October 1652 the crew of another ship that was

---

11 Not to be confused with the commercial directorates such as the Directorate of Levantine Trade mentioned in Chapter One and later treated in section 2.5.

12 Bruijn 1993, p. 27.

13 NA, Archief van de Directies ter Equipering van Oorlogsschepen 1636–57, no. 4-11. The protest is not dated, but must have been sent between March–September 1652.

damaged during a confrontation with the English asked in a petition signed by eighty-nine sailors and officers 'that if your honours want us to return to sea, you provide us with another ship that will be better able to do the enemy harm'.[14]

Despite the bad performance of the *Directie* ships against the English fleet, it took until the end of 1655 before the States General abolished the separate *Directies*. Partly this had to do with the fact that the need for armed protection of the commercial fleet was felt more, not less strongly after the end of the First Anglo-Dutch War. Both in the Baltic area and in the Mediterranean, the need for convoying outstripped the capacity of the financially strained Admiralty Boards.[15] Partly it was the result of the fact that the Admiralty Boards themselves also relied heavily on hired merchant ships, which suffered the same shortcomings as those provided by the *Directies*. An anonymous pamphlet in the form of a letter to the Amsterdam Directors complained about the low quality of the captains serving the Admiralty Boards, and even suggested that to remedy this the *Directies* should be expanded instead of abolished: 'Imagine what good fifty *Directie* ships, properly equipped under the guidance of two directors, would do: the world would be brought under our control'.[16]

The opinion of the author of this pamphlet went against the current. According to the early twentieth-century Dutch historian Johan Elias, the most important lesson drawn by the Dutch from the war was 'that the old axiom was untenable that the merchant fleet, as a reserve for the state navy, should be seen as the backbone of protection at sea'.[17] After intensive lobbying by Admiral Tromp, the States General decided to provide a sum of two million guilders for two major building programmes of in total sixty new warships under control of the Admiralty Boards.[18] With the successful expansion of the fleet under the Admiralty Boards, the *Directies* had become superfluous. The States General ordered the Admiralty Boards,

---

14   NA, Archief van de Directies ter Equipering van Oorlogsschepen 1636–57, no. 5-I. Letter of 15 October 1652.

15   The financial problems of the Admiralty Boards after the end of the First Anglo-Dutch War are clear, among other things, from the stream of requests to the States of Holland, continuing for the entire decade, asking for payment of the provincial arrears in order to pay the suppliers of the three Holland Admiralty Boards. E.g., NA, Archief Staten van Holland, no. 5086, 'Resolutions 1654', 356–7 (18 September 1654), 440 (16 December 1654); no. 5087, 'Resolutions 1655', 220 (14 May 1655), 360–1 (2 October 1655), no. 5088, 'Resolutions 1656', 154–6 (22 July 1656).

16   Anonymous 1653, fol. 3 vso.

17   Elias 1933, p. 90.

18   A detailed account of the campaign waged by Tromp and others can be found in Elias 1933.

with the start of the coming year to extraordinarily equip and effectively send to open sea, and for the time of six months to maintain forty-eight warships ... in the same proportion that the directors had planned in the year 1652, and has been executed by the respective chambers of the same *Directie*.[19]

The abolition of the separate *Directies* for convoying forms an important episode in the naval revolution, bringing the hiring, building and equipment of convoying ships on all major European trading routes under direct state control. It also considerably quickened the transition to a war fleet consisting mainly of purpose-built warships.

It is hard to estimate the impact of this transition on naval expenditure. Hardly any information is available on the relative costs of hiring merchant ships versus ships owned by the Admiralty Boards. However, a comparison on the basis of the sparse documents that are available suggests that the main shift was in the ratio between costs and cannons. For 1642 the archive of the States General contains a calculation of the costs of hiring fifteen merchant-men for operations against the Spanish fleet. For 1658 similar calculations are available for the costs of the 'extraordinary fitting out' of forty-eight ships. Table 2.2 shows the full costs of the employment of the fifteen hired merchant-men. On average, employment of each ship cost the state f5,753 per month. For the 1658 fleet the Admiralty Boards calculated a total of f2,840,500 for all forty-eight ships over a period of ten months, or an average expenditure of f5,918 per ship per month.[20] In 1642 the costs of building and maintaining the ships were carried by the owners and not by the state, but this difference was partly compensated by the fact that the owners of the ships had to receive large sums in compensation if their ships were lost in battle. The main difference between hiring and making, then, seems to have been the enormous shift in size and quality that took place in the intervening years. Based on what is known about the composition of the 1642 fleet, the hired merchant-men must have consisted of ships carrying at the very most 32 to 36 cannons, manned by crews of no more than 140 sailors and soldiers.[21] The planned equipment of 1658 consisted of two ships of 60, nine

---

19   As reported by Secretary Van Slingelandt to the States of Holland, NA, Archief Staten van Holland, no. 5087, 'Resolutions 1655', 415–6 (10 December 1655).

20   NA, Archief Staten van Holland, no. 5090, 'Resolutions 1658', 396–8 (20 December 1658).

21   The 1642 fleet consisted of one ship of 57 canons, one of 46 (both owned by the Rotterdam Admiralty), 9 of 32–6, 49 of 24–30, and 36 of 20–3. De Jonge 1858, p. 754.

TABLE 2.2   *Costs of hiring fifteen merchant-men, 1642 (in guilders)*

Name ship	Period of employment (months)	Rent of ship and crew	Insurance	Extra costs	Total costs
Rooden Leeuw	7	45,500	3,183	2,989	51,672
Engel	6.3	28,500	2,042	333	30,874
Roos	7	45,107	2,881	–	47,988
Tijeger	5.5	20,227	1,536	–	21,764
Prins	7	46,550	3,552	2,268	52,370
Vergulde Pellecaen	7	39,375	2,894	697	42,966
De Swaen	4.3	24,375	1,837	2,038	28,251
St Jacob	6.6	31,840	–	2,538	34,378
Prins van Portugael	7	31,743	1,842	727	34,312
Drie Helden Davidts	7	39,946	3,116	185	43,247
St. Andries	7	46,550	3,015	1,058	50,623
Engel Gabriel	3.7	16,500	1,369	1,765	19,633
Groote St Marten	7	38,648	2,700	675	42,023
Hoope	6.7	29,011	1,922	733	31,666
Neptunus	6.4	20,265	1,034	549	21,848
Total		504,137	32,921	16,554	553,612

SOURCE: NA, ARCHIEF STATEN GENERAAL, NO. 12561.94. 'STATEN OVER MAENTGELDEN VAN GEHUYRDE SCHEPEN INDEN JARE 1642'

of 50, and thirty-two of 40 pieces, manned on average by crews of 202 sailors and soldiers. Only the large return-ships sailing for the East Indies had the capacity to carry such large numbers of guns, and the States General continued to use these ships in warfare far longer than regular merchant ships. But on the whole, the building programmes inaugurated in the 1650s pushed the hired merchant-men out of active service for the navy, and relegated such ships to subsidiary duties such as transport or victualing, for which hired ships were still regularly employed.[22]

---

22   The one important exception to this of course was privateering. This line of business did not play a great role in trade protection, but was important as an instrument of armed competition. The Province of Zeeland in particular became a stronghold of privateering

The concentration of administration, building, equipment, and upkeep of the fleet in the hands of the Admiralty Boards was much more than just the abolition of one particular brokerage institution in naval warfare, or a way to bring costs and quality into line. It signified a decisive change in perceptions of the nature of the fleet, described by Jaap Bruijn as the transition to a 'new navy'.[23] One of the main features of this new navy was its permanent character – unattainable for a navy based on hired ships. At the end of the decade the Admiralty Boards, States General and States of Holland all discussed new ways to make sure that the state 'could at any time have the disposition of a considerable number of sailors, guns of sufficient quality, and robust warships'.[24] To answer to the new needs of a permanent navy, this period saw the rapid erection of impressive new shipyards and storage facilities by most of the Admiralty Boards, geared towards the efficient management of naval stocks and economising in naval production (see Chapter Three). However, while concentrating more power into the hands of the five Admiralty Boards, the States General did not attempt to reform the federal-brokerage composition of these boards themselves. In England, France, and Sweden, the transition to a permanent state-navy later led to attempts at the formation of a specialised naval bureaucracy.[25] In the Dutch Republic, the system of appointing naval councillors with strong connections to the commercial elites as political representatives of particular towns and provinces was firmly maintained. As will be shown in the next sections, the interaction between these temporary naval administrators and merchant companies and directorates was formalised rather than broken down.

There can be no doubt that the transition to the new navy, far from expressing a rift between merchant capital and Admiralty Boards, ushered in a period of the most intense use of the navy for commercial interests. Celebrations of the building in 1656–7 of the formidable Amsterdam naval storehouse by the urban poet laureate Joost van den Vondel stressed that these impressive new facilities were to serve the merchant community at large. In verse that was more functional than poetic, he wrote:

---

ventures with strong ties to the local Admiralty Board. For the strategic functions and practical organisation of privateering, see e.g., Van Meer 1986, Lunsford 2005, and Korteweg 2006.

23   Bruijn 1993, pp. 75 ff.

24   NA, Archief Staten van Holland, no. 5091, 'Resolutions 1659', 241 (11 October 1659).

25   Glete describes the 'naval revolution' as a 'bureaucratic revolution', e.g., Glete 1993, p. 227. See for England: Rodger 2004, p. 43 and p. 109, for Sweden: Glete 2010, p. 308.

My Lords, who were ordered to take care of navigation,
And now, in a pressing hour of need do not have to gather
Naval equipment from every corner or far-away store,
But sleep on the stock, ready for use in your Magazine,
Can man fleet after fleet with more tranquillity than ever before,
Benefitting the merchant towns and installing fear in tyrants at sea.[26]

A few years earlier, another representative of Amsterdam's lyrical establishment had eulogised the commercial advantages of the war fleet in words that were equally patriotic – and, it might be added, in poetry that was equally unimaginative:

By weapons shall you weaken your enemies
Whoever does so with advantage, will remain upright
Navigation is your pillar; if this comes to fall
Your Stock Exchange will collapse, and with it the Nation
No greater loss to a state than the loss of rich fleets
Whoever is great must expand his nation by means of his navy.[27]

Helped by the strong orientation towards naval power of the post-1651 regime, and especially the close personal attention to commercial and naval interests exhibited by grand pensionary Johan de Witt, the reformed navy embarked on a string of campaigns to secure Dutch trade in the Baltic, the Mediterranean, the coast of Africa and the West Indies. When in 1664 this brought forward the inevitable second confrontation between Dutch and English sea power, the Dutch fleet found itself much more prepared than during the First Anglo-Dutch War, and could secure major successes for Dutch trade.[28]

2.2   A Unified State Company for Colonial Trade?

The naval revolution had a profound effect on the relation between the state and merchant companies. To understand the impact, it is useful to briefly consider the prevailing ideas on the military role of the VOC and WIC one step before this transformation. An exceptional, but nonetheless illustrative

---

26   Van den Vondel 1658, p. 3.

27   Vos 1653.

28   Bruijn 1993, pp. 80–3, Jones 1996, p. 217, and Rommelse 2006, pp. 188 ff.

example of the thinking about the relationship between commercial companies and the war fleet from the period preceding the naval revolution was the
debate on the merger of the VOC and WIC into one single company for colonial trade and warfare. This discussion was launched in 1644 by the States of
Holland.[29] The proposal caused a brief furore among directors of the WIC and
their supporters, expressed in numerous pamphlets extolling the benefits of the
creation of such a single state-supported or state-led company. From the other
side, it warranted an extraordinarily curt reply by the directors of the VOC. Both
the recommendations and the rebuttal are instructive on the competing ideas
regarding the relations between companies, investors, and the state then current. They also show the fundamentally different position from which the VOC
and WIC entered the naval revolution.

That the proposal itself belonged to the period when warships and
merchant-men were still considered interchangeable is clear from the arguments of one of the advocates of unification:

> ... [B]ecause of the commerce and navigation exercised in this country
> over the last sixty years, the inhabitants have so much increased their
> means or capital that one can truly say that they own the greatest wealth
> in the world. For if one would seriously investigate this point, one would
> find that they do so because they command over a thousand ships, cap-
> able of usage for warfare ...[30]

According to this writer, the VOC should be viewed as part of this national
power, a power that was based primarily not on state activity but on the
cooperation of armed merchants:

> From the midst of these private persons was erected the VOC, which in
> only thirty years has acquired such power, that it now employs fifteen
> thousand men and hundred-fifty ships, all capable of warfare.[31]

However, the proposed unification should merge trade and state power to an
even higher extent. In the proposal of this writer, the company-to-be would be
organised directly as a section of the state, headed by 'councillors' and 'colleges'
rather than directors and chambers, coming together in a 'Greater Council of

---

29   The episode is discussed at length by Den Heijer 1994b.

30   Anonymous 1644a, fol. A2 vso–A3.

31   Ibid.

the East and West Indies' that should have its meetings in The Hague. At the same time, the States General would accept sovereignty over the territories that until that time had belonged to the respective companies. Remarkably enough for a country still steeped in Hispanophobia, the author was not shy to admit that such a shift from a commercially-run to a state-run organisation of the colonial Empire was meant to mirror the approach employed 'by the King of Castile'.[32]

This author's emphasis on direct state-control was idiosyncratic. But a number of arguments surfaced in all or almost all of the pamphlets of those in favour of unification of the two companies. One was the close relation between success in warfare and expansion of commerce – linking interests of state and interests of trade in the classical Mercantilist fashion. As the directors of the WIC stated in their own defence of unification:

> The interest of state (in this matter) include, that the trade to East India, the coasts of Brazil, Africa and all other neighbouring areas will be vigorously improved, and that our common enemy the King of Spain will be deprived of all means and occasions to harm this state (as much as possible) and thus made impotent. For this aim the unification of the power and means of these two notable companies will be more suitable and strong, than a separate continuation of both, since the results to be expected from the combination of their military forces are better than from their separation, and since the common means will be more easily supported from the benefits of their trade.[33]

Since unification was deemed to be in the trading interests of the nation as a whole, the resistance of the VOC directors to this proposal had to be explained as a selfish move to protect the profits of a single group of traders to the detriment of the country. In the words of one author:

> If the directors and some of the shareholders of the VOC do not want to grant and resolve this [unification in the interest of the nation], yes, if they resist this with body and soul and try to prevent it by any means possible, there has to be a reason or cause for their opposition, and the question that one could pose is which cause. To which the answer is, that I cannot

---

32   Anonymous 1644a, fol. D2 vso.

33   Anonymous 1644f., p. 35.

think of any other cause than their excessive greed, or their fear that their particular interests will be harmed by this.[34]

However, this criticism of the VOC directors also implied a – sometimes tacit, sometimes open – acknowledgement that the two companies were in a fundamentally different position, and that it was the WIC that would profit most from the proposed unification. One of the pamphleteers summed up this difference by stating that

> the VOC is a society of pure trade, while the WIC is more alike and in its action operates more as a company of state, and as a result is much more connected to the political state, and of greater importance.[35]

However, the directors of the WIC emphasised that this was not an absolute difference, but rather one of timing and scale. At an earlier phase in its short history, the VOC also had received substantial state support in order to secure its commercial interests in the East Indies:

> The VOC has been in a poor state, just as the West India Company today, but has maintained itself through God's grace, and the excellent assistance it received from our government. And ever since the establishment of the WIC it has from time to time progressed, while the West India Company on the other hand has regressed to a point where the VOC has been before.[36]

Recognising the unlikelihood that the VOC directors would be willing to abandon their present interests because of the state support the company had received in the past, most of the advocates of unification argued that the state was entitled to subjugate the VOC directors and shareholders and force them into submission either by refusing to renew the VOC charter, or even by disbanding the Company altogether and granting the WIC the rights to trade in Asia.[37] However, at least one author objected that this would cause harm to an even more fundamental interest of the state, namely the security for the rich that their investments and loans were protected at all times against the arbit-

---

34   Anonymous 1644b, fol. D1 vso–D2.

35   Anonymous 1644b, fol. B1. Cf. Anonymous 1644e, p. 10.

36   Anonymous 1644f., p. 24.

37   Anonymous 1644g, p. 51.

rary decisions of policy makers. Retracting the charter in his opinion 'would be the surest way to intimidate all good patriots to stop investing their capital in any company'.[38]

Confident that the state would indeed not intrude upon the investments of the shareholders of the company, the directors of the voc were extremely brief in explaining their rejection of the proposed unification. Their core argument was that after a long period of employing Company money for warfare, the investors now wanted to use the established positions in Asia to engage in the core business for which the voc was set up, i.e., making profits:

> Our affairs in East India, in the course of more than forty years, through many trials and tribulations and with great labour and loss of possessions and blood, have now (by God's blessing) finally come to the point where we can turn to the first aim of the common shareholders in said Company, namely trade, which by continuous warfare until now has been dejected and desperate; to such an extent, that its return-ships now sail undamaged, and yearly fetch so much merchandise from there, as can be absorbed profitably in Europe. Therefore, we are of the opinion that now the time has come to continue this lofty, stabilised, and for the interests of the country long-expected trade, without being distracted by any other point of view than falls within these limits [i.e., the limits of the voc charter].[39]

In a second, even shorter statement, the voc directors alleged that they had the full support of their shareholders in rejecting even the smallest step towards unification. They brushed away the arguments of the wic directors in a manner that exhibited both confidence that the state would not go against their wishes and consciousness of the strength of their position vis-à-vis the rival company:

> The representatives of the voc note that those of the wic do not stop bothering the government with this issue over and over again, to such an extent that there are even pamphlets printed on this. And therefore, following the instructions of their principal shareholders, they are obliged to declare to Your Honours squarely that they do not have or ever will have

---

38   Anonymous 1644 f., p. 7.

39   Anonymous 1644d, fol. A2–A2 vso.

any inclination to agree to such a combination that will of necessity bring to ruin their Company.[40]

After this stern rejection the proposal itself was ultimately shelved.[41] Nevertheless, the episode is significant. It shows that as late as 1644 some Dutch Republican rulers and the WIC directors were still willing to seriously suggest a model for their overseas activity that integrated trade and warfare in one state company much more akin to the tributary model of the Spanish and Portuguese than that of the independent commercial company represented by the Dutch and English East India companies. The directly opposite responses of the directors of the two companies also reveal their very different positions at home and abroad. Whereas the WIC was in need of large-scale state support and willing to reduce its independence in order to obtain it, the VOC had already carved out its own empire and wanted to retain as much control as possible over the balance between trade and warfare. Showing the differences in political strength at home, while the WIC felt the need for an extensive political campaign to get across its preferences to the state, the VOC was confident that it would not need to argue its position in public since the interests of its shareholders would be served by the States of Holland and the States General anyway. The course of the debate makes clear the fundamentally different starting positions from which both companies entered the period of intense naval reorganisation of the 1650s, resulting in very different trajectories in the evolution of the relations between Admiralty Boards and both companies.

2.3   The VOC and the Navy from Symbiosis to Division of Labour

In his major contemporary history of the Company's first century, VOC official Pieter van Dam described the often troubled relation between the Admiralty Boards and the VOC. Not surprisingly, he did so in a fashion that put his employer in the most favourable light:

> According to the charter, the nation is not allowed to lay claim to ships, guns, or ammunition from the Company for its own purposes, except with the Company's consent. But at times when the country was in need, the Company has never refused support, without ever receiving the smallest

---

40   Anonymous 1644d, without page number.
41   Den Heijer 2005, pp. 151–3.

compensation for this. On the contrary, it has sometimes lent out its ships to the state without demanding any rent, or demanding just a small sum; and with regard to the equipment, though the costs have been compensated, this often only happened many years later.[42]

Van Dam ignored the fact that, especially during the first decades of its existence when the VOC's position in Asia had been far from secure, the Company itself had also been the beneficiary of substantial support – military, material, and financial – from the States General. Between 1609 and 1617, the States General had promised a total of ƒ1,740,000 in subsidies, and on several occasions had provided ships, armaments, and at one time even a small fleet to assist in Asian conquest.[43] However, at the time of Van Dam's statement, direct support from the state for the VOC had been reduced to regularly sending out cruisers to escort the Asian return-fleets on the last part of their journey.[44] The reduction of direct military support to this convoying service was the outcome of a gradually developing division of labour, in which warfare in Asia was completely parcelled out to the Company while the state provided protection in European waters.

During most of the seventeenth century, mutual assistance between the Company and the state was the subject of prolonged and often difficult negotiations. These became more intense when there was an acute military threat or when the renewal of the Company charter was under discussion. At such moments, the state felt it had greater leverage and put strong demands on the Company.[45] Until the 1660s the VOC agreed on several occasions to lend its ships to the Admiralty Boards. The four large return-ships provided by the VOC during the First Anglo-Dutch War were the biggest of the merchant ships that sailed out with the Dutch navy. The *Vogelstruys* (Ostrich) and *De Vrede* (Peace) each carried 40 pieces, the *Henriëtte Louise* 40 to 50, and the *Prins Willem* 50 to 60. The Company did not ask any rent, agreed to carry a large part of the financial risks and advanced the entire sum required for wages, victuals and equipment.[46] After the war the repayment of this loan, amounting to almost ƒ600,000, was delayed by the States General and became the subject of a conflict that lasted many years. During the Second Anglo-Dutch War, the material

---

42   Van Dam 1929, p. 362.
43   Enthoven 2002, p. 41.
44   Van Dam 1929, p. 565.
45   Den Heijer 2005, pp. 148 ff.
46   Van Dam 1929, pp. 507–8.

support of the Company for the navy was even more substantial. Despite the building programmes that had made the Admiralty Boards far less dependent on hired merchant-men, at the start of this war they asked and obtained a commitment to provide twenty fully armed and equipped Company vessels to strengthen their squadrons. It has been suggested that the close relations that Holland's leading statesman Johan de Witt maintained with both Company directors and Admiralty councillors were central to the ease with which the state acquired this large scale military engagement. In exchange for the VOC's support, the States General agreed to prolong the Company charter, at that time still valid until 1672, for another thirty years. However, the loss of a large part of the Asian return-fleet during the first year of the war forced the VOC to back out of the agreement. Instead of material support, it now promised to pay a total of ƒ1.2 million in financial aid in the course of 1666 alone.[47]

In hindsight, the move from the provisioning of ships to large-scale financial support in the course of the Second Anglo-Dutch War formed the watershed for direct VOC participation in Dutch naval efforts in European waters. During the Third Anglo-Dutch War (1672–4), no ships were requested. Instead, the VOC went no further than to agree to a loan of ƒ2 million. Even this only came about after a year of to-ing and fro-ing.[48] Significantly, the conditions under which the VOC lent its support made clear that the reluctance to grant this loan had been at least in part due to the feeling among the directors that the interests of the Company itself were not at stake in this war, even though the Dutch Republic was nearly overrun. In exchange for its loan, the directors demanded that an eventual peace would be concluded on terms favourable to the VOC, stipulating:

> ... [S]ince this war did not arise from any action or claims of the kings of France and Britain towards the Company, that in making peace between the highly esteemed kings and this state, the interests of said Company will be well guarded, and nothing will be exchanged or granted that would be of particular harm to the Company ...[49]

When a peace was finally concluded, representatives of the VOC were present in London to assist the diplomats of the Dutch Republic during negotiations. The instructions of the States General to its ambassadors stipulated:

---

47   Staarman 1996, pp. 8–13.
48   Staarman 1996, p. 18.
49   Van Dam 1929, p. 513.

... [T]o confer and concert in everything ... with the directors of the VOC that are present there, and that furthermore aforesaid Highly Esteemed Ambassadors will try to work out, that the regulation of commerce for the Indies will be drawn up in the way that is most advantageous for their commerce.[50]

This was certainly not the first time that the willingness of the VOC directors to give financial support depended on the stake they felt the Company had in the outcome of military actions. Already in 1605, only three years after its foundation, the directors had agreed to subsidise the state with a sum of ƒ125,000 to build a large fleet destined for the Iberian Peninsula, 'considering that it will serve to occupy the river of Lisbon, and hold the carracks that are sent each year to the East Indies'.[51]

Making the willingness to pay contributions dependent on the purpose for which money was raised fitted a more general practice of taxation on commerce. It followed the same logic by which customs paid on imports and exports were earmarked specifically for the protection of overseas trade by the Admiralty Boards. For the directors of the VOC it was normal to view not only individual instances of financial support, such as the ones made in 1605 and during the First and Second Anglo-Dutch Wars, but all the money that the Company paid in taxes as a contribution to the defence of its trade. According to the same reasoning, all military expenses made by the VOC under the formal jurisdiction of the state could be seen as a ground for tax-exemptions. Pointing at their large military expenses on fortresses, soldiers, and wars for territorial control in Asia, the VOC directors frequently tried to evade their full custom duties or exclude themselves from general raises in tariffs.[52]

The shift from material support to financial support that took place between the Second and Third Anglo-Dutch Wars went hand in hand with an attempt by the Admiralty Boards to bypass this area of ambiguity by demanding that henceforward the Company would pay its full custom obligations. With great agility, the directors played out the dual nature of their company as both a private enterprise and a semi-state institution in order to avoid higher taxation. In 1672, when the States of Holland contemplated a forced loan from the Company to alleviate the enormous pressures on the state due to the joint Anglo-French invasion, they objected:

---

50   NA, Archief Staten Generaal, no. 8581. 'Verbaal vande Heeren Corver en andere Hare Ho Mo exs gedeputeerden, 9 April 1675'.

51   Van Dam 1929, p. 486.

52   E.g. Van Dam 1929, p. 410.

> ... [T]hat the Company cannot be considered to be a corpus in and of
> itself since it consists of share-holders, who count their possessions in the
> Company for their own personal and special possessions, from which they
> help to carry the general means.[53]

Merely five years later, in 1677, the directors argued that the VOC should be
exempt from taxation on all outbound goods that were destined for its protection in Asia. Flatly contradicting their 1672 argument, they emphasised that
the Company should not be treated as just the sum of its share-holders, but
as an institution which served the interests of the nation.[54] The fundamental
difference between the Company and a simple combination of private traders,
argued the directors in 1677, lay in the services the VOC provided by its warring activities in Asia. If the Admiralty Boards would persist in their plans, they
threatened, the directors would stop executing these state-like functions and
act 'as private merchants'. To this, they added unconcealed economic black-
mail:

> If it would behave like all ordinary private merchants and would strive
> for nothing but its private gain, without any relation to the state – which
> the Company until this moment has refused to do – it would have the
> same freedom as other merchants not to bring its return goods to this
> country, but could trade them in full or in large part in other countries,
> such as in Cadiz, Italy, and in other places. It is not necessary to prove the
> disadvantage this would bring for the state.[55]

Admiralty Boards and Company agreed to end this permanent haggling in 1683
by establishing that the VOC would pay a lump sum that was ultimately set at
ƒ364,000 per annum instead of ordinary customs. This arrangement remained
in power until the end of the eighteenth century. The Company also paid a far
smaller fluctuating amount for the extraordinary customs (*last- en veilgeld*). A
reconstruction of the finances of the Amsterdam Admiralty Board shows that
between 1681 and 1794, this institution alone received a total of over ƒ22 million

---

53   Quoted in Staarman 1996, p. 22.

54   It is interesting to see how approximately at the same time East India Company advocate
      Josiah Child used the same type of argument, with explicit reference to the Dutch exper-
      ience, to argue for the special status of the EIC within the English trading community.
      [Child] 1681, pp. 6 ff.

55   Van Dam 1929, p. 413.

TABLE 2.3   *Contributions of VOC to Amsterdam Admiralty Board (1681–1794)*

Period	Contribution VOC (in millions of guilders)	Total custom revenue incl. contribution VOC (in millions of guilders)	Share of VOC in total custom revenue (%)
1681–9	1.6	13.4	12.2
1690–9	2.5	18.7	13.4
1700–9	2.1	16.4	13.0
1710–9	1.3	15.5	8.6
1720–9	1.9	14.0	13.5
1730–9	2.3	12.1	18.7
1740–9	1.9	11.4	18.3
1750–9	2.1	11.4	18.3
1760–9	2.1	12.3	17.2
1770–9	2.1	11.6	18.4
1781–9	0.9	9.2	10.3
1790–4	0.9	5.3	17.2

SOURCES: NA, ARCHIEF GENERALITEITSREKENKAMER 1586–1799, NOS. 490–717, RE-CONSTRUCTED ACCOUNTS

from the Company. As a rule, the Amsterdam contribution for ordinary customs amounted to half the total contribution of the VOC, so that it seems safe to estimate that the total contribution for the entire period amounted to about *f*40 million. In the years 1711–13 and 1715–17, the Amsterdam Admiralty Board did not receive its contribution since the VOC and the States General agreed that the Company would pay its entire sum for those years at once to alleviate the financial crisis that had beset state finances (explaining the fall in size of the VOC contribution for the years 1710–19 in table 2.3).[56]

Victor Enthoven has estimated that over the entire seventeenth century, the VOC paid around *f*15 million in customs. This rather low sum reflects the fact that until 1637 the Company hardly paid customs at all, and in the decades after this frequently was in a position to negotiate about the height of its

---

56   De Korte 1984, p. 14. If the payments made in the years 1711–13 and 1715–17 are accounted for in the same ratio as those in other years, the contribution of the VOC to the Amsterdam Admiralty Board for the 1710s would come at a total of *f*2.3 million, or 11 percent of all revenues.

tax contribution. The 1683 agreement brought the share of the voc in total custom incomes more or less in line with or even somewhat above its share in Dutch foreign trade. Femme Gaastra estimates this share at about six percent in 1636, growing to about fifteen percent in 1753. Older estimates, based on voc director Van der Oudermeulen's figures from a late eighteenth-century report, set the share of the voc in Dutch trade during the eighteenth century at an average of thirteen percent.[57] However, it is noteworthy that as a share of their total import value, the customs paid by the voc were much less than those of its British rival. The total gross value of voc imports, over which customs were levied, stood at *f*56 million in the 1730s and *f*74 million in the 1770s. Assuming that the contribution of the voc to the Amsterdam Admiralty Board was half the amount of its total contribution to the navy – as was required – the voc paid 8.2 percent in customs over its imports during the former decade and as little as 5.7 percent during the latter.[58] In comparison, in 1784 the British state *lowered* custom rates on the EIC tea imports to 12.5 percent.[59] The direct influence of voc and wic directors within the Admiralty Boards made it virtually impossible for the Dutch state to raise customs to similar levels.[60]

The shift from material support to lump sum contributions meant that the voc henceforth withdrew from active engagement in Dutch naval warfare in European waters. But the costs of all forms of support for the state taken together were dwarfed by the amount that the voc paid for its own protective ends, both in Europe and in Asia. Femme Gaastra made a tentative estimation of the military costs carried by the Company. Of necessity, this consists of many 'guestimates', but nonetheless the results are significant. According to his calculations, between 1650 and 1700 the Dutch offices of the voc spent about *f*62 million on protection of its ships, and between 1700 and 1796 just under *f*200 million. For the entire period 1613–1792, military expenditure in Asia is estimated by him at a staggering *f*257 million, coming to about thirty percent of all voc overseas investments.[61] High costs were incurred to protect ships laden with valuable cargo on their long journeys to and from Asia, and to ward off incursions by European competitors into its trading empire. But with far

---

57   Gaastra 1994, pp. 25–6.

58   Estimates of gross value of voc imports taken from De Korte 1984.

59   Ashworth 2003, p. 349.

60   In fact, pressure during the second half of the eighteenth century was in the exact opposite direction. See Chapter Five, and Hovy 1966.

61   Gaastra 2002, pp. 87–8.

TABLE 2.4   *VOC warfare in Asia (1602–1785)*

1605–6	Dutch confrontations with the Spanish and Portuguese in Ambon and Malacca
1622–3	Subjection of Malacca
1634	Irregular warfare against the population of Malacca to affirm monopoly trade
1640	Conquest of Galle
1641	Conquest of Malacca, Luanda and Maranhao
1648	Loss of Luanda and Benguela to the Portuguese
1654–8	Conquest of parts of Ceylon, subjection of Malacca
1661–3	War with Chinese emperor, leading to the loss of Formosa
1661–7	Major conquests of Spanish and English possessions, including Makassar, Cochin and Pulau Run
1677–83	Intervention against Javanese contender
1682–4	Subjection of Bantam
1702–13	Intervention in the civil war in Mataram
1703–8	First War of the Javanese Succession, VOC installs favourite candidate to the throne
1719–23	Second War of the Javanese Succession
1741–3	Chinese war in Javanese inlands, new war in Mataram
1749–55	Third War of the Javanese Succession
1755–6	Crushing of revolt in Banten
1762–6	Dutch-Ceylonese war
1782	British conquest of Ceylon
1783–5	Dutch-Burginese war

SOURCES: NO PROPER SUMMARY LISTS OF COMPANY WARS IN ASIA EXIST. THIS PROVISIONAL LIST WAS COMPILED FROM THE PRECIOUS VOC SITE, HTTP://WWW.VOCSITE.NL/ GESCHIEDENIS/TIJDBALK.HTML (ACCESSED 26-11-2014) AND THE INCOMPLETE SUMMARY BY GAASTRA 2003, PP. 60–5

greater frequency than the public image of the VOC as the embodiment of the Dutch 'commercial spirit' suggests, the Company used its military might to act like a state among Asian states (see table 2.4). As Jurriaan van Goor sums up a long line of historiographic debate:

> The VOC offers the strange image of a hybrid political-economic organisation, that was led according to strict economic rules, but that threw itself more often and with more gusto into 'princely adventures' than the

Seventeen Directors in the Netherlands wished for. As much as any Asiatic ruler, [the voc government in] Batavia did not shrink from violence,
when it feared that its reputation was at stake.[62]

The voc retained full control over military engagements in Asia until the
second half of the eighteenth century, when the EIC, with the direct backing
of the British state, started to encroach seriously on the voc hegemony in
the region and the Company at the same time was faced with a stark decline
in commercial profits. First reluctantly, in the aftermath of the Seven Years'
War, and then more vigorously during the 1780s, the Admiralty Boards sent
squadrons to intervene on behalf of the Company.[63] But until that late stage the
persistent point of view of Company directors and the States General seems to
have been that both parties were better off with a full division of labour, with
Cape Hope as the dividing point of competencies.

How much the Company actually benefited financially from its warfare in
Asia depends not only on the returns and dividends of the European-Asian
trade, but also on the still unsettled question of the size of the intra-Asiatic
trade. The ability to ward off state control over Company strategy and trade
revenues in Asia might have been an important motivation for accepting the
enormous military costs involved in the voc's state-like activities in Asia.
Femme Gaastra assumed that decline of the Dutch role in intra-Asian trade
set in before 1700, lending credibility to the contemporary claim that from this
period onwards, the costs of bureaucracy and military expenditure formed a
burden too heavy to shoulder for the Company.[64] But more recent reconstruc-
tions have suggested that the size of intra-Asiatic trade grew at least until 1750,
and that despite some severe setbacks during the second half of the eighteenth century, it retained its importance for the voc right until the end.[65] It
remains an open question – far beyond the scope of this book – whether in
purely economic terms the division of labour that was worked out between
state and Company ultimately benefited voc investors.[66] Examples of directors and shareholders protesting against the large weight of the costs of warfare

---

62   Van Goor 2002, p. 27.
63   Teitler, 2002, and Bruijn 2003. More specifically on the circumstances of the 1759 interven-
      tion: Winius and Vink 1991, pp. 124 ff., and on the impact of Anglo-Dutch competition on
      the ground in the late eighteenth century: Schrikker 2007.
64   Gaastra 2003, pp. 124 ff.
65   Jacobs 2006, and Van Rossum 2011, p. 62.
66   For a summary of the historiography, see Van Goor 2002.

in Asia in Company expenditure can be found throughout the existence of the VOC.[67] But since the alternative of a largely peaceful commercial expansion into an area invested with warring states and already partly colonised by rival European empires was unavailable, these protests remained toothless.

More research into the economic benefits of its political and military position in Asia could further our understanding of why the Company directors did not actively solicit for state support in Asia until the final third of the eighteenth century. For current purposes, it suffices to say that they did not. For the East Indies the strong ties between the monopoly-form of trade, the company-form of economic organisation, and the direct combination of commercial and state-like functions remained intact until the very end of the Company's existence. While rejecting most of its 'brokerage' functions in European warfare in the course of the naval revolution, the VOC carefully maintained its independence from the state in its actions in Asia, carrying the full costs of warfare as an integral and indispensable part of its trade balance.

2.4   The WIC between Private Trade and State Protection

For the WIC such independence of action overseas was never an option. This was not due to any fundamental difference in the Company charter or in the relation between directors and the state envisioned in it, but had everything to do with the different conditions of trade and colonisation in the Atlantic.[68] While the VOC quickly managed to surpass its European rivals in Asia and could deal with its competitors from a position of strength, the WIC's possessions remained heavily contested. Far more than its Eastern counterpart, the Company was a player in the many wars waged by the Republic, whether against the Spanish and Portuguese or in later decades against the English and the French. This forced the directors to rely heavily on military and naval support from the States General, from the use of regular state troops in its struggle against Portuguese colonists in the 1640s and 1650s to the re-conquest of its African slave-port Goree by a navy squadron under Michiel de Ruyter in 1665, and from permanent naval convoys in Caribbean waters to armed support for the planters in their bloody wars to suppress maroon revolts. With such heavy military engagement of the state, the division of labour between colonial warfare under

---

67   Early examples can be found in Gelderblom, De Jong, and Jonker 2011.

68   Schnurmann 2003, p. 493.

Company control and financial support for naval operations in Europe practiced by the VOC was neither attainable nor desirable for the WIC.[69]

Military dependence weakened the WIC's negotiating position vis-à-vis the
state. At the same time its monopoly trading rights were undercut by the private
trading networks of interloping merchants and colonial settlers. The Americas
were easier to reach and Atlantic voyages thus demanded far smaller initial
investments than the long return journeys to Asia. Trade on the West African
coast and in the Americas had already been substantial before the foundation
of the WIC.[70] Large-scale colonisation by the Spanish and Portuguese, and later
the presence of English and French colonists, created competing networks of
trade for private merchants to tap into. Furthermore, the reliance on permanent settlement, combined with the creation of complex slavery-based colonial
societies, gave rise to overseas elites powerful enough to go against the commercial policies of the Company directors at home.[71]

The dual weakness in the face of the state and of private competitors
haunted the WIC from its inception. In the mid-1630s, the Company managed
to gain an important foothold in Portuguese Brazil. The capture of Pernam-
buco and Paraiba in 1634 and 1635 raised great hopes for investors, but the costs
of operations were enormous: the military budget ran at about $f3$ million a
year.[72] A further problem for the WIC was that many Dutch merchants, especially in Amsterdam, had already established relations with the Portuguese and
Sephardic settlers before the conquests. These merchants put up strong resistance against the introduction of a Company monopoly in the newly conquered
territories. Since many of the private traders were at the same time involved
in the WIC, the conflict over monopoly or free trade led to sharp internal
divisions within the Company, pitting the pro-free trade Amsterdam chamber against the pro-monopoly Zeeland chamber. Such sharp divisions between
the regional chambers were much more common for the WIC than they were
for the VOC.[73] Even after the States General had decided in favour of a monopoly in December 1636, this proved hard to enforce due to resistance from
inside the Company and only survived for one year.[74] As one WIC historian
notes:

---

69   As was already noted by Van Rees 1868, p. 180.

70   Emmer 1981, p. 76.

71   De Vries and Van der Woude 1997, p. 401.

72   Bachman 1969, p. 145.

73   Emmer 1981, p. 76.

74   Den Heijer 1994, p. 45.

TABLE 2.5   *Estimate of WIC income, expenditure and damage done to the Spanish and Portuguese, 1623–36 (millions of guilders), based on figures of WIC director Johannes de Laet*

Income		Expenditure		Damage done to the Spanish and Portuguese	
Value of ships taken	5.5	Production of 118 ships of 100–500 lasts	3.0	Value of 547 ships taken or destroyed	6.7
Value of goods taken	30.3	Production of 101 ships of 50–90 lasts	1.0	Value of goods taken	30.3
Value of imports	14.7	Ammunition and repairs	4.8	Destruction of property	7.6
		Victuals	18.3	Loss of income for the Spanish crown	28.5
		Wages	18.1		
		Cargoes	7.0		
Totals	50.4		52.2		73.1

SOURCE: DE LAET 1644, APPENDIX: 'KORT VERHAEL', PP. 1–31

The horns of the Company's dilemma were these: monopoly might better enable the Company to meet its vast military budget, but it would also alienate the Portuguese and discourage immigration from Holland, thereby increasing the necessity for a large military establishment and slowing the reconstruction of the war torn land.[75]

An extensive contemporary estimate made by WIC director Johannes de Laet shows how at this time, the costs and income from war and privateering far exceeded the returns on trade for the Company (table 2.5). The figures are far from comprehensive: De Laet excluded income from state subsidies and connected expenditures, gave incomplete figures for cargoes, and did not include shipping costs for the transport of merchandise. The ƒ35.8 million in prizes conquered on the Spanish and Portuguese that were included in his figures did not accrue to the Company in full, but were redistributed among the WIC, shareholders and the Admiralty Boards. These irregularities stemmed

---

75   Bachman 1969, p. 146.

from the aim of his exposition, which was to show the benefits that the WIC had brought to 'the nation' and the costs that the Company had borne in pursuit of this aim. Nevertheless, table 2.5 gives a good impression of the sheer weight of warfare and privateering as part of Company activities.[76]

Despite huge military investments, the WIC's position remained embattled. Under the belligerent governor Johan Maurits van Nassau-Siegen, family of the reigning stadtholder and member of the military establishment of the Dutch Republic, the WIC managed to gain temporary control over substantial Brazilian possessions. But the eagerness with which the directors jumped at the proposal for unification with the VOC in 1644 showed their awareness of the increasingly precarious situation in their most valuable overseas colony. A string of uprisings of Portuguese settlers culminating in full-scale war in 1645 sounded the death-knell for Dutch rule in Brazil, and gave rise to biting criticism of the policies of Company representatives on the ground.[77] Unable to carry the burden of warfare alone, the directors and shareholders asked for and received large subsidies from the States General (see table 2.6). According to one of their requests, the shareholders 'throw themselves in your [i.e., the States General's] lap, with tears in our eyes, with worrisome hearts, ruined means, desperately, without hope, inpatient, not knowing what to say or do'.[78]

The States of Holland lent support to the Company through the Holland representatives in the States General, promising

> ... that the Highly Esteemed Gentlemen will most seriously observe at the Generalty level that the provinces will regard the work of the WIC as an important part of the state, and will estimate it at its true value, contributing what each of them respectively is due ...[79]

---

76   De Laet's figures are chaotic and sometimes misleading. E.g., the common assertion in the literature, as in Den Heijer 1994, p. 65, that the WIC in this period captured 609 ships is based on adding 62 Spanish or Portuguese ships that, according to De Laet's list, were destroyed, to the total of 547 ships he gives as captured by the WIC. However, more careful examination shows that the 62 ships destroyed were already included in the total figure of 547. Also, many writers accept De Laet's unproven assertion that since the costs of producing and fitting out the WIC fleets apparently did not much diminish the initial WIC capital, they should be brought as a separate post on the account of damage done to the Spanish and Portuguese, bringing its total at ƒ118 million rather than the more careful ƒ73 million entered in this table.

77   E.g., Anonymous 1647.

78   Anonymous 1649, fol. A4 vso.

79   NA, Archief van de Oude West-Indische Compagnie, no. 5, 'Notulen van het Haags Besoigne', 22 September 1651, fol. 59 vso–60.

TABLE 2.6   *State subsidies for the WIC in Brazil, 1645–51*[80]

	Subsidies granted	Subsidies paid up to 1651	Still unpaid in 1651
1645	700,000	700,000	
1646	700,000	700,000	
1647	3,028,612	1,902,726	1,125,886
1648	1,400,000	1,348,179	51,821
1649	1,200,000	1,200,000	
1650	787,012	300,000	487,012
1651	1,987,012		1,987,012
Total	9,802,636	6,150,904	3,651,732

SOURCES: NA, ARCHIEF OUDE WEST INDISCHE COMPAGNIE, NO. 5. 'NOTULEN VAN HET HAAGS BESOIGNE', 15 MAY 1651–2 SEPTEMBER 1654, 'STAET SOMMIER VAN DE PETI-TIEN', FOL. 73–6 AND 'CONCEPT OMME BIJ VOORSLACH ENZ.', FOL. 77–9 VSO, AND NA, ARCHIEF STATEN GENERAAL, NO. 5763, 'INGEKOMEN ORDONANTIES BETREFFENDE WEST-INDISCHE ZAKEN 1651–1652'

Despite state support in the form of men-of-war, soldiers, and an average of close to ƒ900,000 per year in subsidies in the years 1645–51, the WIC did not manage to quell the unrest. Finally, making use of their alliance with the English during the First Anglo-Dutch War, the Portuguese ousted the Company from Brazil in 1654.

The Second Anglo-Dutch War saw new important losses for the Dutch in the Atlantic, especially the loss of the foothold in North America, the settle-ment colony of New Netherland. But in return it also saw the capture of Sur-iname from the English, which became the Dutch Republic's most important possession in the Western hemisphere. Only an ignoramus can now hold the once popular view that trading New Amsterdam for Suriname at the Treaty of Westminster concluding the Third Anglo-Dutch War was a mistake. In the course of the eighteenth century, West Indian trade gained in significance rel-ative to European trade, becoming, in the words of Jan de Vries and Ad van der Woude, 'the most dynamic part of Dutch trade in the eighteenth century'.[81] The Dutch possessions in West Africa, the Caribbean and on the Wild Coast also

---

80   Thanks to Joris van den Tol for pointing out the flaws in an earlier version of this table that appeared in the unpublished dissertation and providing additional source material.

81   De Vries and Van der Woude 1997, p. 447.

became central hubs in the Dutch Republic's extensive engagement in transatlantic slavery.[82]

However, in the long run the WIC was not the main benefactor of the expansion of trade in the hemisphere assigned to it by the charter. When in 1674 the WIC was reconstituted, not only were the territorial and investor base more limited, but the WIC's monopoly was stripped to include only the African trade and the slave trade. Even then, the Company suffered from the same dilemmas that had plagued its predecessor. Protective measures such as the building of fortresses along the African coasts and the sporadic sending out of Company cruisers were directed as much against the Republic's European and native enemies as against Dutch private traders bound for Africa and the Caribbean. Nevertheless, interlopers could use the presence of fortresses of other European nations to provide cover for their activities. They also found substantial support within the state, particularly the Zeeland Admiralty Board, to provide a legal subterfuge for undercutting the WIC.[83] Just as had happened in the 1630s, the divisions between regional chambers helped to undermine the WIC monopoly, only with the roles reversed. Now Amsterdam merchants had the largest investments in the Company and wanted to maintain the monopoly, while many Zeeland merchants shifted between privateering and interloping. The first decades of the eighteenth century saw the loss of the *asiento* to the British as a result of the War of the Spanish Succession and the official opening to private trade of the Company's two remaining monopolies in 1730 and 1734, under sustained pressure from Zeeland merchants and political representatives.[84] With the WIC charter thus stripped, legal private trade was resumed by many Zeeland merchants. A new separate company, the *Middelburgse Commercie Compagnie*, gained the main share of the Dutch slave trade, causing the name of this small Dutch province to be writ even larger in the annals of this great crime.[85] Private trade by the MCC, individual merchants and colonists soon completely overshadowed trade by the WIC.

While losing its dominant position in West Indian trade, the WIC did retain its brokerage function of privately organised armed protection. It kept an important share in the running of Dutch territories in Africa and the Carib-

---

82   Even according to Piet Emmer's notoriously conservative estimates, around 1770 the trade
      in enslaved Africans added 15 percent to the Dutch trade balance. Emmer 2000, p. 173. For
      more up-to-date figures on the economic impact of the slave trade on the economy of the
      Dutch Republic, see Fatah-Black and Van Rossum 2012.

83   Paesie 2008, pp. 48–9.

84   Den Heijer 1997, pp. 304 ff.

85   Reinders Folmer-van Prooijen 2000, pp. 85 ff.

TABLE 2.7   *Convoying ships and cruisers sent out by the Amsterdam Admiralty Board, 1738*

Name ship	Destination	Crew size	Wages (f)	Victuals (f)	Extra-ordinary costs (f)	Total costs (f)
Dolphijn	Morocco and the Mediterranean	151	29,195	23,599	3,649	56,594
Spiegelbos	Morocco and the Mediterranean	150	26,212	21,545	2,874	50,781
Brederode	Mediterranean	271	51,878	44,342	6,063	102,554
De Brack	Mediterranean	100	20,025	16,144	2,294	38,563
Hartekamp	Morocco	150	25,914	20,900	2,360	49,324
Wester-dijkshorn	West Indies	201	37,450	30,327	10,539	78,517
Beschermer	West Indies	201	38,137	30,925	6,389	75,652
		1,224	228,811	187,782	34,168	451,985

SOURCE: NA, ARCHIEF GENERALITEITSREKENKAMER, NO. 548

bean, though often through constructions of shared governance. For example, Suriname was run by the chartered Society of Suriname, in which the WIC, the city of Amsterdam and planter-governor Cornelis van Aerssen van Sommels-dijck initially each owned a 33 percent share.[86] An important source of income for the WIC consisted of its right to levy a special tax on private trade, which brought in f3.3 million between 1730 and the dissolution of the WIC in 1791, in exchange for providing armed cruisers to protect West Indian trade.[87] Even for this task, however, the Company relied heavily on support by the Admiralty Boards. Given the growing importance of this branch of trade, the protection of the West African coast and Caribbean waters took increasing priority in Admiralty expenditure. Even in the quiet years of the 1730s, when expenditure on convoying was seriously cut back, the Amsterdam Admiralty Board regularly fitted out ships for expensive cruising across the Atlantic. Table 2.7 shows that in 1738 West Indian convoying took up about a third of all means and man-

---

86   Schalkwijk 2011, pp. 93 ff. In 1770, the share of the family Van Aerssen van Sommelsdijck was bought by the city of Amsterdam.

87   Den Heijer 1997, p. 372.

power assigned to trade protection by the Amsterdam Board. For many years, this was one of the main forms of armed engagement apart from long wars against Algerian and Moroccan privateers, which also functioned to protect westbound trade. The WIC was sometimes asked to contribute to the costs of convoying and cruising operations that were executed on its behalf. This for example was the case in the second half of the 1760s, when at the request of the WIC the Admiralty Boards decided each in turn to send one ship to the coast of Guinea over a period of six years. The entire costs of this operation were estimated at ƒ695,520, of which the Admiralty Boards would pay ƒ600,000, and the WIC was asked to pay the remaining ƒ95,520.[88]

Despite the growing importance of transatlantic trade, the position of the (reconstituted) WIC in the Dutch system of global power-projection always remained much more marginal than that of its East Indian counterpart. Throughout its existence, the Company was crushed between intense competition from rival empires and their subjects, forcing it to rely heavily on state support, and the easy access to the region for private traders undercutting its monopoly positions. Like the VOC, it consolidated many of its brokerage functions in warfare, but in contrast to its older sister, it gradually lost its hold over trade. Consequently, earlier and more persistently than was the case for the East Indies, West Indian trade became a focus for debates on free trade and abolition of the Company structure altogether.

2.5   European Commercial Directorates as Protection Lobbies

While the VOC and the WIC each in their specific ways maintained strong 'brokerage' roles in the protection of trade in their respective areas, the protection of European trade increasingly became the providence of the state. Early commercial directorates such as the Directorate for Levantine Trade had organised their own convoys, and had also forced merchants to take private protective measures. However, with the intensification of inter-imperial rivalry in crucial trading areas such as the Baltic and the Mediterranean, the securing of armed support from the Admiralty Boards became of increasing importance. The tasks of later directorates, especially those of Eastern and Muscovy trade, as well as those of the Directorate of the Levantine Trade, shifted towards that of organised protection lobbies. They actively petitioned the Admiralty

---

88   NA, Archief Admiraliteitscolleges L, no. 14. 'Notulen Haagse besognes', 5 November 1766, fol. 19–19vso.

Boards, city councils, Provincial States, and States General to fit out ships for their respective trading regions, and cooperated with the Admiralty Boards in determining the practical details of convoying operations. Their influence on the long-term strategic choices of the state in their respective trading regions was much smaller than that of the VOC and WIC.

Trade protection in European waters always had been to an important extent a state affair. The number of ships available for this aim rapidly increased during the first half of the seventeenth century. A 1599 resolution of the States General determined that the five Admiralty Boards would fit out 31 ships, divided over convoys to the Baltic (9 ships), England (7), France (5), Norway (4), Hamburg (3), and 7 ships of the Zeeland Admiralty Board specifically destined for the protection of Zeeland merchants.[89] According to the 1628 war budget, the Amsterdam Admiralty Board alone employed 17 ships for the blockade of the coast of Flanders, 26 for convoying and cruising, and 9 for military transports and protection in internal waters (see table 2.8). Of these various engagements, the stifling of Southern Netherland's trade was the most costly. The ability of the Dutch navy to carry out many tasks at once was based on the large number of ships available, but the sizes of crews specified in the war budget affirm the image of the pre-1660s navy as a mish-mash of small and medium-sized vessels. Only seven ships had crews of over a hundred men. Three patrolled the Flanders coast, and the other four were assigned to take on the Spanish along the Iberian coast.

By the end of the First Anglo-Dutch War, the war budget showed the increasingly global spread of Dutch power projection, with forty-one ships bound for France, the Mediterranean and West Africa, twenty-nine for the Baltic area, twenty-six for Flanders, Britain and the protection of the fishing fleets in the North Sea, and six to the West Indies.[90] As a result of the naval revolution, the number of ships employed for convoying gradually became less, but the size and firepower of the Admiralty ships increased drastically. Up to that time, it had been expected of merchants that they invested heavily in the means for armed protection. When merchants bound for Archangel and Moscow in 1649 requested a regular convoy of several men-of-war to assist them against enemy ships and pirates, the States General instead promised only one 'good and able warship, well equipped and properly manned'. To make up for the weakness of this convoy, they demanded each merchant-man to carry a set number of soldiers, cannons, and ammunition, depending on the size of the ship. Ships

89   Japikse 1930, p. 686.
90   NA, Archief Staten Generaal, no. 8059. 'Staet van Oorlogh te water 1654'.

TABLE 2.8   *Cost and employment of the navy according to the war budget of 1628 (excluding
            Friesland Admiralty Board)*

Destined region	Task	Number of ships	Average size of crew	Total number of men	Projected yearly costs
Coast of Flanders	*Economic blockade*	46	85	3,893	ƒ967,513
Spain		4	106	423	
France		3	73	220	
North Sea and fisheries	*Cruising and*	18	75	1,355	ƒ867,204
Baltic and Norway	*convoying*	4	75	300	
Unspecified		34	71	2,415	
Total		109	79	8,606	ƒ1,834,717

SOURCE: NA, ARCHIEF STATEN GENERAAL, NO. 8049. 'STAAT VAN OORLOG TE WATER, 1628'

that did not answer to those conditions were not only excluded from the convoying service, but were prohibited 'to take on board merchandise as long as there are properly armed ships that require cargo'.[91] However, in areas where traders systematically encountered well-equipped enemy war fleets, convoys based largely on armed merchant-men proved insufficient. Even before the introduction of line-ahead tactics, influential groups of merchants pointed to the inadequacy of the old system of protection and demanded a bigger role for the state. In 1649 Amsterdam Levantine traders petitioned the Amsterdam Admiralty Board, writing:

> The Gentlemen States of this country have had the insight to make regulations for the armament and manning of ships sailing to the Davis Strait,

---

91   Amsterdam City Archive (from here Stadsarchief (SA)), Archief van de Directie van de Moscovische handel, no. 6: 'Ordre ... ghemaeckt op het bevaren van Archangel in Moscovien' [1649].

in order that they may hold themselves against the Turks and other corsairs. And in times of need, the state has been able to use these large
and well-armed ships against its enemies ... But these [armed merchant-
men] are not able to hold out against the mighty armament of French
warships, while the wellbeing of the nation requires that they persist and
that the inhabitants of this nation are protected against all violence ...
Therefore, we request that Your Honours will restore order, with such a
proficient amount of warships and such competencies as necessary, to
end this hindrance and violence of the French men-of-war and to let the
inhabitants of this city enjoy the right of free trade ...[92]

During the second half of the seventeenth century, the Dutch Admiralty Boards
usually sent two convoys each year to the Mediterranean. According to the
English envoy in Tuscany, this was the key factor why after 1648 the Dutch
managed to supplant the English as main traders in the region:

The reason is the Dutch, observing that all foreigners gave greater freights
to our ships than theirs, by reason of the goodnesse of our vessels, they,
partly for their own security, against the Barbary Coast, partly to invite
forraigners to load on their vessels, send out a yearly convoy to protect
theyr ships which takes up all the Spanish money and fine goods from
Spayn for Italy, from Italy for the Levant and agayn from the Levant for
Italy and from Italy to Spayne and in this trade they employ theyr men of
warr.[93]

Thus, lobbying for protection by the Directory of the Levantine Trade proved
highly successful.

   Until the First Anglo-Dutch War, merchants could ask both the Admiralty
Boards and the urban *Directies* to provide armed protection. With the transition to a permanent state navy, the second option was closed. However, as was
the case with the increased use of VOC ships for naval operations in the 1650s
and 1660s, the naval revolution did not all at once lead to a decline in the role
of merchant-men in organised protection. The first response of merchants to
increasing competition was both to ask the state for more intensive and regular
convoying, and to prop up their own defensive measures. A list of the armature

---

92   NA, Archief Directie van de Levantse Handel, no. 236, 'rekesten en missiven', request of
      1649.
93   Quoted in Israel 1989, p. 229.

TABLE 2.9 *Armature of Dutch merchant-men present in the Mediterranean, December 1664*

Number of guns	18	20	22	24	26	28	30	32	34
Number of ships	2	7	2	5	7	31	13	9	6

SOURCE: HEERINGA 1917, PP. 113–15

of Dutch merchant ships present in the Mediterranean area in December 1664, just before the outbreak of the Second Anglo-Dutch War, shows the extent to which merchant-men at that point could still effectively operate as a second base navy (see table 2.9).

At this time, there were a number of short-lived experiments aimed at involving merchants even more closely in formulating the state response to the threats to Dutch trade, filling the gap left by the abolition of the *Directies*. One example of this was the College of Commerce that was established by the Amsterdam burgomasters to 'keep an eye on the conservation and augmentation of the trade of this city'.[94] This college expressly dealt with problems of piracy, the threats posed by armed foreign competitors, and the amelioration of protective measures such as convoying. Characteristically, it was composed of four representatives of the Amsterdam magistrate, and twenty-two representatives of the major Amsterdam merchant groups: two directors of the VOC, two of the WIC, two of the Directorate of the Levantine Trade, two merchants active in the Spanish trade, one in the Portuguese, two in the English, three in the French, three in the Baltic, one in the Moscow trade, a whaler, a cloth merchant, a draper, and a soap merchant.[95] The College made detailed suggestions on issues such as the best location for cruisers and the way in which the Directorate of the Levantine Trade should supervise the armature on board of merchant ships in the Mediterranean.[96] However, after the outbreak of the Second Anglo-Dutch War in 1665, the College stopped working.

The reasons why merchants did not feel an immediate need to replace the urban *Directies* with new permanent institutions seems rather straightforward. At no point before or after this time was the navy employed so resolutely and with such success in favour of the global trading interests of the Dutch. Under the regents' unhampered rule, merchants could be confident they had a government committed, in the words of its leading representative Johan de Witt,

94 Brugmans 1897, p. 206.
95 Brugmans 1897, pp. 211–12.
96 E.g., the advice of 5 February 1664: Brugmans 1897, pp. 226–8.

to ensuring 'that all dangers to the navigation and commerce of the good inhabitants of this nation will be avoided, and no advantages for them will be neglected'.[97] The top merchant families continued to be represented on the Amsterdam Admiralty Board. In 1650 wealthy Levant trader Pieter van Alteren took
the important administrative position of fiscal advocate (*advocaat-fiscaal*),
which he held until 1666. Baltic interests were represented by Admiralty councillors Andries Bicker, who was an active trader in this region, and Cornelis
Witsen, son of a leading grain merchant and prominent participant in the Rus-
sian trade.[98] Individual merchant houses such as that of Momma-Reenstierna,
Grill, Trip and De Geer, with their commercial empires in arms, copper and
iron, had managed to gain great diplomatic and political influence.[99] In the
Baltic, traditionally considered the anchor of the Dutch trading emporium, the
States General engaged in a bout of gunboat diplomacy to break all protective
walls put up by the regional powers.[100] At its peak in 1659 the Dutch Republic had as many as seventy warships in Danish waters.[101] Gerard Brandt, the
seventeenth-century hagiographer of Michiel de Ruyter, wrote that 'the fear of
Holland's weapons, as if signed with the mark of freedom, was powerful enough
... to secure free shipping and trade in the Eastern seas without bloodshed'.[102]
But having the upper hand in the region, the Gentlemen States were not reluct-
ant to engage in actual bloodshed when they felt that the need arose. Attempts
by France and Sweden to use the fallout from the Second and Third Anglo-
Dutch Wars to push the Dutch out of their leading position in the region were
checked by heavy armed intervention, including the landing of a combined
Dutch-Danish force on the Swedish coast in 1676. As Jonathan Israel asserts,
'Dutch naval power was vital to the post-1674 revival of Dutch commerce'.[103]

Fundamental shifts in the balance between geopolitics and trading interests
occurred in the final decades of the seventeenth century as a result of sustained challenges to Dutch commercial hegemony. The political turning point
of 1688, bringing together the Dutch Republic and its main economic compet-

---

97   De Witt to the majors of Amsterdam, 7 April 1657: Fruin 1906, p. 492.

98   Elias 1903, p. 433 (Van Alteren), p. 346 (Bicker), and p. 437 (Witsen).

99   On Trip and De Geer: Klein 1965, p. 98, on Momma-Reenstierna and Grill: Müller 1998,
     pp. 55 ff.

100 For summary accounts, see Bruijn 1993, pp. 83–98, and Tjaden 1994, pp. 85 ff.

101 Glete 2010, p. 111.

102 Brandt 1687, p. 100.

103 Israel 1989, p. 300.

itor England in a Grand Alliance under Stadtholder-King William III, affected core aspects of the strategic geography of naval warfare. More than in the preceding decades, tension arose between the need for sustained intervention of the fleet in great-power struggle and the short-term requirements of trade protection. This tension can best be traced in developments in the Baltic. It is significant that both Directorates for the Eastern trade, one for the Baltic and one for Russia, emerged in the course of the Nine Years' War. Their aim was straightforward: the Directorate for Muscovy Trade initially was named 'Deputies for the Request of Convoy'. Both directorates were modelled along the lines of the Directorate of the Levantine Trade. Their primary aim was to petition for convoys and provide detailed information to the Admiralty Boards on the practicalities of trade – on the diplomatic needs of the commercial communities, the best times for doing business, or the ideal locations for cruising and gathering the return fleets.[104] Three intersecting processes put growing pressure on Dutch Baltic traders, creating the need for such organised lobbying. The Northern War of 1655–60, three Anglo-Dutch Wars, and the Franco-Dutch War of 1672–8 had all temporarily increased insecurity for Dutch merchants operating in the region. But after 1689, with 25 years of Franco-Dutch warfare partially overlapping with the Great Northern War of 1700–21, war became the permanent condition of Baltic trade. This put strong upward pressures on freight and insurance rates. Secondly, the Dutch faced tougher economic competition created by the upswing of English trade in the region. In 1690 Dutch ships for the first time formed only 40 percent of all ships crossing the Sound, and in 1696 this figure even dropped to 25 percent.[105]

Thirdly, and perhaps most importantly, the shifting balance of military power and commercial strength was affirmed in a new political relation between the Dutch Republic and its main competitor for regional influence, England. The Anglo-Dutch alliance of 1689 meant that officially, their fleets now operated jointly both in naval operations and the sending out of convoys in a ratio set at three Dutch ships against five English men-of-war. Initially, it was the city of Amsterdam and its Admiralty Board that lobbied for this arrangement, which was seen as a clever way to divert the costs of protection to the English while continuing to reap protection benefits.[106] There were frequent

---

104   SA, Archief van de directie van de Oostersche handel en reederijen, no. 156, 'Proiect Memorij, hoemen met 12 schepen van Oorloge zoude kunnen convoijeren naar dantzik & Coninkbergen Riga & Revall' (without date).

105   Israel 1989, p. 302.

106   Snapper 1959, p. 185.

TABLE 2.10   *Merchant fleets convoyed in the Baltic area by Dutch squadrons, 1705–11 (east- and westbound)*

Year	Number of convoys	Number of merchant-men convoyed	Total size of convoyed crews	Total number of cannons carried by convoyed ships
1705	1	197	1,713	97
1706	2	159	1,534	275
1707	3	286	2,691	375
1708	4	200	>1,556	>197
1709	3	286	>3,061	>547
1710	6	374	3,931	683
1711	7	664	>5,450	>807

SOURCES: SA, ARCHIEF VAN DE DIRECTIE VAN DE OOSTERSCHE HANDEL EN REEDERIJEN, NO. 165–72

complaints from the War of the Spanish Succession onwards that the Dutch did not even match their minority share in convoying fleets, thereby forcing the English to bear the brunt of keeping Scandinavian waters open for Dutch trade.[107] But gaining short-term competitive advantages on the British by this classic act of free-riding came at a price. The fact that the military allies were at the same time the main economic competitors in the region created the real danger that growing British military and diplomatic presence would be used to gain economic advantages on Dutch traders.[108] That this danger was far from imaginary became apparent already during the War of the Spanish Succession, when the British used the terms of the alliance to enforce a much stricter embargo on carrying Baltic goods to France than the States General desired.[109]

---

107   Hattendorf 2002, p. 193.

108   On the debates this evocated, see Tjaden 1994, p. 117.

109   Bromley 1987, p. 44. The English political economist Davenant already traced the contradictions in the Anglo-Dutch alliance at an early stage: 'Never any League in its Nature was more difficult to hold together, than that which *England* has been lately engag'd in: Trading Countries were to be persuaded to a long War, which they seldom care for: We were to support the Dutch; and the Dutch were to join with us, tho' Rivals and jealous of one another, in Matters relating to Traffick'. Davenant 1698, pp. 90–1.

TABLE 2.11   *Estimated values of goods protected by convoy of 25 July 1709*

Type of goods	Quantity (lasts)	Price on Amsterdam market (guilders / last)	Expected return (in guilders)
Rye	9,232	206.3	1,904,608
Wheat	4,349	299.4	1,302,243
Barley	613.5	130.3	79,915
Line seed	967	9.0	8,713
Buckwheat	365	126.1	46,012
Hempseed	303.8	0.4	120
Flax	21	9.0	189
		Subtotal	3,341,779
Malt, Potash, Tar, Wood, Masts, Piece-goods, Wool, Hemp, 179 iron cannons		Prize or quantity unknown	
		Estimated total	**4,000,000– 5,000,000**

SOURCES: SA, ARCHIEF VAN DE DIRECTIE VAN DE OOSTERSCHE HANDEL EN REEDERIJEN, NO. 172. PRICES CALCULATED ON THE BASIS OF THE PRICELISTS ON THE AMSTERDAM BOURSE, COMPILED BY POSTHUMUS 1943

Of course, this did not mean that the Dutch state withdrew from providing armed protection for Baltic trade altogether. Despite the continuation of warfare and the great financial burden on the Admiralty Boards, the Eastern Directorates managed to secure intensive convoying in the Baltic region (see table 2.10). The lists of armature present on merchant ships provided by the naval commanders of the convoys shows the great distance from the situation of the mid-seventeenth century, when many merchant-men were still so heavily armed that they could be considered part of the convoying force. Now, most merchant-men sailed either unarmed or with no more than two cannons on board. Protection relied far more on the presence of heavily-armed Admiralty ships. More detailed information on one convoyed merchant fleet sailing in July 1709 gives an impression of the enormous value protected by the navy, in this case between *f*4 and 5 million (see table 2.11).

Shifts in power in the long run were decisive in the loss of Dutch trading hegemony in the Baltic 'mother trade'. In the aftermath of the War of the Spanish Succession, the Dutch managed for the last time to briefly gain a fifty percent share of shipping across the Sound. However, once the Great Northern War ended in 1721, Scandinavian traders managed to partially undercut the Dutch. The English profited through favourable trading conditions negotiated in Sweden and Norway. While the absolute number of Dutch merchant voyages through the Sound was larger during most decades of the eighteenth century than during the second half of the seventeenth century, the Dutch share in the total trade gradually fell to just over forty percent in the 1720s and 1730s, and under thirty-five percent in the 1750s and 1760s.[110] During these decades, the armed presence of the Dutch fleet in the region dwindled. The standing of the Dutch navy in the region had declined so much that the sending of armed convoys during the Russo-Swedish War of 1741–3 did not even suffice to end the large-scale attacks on Dutch merchant-men in the region.[111]

These long-term developments in the Baltic area show that in European waters, merchants were much more dependent on direct state intervention for the organisation of violence than either the VOC or the WIC. Brokerage forms of protection, such as the heavy arming of merchant ships, became of less use after the revolution in naval warfare of the 1650s. Trade therefore intersected even more directly than in the colonial areas with inter-state conflict. Especially from the second half of the seventeenth century onwards, merchant directorates adapted to this situation by functioning less as brokerage-type protection agents, and more as protection lobbies.

2.6   Protection Costs and Merchant Interests

There is a persistent strand in Dutch naval historiography that unites eighteenth-century imperial overstretch, a politico-moral degeneration of the rulers of the Republic and the waning of Dutch naval power into a single grand narrative on the loss of Dutch commercial hegemony. The underlying mechanisms linking these diverse factors into one single process of decline can easily be constructed. A secular diminution of Dutch trade, this line of argument holds, led to a fall in custom revenues which formed the main source for financing naval operations for trade protection. The resulting gap in Admiralty finances could only be solved by an injection of state subsidies. But the financial crisis following the War of the Spanish Succession, combined with the 'aristocratisation' of Dutch political elites and their reduced interest in trade, prevented such

---

110   Ormrod 2003, p. 284.
111   Lemmink 1990, p. 172.

financial counter-measures. The effectiveness of Admiralty government was thus undercut, leading to demoralisation and corruption, further affecting the readiness of the Dutch fleet. This negative spiral, it is alleged, proved unbreakable within the old political structures, and culminated first in withdrawal from naval competition and then defeat in the Fourth Anglo-Dutch War.[112]

The source of this grand narrative can be found in the intense political debates of the late eighteenth century. The critiques of the *ancien régime* constructed a binary opposition between the 'golden' seventeenth century, when far-sighted politicians with an eye to commerce employed sea power to protect Dutch trading interests, and the barren eighteenth century when the interests of trade were sacrificed to decadent finance, and corrupt administrators neglected the impediments of naval competition.[113] The basic elements of this view were carried over by nineteenth-century naval historians such as J.C. de Jonge.[114] A moderate version of the same story can still be discerned in Jaap Bruijn's insistence that after the War of the Spanish Succession, the Dutch war fleet degenerated into a 'second rate navy'.[115] This qualification is a generalisation of an argument made in his dissertation on the Amsterdam Admiralty Board in the 'quiet years' from 1713–51. Looking at the 1740s, he concluded that for a string of financial and political reasons '[t]he precarious balance between incomes and expenditure was completely disturbed'. He assumed that this situation was never really repaired, thus laying the basis for the disastrous performance of the Dutch navy during the Fourth Anglo-Dutch War.[116]

The image of Admiralty administrations squeezed between declining customs and political unwillingness to pay subsidies has persisted, despite major criticism of its underlying presumptions. As was already noted in the introduction, modern economic historians have challenged the idea of a secular decline of Dutch trade from the late seventeenth century onwards, instead emphasising continued commercial strength until late in the eighteenth century. Although total custom incomes gradually fell, especially in Holland as the richest and most dynamic province, this fall was far from dramatic.[117] On the other hand, Wantje Fritschy's major reconstruction of eighteenth-century government finances showed that there was no marked decline in willingness to mobilise the

---

112   E.g., Snapper 1959, pp. 160–1, and Bruijn 1993, pp. 145–6 and pp. 160–1.
113   E.g., Leonard Leeb 1973, pp. 86 ff., and Sturkenboom 2008, p. 113.
114   De Jonge 1861, p. 388.
115   Bruijn 1993, pp. 145 ff.
116   Bruijn 1970, p. 168.
117   De Vries and Van der Woude 1997, pp. 495 ff.

still powerful tax base of the United Provinces for warfare.[118] Recent recon-
structions of the finances of the Zeeland Admiralty Board by Wietse Veenstra
seriously question the idea that this institution, one of the least well-funded of
the five Dutch Admiralty Boards, could be described as ineffective or lethargic
around the time of the Fourth Anglo-Dutch War.[119]

Closer examination of the development of the finances of the Amsterdam
Admiralty Board further strengthens these findings (chart 2.1 and 2.2). The basis
for this examination is a full reconstruction of the yearly accounts sent by the
receiver general of this institution to the Generalty Audit Office. Such accounts
are available from 1681 onwards, and run to the fall of the Republic in January
1795.[120] Table 2.12 and Table 2.13 compare these figures for Amsterdam with
Wietse Veenstra's reconstruction for Zeeland, as well as the unreconstructed –
and therefore very rough – figures from the Rotterdam and Northern Quarter
Admiralty Boards. These are the most complete figures to date on naval income
and spending during the 'long eighteenth century', providing a solid base for
the rejection of some of the main assumptions of the older historiographic
tradition on the evolution of Dutch naval power.

---

118   Fritschy 1988, pp. 61–4.

119   Veenstra 2008.

120   NA, Archief Generaliteitsrekenkamer 1586–799, nos. 490–717. The only gap in this com-
       plete series is 1780. For this year, an estimate has been entered based on a note on incomes
       and expenditures that year by fiscal advocate Van der Hoop, NA, Archief J.C. van der Hoop,
       no. 161, 'inkomsten en uitgaven van de Admiraliteit van Amsterdam, 1778–1787'. Recon-
       struction of the accounts is necessary, since the total figures for income and expenses
       given in the summary accounts made by the receivers general often included large (and
       cumulative) sums for the remainders or shortages on the previous accounts, as well as
       some other large irregularities. Annex Three contains a description of the steps taken
       from the 'borderel', the summary accounts drawn up by the receiver general, to the recon-
       struction presented here. A general difficulty with the figures is that according to the
       style of accounting customary in Dutch government finances, expenses were only writ-
       ten down once they were actually paid. Given the frequency of great time-lags between
       the moment of deciding expenses and their actual payment, the accounts do not reflect
       faithfully the expenditures of each individual year. Taking aggregate figures of expendit-
       ure per decade to some extent straightens out this irregularity. A last point to be noted
       is that loans were included in the income figures, since down-payment on loans and
       interest payments could not be separated on the expenses side. My gratitude goes to
       Wietse Veenstra, who was kind enough to provide me with his yearly aggregate figures
       for the Zeeland Admiralty Board, and pointed out some shortcomings in my earlier calcu-
       lations.

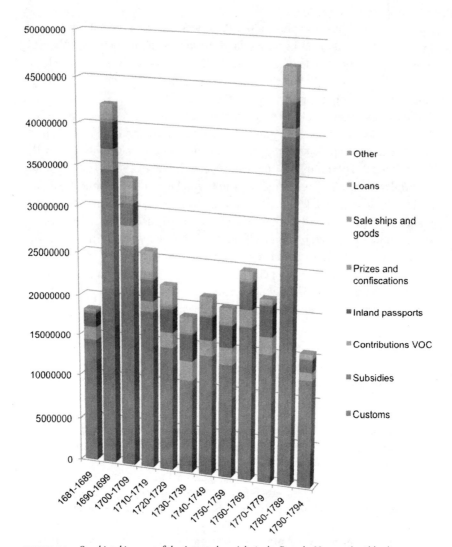

CHART 2.1 *Combined income of the Amsterdam Admiralty Board, 1681–1794 (guilders)*
SOURCES: NA, ARCHIEF GENERALITEITSREKENKAMER 1586–1799,
NOS. 490–717, RECONSTRUCTED ACCOUNTS (FOR PROCEDURE OF
RECONSTRUCTION, SEE ANNEX THREE)

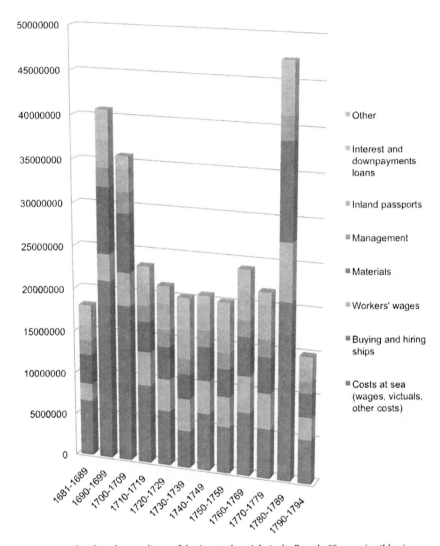

CHART 2.2 *Combined expenditure of the Amsterdam Admiralty Board, 1681–1794 (guilders)*
SOURCES: NA, ARCHIEF GENERALITEITSREKENKAMER 1586–1799,
NOS. 490–717, RECONSTRUCTED ACCOUNTS (FOR PROCEDURE OF
RECONSTRUCTION, SEE ANNEX THREE)

TABLE 2.12   *Total incomes of Amsterdam, Zeeland, Rotterdam, and Northern Quarter Admiralty Boards, 1680–1795 (millions of guilders)*

	Amsterdam (reconstructed)	Zeeland (reconstructed)	Rotterdam (partially reconstructed)	Northern Quarter (partially reconstructed)
1680–9	18.3	3.9	6.6	2.2
1690–9	42.3	11.8	18.6	12.1
1700–9	33.6	7.7	14.0	9.4
1710–9	25.7	5.3	8.8	3.4
1720–9	22.1	3.7	9.0	3.5
1730–9	18.5	3.7	7.0	2.7
1740–9	21.2	6.2	8.9	3.1
1750–9	20.2	4.4	8.1	2.9
1760–9	24.7	4.5	9.9	3.1
1770–9	21.7	4.6	8.8	2.4
1780–9	47.4	7.8	25.3	12.2
1790–5	15.5	2.7	2.1	2.0

SOURCES: NA, ARCHIEF GENERALITEITSREKENKAMER 1586–1799, NOS. 113–332 (ROTTERDAM), 490–717 (AMSTERDAM), 721–943 (NORTHERN QUARTER). AMSTERDAM: 1680 MISSING, 1780 ESTIMATE, 1795 MISSING / ZEELAND: 1795 UP TO MARCH, FIGURES COURTESY TO WIETSE VEENSTRA / ROTTERDAM: 1680, 1703, 1780, 1792–5 MISSING / NORTHERN QUARTER: 1680–4, 1795 MISSING / AMSTERDAM FIGURES ARE RECONSTRUCTED ACCORDING TO THE PROCEDURE EXPLAINED IN ANNEX THREE. ROTTERDAM AND NORTHERN QUARTER FIGURES ARE BASED ON THE TOTALS GIVEN BY THE RECEIVER GENERALS OF THE ADMIRALTY BOARDS, CORRECTED ONLY FOR INTERNAL TRANSFERS ON THE ACCOUNTS AND UNPAID SUBSIDIES. THESE FIGURES THEREFORE ONLY PROVIDE A ROUGH INDICATION. ZEELAND FIGURES COURTESY TO WIETSE VEENSTRA.

TABLE 2.13   *Total expenditures of Amsterdam, Zeeland, Rotterdam, and Northern Quarter Admiralty Boards, 1680–1795 (millions of guilders)*

	Amsterdam (reconstructed)	Zeeland (reconstructed)	Rotterdam (corrected, not reconstructed)	Northern Quarter (corrected, not reconstructed)
1680–9	18.1	4.3	6.4	2.2
1690–9	40.8	12.1	19.3	12.1
1700–9	35.7	7.2	14.5	8.4
1710–9	23.3	4.9	8.2	4.0
1720–9	21.3	4.1	8.9	3.5
1730–9	20.1	3.8	8.2	2.8
1740–9	20.6	5.7	8.9	3.3
1750–9	20.1	4.6	8.0	3.4
1760–9	24.1	4.7	10.1	2.8
1770–9	21.7	4.3	8.7	2.4
1780–9	47.4	7.7	25.2	13.4
1790–5	14.9	2.7	2.6	1.5

SOURCES: NA, ARCHIEF GENERALITEITSREKENKAMER 1586–1799, NOS. 113–332 (ROTTERDAM), 490–717 (AMSTERDAM), 721–943 (NORTHERN QUARTER). AMSTERDAM: 1680 MISSING, 1780 ESTIMATE, 1795 MISSING / ZEELAND: 1795 UP TO MARCH, FIGURES COURTESY TO WIETSE VEENSTRA / ROTTERDAM: 1680, 1703, 1780, 1792–5 MISSING / NORTHERN QUARTER: 1680–4, 1795 MISSING / AMSTERDAM FIGURES ARE RECONSTRUCTED ACCORDING TO THE PROCEDURE EXPLAINED IN ANNEX THREE. ROTTERDAM AND NORTHERN QUARTER FIGURES ARE BASED ON THE TOTALS GIVEN BY THE ADMIRALTY BOARD RECEIVER GENERALS, CORRECTED ONLY FOR INTERNAL TRANSFERS ON THE ACCOUNTS AND UNPAID SUBSIDIES. THESE FIGURES THEREFORE ONLY PROVIDE A ROUGH INDICATION. ZEELAND FIGURES COURTESY TO WIETSE VEENSTRA.

One of the most striking features of the evolution of the finances of the Holland Admiralty Boards is the level of continuity between the late seventeenth and the eighteenth century. The figures for the peace decade of the 1680s are incomplete, since they exclude the year 1680 for Amsterdam and Rotterdam, and the years 1680–4 for the Northern Quarter. But even when compensating generously for these deficiencies, total income and expenditure will not have been above that of the eighteenth-century peace decades of the 1720s, 1760s, or 1770s. The peak in expenditure during the 1780s shows that state finances were sufficiently elastic to respond rapidly to emergencies. In fact, yearly expenditure during the Fourth Anglo-Dutch War was considerably higher than that during the Nine Years' War and the War of the Spanish Succession. In 1782 alone the Amsterdam Admiralty Board spent ƒ8.15 million and the combined expenditure of the three Holland Admiralty Boards can be estimated at around ƒ15 million, an all-time record.

Unfortunately, no comparative figures exist for earlier war decades in the seventeenth century. But it is possible to make an estimate by combining figures for the two main sources of income of the Admiralty Boards, customs and consented petitions. Together, they form a good indication for the limits of naval spending. For the 1650s and 1660s total custom incomes amounted to ƒ17.6 and ƒ16.1 million respectively.[121] Incomes from subsidies are harder to estimate. According to an eighteenth-century summary, the provinces consented to pay a total of ƒ18.8 million for the 1650s and ƒ30.8 million for the 1660s.[122] However, in the seventeenth century as much as in the eighteenth, subsidies were not always paid with great punctuality.[123] Even if this would have been the case, the difference in size of naval expenditure is striking. All Admiralty Boards together (including Zeeland and Friesland) could not have had a budget far exceeding ƒ36.4 million during the 1650s and ƒ46.9 million during the 1660s, against approximately ƒ85 million during the 1690s and ƒ93 million during the 1780s, excluding Friesland. That these figures give a good indication is apparent from the only available full budget for naval expenditure during the First Anglo-Dutch War, summed up in table 2.14. During this year of

---

121   Becht 1908, Table 1 (appendices).

122   NA, Archief Admiraliteitscolleges XXXI, J. Bisdom 1525–793, no. 89. 'Aanteekeningen omtrent de financiën'.

123   As can be seen, among others, from a 1665 report on unpaid subsidies of the inland provinces to the Admiralty of the Northern Quarter, noting over ƒ200,000 in outstanding subsidies going back as far as 1653. NA, Archief Staten-Generaal, no. 9228, 'Verbael van heeren J. de Wit, etc.', 28 March 1665.

TABLE 2.14   *Ex-ante income and expenditure of the five Admiralty Boards, 1654 (guilders)*

	Rotterdam	Amsterdam	Zeeland	Northern Quarter	Friesland	Total
Income						
Customs	402,527	1,331,996	369,880	94,597	60,827	2,259,827
Requested subsidies	323,114	1,017,861	515,800	574,472	212,955	2,644,202
Total	725,641	2,349,857	885,680	669,069	273,782	4,904,029
Expenditure						
Equipment	393,171	1,506,371	581,850	456,324	146,076	3,083,792
Buying of ships	120,000	480,000	210,000	150,000	60,000	1,020,000
Interest on loans	68,581	126,487	26,830	24,165	15,586	261,649
Extraordinary costs captains	9,000	20,000			1,440	30,440
Care for the wounded	15,000		9,000		1,000	25,000
Travel expenses for administrators	19,000	25,000		34,579	8,292	86,871
Costs of administration	18,000		58,000		2,000	78,000
Salaries of administrators	74,889	82,000			38,696	195,585
Restitution customs	8,000				700	8,700
Maintenance of shipyards and ships		20,000		4,000		24,000
Building and replacement of ships		90,000				90,000
Total	725,641	2,349,858	885,680	669,068	273,790	4,904,037

SOURCE: NA, ARCHIEF FAGEL, NO. 1088, 'EXTRACT STAAT VAN OORLOG TE WATER 1654'

intense naval engagement, the total budget of all Admiralty Boards remained just under f5 million, while *average* yearly expenditure by the three Holland Admiralty Boards and Zeeland combined reached f8.5 million during the 1690s and f9.3 million during the 1780s.

Taking this long view, the financial problems faced by the Admiralty Boards in the decades around the middle of the eighteenth century seem much less dramatic than they appeared to Jaap Bruijn, who compared the functioning of the Amsterdam Admiralty Board in this period with the turn of the century high-point of activity. They certainly are not indicative of a trend spanning the entire eighteenth century. The Amsterdam figures in chart 2.1 also disprove the assumed mechanism behind naval decline, the secular squeeze of Admiralty finances. Custom incomes did fall slightly in the decades after the War of

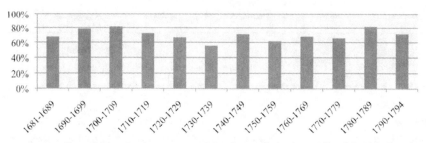

CHART 2.3   *Operations and upkeep as percentage of expenditure, Amsterdam Admiralty Board*
SOURCES: NA, ARCHIEF GENERALITEITSREKENKAMER 1586–1799, NOS.
490–717, RECONSTRUCTED ACCOUNTS

the Spanish Succession, but remained more or less constant at an average of ƒ800,000–1,000,000 per year from the 1730s onwards, still higher than most years before 1680, and partly compensated by the greater regularity in VOC contributions.[124] Political unwillingness to grant new subsidies in the period immediately after the War of the Spanish Succession did contribute to the 1730s and 1740s problems in Admiralty finances. But from the 1760s onwards, this factor seems to have lost its importance, with the Province of Holland stepping in and paying large contributions. During the 1760s the Amsterdam Admiralty Board received ƒ7.8 million in subsidies, a sum unprecedented in peacetime.

The figures also cast doubt on a third aspect of the conventional explanations of eighteenth-century naval involution: a secular rise in the costs of management due to growing corruption. As is shown in chart 2.3, expenditure on operations and upkeep of the fleet fluctuated, but at no point sank below half of naval expenditure, and most of the time lay well above sixty percent (with levels above seventy percent in war decades). Of course, corruption and mismanagement could have led to unnecessary expenditures on materials and wages. But except for – deeply politically motivated – contemporary complaints about inefficiency and corruption, there is no evidence for the assumption that this would have occurred more frequently during the eighteenth than the seventeenth century. As the next chapter will show, the eighteenth century saw important innovations in economic management at the Amsterdam shipyards, partly to counter the financial problems of the Admiralty Boards of the 1730s and 1740s. Up until the 1780s management costs of the Amsterdam Board remained stable at around ƒ200,000 per year.

A final argument for financial decline as the main factor behind the ineffectiveness of the eighteenth-century Dutch navy is that while nominal war levels

---

124   Becht 1908, Table 1.

and peace levels of expenditure did not drop dramatically, inflation made for a sharp decline in real expenditure. Jan Luiten van Zanden's calculations of early modern consumer price indices (CPI) show that between 1680 (a year of low prices) and 1780 overall inflation stood at about twenty percent.[125] However, it is unclear how inflation affected the costs of shipbuilding. As will be shown in the next chapter, wages and expenses on victuals were fixed during the mid-seventeenth century, excluding these items from general price rises. Wood prices, the other large factor in the costs of shipbuilding, did increase. But such an increase could be counteracted by shifting from more expensive Scandinavian wood to cheaper (and lower quality) German wood, as was done by the naval shipyards in the course of the eighteenth century.[126] Any comparison of shipbuilding costs over time is problematic, given the changes in the requirements placed on warships in the course of this period. Nevertheless, there are reasons to assume that for most of the eighteenth century costs did not increase sharply.

During the 1760s the Amsterdam naval shipyard turned out approximately as many ships (18) as during the 1700s (17). On average, these were ships of a larger category. Nevertheless, combined costs of shipyard wages and building materials for the latter decade were lower than for the first decade of the eighteenth century, and only slightly higher than for the 1710s and 1720s when fewer ships were built. Only for the year 1781, at the highpoint of wartime naval expansion, do figures compiled by the Admiralty Boards themselves show an extraordinary increase in the costs of building. At that time, a calculation by Amsterdam fiscal advocate Van der Hoop put the price of a man-of-war carrying seventy pieces at ƒ510,000, almost double the cost of building a similarly sized ship in 1748.[127] But coming back to the main argument, even then high prices did not deflect the Dutch state from launching its largest building programme since the seventeenth century.

---

125   Van Zanden, 'Prices and wages and the cost of living in the western part of the Netherlands, 1450–1800', online database, http://www.iisg.nl/hpw/brenv.php, accessed 26-11-2014.

126   As can be seen from the places of origin of wood acquisitioned by the Amsterdam Admiralty during the Fourth Anglo-Dutch War, NA, Archief Admiraliteitscolleges XXXIX, Van der Hoop, 1524–825, no. 118, 'Rekeningen aangekocht hout Admiraliteit Amsterdam maart 1778-december 1790'.

127   Estimate for 1781: NA, Archief Admiraliteitscolleges XXXIX, Van der Hoop, no. 15. 'Staten van de kostenberekening c. 1770–c. 1795'. Estimate for 1748: NA, Familiearchief Fagel, no. 1075, 'Een lyst van de charters van 's Lands oorlogsscheepen, beneffens de kosten nodig zynde om de zelve te completeeren, op gegeeven door C. Bentam, Mr. Timmerman van 's Lands werf binnen Amsterdam'.

The figures presented in this section in and of themselves do not explain why, in the course of the eighteenth century, the Dutch navy proved no match for the English competitors, and in terms of size fell behind those of France (by the mid-1720s), Spain (during the 1730s and again from the mid-1750s onwards), and Russia (by 1775), turning it into the fifth largest navy of Europe by 1785–90.[128] But they do show that a decline in financial capabilities of the Dutch Republic do not form a likely explanation. Rather, the explanation should focus on the sharp upward shift in naval spending by the competing powers, and the reasons of the Dutch Republic not to follow suit.[129] The expansion of war fleets that is sometimes described as the 'second naval revolution', leading to the creation of standing navies of 150 ships or more by the second half of the eighteenth century, was driven by the competition between Britain, France, and Spain.[130] As the previous section has shown, for most of this period the Dutch could operate under the umbrella of British naval supremacy. This meant that Dutch commercial interests could rely on the British fleet to keep at bay the Bourbon competitors, while pressuring the state to re-arrange the existing war fleet for direct trade protection by cruising and convoying only. The increasing weight in naval expenditure on expensive long range convoys to the West Indies and the large outlays on low-intensity warfare against Moroccan and Algerian privateers can be explained in this light. Far from being a turn away from the priorities of merchant capital, the shifting pattern of naval expenditure during the eighteenth century reflected the growing importance of cross-continental trade within the overall trade balance, as well as the wish of European merchants to cut costs on expensive convoying operations and act as free-riders on British power. Instead of proving a growing rift between merchants and naval administrators, the transformation of the Dutch fleet from an instrument of great-power competition to a mere auxiliary force for the protection of trade routes reflected the continued weight of the short term interests of active merchants in the setting of naval priorities.[131] Operating a 'light' rather than second rate navy allowed the Dutch Admiralty Boards to

---

128   Glete 1993, p. 311.

129   Patrick O'Brien estimates that British taxation, geared in large part towards the mainten-ance of this naval supremacy, increased fifteen-fold between 1688 and 1815. O'Brien 2002, p. 250. Also see figure 4.1, Brewer 1988, p. 90.

130   For the long-term effects of this contest for British economic position, see Baugh 1994 and Baugh 2004.

131   The successful opposition of merchant lobbies to custom increases during the second decade of the eighteenth century is outlined in Meijer 1995.

fulfil their role in supporting commercial interests, without having to resort to an unpopular increase in customs that would have been necessary to match British, French, and Spanish fleet building.

Thus, the policy of armed neutrality followed by the Dutch Republic in European waters did not meet with sustained opposition within merchant circles. The same commercial influence over the Admiralty Boards that allowed for a careful balancing of profit and power, long-term interests of the ruling class and short-term considerations at the height of the Dutch cycle's second, hegemonic phase, produced the one-sided stress on short-term profits over power projection associated with the third phase of the cycle that produced the gradual withdrawal of the Dutch Republic from direct great-power competition. If there were any doubts about the wisdom of this policy, they came from statesmen weary of the long-term strategic effects of such systematic disengagement from great-power struggle. Only in the course of the 1750s did the political moods among important segments of the Dutch ruling class start to shift in a decidedly anti-English direction.[132] Even then, it seemed much more profitable to try and undercut British trade by using the cover of neutrality than by direct confrontation.[133] When in the late 1770s and 1780s the Dutch, at their loss, found out that such confrontation had finally become inevitable, they were unable to replace a lean and mean fleet of convoyers and cruisers with the heavily armed battle fleet needed for full-scale war. Paradoxically, it was the eighteenth century efficiency of Admiralty Boards in trade protection, not their lack of it, which prepared for the humiliating defeat of the Dutch navy in the Fourth Anglo-Dutch War.

Conclusions

The spectacular rise and gradual loss of Dutch hegemony at sea formed one of the crucial underpinnings of the Dutch cycle of accumulation. Trade protection by definition required close cooperation between merchants and the state in the organisation of violence. But the nature of this cooperation changed substantially as a result of the naval revolution of the 1650s and 1660s. During the first half of the seventeenth century the interchangeability of merchant fleets and war fleets had been the backbone of Dutch commercial hegemony, enabling the Republic to expand its commercial presence and its armed

---

132   Van Sas 2003, pp. 35 ff.
133   Carter 1971, pp. 103 ff.

reach in tandem. A string of Dutch-centred trade wars, running from the First
to the Third Anglo-Dutch War and focused on the main European areas of
trade, completely altered the equation. The introduction of line ahead or line
of battle tactics in the course of the First Anglo-Dutch War and the ensuing
period of intense inter-state competition at sea in the long run rendered armed
merchant-men close to obsolete in European naval conflict. However, the successful replacement of the old navy consisting in large part of hired or borrowed
merchant ships by a permanent and professional war fleet did not end the
intimate relation between Admiralty Boards and merchants, as Snapper suggested in his classic study on Dutch war and trade. In fact, during the second
half of the seventeenth century the navy was employed most assertively and
successfully as an instrument for securing Dutch commercial interests in the
Baltic, Mediterranean, and along the African coast. Meanwhile, the colonial
companies retained their strong state-like functions in organising warfare beyond Cape Hope and in the wider Atlantic.

What did change were the institutional forms of the interaction between
merchants and the state. The new forms of cooperation that arose differed for
the four main geographic areas of Dutch overseas trade; the East Indies, the
Atlantic, and the Baltic and Mediterranean. For the VOC, a situation of symbiosis in which Admiralty Boards and the Company had exchanged military,
material, and financial support on a case to case basis was replaced by a strict
division of labour, in which the Company 'bought off' its naval obligations in
European waters by regular financial contributions while retaining full independence of action in Asia. The dominant position that the Company had
achieved in Asia by the second half of the seventeenth century and its political influence within the Dutch state allowed it to hold on to its brokerage roll
of commercial enterprise and war maker. Keeping the state at bay meant that
in all its ventures, the Company could put profit first. While debates on the
economic usefulness of its military adventures resurfaced on more than one
occasion, the division of labour between Company and state thus created only
broke down in the second half of the eighteenth century. That the WIC was
in a very different position is apparent from the enthusiasm with which its
directors jumped to the 1644 proposal of a merger of VOC and WIC into one
state company for colonial warfare. The strength of European military competition on the African coast and in the West Indies, as well as the ease with
which private traders could penetrate these regions, made the Company per-
manently dependent on state support for warfare as well as the defence of its
monopoly. Re-established as the Second WIC in 1674, the company was gradually forced to share its trade with private merchants in all major areas under
its charter, including the slave-trade. Classical brokerage functions such as the

maintenance of fortresses and the organisation of convoys in exchange for taxation rights formed a growing share of WIC income in the eighteenth century. In
the course of the century, Admiralty Boards increasingly turned their attention
to the Atlantic area of Dutch overseas trade. But after the loss of its monopolies, this protection benefitted the Company, colonists and private traders alike,
weakening the ties that had previously existed between the WIC and the state.

In European waters, merchants had been able for a long time to secure their
protection through private initiative and localised brokerage institutions such
as the urban *Directies*. Early forms of merchant self-organisation like the Directorate for the Levantine Trade lobbied for protection, ensured that merchant
ships bound for their respective regions followed the rules for manning and
armature, and maintained diplomatic relations. But their independent role in
warfare was always more limited than that of the VOC and WIC. The priority
given by the state to the protection of European trade meant that in the most
important geographic theatre, the Baltic, separate merchant organisations did
not even arise until the very end of the seventeenth century. When they did,
in the context of the Anglo-Dutch naval alliance and severe politico-military
threats to Dutch trading dominance, they were designed not as classical brokerage institutions but as protection lobbies that petitioned the Admiralty Boards
to organise state convoys.

Through these very different institutional arrangements, competing groups
of merchants managed to secure continued state support for their trading
interests. The federal-brokerage character of the state was not abandoned,
but redefined by the increase of naval competition during the second half of
the seventeenth century. In contrast to long-held views in Dutch naval historiography, the evolution of Admiralty income and expenditure during the
long eighteenth century affirms that the state continued prioritising the armed
protection of trade for the benefit of Dutch commercial capital. Shifts in the
regional pattern of naval investment – from the Baltic-Mediterranean axis to
the far end of the Mediterranean, the African coast, the West Indies and finally
the East Indies – reflected and consolidated underlying changes in the geography of Dutch trade. The creation of separate institutional arrangements for
all main areas of trade meant that each group of merchants could compete for
political influence on its own terms. While this ensured that the short-term
interests of the main merchant groups were well-served, the organisational
structure of the relations between Admiralty Boards and merchants proved
less suitable for designing integral long-term strategies for international commercial rivalry. The needs of power projection and trade protection, closely
aligned at the highpoint of the Dutch cycle, began to be pulled in different directions. The way that naval institutions were tied to the competing groups of

merchants tended to strengthen this divergence. But as long as trade continued to go strong, the need for overriding strategies to challenge this trend was not considered with great urgency by Dutch Republican statesmen and capitalists. Only the impending clash with Britain in the 1770s convinced sections of the Dutch ruling class of the need to recreate the links between trade protection and power projection that their own interests had led them to ignore during the preceding period.

Production, Supply, and Labour Relations at the Naval Shipyards

Few, if any, investments in material goods in the early modern period were of the size of building and equipping fully armed war ships.[1] Navies depended on sustained interaction with their economic hinterlands on a scale hardly matched by other state institutions. Whereas the last chapter dealt with the evolution of the relations between Admiralty Boards and merchants in commercial protection and warfare, this chapter examines the economic impact of the naval economy on the development of capitalist structures in the home economy. After the naval revolution of the 1650s and 1660s with its associated launch of major in-house shipbuilding programmes, the Amsterdam naval shipyard became the second biggest production facility within the Dutch Republic, only surpassed by the VOC shipyard. The shipyards of the other Admiralty Boards were smaller, but nevertheless remained among the biggest manufacturing enterprises of their respective regions.

Naval shipyards are the laboratories for historians of modernisation processes, the evolution of administrative cultures, and the development of capitalist relations. The sheer size of naval shipyards all around the early modern world meant that they brought together hundreds or even thousands of workers at the same premises in an area when most production was still fragmented and small-scale. This created unique complexities in the nature of planning, costing, and coordination. Managers and workers fought over the implementation of technological innovation in a sector still dominated by craft labour. It created huge strains on labour relations as well as friction between state demand and private suppliers.[2] Whereas in the past much of the literature on war and state formation concentrated heavily on finances, production, and supply for warfare on land, in recent years naval institutions have become the focus of an increasing number of studies on the evolution of states, bureau-

---

1 As estimated by Brewer 1988, p. 34.

2 These themes are prominently addressed in recent studies on the Venetian arsenal, such as Davis 1991, Davis 1997, Zan 2004, and Zambon and Zan 2007, and on the Royal Dockyards, Morriss 1992, Knight 1999, and Linebaugh 2006.

cracies, and practices of contracting.[3] These debates, however, have as yet largely passed by Dutch historiography on the naval shipyards. Labour relations, supply systems, and management culture have been far more central in investigations of the VOC and of smaller private yards than they have been for the Admiralty Boards.[4] Like the debate on the employment of the navy in commercial protection, the debate on the functioning of naval shipyards is still heavily influenced by the image of a binary opposition between the market-oriented practices of the seventeenth century and the supposedly financially hamstrung, nepotism-infested and lethargic practices of the eighteenth century.[5] This story fits well into nationalist as well as liberal meta-narratives, in which the glorious days when the Dutch ruled the seven seas were undercut by self-serving bureaucrats who managed to replace the frugal merchants at the head of naval direction. Only very recently have historians started to nuance this view, for example by pointing out that in shipbuilding practices at the naval shipyards the eighteenth century was not as stagnant as was long assumed.[6] The previous chapter showed how the shifts in employment and make-up of the fleet were much more adapted to the needs of merchant capital and much less driven by 'economic decline' than is often suggested. It argued that far from arising from the removal of merchant capitalists from the helm of state it was their continued power over the state, guaranteed through federal-brokerage arrangements, that caused unbridgeable tensions between the sectional interests of individual groups of merchants and the long-term strategic interests of the Dutch ruling class. Similar conclusions can be drawn for the functioning of the Admiralty Boards in their relation with the home economy.

---

3   E.g. Glete 1993, Harding 1999, Bruijn 2000, Rodger 2004, Kirk 2005, Glete 2010, and Knight and Wilcox 2010. Older literature addressing such questions in great detail includes: Elias 1933, Mémain 1936, and Pool 1966.

4   For the VOC, see the essays collected in Wieringa 1982, Werkgroep VOC-Oostenburg 1986, Gawronski 1996, and Lucassen 2004. For private shipbuilders, see: Van Kampen 1953, Unger 1978, and the sections on shipbuilding of De Vries and Van der Woude 1997, pp. 296–300.

5   The main work setting out this view remains Bruijn 1970. Most studies on the other Admiralty Boards consisted of short articles, often highly episodic in nature. E.g., Thurkow 1945, Van 't Zand 1998, Enthoven, 2003, Roodhuyzen-van Breda Vriesman 2003. Relevant research into the functioning of the Zeeland Admiralty Board has been done in the rich Zeeland Provincial Archive in recent years, contesting the idea that this smaller Admiralty Board became lethargic and fully inefficient during the eighteenth century. Otte 2004, Veenstra 2008.

6   For the old view of stagnation, see Voorbeijtel Cannenburg 1924. For a recent, more nuanced approach see Hoving and Lemmers 2001.

To examine the evolution of the naval economy, this chapter falls into two parts. The first focuses on supply. It studies the diverse but connected issues of accounting culture (section 3.1), the general organisation of supply (section 3.2), and the structure of supply networks mobilised for the acquisition of different types of goods (section 3.3). The second part of the chapter looks at the organisation of production at the shipyards themselves. It starts from an examination of the size of production and the shipyard workforce (sections 3.4 and 3.5), and continues with investigations into the interaction of shipyards and the labour market (section 3.6), the development of hierarchies at work (section 3.7), attitudes to labour (section 3.8) and the evolution of ideas on the application of science and experimentation in shipbuilding (3.9). Most attention will be given to the Amsterdam shipyard, by far the largest naval institution of the Dutch Republic. However, comparisons with the smaller shipyards will be included to draw attention to the consequences of the differences in scale and the implications of the federalist divisions between Admiralty Boards for production and supply. By taking this broad view of the functioning of the naval economy, this chapter can show how market-oriented systems of pricing, costing, and accounting, as well as capitalistic attitudes to the organisation of production and the workforce, were carried over from the seventeenth into the eighteenth century. Again, the close connections between state administrators and economic elites typical for the federal-brokerage structure of the Dutch Republic remained an important factor in determining the direction of development of production and supply.

3.1   Capitalist Rationality, Accounting, and the Naval Revolution

The centralisation of naval production and supply in a small number of large facilities that resulted from the naval revolution was accompanied by a real shift in administrative practices and attitudes to state management. John Brewer has pointed out the centrality of accounting structures to the functioning of fiscal-military states:

> Of course, the fiscal-military state presented a different face to civil society ... than it did to the world at large. On the frontiers of the empire, in Europe and on the high seas it relied on the coercive brute force deployed by all the main military powers; but at home state power worked more subtly and less obtrusively. Its key technology was not derived from the arts of war but from the counting-house – slips of paper rather than shot and cannon, slide-rules rather than the blades of swords. Its

ethos was that of bookkeeping, penmanship and political arithmetic, its ambiance entirely compatible with commercial society. Yet its unobtrusiveness did not preclude remarkable powers of surveillance: basic measuring skills, aided by calculus, the measuring rod and the slide-rule, together with exacting standards of bookkeeping, enabled the state and its functionaries to observe and record an astonishing amount of activity.[7]

It is no coincidence that three of the driving figures in this process – Jean Baptiste Colbert, Samuel Pepys and Johan de Witt – all combined great influence on the general course of state policy with direct involvement in naval reform.[8] But in the Dutch Republic reforms in Admiralty administration pre-dated the tactical revolution by half a century, making standardised bookkeeping practices, strict centralised control over accounts, and active price comparison central to managerial choices. Already before the 1650s, Dutch naval administrators built on the achievements in accounting of the Italian city states and on a widespread culture of using advanced mathematics in state tasks in order to rationalise government administration.[9]

The high level of involvement of people steeped in commercial practices in politics made Dutch statesmen and officials susceptible to innovations in this area. In the words of historian Jacob Soll: 'The *ars mercatoria* was a rich part of everyday urban life and an essential element of state government. The Dutch ruling elite was familiar with the minutiae of finance, industry, and trade'.[10] The intimate relation between merchant practices and administrative attitudes is borne out by contemporary sources. A revealing set of notes of Stadtholder Maurits's mathematician Simon Stevin conveys the content of a discussion between himself and 'His Princely Grace' around the turn of the seventeenth century. In his rendering of the debate, Stevin explains the advantages of replacing the traditional system of accounting for the princely domains with Italian style double-entry bookkeeping used by merchants. Up to that time, bailiffs of the domains had included income and expenditure in one single column, determining the balance by a simple process of adding

---

7   Brewer 1994, pp. 60–1.
8   For De Witt: Oudendijk 1944, p. 98 and p. 155, Panhuysen 2009, pp. 123 ff. For Pepys: Tomlinson 1979, p. 112. For Colbert: Taillenitte 1985 and Jacob Soll 2009, pp. 50 ff.
9   On the wider significance of accounting and mathematics in creating a 'rational' culture of government and trade, see Pocock 1975, Smith 1984, and Bryer 1993.
10   Soll 2009, p. 225.

and subtracting. At the start of the stylised 'conversation', Stevin gives the reasons why a merchant would prefer the double-entry system over the system commonly used in state administration:

> First, so that he always knows how much money his treasurer has, or ought to have, in his cash register, which is now unknown to the Prince and his treasurer ... Also, the merchant has a handy certainty of all goods handed over by him to the control of his factors, whereas the Prince in all commodities supplied to him must rely on the information of his officers. Thirdly, the merchant always has a clear view, not only of the remainders on the accounts of his debtors and creditors, but also of the stock of all goods that he should have in his possession, the profits or damages incurred on every category of goods. And he obtains all of this with such short shrift that can be held for impossible if the ordinary method of accounting of the bailiffs would be applied to a large trade.[11]

Stevin thus laid much stress on the connections between commercial accounting, orderly management of stocks, and the possibility to gain a separate overview of costs and profits for the discrete elements of business included in the accounts. This cut two ways. Not only would proper accounting enable administrators to make far more precise economic judgments. It also enlarged state control over the administrating officials themselves, diminishing the possibilities for fraud. As Stevin put it, 'bookkeeping is a well-known means to force unjust people with violence to behave justly, out of shame and fear of what might follow'.[12] According to his own rendering, Stevin managed to convince Maurits of the usefulness of his suggestions, and with the help of 'an experienced accountant in trade' he wrote an annotated model account for the princely domains. In 1604 Stevin's system of accounting was put into practice for the first time.[13] Significantly, a thorough reform of the system of naval accounting was proscribed by the States General in the same year.

The 1597 instructions for the Admiralty Boards had already summoned that proper accounts should be kept of every area of Admiralty income and expenditure, from the collection of customs and the sale of confiscated goods to the

---

11   Stevin 1649, pp. 3–4. The notes were first published after Simon Stevin's death by his son Hendrick.

12   Stevin 1649, p. 10.

13   Stevin 1649, p. 13.

acquisition of ammunition and the hiring of ships. It was the task of the receiver general of each of the five Admiralty Boards to turn these separate accounts into general reports. Every six months, the accounts should be sent to the States General, no later than three months after the end of the period covered therein. The aim of this was 'that the Gentlemen States General from time to time will have perfect knowledge, both of the income and the expenditures'.[14] These instructions did not establish general rules for the style of accounting. But in 1604 the States General delegated a commission to work out a standardised system of accounting for all five Admiralty Boards. The aim was 'that the entire administration of income and expenditure of each board will be brought on one account by the receiver general'.[15] The report of the commission, accepted by the States General, contained detailed prescriptions on how the accounts should be subdivided into separate posts or *summae*, established that the receivers general should keep proof of all expenditures mentioned in the accounts for control by the Audit Office, and also determined that every ledger should contain a summary report (*borderel*) following the same subdivisions as the account books themselves.

The result of these interventions in Admiralty management was a system of accounting that was extremely well-ordered for its time. The only other place where completely standardised bookkeeping was applied to naval management at such an early date was Venice, where the senate had already decreed regulation much akin to the Dutch system in 1586. Accounting historians Zambon and Zan have rightly pointed to the great significance of this regulation, arguing 'that the Venetian Senate was clearly posing the problem of costing and the efficient use of resources within the Arsenal'.[16] In a fascinating history of the role of the printed word in the development of East India trade, Miles Ogborn emphasises the function of accounts as a way to achieve managerial control of means, material, and men, focusing on the second half of the seventeenth century as a period of rapid development of administrative practices by the English East India Company.[17] As the discussions between Simon Stevin and Maurits show, very similar aims motivated Dutch administrators in the improvement of bookkeeping practices. Unfortunately, most of the accounts of the period before 1680 have been lost, except for those of the Zeeland Admir-

---

14 Staten Generaal 1689, p. 13.

15 NA, Archief Staten-Generaal, no. 12561.14, 'Poincten van Advijs, waer near de Heeren van den Admt hun sullen reguleren int dresseren der selver reeckeningen'.

16 Zambon and Zan 2007, p. 108.

17 Ogborn 2007, pp. 83 ff.

alty Board. But the almost complete series of ledgers of the receiver general that remain for the last decades of the seventeenth and most of the eighteenth century show that with a few minor variations, the system designed at the start of the century was maintained by all five Admiralty Boards. The introduction of this unified system of accounting helped to rationalise management of naval affairs both for the state as a whole and within the separate Admiralty Boards. For the state, it enhanced the possibilities of comparison and control.[18] For the individual Admiralty Boards, it helped in the development of internal costing methods based on calculating comparisons of expenditures over time and in different branches of naval production and supply.[19]

At the time of the naval revolution of the 1650s and 1660s, then, the Dutch Admiralty Boards already possessed important administrative tools to enhance cost-cutting management practices. But it was the building of large centralised shipyards and storehouses in the period between the First and Second Anglo-Dutch Wars that enabled naval administrators to really bring these methods to fruition. The Amsterdam shipyard and storehouse provide the best illustration of the advantages of concentrating all naval activity in one location. During the first half of the seventeenth century, the Admiralty shipyard and storehouse were cramped in amidst VOC and private shipyards in a small area

---

18 Comparisons of the efficiency of the different Admiralty Boards based on their accounts survive for example for the early 1680s, the 1750s and the 1780s. Resp. NA, Archief Van der Hoop, no. 160. 'Staet ende memorie van de ontfangh ende de lasten' (1681–5), no. 153. 'Secrete missiven van de Admiraliteiten op de Maaze, te Amsterdam en in het Noorder Quartier, 30 Juny 1751', and no. 151. 'Missive en memorie door zyne Hoogheid den heere Prince van Orange en Nassau aan hun Hoog Mogende op den 7 October 1782 overgegeven'. At the end of the eighteenth century, there were even cases where pre-printed administration forms were sent to the Admiralty Boards to fill out. NA, Familiearchief Steengracht, no. 157 'Notities betreffende de vordering'.

19 Especially for the second half of the eighteenth century there is abundant evidence of this use of the accounts to make projections on the future costs of building and equipping ships, determining the desired price, and seeking ways to increase economic efficiency. E.g., NA, Archief Admiraliteitscollecties XXXII, Pieter van Bleiswijk 1690–1787, no. 6. 'Stukken betreffende de aanbesteding', containing detailed estimates of the costs of building ships of different charters, and comparisons of those estimates with the actual offers made by shipbuilders and suppliers in the process of public tender. However, the availability of similar lists from the seventeenth century suggests that the practice of internal costing was well developed at a much earlier stage. E.g., the calculations made for a ship of 170 ft from 1667, NA, Admiraliteitscolleges XXXI, J. Bisdom 1525–1793, no. 117. 'Stukken betreffende constructie'.

at what were then the eastern outskirts of the city.[20] The storehouse was so small that the Admiralty Board was forced to hire a number of private warehouses in different parts of the city, making it harder to keep a precise overview of stocks. The wharf itself was more suitable for maintenance than for the building of large ships. Already in 1648 the Admiralty directors had petitioned the Amsterdam city council for the right to build a new storehouse, but this was refused. However, under the impression of the First Anglo-Dutch War the Amsterdam burgomasters changed their minds and allocated an area called Kattenburg – one of three newly created artificial islands in the main waterway the IJ – to the building of both a new storehouse and a shipyard 'of astounding length'.[21] Shortly after the Admiralty Board started moving its facilities, the VOC acquired the adjacent island (Oostenburg). The two islands, separated from the rest of the city by bridges, now became the heart of Amsterdam's shipbuilding industry.

The first building that was erected was the naval storehouse. The total costs of the facility came at just under f400,000, and after placing the first stone in September 1656 the building was made ready for use in a remarkably short period.[22] According to Dapper's contemporary history of Amsterdam, the concentration of all naval facilities around this single imposing building was motivated by both practical and financial advantages:

> ... [F]irst, to keep all the prerequisites for war that are needed for the equipment of warships together at short distance in one place. On the other side to avoid the high costs of renting warehouses and cellars, in which all shipbuilding tools and battle-gear were stored, spread out over the whole city. Because the yearly costs of this were so high ... that the money laid out on the building of this edifice will be paid off within five years.[23]

---

20   The storehouse was situated at Uilenburg, the wharf at Rapenburg. Wagenaar 1765, p. 78. From 1608, the VOC shared the same terrain at Rapenburg. De Haas 1982, p. 63. Throughout this chapter, the term 'private shipyard' will be used for the many independent shipbuilding enterprises producing for an open market, not for the VOC-shipyards which functioned as embedded institutions within the larger framework of this specific monopoly trading company. Also De Feyter 1982, p. 155.

21   Wagenaar 1765, p. 80.

22   Bonke 1986, p. 43, and De Meer 1994, pp. 25–7.

23   Dapper 1663, pp. 452–3.

In all its features, the four-storey building was to exude power and wealth. Its frontispiece represented the protection of seafarers, and the lines by Amsterdam's celebrated poet Vondel under a painting in the conference room stressed the centrality of the new navy for the Republic:

> Now will no sea beast dare to move his fins at sea,
> Thus grows our trade, for the expansion of the state.[24]

In another poem celebrating the building, Vondel expressed the connection between the institution, the power of the Republic, and economic prosperity in even starker terms: 'Thus keeps a magazine, a house, the wealth of the nation in place'.[25]

Other Admiralty Boards followed suit and built their own central storehouses and shipyards, albeit on a smaller scale. These buildings formed the backbone of the efforts to produce a new navy. Even a century after the erection of the Amsterdam naval storehouse, one British observer could write of the methods for storage and safety and the internal organisation employed there:

> They have admirable Methods in preserving their Ships when built, and their Magazines are in good Order, every Ship having an Apartment to lay up all Equipage in; and at the Top of their Magazines are vast Cisterns, which are kept constantly full of Water, having Pipes into every Apartment, to let it down upon Accident of Fire. And there is in their Magazines a Nursery Room, where a Woman keeps an Office, to feed, at certain Hours of the Day, a great Number of Cats, which afterwards hunt among the Store, for Mice and Rats.[26]

And another British visitor mused:

> The Contrivance of this House is admirable ... The Arms and Stores belonging to the Ships, are kept in excellent Order in several Chambers. The Keepers are shy of shewing the House, though they need not be ashamed of any Thing that belongs to it. The so much boasted Arsenal of *Venice* is not comparable to it, though there are four other lesser Admiralties, or Docks, belonging to the Republick, besides this of *Amsterdam*.

---

24   Wagenaar 1765, p. 81.
25   Van den Vondel 1658, p. 13.
26   Poole 1750, p. 184.

> The Buildings and Docks of *Woolwich* and *Chatham* are indeed handsom, and well provided with naval Stores; but their Situation will not admit of the Neatness and Order conspicuous in the other.[27]

This ruthless pursuit of managerial 'neatness and order' became the hallmark of Dutch naval administration across the board, and was characteristic for a culture of management bent on a form of economic efficiency derived from commercial practices as the guiding principle in the execution of state tasks.

3.2 Personal Networks and Market Practices

The adoption of commercial accounting of course was not the only link that connected Admiralty administration to the logic of the market. The personal involvement of leading merchants in the direction of the navy did not only influence the employment of the war fleet abroad, but also the management of naval resources at home. One of the institutional disadvantages inherent in this direct involvement of capitalist elites in the management of naval production and supply was that of in-trading. The 1597 instruction for naval administrators contained a number of clauses directed against the personal involvement of councillors and other servants of the Admiralty Board in economic activities related to the affairs of the navy. The oath sworn by all Admiralty councillors summoned:

> [t]hat they shall not participate, directly or indirectly, in *tax-farming*, or collection of customs or other general means, nor in the *supply of gunpowder, scarp, guns, weapons, butter, cheese*, or any other victuals, or in commercial services, or in selling goods to the public.[28]

But of course they did. In 1626 the Rotterdam Admiralty Board became the centre of major proceedings for fraud by its staff. The case had been brought to the courts when rumours started to spread among the populace of Rotterdam that naval administrators enjoyed incomes far greater than they were officially entitled to. One of the leading Admiralty functionaries, the fiscal advocate, as well as several councillors were found guilty of participating in the buying and selling of confiscated goods and receiving bribes. They were sen-

---

27 Anonymous 1743, pp. 370–1.
28 'Instructie voor de Collegien ter Admiraliteyt', 13 August 1597, Staten Generaal 1689, p. 26.

tenced to long detention, were banished for life, and received tens of thousands of guilders in fines. But as the contemporary historian Lieuwe van Aitzema made clear, the sentences were as much directed at shielding the system as a whole from popular wrath as they were at punishing the culprits. 'For if there would have been an examination of all councillors and magistrates in the same way according to their instructions, one might well say *Domine quis sustinebit* [Lord, who would remain standing]'.[29] Despite frequent reissuing of the rules as well as sharpening of the wording of the oath for functionaries, in-trading remained a reoccurring phenomenon well into the eighteenth century.[30]

However, parallel to what Michiel de Jong has argued in his study of the arms trade in the Dutch Republic, the tendency to see personal intervention of state administrators only as a source of corruption or waste is based on an anachronistic view with strong overtones of a neo-liberal rejection of the state as inherently rapacious, contrasted to an inherently efficient and non-corrupt market.[31] A sharp separation between state and market simply did not exist, and in fact direct connections between officials and merchants created venues of profit for members of the ruling class inside and outside of the state. Pieter de la Court stressed that precisely because of such links, Holland officials in general were much better able than their counterparts elsewhere to mobilise funds and acquire goods at low prices:

> The ... fruit of free government before and during the [second] English war, is that the States of Holland as well as their Government have been able to gather all necessities, even before need arose. This precaution was combined with two others, namely in the first place that everything was bought and paid with ready money, and in the second place that the commission to execute this was given to plenipotentiaries representing those cities for which a good outcome of these affairs was of prime importance ... This was the cause why Holland, to the surprise of the entire world, during all emergencies of war could procure the means and finances to

---

29 Van Aitzema 1669a, pp. 529–30.

30 One of the most spectacular cases of the eighteenth century involved Amsterdam master of equipment Willem Sautijn and master shipwright John May, who together with three other officials were guilty of large-scale embezzling of goods that belonged to the wharf and fiddling the accounts. Despite all evidence, none of them were found guilty, but the clerks who had acted as whistle-blowers lost their jobs. Bruijn 1993, pp. 164–5.

31 De Jong 2005, p. 92.

temporarily bear the shortages of the Admiralty Boards and the other provinces, and to supply at lower prices than ever in times of peace the canon, scarp, gunpowder, and victuals.[32]

Personal profiteering, even outright corruption, and the introduction of stricter economies in the management of state funds often went hand in hand.

Contacts between the state and markets always were in part shaped by the personal networks of administrators. Various measures were taken to check the tendencies towards favouritism inherent in such an organisation. Apart from tight administrative control, the most important of these was the use of public auctioning to ensure that buying and selling took place at the most advantageous price. Central regulation was first developed for the sale of Admiralty goods, an area that was particularly vulnerable to in-trading. The instruction of 1597 decreed that all selling of prizes and confiscated goods should take place in this way. It also specified the conditions under which the auctions should take place. Day, time, and location had to be announced well in advance through placards posted in all cities at one day's travelling distance from the Admiralty town. The auction itself should be held in the presence of a number of Admiralty councillors who had to make sure that the sale would go to the highest bidder, and that a detailed register of all transactions would be kept.[33] As the Rotterdam case of 1626 shows, the latter condition was not in itself sufficient to prevent fraud. Nevertheless the widespread use and developed regulation for auctioning show a perception on the part of central administrators that such forms of favouritism could be counteracted by market competition.

The same logic was extended early on to the field of contracting. Auctioning of contracts became the standard practice for many different types of acquisitions. Procedures for public tendering were most elaborate for entire ships or hulls. The strong personal influence of the master shipwright on the shipbuilding process and the properties of the end-product made it difficult to determine at what point exactly the terms of the contract were met. To avoid endless conflict, the terms of the offer were set meticulously. One such offer, put out by the Northern Quarter Admiralty Board and finished in September 1653, contained over forty conditions for 'a warship, built in the way of a ship of 200 lasts as used by the VOC, length 130, width 32 ½ Amsterdam feet'. The conditions specified the exact measures of the ship and all its individual parts, the thickness

---

32   Kernkamp 1935, p. 179.
33   'Instructie', in Staten Generaal 1689, pp. 36–7.

of the wooden beams used in construction, the internal architecture, and all other prerequisites 'up to the point where the ship can take sea'. Once the ship was built, Admiralty officials checked whether all conditions had been met by the contractor. In the case of the 1653 tendering, a handwritten statement by the master shipwright of the Northern Quarter Admiralty Board testified under oath that the new warship had been built by a master shipwright from Hoorn 'in conformity with the offer'.[34] Conditions for Admiralty control over the execution of the contract, however, could also be used to tamper with the rules of tendering to the lowest bidder, as is clear from a case described by Johan Elias. In January 1654 the Rotterdam Admiralty Board tendered for the making of four hulls of 136 feet. The States General had demanded that these contracts would go to the lowest bidder, and therefore that shipwrights from the shipbuilding areas in the Northern Quarter of Holland would be allowed to take part in the auction. The Rotterdam Admiralty councillors, in favour of employing shipbuilders from their own region, proceeded to put into the contract a condition stating that the hulls

> should be made under supervision of aforementioned board, and launched at the easiest place for their Highly Esteemed Gentlemen to hold precise day to day inspections of the work in progress, [checking] ... whether everything is made and done according to the offer ...[35]

The terms of this condition made sure that shipbuilders from the Northern Quarter were prevented from bidding. As a result, the Rotterdam Admiralty Board bought the four hulls for ƒ32,500 apiece, while similar contracts in Amsterdam went for ƒ28,500 and in the shipbuilding town Zaandam even for ƒ27,500.[36]

From ships and hulls, the practice of public tendering was extended to many smaller contracts. This strengthening of market-orientedness continued well into the eighteenth century. The 1744 regulation of the Amsterdam shipyard stated

> That an experiment shall be taken ... to regulate the supply of all products from now on not through permanent suppliers, but through inscription

---

34   NA, Archief Staten-Generaal, no. 12561.120.2. 'Forma vant besteck omte maken een schip van oorloge'.

35   Elias 1933, p. 142.

36   Ibid.

on the basis of posters and notification in the papers, made public a convenient time in advance. And [only] for those deliveries that merely consist of small quantities of little consideration, or that can only be tendered to two or three bidders, shall the contract be given to a fixed person. But also for such a tendering, [the Admiralty Board must] gather as many people as possible trading in this product.[37]

This decision to open up almost every area of supply to direct market competition was taken at a moment when the Amsterdam Admiralty Board was operating under great financial restraint, as part of a thoroughgoing programme of financial restructuring undertaken by the Admiralty councillors during the 1730s and 1740s – underlining that Admiralty administrators saw a strong connection between using market competition in supply and economising management at the shipyards. The use of tendering as a way to force down costs can also be seen from its application by the Rotterdam Board in 1782 for the rebuilding of part of the naval storehouse. Seven bidders applied to do masonry, at prices ranging from f9,900 to f12,619. Bids for carpentering work varied as much, with sixteen carpenters committing to prices ranging from f3,747 to f5,820. The names of three of the lowest bidders were underlined, signifying that they were eligible for the job, though for reasons that remained unspecified the contract for masonry did not go to the one offering the very lowest price, but to a contractor bidding the slightly higher sum of f9,988.[38]

Throughout the eighteenth century, the Admiralty Boards employed the method of public tendering widely and with growing sophistication. Even in 1781, when the need to build quickly in order to meet the necessities of war put great upward pressure on prices, Rotterdam Admiralty councillors ostensibly made conscious use of the tendering process to obtain the best deal within the given circumstances. On 4 April 1781 four deputies of the States General joined Rotterdam fiscal advocate Bisdom, master of equipment Van Staveren, master shipwright Van Zwyndrecht, and nine Admiralty councillors, 'seated according to the rank of their provinces and towns', to receive the bids for the building and equipment of two ships carrying 60 and 70 pieces respectively. The bidding started with a reading of the conditions for tendering. Beforehand, the deputies of the States General and representatives of the Rotterdam Admir-

---

37 NA, Archief Van der Hoop, no. 153. 'Secrete Missive van de Admiraliteit Amsterdam', 30 June 1751, 86.

38 NA, Archief Admiraliteitscolleges XXXI, collectie J. Bisdom, no. 205. 'Stukken betreffende het Admiraliteitsmagazijn'.

alty Board had agreed that if the bids would contain 'such a reasonable price
that no objections could be raised', the contract would be granted immediately. In order to determine this 'reasonable price' a calculation of prices for
the hull and equipment of different sizes of ships was included in the documents, based on tendering contracts from the pre-war year 1779. If the bids
would exceed those prices 'but not all too excessively', the contracts would
only be awarded after three days, giving time for consultation with the States
General. If all bids would exceed the calculated price by a large margin, fourteen days would be taken 'in order to await the results of tendering by the
Amsterdam Admiralty Board'. Of the three bidders for the hull of the smaller
ship, Jacob Spaan from Dordrecht offered the most favourable price. However,
at ƒ323,365 this was still almost one and a half times as high as the price
indicated by the calculation from 1779. Apparently this was still within the
range of expectations, since the delegates announced to give Spaan a definit-
ive answer after three days. After the meeting was over the delegates agreed
to advise favourably on giving Spaan the contract 'because of the circumstances at the time, and the impossibility to execute all building at the nation's
shipyards with the required speed', but to keep the price secret in order not
to influence the tendering a few days later in Amsterdam for a ship of similar
size.[39]

The decision on the bid for the larger ship proved more difficult. The
cheapest offer was that of Jan Schoute from Dordrecht, who at ƒ520,000 demanded double the price of a ship of 70 pieces before the war. In this case, the
delegates demanded a fourteen-day waiting period before announcing their
decision. Thereafter, Schoute agreed 'both by word of mouth and in writing' to
lower his bid to ƒ460,000, but the delegates still considered this price excessive
and therefore discouraged giving the contract to any of the bidders, suggesting that the tendering process be started anew.[40] Around the same time the
Rotterdam Admiralty Board received the outcome of the tendering process
in Amsterdam, where a hull for a ship of 60 pieces had been contracted for
ƒ278,400, and for a ship of 70 pieces for ƒ410,000.[41] The Rotterdam deputies

---

39   NA, Archief admiraliteitscolleges XXXII, collectie Van Bleiswijk, no. 6. 'Secrete missive',
      5 April 1781.
40   NA, Archief admiraliteitscolleges XXXII, collectie Van Bleiswijk, no. 6., 'Missive van de
      Admiraliteit op de Maze', 13 April 1781.
41   NA, Archief admiraliteitscolleges XXXII, collectie Van Bleiswijk, no. 6., 'Notitie waar voor
      alles is aanbesteed voor een schip van Oorlog van 70 stukken'. The conditions and outcome
      of tendering for the Amsterdam ships can be found in NA, Archief Fagel, no. 1096.

themselves had already expected the large price difference with Amsterdam, which they ascribed to more lenient conditions in the offer.[42]

The latter example shows to what extent calculation on the basis of past prices, comparison with the prices obtained by other Admiralty Boards, and strictly regulated forms of public tendering had become standard procedure in naval administration. Even under duress of war such practices were not replaced by a simple reliance on direct connections with privileged contractors. While strongly tied to local commercial networks, personal preferences were channeled through and held in check by a developed capitalist culture of accounting and public tendering. But the example also shows that the use of auctioning in itself was not a sufficient guarantee that ships and goods could indeed be obtained at the desired price. Market conditions varied per product, for the different localities of the Admiralty Boards, and for periods of peace or war, demanding very different approaches to contracting.

3.3   Different Products, Different Systems of Supply

Practices for acquisitioning varied substantially for different types of goods, depending on the size of demand and the structure of the market. Table 3.1 contains the reconstruction of the Amsterdam Admiralty accounts for a number of selected expenses from 1681–1789. Unfortunately, it is not possible to obtain such complete series of figures on Amsterdam expenditure for an earlier period. But the table gives a good indication of the relative weight of different types of goods on the Admiralty accounts. Three categories of goods bought by the Admiralty Board will be more thoroughly examined here: victuals, expensive bulk goods such as wood, and finally less expensive types of goods, acquired either in bulk (as for example was the case with nails, included under ironware), or in small quantities.

Victuals
Making up a total of 14.8 percent of all of Amsterdam's expenditure, victuals invariably formed the largest category of goods supplied to the navy. Throughout the existence of the Republic, victualling remained a fully privatised activity, bypassing Admiralty administration. Captains were given a fixed amount of money per crew member per day (initially five *stuyvers*, later seven), and

---

42   NA, Archief admiraliteitscolleges XXXII, collectie Van Bleiswijk, no. 6. 'Secrete missive', 5 April 1781.

TABLE 3.1   *Amsterdam naval expenditure on selected goods, 1681–1789 (millions of guilders)*

	1681–1689	1690–1699	1700–1709	1710–1719	1720–1729	1730–1739	1740–1749	1750–1759	1760–1769	1770–1779	1780–1789	Total	As % of total exp.
Victuals	2.8	8.2	7.5	3.1	3.7	1.8	2.0	3.0	2.9	2.2	5.9	43.2	14.8%
Wood	1.3	2.3	2.0	0.9	1.9	1.6	1.8	1.7	2.3	2.1	5.3	23.3	7.9%
Rigging, rope, hemp	0.7	2.1	2.2	0.7	0.6	0.3	0.7	0.4	0.8	0.7	1.4	10.7	3.6%
Iron and ironware	0.4	0.8	0.7	0.2	0.4	0.3	0.4	0.4	0.4	0.4	1.3	6.0	2.0%
Ammunition	0.5	1.1	0.8	0.1	0.3	0.1	0.3	0.3	0.4	0.4	1.6	5.8	2.0%
Cloth and sails	0.3	0.7	0.7	0.3	0.2	0.2	0.3	0.2	0.4	0.2	0.5	3.8	1.3%
Complete ships	0.4	0.4	0.1	0.0	0.0	0.0	0.0	0.0	0.0	0.1	1.9	2.8	1.0%
Expenditure on main types of acquisitions	6.3	15.6	13.9	5.4	7.1	4.3	5.6	6.0	7.1	6.1	18.0	95.4	32.5%
Total Admiralty expenditure	18.0	40.8	35.7	23.3	21.2	20.1	20.6	20.1	24.1	21.7	47.4	293.3	100.0%

SOURCES: NA, ARCHIEF GENERALITEITSREKENKAMER 1586–1799, NOS. 490–717, ESTIMATE 1780 BASED ON NA, ARCHIEF ADMIRALITEITSCOLLEGES XXXIX, VAN DER HOOP, NO. 17

had the responsibility to take care of provisioning on their own account. Lists were provided determining the amount of each type of victuals that had to be on board their ships.[43] But captains were free to choose their own suppliers, and could cut back on expenses by buying low quality products. Because of the decentralised organisation of this type of supply very little source material is available about the exact ways in which this was done and the profits that could be made. An – albeit denunciatory – pamphlet of the late eighteenth century estimated the profits that a captain of a large man-of-war carrying sixty pieces could make per year as at least ƒ19,000.[44] Though this seems an

43   UB, Universiteit van Amsterdam, Bijzondere Collecties OF63/985, *Extracten uit het register van de resolutiën der Staten Generaal en uit de notulen van de Admiraliteit te Amsterdam, alle betr. zeezaken [1671–1780]* (Henceforth: UB-BC), *Extracten*. 'Specifications 1777'.

44   Anonymous 1779, pp. 22–4.

unrealistically high sum, in general victualling was considered to be a way for captains to make major profits. It is well known that during the seventeenth century Michiel de Ruyter, the most famous admiral of the Dutch Republic, made tens of thousands of guilders on victualling. But long delays in the payment of victualling money by the Admiralty Boards, forcing the captains to place large loans with *soliciteurs*, or sharp increases of food prices at times of war, could also make victualling a source of loss.[45] The decentralised system of victualling almost certainly favoured traders in foodstuffs in the Admiralty towns and other port cities. The two remaining 'victualling books' for De Ruyter's flagship *De Zeven Provintiën* from 1666 and 1672 show that he bought victuals mainly from traders in his hometown Amsterdam and in Hellevoetsluys, one of the principal navy ports. In some cases, he placed very large orders, such as one with baker Cornelis Verstege for 19,439 pounds of hard tack, at a total sum of ƒ1,371.[46] A description of Amsterdam of about the same time notes that at the Angeliers Channel near the IJ (the main Amsterdam waterway) 'live the biscuit-bakers, who make ship's biscuit; the bakeries are very big, with as much as ten or twelve ovens'.[47]

It remains a matter of speculation why the Admiralty Boards did not try to gain a firmer hold on victualling by setting up their own centralised supply system. The Amsterdam chamber of the VOC did centralise this branch of supply, running its own butchery within the Company storehouse.[48] One advantage of fixing the amount of money per head of the crew was that the hazard of sharp rises in food prices at times of war was put on the captains, who in turn could let their crews bear the burden by providing lower quality goods. But of course, there was a limit to such a strategy, if not made apparent by open mutiny than still present in the danger that failure to supply in time could slow down operations. If anything, such a system of decentralised victualling presupposed a highly developed market in agrarian supplies that could respond to large spikes in demand. It also demanded that the captains themselves were well to do entrepreneurs, and had easy access to large amounts of credit to overcome the arrears of the Admiralty Boards. All of these circumstances of course were characteristic of the situation in the Dutch Republic. Even the aforementioned highly critical anonymous pamphlet from 1779 admitted that if these conditions could be met, the system actually ran rather smoothly:

45   Bruijn 1994, pp. 119 ff.
46   NA, Collectie De Ruyter, 1633–1683, no. 125, 'Specificatie van de victualien', 1666.
47   Fokkens 1662, p. 92. Thanks to Clé Lesger for pointing me towards this useful reference.
48   Gawronski 1996, p. 65.

As soon as the suppliers hear that a captain has been appointed a ship, knowing that he has means of his own and pays promptly, they each try to get into his favour, and offer him their samples of what they know the captain needs for his crew, of which he buys the best and cheapest, making conditions in advance that if the commodities sold do not equal the samples in quality, the sellers can be sure to receive them back. And in this way, the suppliers, although they make only a small profit, do not have the audacity to send goods to the ship that do not have the same quality as the samples. And the crew that sails with such a captain can be confident not to be forced to eat old, rotten or bug-infested food.[49]

But according to the pamphlet, the opposite was true for captains who were known to possess poor credit:

... [N]o supplier will look at him, and if he wants to have victuals for his ship, he will have to go out himself looking for traders who want to supply him with food on credit, which often costs such a captain great troubles before he gets ready and makes his head spin with all the conditions, clauses, and notes that these suppliers send him, before they are willing to supply the required provisions.[50]

Even in these conditions, however, the Admiralty Boards were more or less shielded from malfunctions in the supply system. Crews bore the brunt of supply failures in the form of malnutrition, while the captains were the ones to face their wrath. Meanwhile, though firm evidence of this is lacking, the presence of quite a number of large oxen-traders among the Amsterdam Admiralty councillors suggests that keeping victualling out of the formal chain of supply – and thus outside the books – could create lucrative loopholes for in-trading by the naval administrators.[51] This might be one more reasons why a more centralised system of supplying victuals was not introduced, despite the shortcomings of the existing arrangement.

---

49   Anonymous 1778, p. 67.
50   Anonymous 1778, p. 68.
51   E.g. Hiob de Wildt, the influential secretary of the Amsterdam Admiralty from 1671 to 1704, who was registered as an ox trader and according to the 1674 tax register owned an ample ƒ170,000. Elias 1903, pp. 392–3.

Wood

For large, expensive bulk goods such as the high standard oak used for the building of ships of the line, Admiralty Boards relied on a much more limited number of suppliers than were involved in providing captains with victuals. Before the late 1660s, when shipbuilding was mostly done on private shipyards, the acquisition of wood was often left to the shipwrights who managed to obtain the tendering contracts. The accounts of the master of equipment in the Zeeland Admiralty town Flushing, for example, show the two master shipwrights Pieter Leynssen and Crijn Cudde receiving compensation for wages they paid out as well as for the supply of wood.[52] But after the onset of major in-house shipbuilding programmes in the 1660s, the Admiralty Boards became increasingly large players on the wood market in their own right. Since almost all wood used in shipbuilding had to be imported from Scandinavia, the Baltic region, and Germany, wealthy international merchants dominated this line of supply.[53] Over the course of the seventeenth and eighteenth century, this led to frequent fears of large wood-traders forming a cartel against the Admiralty Boards. This was an element of lieutenant admiral Schrijver's long critique of naval affairs from the 1750s.

> It is well known to everybody that in their trade of shipbuilding oak, the buyers for centuries have been cheated in the most awful way ... And it is still daily practice that this wood is sold a capital above its value to the profit of the sellers, often supplying rotten wood instead of good quality wood, to the ruin of the account of the navy and the voc.[54]

Schrijver proposed the introduction of the taking of an obligatory oath against monopoly practices. But the Amsterdam Admiralty Board also devised some more substantial means to counter the combined power of the large wood traders. One was to use active price comparisons to force merchants to offer discounts. The archive of late eighteenth-century fiscal advocate Van der Hoop contains various notes in which the prices asked by merchants are compared to those actually paid, in one case establishing a difference of more than thirteen percent to the advantage of the Admiralty Board.[55]

---

52   Zeeland Provincial Archive Middelburg (from here RAZ), Archief Rekenkamer C, no. 35520. 'Equipagerekening Vlissingen 1665'.

53   Lesger 1992, p. 107.

54   NA, Familiearchief Fagel, no. 1077. 'Versameling van Annotatien omtrent veele Saken Rakende den Zeedienst en Scheeps-Bouw', vol. 3, p. 125.

55   NA, Archief Admiraliteitscolleges XXXIX, J.C. van der Hoop, no. 118. 'Vergelyking tusschen den Eysch en de Prys van 't ingekogten Eikehout', 5 December 1781 to 11 December 1783.

TABLE 3.2   *Largest wood-suppliers of the Amsterdam Admiralty Board, March 1778–December 1790 (thousands of guilders)*

Name supplier	1778*	1779	1780	1781	1782	1783	1784	1785	1786	1787	1788	1789	1790	Total
Pieter van der Stadt	67.2	70.2	21.9	336.5	323.8	103.9	16.0	7.3	0.9					947.7
Benjamin van Luneschlos				112.4	273.9	124.5								510.8
Gerrit Braamcamp	22.3	21.1	18.9	112.8	6.4	57.6	59.8	29.6	26.6	32.3	5.7	1.0		394.2
The widow and heirs of Jan Frederiks	52.8	33.6	21.6	77.1	124.9	22.4	6.7							339.1
Jacob Hagen	55.2	54.3	37.3	107.1	53.7		2.8							310.4
Dirk van der Plaat	25.5	19.1	9.0	41.0	1.3		2.2	34.7		16.2	23.8	35.7	30.2	238.8
Gerrit van Harlingen				5.9	129.9	18.7	9.3	1.0			10.4	6.4	0.1	181.7
Pieter Kuijper							32.1	23.1	15.5	25.2	19.9	41.2		157.0
Casper Kreeft									25.7	71.4		15.0	30.0	142.1

* (Mar. – Dec.)

SOURCE: NA, ARCHIEF ADMIRALITEITSCOLLEGES XXXIX, J.C. VAN DER HOOP, NO. 118. 'REKENINGEN AANGEKOCHT HOUT ADMIRALITEIT AMSTERDAM MAART 1778–DECEMBER 1790'

The ability of the Amsterdam Admiralty Board to enforce lower prices rested on the availability of a large number of potential suppliers, combined with an active strategy of diversification between suppliers. An overview of accounts from March 1778 to December 1790, including the crucial years of the Fourth Anglo-Dutch War, show that the Amsterdam Admiralty Board traded with no less than forty-eight wood merchants. Eighteen of those can be considered large suppliers, making deliveries worth *f*10,000 or more in at least one of those years. Nine of the wood traders made average yearly deliveries of more than *f*10,000 taken over the entire period. But as table 3.2 shows, none of these very large traders were active for the entire period. The size of their supply contracts varied substantially from year to year, and in no single year did one single trader completely dominate supply to the Admiralty Board. The fact that the Amsterdam Admiralty Board was not their sole client must have helped the merchants involved survive such large shifts in demand. In 1781 four of the biggest wood-suppliers to the Amsterdam chamber of the VOC also made substantial deliveries to the Admiralty Board.[56]

The ability of the Amsterdam Admiralty Board to actively switch between large suppliers rested on its close proximity to the main centres of wood trade in the Dutch Republic. The smaller Admiralty Boards, particularly those of Zeeland and Friesland, had to buy wood at longer distances and in all likelihood were much more vulnerable to the monopoly practices of traders. For the Friesland Admiralty Board wood supply became a major problem in the run-up to and during the Fourth Anglo-Dutch War.[57] The ensuing problems show how completely dependent the Friesland Admiralty Board had been on the Amsterdam market. In the course of the war the Friesland Board had completely ceased payments to its main wood supplier, the widow of wood merchant Jan Frederiks, who also acted as a large supplier to the Amsterdam Admiralty Board during the same period. Her request to the States of Holland asking for support listed the phenomenal sum of ƒ945,950 in outstanding bills.[58] A similar request of 28 creditors of Frederiks show that among those implicated in the Friesland forestalment of payment were the leading merchant-bankers De Neufville and Van der Hoop, as well as the large wood merchants Bontekoning and Van der Poll, who were both involved in supplying both the Amsterdam Admiralty Board and the VOC.[59]

Smaller Supplies

In contrast to the mighty merchant houses involved in supplying wood, by far the largest group of traders supplying the Admiralty Boards consisted of small or middle-size merchants and artisans who did not trade for more than ƒ10,000

---

56   NA, Archief VOC, no. 7165. 'Journaal boekhouder VOC juni 1780-mei 1784' and NA, Archief Admiraliteitscolleges XXXIX, Van de Hoop, no. 118, 'Nota over Prijsen, en quantiteit van swaar hout in 1781 bij het Ed Mog Coll ingekogt, en ontfangen'. The four suppliers are Cornelis van Bavel, (selling ƒ36,876 and ƒ24,859 worth of wood to the Amsterdam chamber of the VOC and the Amsterdam Admiralty Board respectively), the firm Bontekoning & Aukes (ƒ51,738 and ƒ5,122), Herman van der Poll (ƒ21,161 and ƒ18,156), and Pieter van de Stadt (ƒ11,959 and ƒ649,058). Due to a difference in style of administration used in the two documents yearly figures diverge from those cited in table 3.2.

57   Roodhuyzen-van Breda Vriesman 2003, p. 105.

58   NA, Archief admiraliteitscolleges XXXII, collectie Van Bleiswijk, no. 35. 'Extracten Resoluties Staten van Holland', 18 March 1784 and 4 August 1784.

59   NA, Archief admiraliteitscolleges XXXII, collectie Van Bleiswijk, no. 35. 'Extracten Resoluties Staten van Holland', 29 June 1785.

TABLE 3.3   *Distribution of suppliers to the Amsterdam and Zeeland Admiralty Boards*

	Number of large suppliers (>ƒ10,000)	Share in total supply	Number of middle-sized suppliers (ƒ1,000–ƒ10,000)	Share in total supply	Number of small suppliers (<ƒ1,000)	Share in total supply
Zeeland 1665 (Veere branch, Flushing branch, and receiver general)	19	72%	50	23%	152	5%
Amsterdam 1691 (full account)	23	66%	107	29%	133	5%
Zeeland 1781–4 (only receiver general)	6	64%	29	29%	69	7%
Zeeland 1781 (Flushing branch)	0	0%	9	39%	91	61%
Amsterdam 1790 (full account)	16	59%	72	34%	109	7%

SOURCES: NA, ARCHIEF ADMIRALITEITEN, NO. 1930 (AMSTERDAM 1691), NO. 1941 (AMSTERDAM 1790), RAZ, ARCHIEF REKENKAMER C, NO. 6980 (RECEIVER GENERAL 1665), NO. 38060 (VEERE 1665), NO. 35520 (FLUSHING 1665), NO. 8050 (RECEIVER GENERAL 1781–4), NO. 36930 (FLUSHING 1781)

per year, and who often traded for less than ƒ1,000. Table 3.3 gives some figures for the distribution between large, middle and small size suppliers of the Amsterdam and Zeeland Boards for the seventeenth and eighteenth century. The large number of small traders involved indicates the great importance of naval supply for the development of local artisan economies. This was especially true in small towns such as Veere or Flushing, where a substantial part of the labouring and artisan communities were involved in supplying small ironware or textiles for the making of flags, transporting goods, or held temporary jobs as subcontracting painters, woodcarvers or carpenters. Such small artisans were unable to exert the same pressures on Admiralty Boards as the large suppliers in order to enforce favourable prices. They were also more vulnerable to the long delays in payment customary in naval supplying. However, thanks to their proximity to the Admiralty Boards and the influence that the Dutch political system allowed to the middle and upper layers of the artisan community at the local level, small suppliers still managed to gain some economic protection.

The resolutions of the Zeeland Admiralty Board of the 1650s and 1660s contain many examples where the receiver general acted at the request of individual merchants to grant them down-payments on the arrears of masters of equipment.[60] Similar protective measures were taken in Amsterdam. The 1744 regulation that opened up small supplies to public tendering at the same time stipulated a fine of three percent above the original price for each year of arrears suffered by traders.[61] Other forms of protection included compensations for price fluctuations. A Zeeland resolution of 22 January 1657 granted a supplier of iron nails who had waited since 1654 for payments for his deliveries that the nails would be bought at current market prices rather than the prices of 1654, thereby compensating for the stark rise in prices since the deliveries were made.[62] Similar forms of local protection were still employed a century later, even in Amsterdam where the Admiralty Board could choose from a much larger pool of small suppliers. In 1779, for example, the Amsterdam Board accepted the request of suppliers of nails to compensate them for the price rise of fuels since their contracts were granted by adding half a guilder per ship-pound to the previously established price for the duration of the entire year.[63] Such protective measures show that the Admiralty Boards had some concern for the long-term maintenance of their supply networks, not only where large and powerful merchants were involved, but also touching the interests of the large mass of local small suppliers.

One common factor underlying all these different approaches to supply was the ease with which the Admiralty Boards could find credit, and the trust this produced in suppliers that eventually their concerns would be met by the state. In this sense, the troubles that the Friesland Admiralty Board generated for its major wood supplier were a real sign of crisis, conflicting with the long-established reputation of Dutch public institutions. At the end of the seventeenth century, one British observer had noticed:

---

60   E.g. NA, Archief Admiraliteiten, no. 2476. 'Resoluties Zeeuws admiraliteitscollege 1657', fol. 30, 32, 95, 108 vso.

61   NA, Archief Van der Hoop, no. 153. 'Secrete missive', 30 June 1751, 86.

62   NA, Archief Admiraliteitscolleges, no. 2476. 'Resoluties Zeeuws admiraliteitscollege 1657', fol. 12.

63   NA, Archief Admiraliteitscolleges XXXIX, J.C. van der Hoop, no. 117. 'Extract resolutie', 9 December 1779.

> The Lords of the Admiralty follow the same Methods which the States General observe, as to their publick Bonds, and go through this great Charge by the good Management of their Credit; for though it be true, that they are indebted great Sums of Money, yet they never want a Supply, nay, Moneys are often forced upon them by rich Merchants, who send in their Moneys and only take the Admiralties Bonds, with which they afterward pay their Customs, when their Ships arrive; at which Time the Admiralty allows them Interest for the Time they have had their Money. And this is what makes the Admiralty's Bonds more valued than ready Money, for it saves the trouble of telling: And such is the Credit of the Admiralty, that when they have occasion for any Goods the People strive to furnish them, and rather take their Bonds than Money, because they get Interest: And all other Assignments upon the Admiralty are very punctually paid, and without Exchequor Fees; for they are Sworn Officers, who are forbid to receive any Moneys for Fees, being contented with the Salary they have from the States.[64]

The great differences in organisation of supply for different types of goods underlines a conclusion drawn by Michiel de Jong in his study of the Dutch arms trade during the first half of the seventeenth century. De Jong noted that the complex nature of early modern markets forced the state to operate in a highly diversified way. Whereas in the provision of iron, canons, and guns state storehouses depended on the activity of large internationally operating merchants such as Trip and De Geer and good connections to industrial peripheries such as Liège and Sweden, for many other types of goods the state relied on locally-oriented small scale handicraft production involving large numbers of artisans. The difficulty of sustaining supply networks while payment by the state remained highly erratic required creative ways of leaning on merchants' ability to survive on credit without over-extending such reliance to the point where the supply networks would collapse. Doing so demanded a level of flexibility in operating on the market – as well as direct state support and a diversified system of state finance – for which the close personal connections between the state and economics elites proved an asset.[65] Certainly they also provided venues for corruption and in-trading. But these phenomena did not cancel out the real benefits for the state of the direct involvement of capitalist elites. However, on a more fundamental level the federal-brokerage prism through

---

64   Carr 1744, p. 10.
65   De Jong 2005, pp. 348–50.

which this interplay was organised did produce great differences in market-
access for the five Admiralty Boards. Systems of state supply thus tended to
strengthen regional economic divisions, rather than breaking them down.

3.4   Naval Shipyards as Centres of Production

Naval shipyards not only influenced their surrounding economies as large-scale
buyers, but also acted as large-scale producers in their own right. The Amsterdam shipyard became the second biggest production facility in the whole of
the Dutch Republic, only surpassed by the adjacent and in many ways similarly
organised shipyard of the VOC. The wharf stretched out over a length of 1,500
Amsterdam feet (± 425 m), and was surrounded by a large wall. For most of the
1650s the terrain on which the naval shipyard was erected had been occupied by
private shipyards working as sub-contractors for the navy. In 1660 the Admiralty
councillors bought it from the city for the sum of ƒ60,000.[66] Just as the building
of the adjacent naval storehouse, the move was closely connected to the new
phase in naval competition that had started with the First Anglo-Dutch War.

The architecture of the shipyard reflected the many productive functions
that it brought together in one place. On entering from the street side, one
first came at a square at which the workmen gathered at payday. Surrounding
the square were houses of managing personnel, such as the two 'under-masters
of equipment' and the master shipwright. At the other side were several brick
sheds, one of which was used for the drying, heating and bending of wood.
There also were numerous workshops:

> Here, there is a large blacksmith's shop, where anchors and many iron
> tools are made. Furthermore, there are special workshops for tin makers,
> sword smiths, carpenters and wainscotters, boat makers, gun-carriage
> makers, painters, mast makers, tackle makers, bricklayers, plumbers, oar
> makers, coopers, etc.[67]

A second four-storey warehouse was built at the other end of the terrain, mainly
destined for the storage of voluminous pieces of equipment such as iron ballast,
cables and rigging, and again housing a number of different workshops. In front
of the wharf, there were slipways for larger and smaller ships and a floating

---

66   Bontemantel 1897, p. 497, and Lemmers 2005, p. 32.
67   Wagenaar 1765, pp. 81–2.

dock. Next to the second storehouse was a cannon-foundry, and in front of it the large crane that was the most important labour-saving device on the shipyard.[68]

There were many similarities between the new Admiralty wharf and that of the VOC, the construction of which started only two years later. In 1662 the Company directors were authorised to build a large storehouse. Its design was rectangular, not the square monolith that was its mirror institution, but its dimensions were practically the same (according to Wagenaar, the naval store-house measured 44,000 square feet, while a map of the architect showed the VOC storehouse to be 44,520 square feet).[69] The actual shipyard was somewhat smaller in ground surface than the Admiralty wharf, but did provide enough room for a large number of artisans' workshops. In contrast to the Admiralty Board, the VOC did possess its own wood-sawing mill (which the Admiralty Board acquired only at a much later date), butchery, and a special building for the refinery and storage of tar.[70] In 1660, the VOC and the Admiralty Board decided to erect one joint building for their two rope factories.[71]

The new facilities created the preconditions for a complete shift in naval production. Before 1660 the Amsterdam Admiralty Board had been dependent on private shipbuilders for the production of men-of war. But this changed with the move to Kattenburg. Already during the Second Anglo-Dutch War, the Admiralty Board could take control over the production and repair of a large number of its own ships. In 1665 alone, it produced one ship of the first charter, two of the second charter, and two of the third charter on its own premises. At its seventeenth-century peak during the 1690s, the Admiralty Board was able to produce an average of four large warships a year. The overall number of large East India ships produced at the Amsterdam VOC wharf during the one and a half centuries of its existence far surpassed the number of chartered men-of-war produced by the navy (see table 3.4 and charts 3.1 and 3.2). But at times of war, the Admiralty Board was capable of producing on as large a scale as the VOC. Moreover, the shipyards were not only used for building new ships but also for running maintenance work on existing ships throughout the year. When the French master shipwright Blaise Ollivier visited Amsterdam in

---

68   Ibid.
69   Wagenaar 1765, p. 80, and De Haas 1982, p. 68.
70   The collection of Johan Cornelis van der Hoop in the archive of the Admiralty Boards con-
       tains documents considering the advantages of buying wood-sawing mill *De Groote Otter*,
       which later indeed was in the possession of the Admiralty. NA, Archief Admiraliteitscol-
       leges XXXIX, J.C. van der Hoop 1524–1825, no. 157.
71   De Haas 1982, pp. 72–4, and Gawronski 1996, pp. 76 ff.

TABLE 3.4   *Number of ships built per decade by the Amsterdam Admiralty shipyard, Rotterdam Admiralty shipyard, and the VOC shipyard, 1661–1780*

Years	Amsterdam Admiralty shipyard	Rotterdam Admiralty shipyard	Amsterdam VOC shipyard
1661–70	24	9	43
1671–80	16	4	43
1681–90	23	10	34
1691–1700	43	22	55
1701–10	17	13	57
1711–20	16	1	41
1721–30	14	4	34
1731–40	20	3	49
1741–50	10	5	53
1751–60	18	6	29
1761–70	18	4	28
1771–80	8	4	27
1781–90	30 (est.)	19	33
Total 1661–1790	227 (est.)	104	526

SOURCES: NA, ADMIRALITEITSCOLLEGES XXXII, PIETER VAN BLEISWIJK 1690–1787, NO. 10. 'LYST DER OORLOGSCHEEPEN & FREGATTEN, GEBOUWD DOOR HET COLLEGIE TER ADMIRALITEIT VAN AMSTERDAM ZEEDERT AO 1654 TOT DEN JAAREN 1780', REIJN 1900, PP. 103–12, AND J.R. BRUIJN, F.S. GAASTRA, AND I. SCHÖFFER, *DUTCH ASIATIC SHIPPING*, ONLINE DATABASE, HTTPS://WWW.HISTORICI.NL/RESOURCES/DUTCH-ASIATIC-SHIPPING -17TH-AND-18TH-CENTURIES (ACCESSED: 26-11-2014)

August 1737, he noted that one of the four slipways was in use for the building of a large ship, and the other three for maintenance work on three smaller yachts, so that even in a year in which no ships were actually finished, all slipways were in use.[72] The answers of the Amsterdam Admiralty Board to a questionnaire on building and repair at the shipyards shows that the repair of old ships took more than a quarter of all wage costs in 1776, and over a third in 1780.[73]

---

72   Roberts 1992, p. 317.

73   NA, Archief Van der Hoop, no. 151. 'Bylaagen behoorende tot de Missive en Memorie door Zyne Hoogheid den Heere Prince van Orange en Nassau aan hun Hoog Mogende op den 7 October 1782 overgegeven', pp. 71–2.

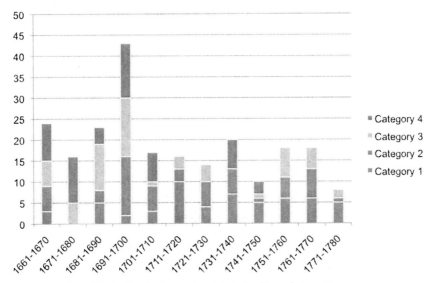

CHART 3.1   *Warships built at the Amsterdam Admiralty shipyard, 1661–1780*
SOURCE: NA, ADMIRALITEITSCOLLEGES XXXII, PIETER VAN BLEISWIJK
1690–1787, NO. 10. 'LYST DER OORLOGSCHEEPEN & FREGATTEN, GEBOUWD
DOOR HET COLLEGIE TER ADMIRALITEIT VAN AMSTERDAM ZEEDERT AO
1654 TOT DEN JAAREN 1780'. SEE EXPLANATORY NOTE ON NEXT PAGE.

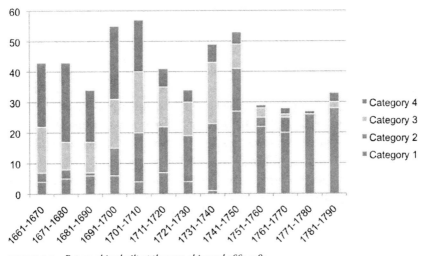

CHART 3.2   *Return ships built at the VOC-shipyard, 1661–1780*
SOURCE: J.R. BRUIJN, F.S. GAASTRA, I. SCHÖFFER, *DUTCH ASIATIC SHIPPING*,
ONLINE DATABASE, HTTPS://WWW.HISTORICI.NL/RESOURCES/DUTCH
-ASIATIC-SHIPPING-17TH-AND-18TH-CENTURIES (ACCESSED: 26-11-2014). SEE
EXPLANATORY NOTE ON NEXT PAGE.

Note on charts 3.1 and 3.2: Both charts only contain the larger ships built at the shipyards, not the small yachts and challops. The VOC list also does not include four small mail ships, or ships that were built for other users than the VOC. The subdivision in categories is the one used in DAS, and is based on estimated tonnage. Category 1 are the largest ships of over 1000 tons, category 2 ships of 800–1000 tons, category 3 of 500–800 tons and category 4 the smaller ships of less than 500 tons. These categories do not neatly match the division in charters used for warships, based on numbers of cannons rather than tonnage. Since no tonnage was available for the ships built at the Admiralty wharf, an approximation was used based on the dimensions of the ships. Of course this does not give tonnage figures, since for this the square dimensions (length × weight × height, or $l \times w \times h$) have to be adapted for the form of the hull. However, since the aim here is only to make a comparison with the large categories applied to VOC ships in DAS, also based on a simple adaptation of $l \times w \times h$, this very rough measure for calculation suffices. Based on the dimensions of a selection of VOC ships for each category, the division used to categorise Admiralty ships was: Category 1: $(l \times w \times h) >$ 105,000 cubic ft, category 2: 105,000 cubic ft > $(l \times w \times h) > 80{,}000$ cubic ft, category 3: 80,000 cubic ft > $(l \times w \times h) > 50{,}000$ cubic ft, category 4: $(l \times w \times h) < 50{,}000$ cubic ft.

⁘

The expansion of naval facilities that took place in Amsterdam in the 1650s and 1660s created a huge gap in capacity with the other naval shipyards. Important extensions of their facilities were made by the Admiralty Boards of Rotterdam, Zeeland, the Holland Northern Quarter and Friesland, but all of these were dwarfed by those of Amsterdam. Furthermore, most of them did not exhibit the same concentration of facilities reached in Amsterdam, where storage and shipbuilding were all centred on one single terrain. In the Northern Quarter and Zeeland, institutional barriers prevented drawing together all facilities in one single place. In the case of the Northern Quarter, the fact that Hoorn and Enkhuizen took turns as the site of the Admiralty Board was a strong reason for maintaining facilities in both towns.[74] None of the two possessed its own wharf, and even the storage facilities were rather limited. So little maintenance work took place there that the Admiralty Board reported in 1751 that the naval storehouses were practically empty. Any new plans for building would have to be fulfilled by contracting private yards.[75] In Zeeland, the political influence

---

74   Thurkow 1945.

75   NA, Archief Van der Hoop, no. 153. 'Secrete Missiven', 30 juni 1751, p. 100.

in the Admiralty Board of competing towns allowed Vlissingen, Veere, Middelburg and Zierikzee each to hold on to their own slice of equipping ships. The building and maintenance of larger ships took place primarily in Veere and Vlissingen, and for most of the eighteenth century only in the latter.[76] The advantage of Vlissingen over the other Zeeland harbours was due to a large and costly modernisation undertaken at the end of the seventeenth century. From 1705 onwards, this town even had its own dry dock. However, due to financial problems the building of new ships was reduced to a minimum. Between 1714 and 1795, the Zeeland Admiralty Board only oversaw the building of nineteen ships of the line on its own wharfs.[77]

The Rotterdam Admiralty Board also divided shipbuilding and maintenance over two different locations, but this was for practical rather than institutional reasons. Hellevoetsluys, situated near the estuary of the Meuse, had become one of the main bases of operation of the Dutch fleet, so it was only logical to maintain a large dock, storehouse, and some facilities for maintenance there. Shipbuilding was concentrated in Rotterdam where the Admiralty Board possessed a shipyard with three slides of 140–50 feet in length and 40 feet in width.[78] At approximately the same time as the building of the Amsterdam storehouse, the Rotterdam Admiralty Board also built two new storehouses and a large crane to load and unload heavy anchors. A year later a cannon foundry was built nearby.[79] In 1737 the French shipwright Blaise Ollivier judged the Rotterdam facilities to be 'peu considerables'.[80] Nevertheless the Rotterdam shipyard remained the second largest naval shipyard, producing over a hundred warships (disregarding ships carrying less than ten pieces) between 1660 and 1790 (see table 3.4).

Lastly, the case of the Friesland Admiralty Board illustrates well what devastating effects the long eighteenth-century lull in large-scale shipbuilding had on the readiness of more peripheral naval facilities. In order to be able to execute the large programme of shipbuilding that took place between 1779 and 1785, resulting in the building of twelve ships of the line on the naval wharf, the Admiralty Board had to completely renew its shipyard and harbour. Four new slipways, a carpenter's shed and a loft for the laying out and storage of ship moulds were erected, and the harbour and major passageway were dredged.[81]

---

76   Vlaeminck 2005, pp. 76–9.
77   Vlaeminck 2005, p. 83.
78   Roberts 1992, p. 317.
79   Van Spaan 1738, pp. 384–5.
80   Roberts 1992, p. 317.
81   Roodhuyzen-van Breda Vriesman 2003, pp. 99–100.

Despite this effort, the passage way proved not wide enough for the two largest ships of seventy pieces. The ships never left the harbour, and in 1792 were taken apart without ever having been used.[82] Unsurprisingly, this fiasco became one of the major exhibits in the discussions on the incapacity of Dutch naval institutions outside Amsterdam and Rotterdam that raged at the end of the eighteenth century.

3.5   Shipyards and Their Workforce

Together, the Admiralty Boards and the VOC laid a large claim on the labour market. Private shipyards in Amsterdam, the shipbuilding area of the Zaan, and Rotterdam usually employed around a hundred workers at most.[83] The Amsterdam naval and VOC shipyards at Kattenburg and Oostenburg were of an altogether different category. During the eighteenth century, the Amsterdam chamber of the VOC employed between 1100 and 1300 workers at their shipyard and storehouse.[84] For the Admiralty shipyard, the figure of 'more than a thousand' is mostly maintained.[85] As an average, this is probably correct. But at least at one point during the eighteenth century, at the start of the Fourth Anglo-Dutch War, the Amsterdam shipyard included on its payroll almost double that number, temporarily making it the largest single employer of the Dutch Republic.

A detailed picture of the total number of workers and the internal make-up of the workforce can be obtained from two documents, both from the eighteenth century. The first is a report for the States General from 1751, giving extensive information on the employment at the different departments of the wharf and storehouse for the years 1733 and 1744. The second is a complete account of all the salaries and wages paid to officials and workers of the Amsterdam Admiralty Board in 1781. The extensive information on the number and different type of workers produced by these documents is summarised in table 3.5.

82   Roodhuyzen-van Breda Vriesman 2003, p. 107.
83   Deurloo 1971, p. 8, and Van Kampen 1953, p. 48.
84   Van Dillen 1970, p. 400, Gaastra 1986, p. 79, Gaastra 2003, p. 163, and Gawronski 1996, p. 113.
85   Deurloo 1971, p. 7.

TABLE 3.5   *Workers and supervisors at the Amsterdam naval shipyard and storehouse*

	1733	1744	1781
A. Shipbuilders			
Shipwrights	266	166	648
Shipwrights' helpers			56
Boat makers	87	33	99
Wainscotters		10	27
Sawyers	29	12	14
Tool makers		6	8
Wood drillers	14	8	21
Wood workers	59	19	81
Mast makers	15	14	32
Chip gatherers	72	29	16
Wood cutters	26	1	9
Sub-total A	**568**	**298**	**1011**
B. Other craftsmen			
Carpenters	14	14	41
Rolling stock makers	9	6	8
Blacksmiths	27	18	40
Tin makers	4	5	7
Painters	17	9	15
Bricklayers	11	11	14
Tackle makers	9	10	11
Plumbers	3	3	4
Oar makers	5	4	5
Coopers	16	13	16
Stone turners	4	5	7
Tar cooks			2
Compass makers	2	2	1
Sword makers and their helpers	8	5	5
Saddle makers			1
Sail makers	23	21	42
Sail makers' helpers	6	5	2
Clog makers		1	1
Sub-total B	**158**	**132**	**222**

TABLE 3.5 *Workers and supervisors at the Amsterdam naval shipyard and storehouse* (cont.)

	1733	1744	1781
C. Other workers, mainly unskilled			
Carriers	283	146	518
Beer carriers			23
Unspecified workers	5	28	7
Pump servants	6	22	14
Rowers	15	15	14
Skippers, boatmen and sailors on yachts and transport ships	43	61	38
Sub-total C	352	272	614
D. Supervisors and guards			
Supervisors (masters, their servants, commanders, vice-commanders)	62	66	73
Guards	56	52	42
Porters	4	5	6
Other controlling personnel	0	1	2
Sub-total D	122	124	123
Total (A + B + C + D)	1200	826	1970

SOURCES: NA, ARCHIEF J.C. VAN DER HOOP, NO. 153. 'SECRETE MISSIVEN', 30 JUNE 1751, AND NA, ARCHIEF ADMIRALITEITSCOLLEGES XXXIX, J.C. VAN DER HOOP (1524–1825), NO. 104. 'TRACTEMENTEN & EMOLUMENTEN VAN ALLE DE HOOGE & LAAGEN BEDIEN-INGE VAN HET EDEL MOGEND COLLEGIE TER ADMIRALITEIT RESIDEERENDE BINNEN AMSTERDAM. MITSGADERS DE DAGLOONEN DER WERKLIEDEN OP S LANDS MAGAZYNE, TIMMERWERFF, LYNBAAN & GESCHUT WERFF'

These figures show the great flexibility of the number of workers employed. In 1733 the size of the workforce at the Admiralty shipyard must have been approx-imately equal to that of the VOC. Between 1733 and 1744 the Admiralty Board laid off almost a third of its workforce, reflecting the sharp decline in output of newly built ships during the 1740s. Meanwhile the VOC-wharf expanded due to a boom in shipping. In the run-up to and during the Fourth Anglo-Dutch War, when the Amsterdam Admiralty Board engaged in a major programme of ship-building at the same time as having to manage the equipment of the existing war fleet, total employment once again rose steeply. The total size of the work-

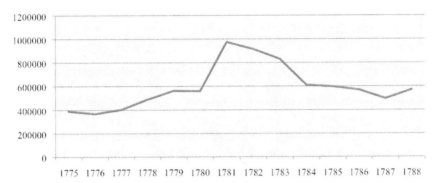

CHART 3.3 *Expenditure on wages by the Amsterdam Admiralty Board, 1775–88 (guilders)*
SOURCES: FIGURES FOR 1775–9 AND 1781–8: NA, ARCHIEF
GENERALITEITSREKENKAMER, NO. 587–99. FIGURE FOR 1780: NA, ARCHIEF
J.C. VAN DER HOOP, NO. 166. 'MISSIVES DER COLLEGIEN TER ADMIRALITEIT
MET DE LYSTEN VAN DE SCHEEPEN WELKE BY HAAR ZYN AANGEBOUWT EN
GEKOGT, ALS MEEDE VAN HET GEENE ZY IN GEVOLGE DE PETITIEN
GENOOTEN HEBBE, EN VAN HET GEENE HUN NOG IS COMPETERENDE,
31 AUGUSTUS 1784'

force at the navy shipyard and storehouse now temporarily greatly surpassed the number of workers employed at the VOC shipyard. The speed of expansion and contraction before and after war can also be gauged from the expenses on labour costs. One of the standard posts on the receiver general's yearly accounts to the Generalty Audit Office was reserved for 'wages of shipwrights and carriers'. This post in fact included the wages of all non-managerial personnel at the naval shipyards (shipyard managers were included under the heading of salaries, '*tractementen*'). Chart 3.3 shows the development of wage costs on the Amsterdam accounts between 1775 and 1788. From less than ƒ400,000 a year, they rose to just short of a million guilders in 1781 when employment at the shipyard reached its eighteenth-century highpoint. This figure again affirms the large capacity of the Admiralty shipyard. In his summary of the VOC ledgers for the eighteenth century, De Korte gave the average annual wage costs as under half a million guilders before 1730, than rising to ƒ530,000–ƒ550,000 until 1780, falling back to ƒ500,000 a year in the 1780s.[86] Gawronski has suggested on the basis of a different account that the wage costs during the shipbuilding boom of the 1740s might have been close to a million guilders for the VOC as well, but as he points out, these figures probably include all sorts of non-wage expendit-

---

86   De Korte 1984, appendix 12A and 12B.

ures.[87] However, the workforce of the naval shipyard was subject to much larger fluctuations than that of the VOC shipyards. During the 1780s, as soon as the war ended, wage costs were brought back to their pre-war level.

In comparison to the size of the workforce of the other Admiralty Boards, the Amsterdam naval shipyard was a Moloch. The smallest numbers were employed by the Admiralty Boards of the Northern Quarter and Zeeland. The Admiralty Board of the Northern Quarter did not possess its own wharf, and even in 1680, when its role in equipping was still bigger than during the eighteenth century, it only employed two shipwrights, one cannon founder and twenty-four carriers in permanent service.[88] A careful estimate of the workforce of the Zeeland Admiralty Board shows that even in the war years 1654 and 1665–6, the different naval establishments did not employ much more than some tens of workers at their shipyards.[89] This must have dropped to an absolute minimum in the course of the eighteenth century, when the Zeeland Admiralty Board often carried out hardly any shipbuilding and maintenance work. From January 1781 to July 1784, in the midst of the Fourth Anglo-Dutch War, the master of equipment of the Vlissingen shipyard noted a total of about ƒ220,000 for 'wages of shipwrights, blacksmiths, carriers, and other workers', or an average of just over ƒ60,000 per year.[90] This made even the biggest Zeeland shipyard considerably smaller than the VOC shipyard in Middelburg, which employed about 600 workers in 1790.[91]

The Admiralty Boards of Friesland and Rotterdam employed more workers, the latter being the largest of the two. For Rotterdam, two handwritten transcriptions from the late eighteenth century survive, containing both ordinary and extra-ordinary expenditure of the Rotterdam receiver general over a number of selected years. These include the early years 1642, 1668, and 1675, for which no accounts are present in the archive of the Generalty Audit Office. The documents also split the wage costs for the facilities at Rotterdam and Hellevoetsluys. Table 3.6 summarises the information on total wage costs they provide. For 1751 a report of the Admiralty Board of Rotterdam on the state of the naval shipyards provides more detailed information on employment, giv-

---

87   Gawronski 1996, pp. 46–7.
88   NA, Archief Van der Hoop, no. 163. 'Staet van de Tractementen, Emolumenten, Necessiteyten, Vacatien, ende andere onkosten ten laste van het Collegie ter Admiraliteyt in West-Vrieslandt ende het Noorder-Quartier, 1680'.
89   Strubbe 2007, p. 121.
90   RAZ, Archief Rekenkamer C, no. 36930. 'Account of Maarten Haringman, Master of Equipment in Vlissingen', 1781–July 1784.
91   Gaastra 2003, p. 145.

TABLE 3.6   *Sums paid on wages by the receiver general of the Rotterdam Admiralty Board, selected years (guilders)*

	1642	1668	1675	1683	1712	1721	1750	1776	1782
Wage costs in Rotterdam	24,615	20,257	3,119	11,722	8,079	40,332	51,405	65,731	287,359
Wage costs in Hellevoetsluys	0	24,813	3,304	40,748	2,408	36,138	51,805	55,230	123,380
Wage costs at the rope factory	0	0	0	0	7,187	1,460	2,246	3,776	7,662
General wage costs (location unknown)	26,535	45,523	18,070	2,536	17,473	3,000	2,750	1,859	26,740
Total	51,150	90,593	24,493	55,006	35,147	80,930	108,206	126,596	445,141

SOURCES: NA, ARCHIEF ADMIRALTIEITSCOLLEGES XXXVII, VAN DER HEIM, NOS. 365–6. 'ORDINARIS EN EXTRA-ORDINARIS REKENINGEN VAN DE ONTVANGER GENERAAL VAN DE ADMIRALITEIT OP DE MAZE, 1642–1782'

ing a combined total of just over 225 workers, of whom 25 were supervisors, at the two locations.[92] At the start of the Fourth Anglo-Dutch War wage costs at the Rotterdam shipyards and storehouses almost quadrupled. This expansion was proportionally bigger than that of the Amsterdam shipyard during the same year. Making a rough estimate based on these available figures, it is safe to assume that all five Admiralty Boards taken together employed no more than between 1200–1500 workers during the quiet 1740s, but expanded their workforce to somewhere between 3000–3500 at the start of the Fourth Anglo-Dutch War, reducing it again quickly once the war was over.

3.6   Admiralty Boards and the Labour Market

How did the Admiralty Boards recruit these large numbers of often specialised workers? Economic historians Jan de Vries and Ad van der Woude have stressed the 'modern' nature of the Dutch labour market. As characteristics of

92   NA, Archief Van der Hoop, no. 153. 'Secrete Missiven', 30 juni 1751, pp. 11–21.

this developed market they pointed to the strong internal segmentation, high wage levels and the combination of large-scale unemployment and temporary, season-bound labour shortages, which were met by employing cheap migrant labour.[93] Labour historian Jan Lucassen emphasised the fact that the Dutch Republic was perhaps the only country before the industrial revolution with a fully 'free' labour market, meaning that economic force had replaced physical force, bondage, and penal law as prominent instruments in recruiting labour power. Personal arrangements between masters and servants or employers and their workforce were replaced by impersonal relations.[94] Furthermore, recent literature shows that the proliferation of guilds during the sixteenth and seventeenth centuries did not contradict or impede this development.[95] As one of the largest manufacturing employers of the Dutch Republic, the Amsterdam naval shipyard forms an important case study for these claims.

The number of different jobs among the shipyard's workforce meant that it strongly reflected the existing social segmentation of the labour market. Descriptions of labour relations at the shipyards often concentrate exclusively on the position of shipwrights. With a daily wage of thirty *stuyvers* in summer and twenty in winter, they formed the best paid section of the Admiralty workforce. However, the majority of the workforce worked for wages far below this level. Table 3.7 gives an impression of the internal wage differentiation among workers at the wharf. As was true for most sections of the urban working classes, nominal wages remained remarkably stable from the middle of the seventeenth century until the nineteenth century, so that this table can be safely taken as an indication for the entire period under investigation.[96] But because workers were paid per day, equal wage rates could conceal great fluctuations in income. The table gives two different calculations. The first is the income that theoretically was obtainable when working the maximum number of working days per year, based on a working week of six days and subtracting holidays. The second is the income calculated on the basis of the number of working days

---

93   De Vries and Van der Woude 1997, p. 654.

94   Lucassen 1995, pp. 394–6. As Lucassen himself pointed out, this freedom did not extend to the Dutch possessions overseas. Furthermore, sailors and soldiers frequently suffered forced methods of recruitment through the practices of so-called 'zielverkopers' (a pun on the double meaning of the Dutch word 'ziel', which at that time could be used to signify both 'soul' and 'seal'), who used debt as an effective means of impressment.

95   Unger 1892, p. 22, De Munck, Lourens, and Lucassen 2006, Epstein and Prak 2008a, p. 21, and Lis and Soly 2008.

96   Deurloo 1971, pp. 28–9, and De Vries and Van der Woude 1997, pp. 646–7.

TABLE 3.7   *Wages of different categories of labourers at the naval shipyard, 1781*

	Wage (summer/winter)	Income based on 306 (max) working days	Income based on 226 working days
Shipwrights and other skilled craftsmen	30 / 20 st	ƒ421	ƒ311
Painters, bricklayers, plumbers and other semi-skilled craftsmen	24 / 18 st	ƒ344	ƒ254
Carriers and other unskilled workers	16 / 14 st	ƒ237	ƒ175
Apprentices, beer carriers, etc.	8 / 6 st	ƒ115	ƒ85

SOURCE: NA, ARCHIEF ADMIRALITEITSCOLLEGES XXXIX, J.C. VAN DER HOOP (1524–1825), NO. 104. 'DAGLONEN'

mentioned in a request of shipwrights to William IV from December 1749. Apart from Sundays and holidays, workers complained of the many days involuntarily lost because of rain or high water (45), sickness, or the lack of work (36).[97] The actual yearly income is likely to have been somewhere between these two extremes. Together, these figures give a good impression of the high level of internal segmentation among shipyard personnel, strengthened by the existence of a large number of intermediate scales.

For those who managed to attain permanent contracts, employment at the Admiralty yard often paid better than the day rate suggests. This is due to the many hidden forms of payment that existed. A payroll of the Rotterdam Admiralty Board from March 1751 shows that many guards, though formally on daily pay, actually received this wage thirty-one days a month, plus ten *stuyvers* for every night watch. In this way, all twenty-three guards received a monthly wage of over thirty guilders, more than many of the skilled craftsmen employed by the Admiralty Board.[98] Becoming a guard for the Admiralty Board thus

---

97   NA, Archief van de Stadhouderlijke Secretarie, 1600–1795, no. 467. 'Request aan Willem IV van 6 december 1749', also referred to in Deurloo 1971, p. 29.

98   NA, Archief Van der Hoop, no. 153. 'Lyste van de losse en vaste bediendens, en wat ieder wint', pp. 3–7.

became a career opportunity for lower-paid workers. Cornelis van Oeveren, who was a not unsuccessful cart maker in Rotterdam before 1747, used the clout he had acquired during the Orangist revolt of that year to attain a position as a guard, and according to his own testimony fared well from it.[99] Similar advantages were common in Amsterdam as well, although during the 1740s the Admiralty Board tried to limit the number of people on seven days' pay to a small group of people who either actually remained active the whole week, or were 'of special knowledge and capacities'.[100]

However, the position of these relatively well-paid workers tells only half the story. This is shown by the detailed wage administration of the rope factory of the Amsterdam Admiralty Board. On the upper end of the scale, the wage lists include Steven Duijm, who was already employed in a supervising position at the time when the first available list was made up in 1719, and who retained this function at least until 1752. Duijm received a wage of twenty *stuyvers* a day, later raised to twenty-five *stuyvers*, for 366 full days per year. This brought his yearly income at maximum to the ample sum of ƒ481,25.[101] However, wages of most workers stood at fourteen to sixteen *stuyvers*, and there were also many on the list (probably children or apprentices) not paid more than five or six *stuyvers*. Furthermore almost all workers received pay only for the days worked, and most were employed irregularly. The 1730 wage administration, for example, shows how the ordinary worker Jan Poortman was employed during each of the thirteen pay periods, but not for the full length of each period. In total, he worked just over 250 days for sixteen *stuyvers* in summer and fourteen *stuyvers* in winter, bringing his yearly income to ƒ206. Of the seventy-nine workers on the 1730 wage list, only thirty-seven were in such 'permanent' employment, defined here as having some work during at least ten out of thirteen pay periods. Their average yearly income from the rope factory amounted to ƒ178 guilders.[102] It is impossible to tell whether these workers could add to their incomes by other means, but the figures do attest to the great dependence of the Admiralty Board on low-paid, temporary or even day labourers on very insecure incomes. Alternately, the fact of this continued dependence also suggests that on the developed labour market of the Republic, these low wage workers could be found with relative ease, such that there was no need for the Admiralty Boards

99   [Van Oeveren] [1787].

100   NA, Archief Van der Hoop, no. 153. 'Secrete Missiven', 30 June 1751, p. 74.

101   NA, Archief van de lijnbaan in Amsterdam 1712–1892, no. 8–10. 'Betalingsboek spinders en draijers', 1719–27, 1727–34, and 1735–53.

102   NA, Archief van de lijnbaan in Amsterdam 1712–1892, no. 9. 'Betalingsboek spinders en draijers', 1727–34.

to offer more stable working conditions. This situation must also have prevailed for carriers, at most times the largest single group of workers at the shipyard and storehouse. As a study of representations of labour in the Dutch seventeenth century notes, carriers were the 'omnipresent stage extras' of the Dutch 'Golden Age'.[103] Several types of carrying labour, such as that of rye and peat, were organised into rather influential guilds, but carrying on the naval shipyard was done by non-guild workers. With large numbers of urban poor and recent immigrants from low-wage regions, their labour power was in chronic oversupply and came cheap.

The existence of bonuses and internal career opportunities for a select group within the workforce must have made the Admiralty Board a relatively attractive employer for some. Furthermore, in binding its workforce economically it could make tactical use of the fact that it operated not one, but two recruitment systems for cheap labour: one on land, the other at sea. This became of particular importance after the 1720s when the number of ships sailing for the navy declined. Letting go of all experienced sailors would have been a dangerous step, given the sharp competition the naval authorities faced from the merchant fleet and the VOC in the area of recruitment of sailors. Thus, the Admiralty Board decided to establish special work gangs of carriers (so-called *vemen*) consisting solely of non-commissioned officers (NCOs). The condition for admission was that these NCOs would not refuse to sign up for the navy when the occasion arose, and would not take employment with any other company without prior knowledge of the Admiralty Board.[104] In 1733 the same arrangement was extended to sailors who had served the fleet during at least two voyages, were between eighteen and fifty years of age, and could show a declaration of good behaviour from their officers. Most non-skilled jobs at the shipyard were opened for these former seafarers.[105] In 1744, when there was greater need to preserve able sailors given the Dutch implication in the War of the Austrian Succession but fewer available positions on the wharf, the directors limited access to the gangs to 'the very best men'. They asked officers to draw up lists of their sailors in order to decide who would be given jobs on shore.[106]

In this way, the Amsterdam Admiralty administrators could make use of internal shifts in supply and demand of labour power, using economic means to guarantee a reservoir of experienced seafarers. What they could not do,

---

103   De Vries 2004, p. 196.
104   NA, Archief Van der Hoop, no. 153. 'Secrete missiven', 30 June 1751, p. 25.
105   NA, Archief Van der Hoop, no. 153. 'Secrete missiven', 30 June 1751, p. 36.
106   NA, Archief Van der Hoop, no. 153. 'Secrete missiven', 30 June 1751, p. 68.

however, was use force to impress these same workers whenever they felt the need. The unattractiveness of life on board of warships – with its high mortality rates, horrid quality of food and harsh discipline – made many NCOs decide to ignore the conditions of their employment at the wharf. In 1762 the Admiralty Board decided to start diminishing the number of officers on the yards, noting

> the difficulties that have risen in making the NCOs serve on the new ships, because they often decline to do so; and though they are dismissed from the nation's wharf, they then have often already drawn money [meaning their wages] from this wharf for years, without in the end serving the beneficial purpose of this Board.

Signifying the relative ease with which workers moved in and out of employment, the Admiralty Board also had to order that NCOs who had been previously dismissed from the shipyard for refusing service could not be re-admitted into service at the wharf at a later stage.[107]

More difficult than the securing of low- or unskilled labour was the recruitment of skilled shipwrights. According to the figures of the demographic historian S. Hart, based on the records for marriages and therefore incomplete, there were around a thousand skilled shipwrights in Amsterdam during the second half of the seventeenth century.[108] Around the middle of the eighteenth century the shipwrights' guild had some 1500 members, including both masters and journeymen.[109] While traditionally masters and supervisors had played a big role as intermediaries in the recruitment of personnel, the appointment of set places where workers could solicit for employment signals a transition to more impersonal practices. The eighteenth-century historian of Amsterdam Jan Wagenaar described how this form of recruitment worked:

> Shipwrights who are looking for employment must gather in the morning half an hour before the sounding of the bell of the Admiralty wharf at the Kadyk near the Kattenburg Bridge, or at the start of the Bicker-street, and in the afternoon, between twelve and one, at the New Bridge. They are not allowed to accept employment along the way, or at any other place.[110]

---

107   UB-BC, *Extracten*. 'Extract from the minutes of the Amsterdam Admiralty Board, 9 February 1762'.
108   Hart 1976, p. 129.
109   Wagenaar 1765, p. 461, and Bos 1998, p. 90.
110   Wagenaar 1765, p. 460.

However, it is quite possible that this method of recruitment reflected the rather unfavourable conditions of the mid-eighteenth century, when many shipwrights at the Admiralty wharf had lost employment due to recent reductions of the workforce. The large demand of the two big shipyards and the limited number of skilled workers meant that at other times the Admiralty Board and the VOC had to engage in serious competition with the private shipyards. These yards paid higher day wages, and often added better possibilities to achieve bonuses. Support from the town government in part helped to shield the big wharfs from this competition, often at the cost of their workers. Private shipyards were prevented from hiring unemployed shipwrights from the VOC or Admiralty yards as long as shipwrights who used to work on private yards were available. If this was not the case, former VOC or Admiralty workers were allowed to work for selected masters only, and on the condition that they could be rehired by the two 'principle wharfs' as soon as this was considered necessary.[111] Furthermore, the Admiralty Board and VOC were exempted from the rule that new ships could only be built by workers that were members of the guilds. This exemption was strongly contested by guild members since wages for non-guild workers were lower than those for guild workers, but without success.[112] In 1781 the Amsterdam Admiralty Board employed 281 non-guild shipwrights, alongside the 367 members of the guild.[113]

Finding enough skilled workers to work at the yards at times of war could prove very hard indeed. Both the Amsterdam and Rotterdam Admiralty Boards blamed their slowness in building new warships in the run up to the Fourth Anglo-Dutch War on a lack of skilled personnel. According to the Amsterdam Admiralty Board, building could have been taken to hand at full speed

> if the lack of shipwrights in the years 1777, 1778, 1779, and 1780, caused by the many merchant ships that were built and repaired, would not have hindered us; a problem which, despite of all attempts of and orders to our master shipwright to recruit more labourers, we could not remedy.

Only when commercial shipping plummeted because of the arrival of war, leading to the layoff of many workers at the private shipyards, did the Amsterdam Admiralty Board manage to find enough workers to start its building

---

111   Ibid.

112   NA, Archief Stadhouderlijke Secretarie, no. 467. 'Request aan Willem IV van 6 december 1749'.

113   NA, Archief Admiralty Colleges XXXIX, J.C. van der Hoop, no. 104. 'Dagloonen'.

programme at full speed.[114] This suggests that the Admiralty Board did not have many means to manipulate the labour market before a change of conditions led to an increase in availability of skilled labour.

Problems were even greater for the Rotterdam Admiralty Board, which had to resort to a series of more drastic measures to attract shipwrights. In the quiet years since the Seven Years' War, the Admiralty councillors alleged, the position of the Admiralty Board on the labour market had sharply deteriorated. There were rumours suggesting that many unemployed shipwrights had emigrated to the East Indies or taken employment at sea. Others had left the Admiralty Board to work for private shipyards where they could earn better bonuses over and above their regular wage. The result was that when the Admiralty Board needed to expand its workforce during the second half of the 1770s, it had to offer passes for workers from outside the Republic, employ unqualified carpenters, wagon makers, and mill makers as shipwrights, and force those who were already employed by the Admiralty Board to work on Sundays and at night hours. Significantly, the Rotterdam Board offered premiums to master shipwrights, supervisors, and under-supervisors if they managed to recruit workers, showing that at the smaller Admiralty shipyards these groups probably retained a strong role as intermediary links to the labour market. When none of this proved sufficient to solve the labour shortage, the Admiralty Board requested the States of Holland to order the bosses at the private wharfs to yield one-fourth or one-fifth of their workers to the Admiralty shipyard, a measure that also had been in place during the war year 1747–8. The owners of the private yards offered a compromise, promising to send one in six of their workers.[115]

An interesting question is why such sharp shifts in the balance of supply and demand on the labour market did not lead to any fluctuations in the nominal wage rate. One of the possible answers lies in the good conditions of shipwrights as compared to other workers, as Lucassen pointed out for the roughly 350 skilled workers at the VOC yard. Not only was their wage rate higher than that of most skilled workers, they also enjoyed favourable secondary conditions such as severance pay and old age provisions.[116] In 1781 a total of seventy-two former workers at the Admiralty wharf and storehouse received such 'pensions'. Nevertheless, with unchanging nominal wages inflation could have a serious impact on living conditions, raising the question why a relatively powerful

114   NA, Archief Van der Hoop, no. 151. 'Bylaagen', pp. 63–4.
115   NA, Archief Van der Hoop, no. 151. 'Bylaagen', pp. 34–6, and pp. 56–7.
116   Lucassen 2004, p. 29.

group of workers would not try to compensate for this by demanding higher wages. Another factor should therefore be taken into account: the dampening of wage pressures by the large potential differences between wage rate and actual income due to fluctuations in the occupation rate.[117] When high inflation coincided with an expansion of the number of days worked, a decline in real wages did not have to signify an actual decline in income. Especially for workers at the naval shipyards, it is likely that price increases and increasing labour intensity often coincided. While prices remained relatively stable during peace years well into the eighteenth century, periods of sharp inflation until that time always coincided with wars in which the Dutch Republic was involved. During these periods the Admiralty shipyards worked at full speed. Only from the 1740s onwards was this pattern broken. The combination of the policy of neutrality of the Dutch Republic and the prolonged financial distress of the Amsterdam Admiralty Board resulted in a series of sharp attacks on the secondary benefits of shipyard workers and decreasing employment, coinciding with steep inflation. It seems no coincidence that by the end of this decade shipwrights systematically started putting forward wage demands for the first time. However, the long and severe depression in the manufacturing sector during the second half of the eighteenth century did not prove conducive for winning their demands.

Overall, the recruitment and employment of workers by the Amsterdam Admiralty Board shows the advanced nature of Dutch labour markets. Both because of their size and because of their backing by the state, the Admiralty Boards could and did try to manipulate the supply and demand of labour, often at the cost of the freedom of movement of their workers. But despite the apparent rigidity of the wage system, they did so primarily by economic means. Large differences in internal wage scales, the use or restriction of bonuses, promising long-term employment or effectively using the threat of unemployment, and the existence of possibilities for internal replacement of labour helped to stabilise the Admiralty workforce, despite major fluctuations in the level of production at the wharf. Where the state did intervene, it was by granting the Admiralty Board and VOC the right to circumvent guild regulations for employment. Both institutions could thus make use of the dampening effect of the guild's system for mutual aid on labour unrest, without suffering restrictions on their own use of non-guild labour.

---

117   The significance of this factor was already pointed out by Noordegraaf and Van Zanden 1995, p. 425.

Important aspects of the nature of the labour force at the Amsterdam naval shipyard still remain to be investigated, such as gender divisions, the use of child labour, and the role of foreign recruitment. The Amsterdam Admiralty Board must have employed many women, though probably mostly not as shipwrights. A list of persons receiving money as former workers from 1680 contains fifteen women, excluding the widows of high officers, as against thirty-seven men.[118] As to migrant labour, its extensive use at the VOC shipyard makes it most likely that it formed an important source of labour for the Admiralty Board as well.[119] During the sharp labour shortage in the run up to the Fourth Anglo-Dutch War, Admiralty administrators indeed actively sought to recruit foreign workers, using agents abroad to solicit for shipwrights. Further research on such issues is likely to strengthen the image of the Amsterdam shipyard as operating a highly flexible and differentiated system of recruitment, reflecting the early capitalist structure of Dutch Republican labour relations.

3.7   Combination, Coordination, and Control

The prominent role of naval institutions in the development of labour relations was not restricted to their position on the labour market. In his study of shipbuilders at the Venetian Arsenal, Robert C. Davis has rightly stressed their importance for the history of the organisation of work itself:

> Seemingly defined by bureaucratic and military structures and operating largely independently of the workings of profit and the marketplace, such large, state-run shipyards have generally not appeared especially central to the key social and economic determinates of the industrializing process. Nevertheless, the massive, concentrated workforces of large manufactories like the Arsenal presented for the first time kinds of management and labor problems that would be much more typical of the industrial factory than of the putting-out system: the disciplines of wages

---

118   NA, Archief Van der Hoop, no. 161. 'Notitie van Tractementen en Pensioenen, in den jare 1650 gelopen hebbende tot lasten van het Collegie ter Admiraliteyt, residerende binnen Amsterdam, en hoe die successivelijck vermindert, vernieticht, verhooght of nieuwelijcks inghevoert souden moghen zyn tot het eynde van het jaer 1680', pp. 14–15.

119   Research on the far more complete lists of workers of the VOC shows that a high percentage of the craftsmen who lived and worked in the quarter of Kattenburg and Oostenburg were in fact of foreign origin. Opper 1975, pp. 114 ff.

and time, the need for coordinated work gangs, and the formation of specialized and uniform 'company towns' on the fringes of the work-place.[120]

In this sense the Amsterdam naval shipyard was certainly comparable to the famous Arsenal. Between 1650 and 1795 important changes took place in the organisation of shipbuilding, the relations between master craftsmen and ordinary workers, and the enforcement of labour discipline. However, there were large differences with the operation of modern factories as well. The most significant of those was the subordinated role of machinery, technology, and technological change. Economic historian Van Dillen described the structure of early modern shipbuilding as that of 'manufacture or the non-mechanised enterprise', and this feature of work at the naval shipyards remained basically unchallenged throughout the period under examination.[121] Attempts to gain in speed and cost-efficiency thus seem to have remained focused on the triad of combination, coordination, and control of labour characteristic of the manu-facture organisation of production, rather than the systematic introduction of labour-saving devices characteristic of industrial capitalism.[122]

One of the most important leaps in efficiency in naval shipbuilding undoubtedly was the result of the move to Kattenburg itself. Apart from allow-ing all equipment to be gathered at one place, reducing storage and transporta-tion costs and enhancing the precision of administration, the new, much larger naval terrain also made it possible to concentrate and combine all sorts of sec-ondary functions of shipbuilding in one location. The process of building and fully equipping a ship involved many different crafts. Tasks such as the produc-tion of tackle, anchorage and other ironwork, sails, and the making of prows and other embellishments, remained the work of small numbers of artisans and their apprentices. Most private shipbuilding companies at this time relied on independent, off-yard craftsmen for these types of labour.[123] In the Amster-dam naval facilities, as at the voc wharf, the different crafts were physically united with the primary functions of shipbuilding. Architect Daniel Stalpaert's own drawings already show the inclusion of a sail-makers' shop inside the naval

---

120   Davis 1991, p. 7.

121   Van Dillen 1970, p. 400. On the lack of technological change in shipbuilding after the first half of the seventeenth century, see Unger 1978, p. 41 and p. 86.

122   The main exception being the use of wind power in sawing, an innovation that stemmed already from an earlier date. Unger 1978, p. 7.

123   Van Kampen 1953, pp. 155 ff.

storehouse.[124] The incorporation of new crafts into the naval establishments was an ongoing process. In 1650 the work of a carpenter (or carpenters), roofer, glassmaker, plumber, and coffin maker were mentioned not under general wage costs but as accidental expenditure, including both their wages and materials. In 1680 this was the case for a bricklayer and a glassmaker, but the others had disappeared from the list, suggesting their inclusion under general wage costs.[125] In 1662 a resolution granted a wage increase of 150 guilders a year to a master carpenter, proving that this function had already been created before that year.[126] The lists of workers of the middle and late eighteenth century, summarised in table 3.5, show the measure of integration and internal differentiation of the Amsterdam Admiralty workforce. Only a minority of highly specialised jobs, such as the work of glassmakers, was still done off-yard at the end of the eighteenth century.[127]

The smaller Admiralty Boards did not achieve the same heights in combining different forms of labour as the Amsterdam Board. The shipyards of Zeeland never managed to lose their dependence on off-yard craftsmen for auxiliary tasks. But the dockyards at Rotterdam and Hellevoetsluys did see some development in this direction. In 1655 the States General had ruled that the Rotterdam Admiralty Board could employ not more than one sail maker for the purpose of repair. The making of new sails, rigging, anchorage, tackle, and carpenters' work, as well as any large repairs on ships should be tendered to contractors.[128] But by the middle of the eighteenth century, the same institution employed several sail makers, carpenters, coopers, a master blacksmith with nine servants in Rotterdam and three blacksmiths in Hellevoetsluys, block makers, and a master painter with an apprentice and four servants. The fact that they ceased to operate as independent craftsmen and were now in full service of the Admiralty Board also appears from the ruling that prohibited the master painter from doing work for any off-yard clients.[129]

---

124   D. Stalpaert, 'Plattegrond van het magazijn met bruggen en huisjes', 1656, SA, Collectie bouwtekeningen, no. 010056916934.

125   NA, Archief Van der Hoop, no. 161. 'Notitie van Tractementen en Pensioenen Amsterdam', p. 10.

126   NA, Archief Van der Hoop, no. 161. 'Notitie van Tractementen en Pensioenen Amsterdam', p. 4.

127   The 1781 account of the Amsterdam receiver general include a payment of f1218 for glasswork to Benjamin van Oort. NA, Archief Generaliteitsrekenkamer, no. 592. 'xve ordinaris Reekening van Mr Joan Graafland de Jonge'.

128   Staten Generaal 1701, fol. 392 vso.

129   NA, Archief Van der Hoop, no. 153. 'Secrete missiven', 30 June 1751, p. 17.

The drawing of all these different functions of production into one single institution, separated both physically and symbolically from the outside world by its walls, set the stage for new approaches to the organisation and supervision of production. Amsterdam again provides the clearest example. Important changes in internal hierarchy took place at the same time as the move to new facilities and the increase in shipbuilding at the Admiralty wharf at Kattenburg. The highest official working on the naval shipyard was the master of equipment. Before the move to the new facilities he had received f400 above his regular salary of f2400 for the renting of a house. But from 1656 onwards the master of equipment lived in a house on the shipyard itself, enhancing his ability for control. In 1662, around the time that shipbuilding at the naval yard took off on a large scale, his salary was raised by 600 guilders a year to the ample sum of f3000. This was motivated by 'the growth of equipment and the big change of this Board in the last few years, by which his task had become noticeably enlarged'.[130] In February of the same year, two under-masters of equipment, an accountant for the naval storehouse, and one for the shipyard were added to the payroll at a yearly salary of f1095.[131]

Through the master and under-masters of equipment, the Admiralty Boards gained far greater control over the entire process of production than they had had previously. The description of the functioning of the smaller Rotterdam shipyards in the eighteenth century makes clear how far-reaching the ideal of supervision was:

> The storehouses and dockyards of Rotterdam and Hellevoetsluys, which are entrusted to the care of the Admiralty Board of the Meuse, are in the first place and immediately governed by the Board itself, outside whose knowledge the servants are hardly allowed to do anything, except small repair ...[132]

The master of equipment was to implement this strict control by his permanent presence on the naval facilities:

> ... [H]e must be at the wharf or storehouse daily, in order to advance the equipment and shipwrights' work, and to make sure that the bosses and

---

130   NA, Archief Van der Hoop, no. 161. 'Notitie van Tractementen en Pensioenen Amsterdam', p. 1.

131   Ibid.

132   NA, Archief Van der Hoop, no. 153, 'Secrete missiven', 30 June 1751, p. 11.

workers keep to their duties, and if he discovers any disorders, or finds
anyone disobedient, he has to immediately notify the Board.[133]

Of course, certainly at the Amsterdam shipyard, control over the entire workforce could not be gained by a staff of one master of equipment and two under-
masters. Accountants, supervisors, and guards all had a function in restructuring the hierarchy of work. One of the main changes in this area was the
elevation of the position of the master shipwright to a level far above that of
ordinary workers. Before the move to Kattenburg the master shipwright had
received a day wage of fifty *stuyvers* (*f*2.5) in summer and winter. This was
about double the wage earned by ordinary shipwrights, but the fact that the
master was still nominally paid for a day's work shows how similar their positions still were. In 1654 a gratification of *f*200 per year was granted for 'ordinary
and extraordinary services', increasing the social difference. But the real change
came in October 1661, when the master shipwright was granted a yearly salary
or *tractement* (the term itself marking the difference with a worker's wage) of
*f*1800. Such an income, about six times as high as that of an ordinary worker,
put him far above the shop floor in social terms.[134] From that moment on master shipwrights had joined the ranks of higher management of the shipyard.
This process of differentiation continued during the eighteenth century. By 1781
the salary of the master shipwright stood at *f*2500, supplemented by an allowance for the rent of his house, several gratifications, and a reward for every ship
built at the wharf. His staff joined in this advance. Before 1733 his first journeyman, oldest journeyman, and ordinary journeyman all earned approximately
one and a half times as much as ordinary shipwrights, while his clerk earned
the equivalent of a workers' wage. By the end of the century the first journeyman earned more than *f*1100 (including gratifications) and lived in a house free
of rent at the shipyard, while the others received salaries of *f*730, about twice
the amount of an ordinary shipwright.

While those master craftsmen who managed to move up in the chain of command and obtain controlling positions over the work process as a whole saw
structural improvement in their salaries, those who became mere supervisors
or coordinators often faced a decline in status and income. This is particularly true of the shipwright's bosses or *commandeurs*. Master shipwrights who
owned their own yards often held a social position that was more akin to that

---

133   NA, Archief Van der Hoop, no. 153, 'Secrete missiven', 30 June 1751, p. 14.
134   NA, Archief Van der Hoop, no. 161. 'Notitie van Tractementen en Pensioenen Amsterdam',
      p. 4.

TABLE 3.8   *Yearly income of bosses at the Amsterdam naval shipyard in the eighteenth century (based on 226 working days)*

	1733	After 1733	1781
Blacksmith's boss	531	664	797
Mast makers' boss	593	531	531
Sail makers' boss	478	611	531
Boat makers' boss	445	664	505
Shipwright's boss	445	478	478
Carpenter's boss	478	531	478
Block makers' boss	624	531	478
Painters' boss	437	531	398
Carrier's boss	n.a.	n.a.	318

SOURCES: NA, ARCHIEF J.C. VAN DER HOOP, NO. 153. 'SECRETE MISSIVEN', 30 JUNE 1751, AND NA, ARCHIEF ADMIRALTEITSCOLLEGES XXXIX, J.C. VAN DER HOOP (1524–1825), NO. 104. 'DAGLONEN'

of well-to-do citizens than to that of ordinary craftsmen.[135] But in the course of the seventeenth century on the larger shipyards, including large private shipyards, they started to leave direct control over the workforce to their jour-neymen. These functioned more as gang leaders than as traditional craftsmen, a functional shift signified by the use of the term *commandeur*. Sub-bosses were called *Javanen* (Javanese), perhaps referring to the authoritarian labour regimes implemented by the Dutch in Asia. With 44 workers per boss in 1733 and 58 in 1781, the *commandeurs* at the naval shipyard controlled a workforce that was akin to that of a large or medium sized shipyard. But with thirty-six *stuyvers* in summer and twenty-six in winter (after 1733 raised to thirty-eight and thirty *stuyvers* respectively), their wage stood much closer to that of the ordinary workers below them, and at the same level as that of guild members on private wharfs.

Table 3.8 shows the fluctuations of income of a number of bosses in other crafts, ranked according to their 1781 income. As can be seen from this table only the blacksmiths' boss, sail-makers' boss, and boat-makers' boss made considerable gains over the course of the eighteenth century, maybe due to the fact that their workshops always remained more or less separate islands

---

135   Van Kampen 1953, pp. 178 ff., and Deurloo 1971, p. 21.

within the shipyard organisation. Some, such as the bosses of mast makers, block makers, and painters, suffered a marked decline in income. The others had incomes from wages that were the same or only slightly higher at the end of the eighteenth century than at the start, around one and a half times that of their subordinates.

Probably as significant for their income position as their formal wage was the attack on bonuses and gratifications that took place from the 1730s onward. The spike of most *commandeurs'* incomes after 1733 is due to the fact that before that time many bosses and some selected workers had received gratifications in the form of firewood or candles. The regulation of 1733 ruled that the gratification in firewood would be replaced by a sum in money, varying from twenty to fifty guilders, but it is likely that these sums were often below the actual value of the previously earned rewards in kind. The right to receive candles would be 'mortified', meaning that it was kept in place for those who already possessed this right but not for their successors.[136] New regulations introduced in 1744 limited the entitlement to a monetary compensation for firewood to a select group of managers, consisting of the master and under-master of equipment, the master shipwright and his oldest apprentice, the clerk (*commis*) of the wharf, one skipper, and the controller of the nail shed.[137] For *commandeurs* the taking away of their entitlement to firewood signified a real shift. They had gradually been degraded from specialised craftsmen to high-paid workers in supervising positions. In August 1748, when workers of the shipyards marched through Amsterdam in support of the Orangist revolt against the city governors, one observer notes the presence of 'all the masters of the wharfs'.[138] Earlier that year, the directors of the naval shipyard had found it necessary to summon all *commandeurs* and read them the States General's declaration against seditious movements, to which they added their own 'serious threats'.[139] It is hard to imagine that the semi-proletarianisation of those most directly responsible for the coordination and control of work would not have played a role in the radicalisation of the shipyard workforce.

---

136   NA, Archief Van der Hoop, no. 153. 'Secrete missiven', 30 June 1751, p. 41, and pp. 54–6.

137   NA, Archief Van der Hoop, no. 153. 'Secrete missiven', 30 June 1751, pp. 74–6.

138   Fuks 1960, p. 79.

139   Ypey 1789, p. 142.

3.8   Of Time, Theft, and Chips

The restructuring of labour relations on the shipyards did not go unchallenged, especially since it raised both wage issues and powerful notions of the 'ancient rights' of guild workers. On 6 February 1749 between six and seven in the evening, lieutenant admiral Cornelis Schrijver faced an uncommon adversary. Schrijver was a highly respected naval officer, though posterity remembers him better for his achievements behind an administrator's desk than for his deeds at sea.[140] In this particular mission, the Amsterdam Admiralty Board had again called on him more for his diplomatic than for his martial capacities. In the charged atmosphere that had held the Republic in its grip since the stormy, protest ridden advent of William IV to the Stadtholderate in 1747 – especially in Amsterdam where a popular Orangist revolt had led to the abdication of part of the city council in the late summer of 1748 – Schrijver had to convince the shipwrights of the Admiralty shipyard that there was no room to give in to their demands on pay and working conditions. To add to his discomfort, the shipwrights had sent a hero of their own, Jan Martini, to head a delegation of six negotiators. Martini was not a shipwright, but had been one of the leaders of the radical fraction of the Revolt the previous year. He had even led a demonstration of two thousand Admiralty and VOC workers through Amsterdam, dressed in traditional shipwrights' garb, to the great distress of defenders of law and order on both sides of the main political dividing line.[141] As could be expected from such a firebrand, when the delegation had come to Schrijver's house on the fifth of February to list the shipwrights' demands, 'aforementioned Martini absolutely refused to listen to anything, no matter what persuasive reasons the undersigned brought forward'.[142] When his, in his own opinion, persuasive reasons did not seem to impress his adversary, Schrijver resorted to open threats. The Admiralty Board and the VOC, he explained, could not be forced into granting demands either by the shipwrights, or even by city government, 'which had power only over its citizens ... but not in any way over the Admiralty Board and the Company'. Higher wages, in this case two *stuyvers* a day for guild members, would lead to instant ruin, causing

---

140   Bruijn 1973, pp. 161–75.

141   Anonymous 1748, p. 107 and p. 111, and Geyl 1936, p. 56 and p. 95.

142   NA, Familiearchief Fagel. no. 1099, 'Raport van den Luijtenant Admiraal Cornelis Schrijver omtrent zijn wedervaren met de clouwers van het scheepstimmermans gilden'.

the wharf to come to a standstill, for lack of the necessary funds to buy wood and pay the shipwrights their daily wages; particularly when the Admiralty Board would further be burdened ... if the shipwrights would gain the upper hand, and came to carry through their demands by force and violence.

And so, the next day, a group of fifty or sixty shipwrights led by Martini returned to Schrijver's house,

shouting out in a violent way, with swearing, raging and the most unmentionable curses and threats: yelling that undersigned [Schrijver] had no business engaging himself with their guilds. And having lit a fire of wood curls, they burned a printed plan that was written by undersigned to make them and their heirs forever happy.[143]

Unable to bring together these diverging views on eternal happiness and the two *stuyvers* wage raise, the shipwrights later that year turned directly to the stadtholder. In December 1749 they presented him with a request complaining about wage levels that were considerably lower than those among private sector shipwrights, exemptions that allowed the Admiralty Board to employ non-guild labour, irregular payment, and the low quality of beer served during work. However, unlike Martini and his delegation, William IV did have an ear for Schrijver's persuasiveness, and only encouraged the Admiralty Board to comply with the demands on beer and regular payment. As far as the wage raise was concerned, he explained that 'his Highness was not unwilling to take favourable reflection on it when times get better'.[144] Day rates of Amsterdam shipwrights remained unchanged until the second half of the nineteenth century.

The disciplining of the workforce at the naval shipyards according to the requirements of large scale manufacture was a long and uneven process. It did not only involve the introduction of new hierarchies, but also the challenging of long-held perceptions of the nature of work, time, leisure, property, and consumption of alcohol and tobacco on the job. Resistance ranged from the most individual methods, such as absenteeism and theft, to collective action in the form of strikes and involvement in political protest. Such themes play a large role in the historiography of the 'making of the working class', but have

---

143   Ibid.

144   NA, Archief Stadhouderlijke Secretarie, no. 467. 'Request aan Willem IV van 6 december 1749'.

hardly been researched for the early modern Dutch Republic.[145] The typical approach for the Netherlands remains the one recently summed up by Jan de Vries, who agrees that eighteenth-century labour patterns underwent revolutionary changes, but criticises what he sees as the 'pessimist' view, instead insisting that workers benefitted from these changes even when they had to be enforced: 'After the manner of Ulysses requesting to be tied to the mast of his ship as it sailed past the sirens, factory discipline forced workers to do what they wanted to do but could not do unaided'.[146] However, it is hard to read this repressed urge for discipline from the actions of the labourers involved. During the eighteenth century, shipwrights gained a name for themselves as the most unruly section of the Amsterdam population. While much attention is given in Dutch historiography to the ideological component of this radicalisation, stressing the role of shipwrights in the 'Orange revolutions' of 1747–8 and 1787, the fact that the naval and VOC shipyards were at the same time in the forefront of the abolition of craft practices and their replacement by more elaborate forms of collective labour discipline has been virtually overlooked.

The transformation that took place in the position of shipyard workers can be summarised along the lines of a threefold shift, involving the introduction of new forms of time management, strong measures against practices that management defined as theft, and the loss of the labourer's control over tools and other materials used in production. As E.P. Thompson noted, the development of new notions of labour time was intimately connected with the development of manufacture on a large scale.

> Attention to time in labour depends in large degree upon the need for the synchronisation of labour. But in so far as manufacturing industry remained conducted upon a domestic or small workshop scale, without intricate subdivision of processes, the degree of synchronisation demanded was slight, and task-orientation was still prevalent.[147]

Not surprisingly, given their size and the level of combination and internal coordination, the Amsterdam naval and VOC shipyards pioneered a system of strict time management. Symbolic for this was the inclusion of a large clock above the gate to the shipyard. Before the move to Kattenburg, no clock setter is mentioned in the account of personnel, but in 1680 a clock setter was employed

---

145   E.g., Thompson 1963 and Rule 1981.
146   De Vries 2008, p. 115.
147   Thompson 1991, p. 370.

for the yearly fee of ƒ80.[148] From that time onward, strict rules applied for the exact length of the working day. Jan de Vries has calculated that between the sixteenth century and the 1650s, the number of working hours for manual labourers in general increased by twenty percent, from 3,100 to 3,700 working hours per year.[149] One surviving copy of the rules for work at the shipyard, from the rather late date of 1788, stated exactly the hours at which a bell should ring to mark the start and end of the workday, the morning break of half an hour and a break at noon of an hour. The length of the workday, excluding breaks, varied from 8 hours in January (at winter wage) to 11.5 hours from April to the end of September (at summer wage).[150] Incidentally, this means that for all workers except for a skilled 'elite', wages per hour were much lower in summer than in winter. With large clocks at the entrances of the naval shipyard, the VOC shipyard, and at the tower of the church that was built right in between the two in the late 1660s, the daily passage of workers as well as their supervisors was always marked by time.

One indication of the success in demarcating the labour day, as well as the exceptional nature of this achievement, is a remark in a request made by skippers in 1731:

> ... [T]hat at the naval and company yards there is observed a good order in arriving at work and quitting, as well as in the timing of breaks, while the journeymen at the [private] yards at which the suppliants are forced to have their ships built, come and go and have their breaks as long and protracted as they please ...[151]

How deeply notions of time and discipline had become ingrained in the minds of the shipyard workers appears from a strike in Rotterdam in 1784. On 8 March, the birthday of Stadtholder William V, they staged a rowdy celebration in the yard involving lots of drink. After wresting involuntary 'gifts' from a number of the bosses and the master shipwright, the crowd was granted leave at three in the afternoon. They then marched to the adjoining VOC yard and proceeded

---

148   NA, Archief Van der Hoop, no. 161. 'Notitie van Tractementen en Pensioenen', p. 6 and p. 11.

149   De Vries 2008, p. 89.

150   NA, Archief Van der Hoop, no. 146A. 'Reglement voor s'Lands werf, Eerste Deel, Rakende de Equipagie-Meester en de algemeene Ordres', p. 5. Similar working hours applied in Hellevoetsluys around 1750. NA, Archief Van der Hoop, no. 153, 'Secrete missiven', 30 June 1751, p. 19.

151   Quoted in Van Kampen 1953, p. 174n.

to the private shipyards in another part of town, while shouting 'it strikes' (meaning 'the clock strikes for leaving work'). After that, some young workers broke into the Schiedam gate, where they sounded the bells.[152]

Usually resistance against strict enforcement of labour time took a less frivolous and more individualised form. Unannounced absenteeism remained one of the great concerns of shipyard administrators. This was very clear during the 1730s and 1740s, when over-employment and the low level of work caused many workers to skip days, while still demanding their full pay. The *commandeurs* had the task of carefully administering the exact number of days worked, for which they used a so-called 'checkers-board'. This was a square on which they could mark the days for each labourer with crosses. Apparently, however, there were reasons not to trust the accuracy with which the bosses carried out this task, since in 1733, new rules for work at the shipyard demanded an oath from them stating:

> ... [T]hat I will not mark anyone as having worked on the naval yard, apart from those who effectively have worked there in the service of the nation during the complete prescribed time, and in the same function as is expressed on this list. That if I discover any mistakes in this work, I will immediately give notice of this to the proper authority, and further behave as a loyal *commandeur* is supposed to.

The checkers-boards had to be handed over to the master shipwright or the deputy-masters of equipment for control.[153]

Apart from absenteeism, theft was a major issue in eighteenth-century labour relations. As Peter Linebaugh showed for England, this was not only a result of pilfering being an easy way to supplement low wages, but also of colliding views on the nature of property itself. Waste materials such as unusable pieces of wood (chips or curls) often were seen as rightfully belonging to the craftsmen. This encouraged the bad handling of materials, since all spoiled pieces of wood could be appropriated by the shipwrights for their own use. The 'battle over chips' preoccupied management at the English shipyards for the entire eighteenth century – in 1768 even leading to soldiers being employed against shipyard workers.[154] Naval administrators in the Dutch Republic were far more successful on this account than their English counterparts. Already in

---

152 Van Kampen 1953, pp. 175–7.
153 NA, Archief Van der Hoop, no. 153, 'Secrete missiven', 30 June 1751, pp. 42–4.
154 Linebaugh 2006, pp. 378–82.

1671, former Amsterdam Admiralty councillor Nicolas Witsen could write about the great economy attained on Dutch wharfs, compared to the wastefulness in other countries. In his then famous manual for shipbuilding, he ascribed this particularity to the frugal mentality of Dutch labourers:

> From which follows, that even if a stranger would keep in mind all rules for building, they could not serve him ... unless he would see chance to equal the nature of the people, with which he has to work, to the thrifty and clean disposition of the Hollander, which cannot be done.[155]

This attitude of the worker was at least partly enforced by the tighter administration and greater care in the storage of raw materials, semi-finished products and excess equipment that was introduced with the move to Kattenburg.

Order was a powerful weapon for management in the fight against workers' appropriation of part of the stock. It is noticeable that in 1733, when the entitlement to firewood was replaced by a gratification in money, this right was already limited to a small section of the workforce, and the distribution was administered according to set rates that varied according to one's position in the shipyard hierarchy. The anarchic practices at English shipyards, where workers at one point were able to carry out on their backs 40 percent of all wood ordered for the building of a third-rate ship, were absent in Amsterdam.[156] Instead, a special category of workers (called *spaanderrapers* or chip gatherers) belonging to the lowest-paid section of the workforce was appointed to collect chips. Set amounts of firewood divided into a *schuitje* (worth about twenty guilders), *roodgat* (about thirty guilders), or *boot* (about fifty guilders) were distributed among 165 selected members of personnel, mainly belonging to the administrative cadre and the workmen's bosses at the wharf. The only sections of workers entitled to firewood were guards, privileged servants of the staff, and a small group of workers such as cooks and fire makers who could probably have easily taken firewood for themselves anyhow. The total costs of these gratifications came to about ƒ4000.[157] In 1744, when the right to gather chips was restricted to a small section of higher management, it was also decided that the Admiralty Board would no longer buy any firewood but instead would only use waste from the wharf. Shipyard waste was now officially turned into a commodity, in a ruling stating that

---

155   Witsen 1671, 'Introduction'.
156   Linebaugh 2006, p. 380.
157   NA, Archief Van der Hoop, no. 153, 'Secrete missiven', 30 June 1751, p. 56.

even the chips and waste of the wharf will be sold, as it is, without cleaving either the chips or the blocks, but that both in the boardroom and the departments, as well as in the Admiralty residence in The Hague, only the best chips and waste of the wharf will be burned ...[158]

Apparently this ruling was applied with success. Yeoman Lott, an English naval administrator visiting Holland in the 1750s, admiringly wrote about the 'peculiar attention' paid at the Amsterdam shipyard to waste management 'prohibiting any Kind of Wood whatever, or Stores of any Kind, to be carried out of their Dock Yards by the Workmen, under the Perquisite of Chips, &c'.[159]

Control against the unlicensed appropriation of shipyard goods was also extended or strengthened in other areas. During the 1730s and 1740s many rules were introduced for the supervision and precise administration of goods that were not in current use. In 1748, for example, a shipwright was appointed for every ship that lay in the docks, with a duty to remain on this ship from the sounding of the bell in the morning to the closing of the yard in the evening. One of his tasks was

to take care that nothing is stolen or goes missing from this ship, to which aim a proper inventory will be made of all goods that are present on this ship in the dock. And of this inventory one copy will remain in the possession of the master of equipment, and one of the shipwright on this ship.[160]

Similar rules were introduced for the unloading and offloading of victuals and equipment.[161]

Of particular interest are the attempts to limit workers' access to those goods that were traditionally seen as belonging to them only. One was the beer consumed during work, the other the simple tools that were used in production. As a compensation for the absolute prohibition of smoking on shipyards, guild rules from the seventeenth century onwards had provided the workers with free access to beer as a 'refreshment beverage'. Given the physical character of shipwrights' labour, usually taking place in the open air, unlimited

---

158   NA, Archief Van der Hoop, no. 153, 'Secrete missiven', 30 June 1751, pp. 76–7.

159   Lott 1777, p. 5.

160   UB-BC, *Extracten*. 'Extract minute Amsterdams Admiraliteitscollege', 30 May 1748.

161   UB-BC, *Extracten*. 'Extract minutes Amsterdams Admiraliteitscollege', 21 April 1734 and 29 August 1749.

access to beer was seen as an essential right. However, already at the end of the seventeenth century, Van Yk's manual for shipbuilding had advised:

> ... [N]ot to allow that any beer will be carried along the wharf or around the place of work in jugs, but rather to summon everyone to drink in front of the barrel; because in this way, he [the master shipwright] will not only spare the wage of beer carriers, but also much beer, since most will be ashamed to walk away from their work too often under the eyes of the master.[162]

The naval and VOC shipyards had found an even easier solution to the problem of excessive drinking during work: providing beer that was undrinkable. In their request to William IV of December 1749 workers complained about the low quality of their 'refreshment drink', 'being for a long time so bad that it cannot be used, and having given many diseases and inconveniences to those who for excessive thirst were nonetheless forced to drink it'.[163] Conceding to their complaint, the stadtholder summoned the shipyard administrators to make sure that from that moment on, good quality beer was provided to the workers. Interestingly enough, the list of workers of 1781 shows the employment of twenty-five 'jug-fillers' (*kantappers*), which had not been present at the wharf around the time of the workers' complaint.[164] This could point in two very different directions. One possibility is that on the issue of drink, workers' protest had resulted in a return to the seventeenth century practices that Van Yk had denounced. But it is also possible that the opposite happened, and management had used the introduction of better quality beer as an excuse for rationing. Unfortunately, the sources do not provide a direct answer on this matter.

More straightforward is the introduction of twelve *lappen* or guards of the tools around the same time. With a day wage at the same rate as shipwrights, these were considerably better paid than ordinary guards who received no more than sixteen *stuyvers* a day in summer and fourteen in winter. The introduction of this group of well-paid supervisors must have signified a lessening of control of the workforce over the tools they used. Traditionally, the smaller tools that shipwrights worked with had been in their own possession, while

---

162   Van Yk 1697, p. 24.
163   NA, Archief Stadhouderlijke Secretarie, no. 467. 'Request aan Willem IV van 6 december 1749'.
164   Given their wage of 5 to 7 *stuyvers* a day, probably children.

the larger tools were supplied at the wharf.[165] How freely the shipwrights, or 'axes' (*bijltjes*) as they were popularly called, had previously commanded these simple tools appears from their role in the Orangist revolt of 1748. At several strategic turning points, the dividing line between moderates and radicals had been drawn over the question of whether the 'axes' should demonstrate with or without their axe.[166] But the employment of a number of specified 'toolmakers' among the Admiralty workforce after 1744 signifies that tools were increasingly supplied by the shipyard and considered its property.

By the end of the eighteenth century there was no other sector of industry in the Dutch Republic where craft practices in production had so successfully been challenged and replaced by new conceptions of time management, property, hierarchy, and control as at the large naval shipyards. While shipbuilding manuals from the seventeenth century show that shipyard managers could start this transformation from a more advantageous position than their English counterparts, the crucial years in the transition were centred around the 1730s and 1740s, or the so-called 'quiet years'. The financial crisis that beset the Admiralty Boards was a strong motivation for naval bureaucrats to challenge practices that they considered wasteful and costly. They did so with a vigour that they never managed to muster in reviewing other potentially costly and wasteful areas of naval production, such as the costs of the shipyard bureaucracy itself, and with considerably more success.[167] The 1740s low in naval shipbuilding must have strengthened the position of management vis-à-vis the shipyard workforce. When in September 1749 the shipwrights rallying in front of Schrijver's house cried out that he should respect their rights as guild workers, this was much more than the rehearsal of a well-known theme.[168] It also referred to a whole catalogue of recent defeats, which the shipyard workers hoped but ultimately failed to redress.

3.9   Neptune's Trident and Athena's Gifts

An influential thesis on the industrial revolution in England focuses on the 'gifts of Athena', the emergence of a specifically British combination of theoretical science and practical, experimental knowledge at the point of production.

---

165   Unger 1978, p. 61.

166   Anonymous n.d., pp. 148–9. A year earlier, shipwrights in Zierikzee had turned out for an Orangist protest 'with their axes at their shoulder'. De Kanter 1795, p. 176.

167   Bruijn 1970, p. 62.

168   Dekker 1982, p. 79, and Deurloo 1971, pp. 56 ff.

According to this theory, around 1750 an 'industrial enlightenment' started to bridge the two and provided the intellectual background to the ensuing surge of inventions.[169] Though less significant than the changes in the organisation of labour relations, the slowly changing attitudes to the practical application of science and experimentation of the master shipwrights at the Amsterdam and Rotterdam Admiralty Boards suggest that the basic elements of this fusion were available in the Dutch Republic, even in a period of industrial retardation.

Compared to the situation after the industrial revolution, innovation in early modern shipbuilding was a slow process. As a means of increasing productivity, technological change and the application of new scientific knowledge were of less significance than the changes in the organisation of the labour process that have been examined in the previous sections.[170] During the seventeenth century, the Admiralty shipyards benefitted from the advanced nature of Dutch shipbuilding in general. However, most of these advances had been made already before the 1630s.[171] In the eighteenth century innovation in shipbuilding slowed down markedly.[172] This resulted in heated debates on the relative merits of English and French shipbuilding methods in comparison to the long-established Dutch practices, in particular after the employment of three English shipwrights at the Amsterdam Admiralty shipyard in 1727.[173] Most of these debates concentrated on the use of 'ship drawings' and the application of advanced scientific theories, in particular mathematics, in ship design.[174] The intensity of the controversy, pitting administrators and master shipwrights of the Amsterdam and Rotterdam Admiralty Boards against each other, has caused this aspect of shipbuilding to be the subject of a long line of historiography.[175] This section will summarise some of the outcomes of these investigations, but also broaden the subject to a number of other, related areas of technological change and the application of science.

The principal instrument employed in shipbuilding throughout the early modern period remained the human body itself, 'a poor engine', as Braudel put it.[176] According to Cornelis van Yk:

---

169   Mokyr 2002, p. 36, and Mokyr 2009, pp. 79 ff.
170   On the interrelation between craftmanship, technology, science, and design in early modern shipbuilding, see McGee 1999.
171   Davids 2008a, pp. 140–1.
172   Unger 1978, p. 41 and p. 86.
173   Bruijn 1970, pp. 9 ff.
174   See in particular Hoving and Lemmers 2001.
175   See ibid. for a summary of the historiographic debate.
176   Braudel 1974, p. 246.

[A]mong all forms of manual labour, I do not know of any in which the human body is exercised and trained in so many ways as in ship carpentry; since one has to work sometimes standing, sometimes sitting or crawling, and even lying down; now carrying heavy wood on the shoulders; than lifting things under hand, in front of the body. Furthermore, heaving, tallying, pulling, hauling, climbing, clambering, sowing, cutting, knocking bolts, wringing, wresting, and applying force in uncountable ways, is the content of daily work. So that the clothes are torn from the limbs, and by this strong training, the complete body becomes hollow from head to toe ...[177]

The central role of the shipwrights and their individual capacities in production was connected to the nature of the production process of the wooden ship. Until the arrival of English masters in 1727, Amsterdam shipbuilders had used the 'shell-first' method. The main characteristic of this method was that the hull was built from the ground up, using a set of simple rules of thumb to determine the exact shape and proportions. Such simple rules, reproduced in manuals, only provided for a more or less unspecified standard ship.[178] To determine the precise characteristics of the ship, for example to distinguish between a bulky merchant ship and a fast sailing man-of-war, these rules of thumb were adjusted according to the individual tastes of the master shipwright during the building of the ship itself.[179] Experience and craftsmanship decided whether this was done with success, and adaptations of the design still took place during the fitting of the available pieces of wood for the hull, making great demands on the judgment and precision of individual workers and their supervisors. Many tools that were used were specifically geared towards this process of on-the-spot adaptation, a practice that was developed to a high level of perfection in the Dutch Republic. Blaise Ollivier, the French naval official who visited the Dutch shipyards in 1737, was surprised to find instruments for the hauling and setting of planks that he had never seen in France, and which in his eyes were also preferable to similar instruments used in England.[180]

Some important labour-saving devices could be easily integrated into this form of production. This is particularly the case for the use of sawing mills and cranes, innovations that were introduced in private shipbuilding in the

---

177 Van Yk 1697, p. 31.
178 E.g. Allard 1695, pp. 33–9.
179 Hoving and Lemmers 2001, pp. 21–2.
180 Roberts 1992, pp. 333–4.

Dutch Republic long before they became common in other countries.[181] The VOC and Admiralty shipyards took over these developments from the private sector, and could use their far larger capital outlays to apply them on an even larger scale. Dutch success in combining these elementary machines and the merits of craftsmanship made Dutch shipwrights much sought-after among their seventeenth-century competitors.[182] However, a century of technological leadership also fostered attitudes to shipbuilding based on the time-tested centrality of the master shipwright and his experience, and a strong hostility to any practice that would diminish their role. The elevation of master shipwrights to high bureaucratic positions that has already been examined in section 3.7 further strengthened their personal influence on the shipbuilding process. A gradual loss in leadership occurred, that gained strong influence on popular consciousness by the long eighteenth-century debate on ship drawings.

The issue of mathematic design in shipbuilding is so important, because it signifies a major step in the mutual integration of science and experience (instead of their traditional opposition) as factors in the production process. Building according to design also allows for a way of preserving and adapting knowledge from one ship to the next, opening up a whole new space for long-term innovation. Thirdly, once designs become the property of the owners or directors of an institution rather than the master craftsmen, this structurally alters the power relationships within the enterprise.[183] Both in England and in France, mathematic designs were used from the late seventeenth century onwards, a practice that was gradually improved in the following decades. According to the traditional view, debates in the Dutch Republic became polarised between the Amsterdam-based advocates of the 'modern' English fashion of shipbuilding, and traditionally-minded masters in the rest of the country. Emblematic for this opposition became the bleak description by Cornelis Schrijver of the shipbuilding practices that were current in Amsterdam before the employment of the three English masters. The older Dutch masters had learned their trade at the private shipyards in the industrial Zaan-area, where, according to Schrijver,

> the usual answer to the question for the reason why one ship proves to be so much better than another, is: 'Yes mate! It did not want to fall from the axe in another way'.[184]

---

181   Unger 1978, p. 7.
182   Davids 2008b, p. 296, and Glete 2010, p. 337.
183   McGee 1999, pp. 222 ff., and Hoving and Lemmers 2001, p. 22 and p. 142.
184   NA, Familiearchief Fagel, no. 1099. Cornelis Schrijver, 'Informatie over eenige wynige

However, Hoving and Lemmers have brought important nuances into this story. First, it is not true that the use of designs was absent outside Amsterdam. Already in 1725, two years before the introduction of 'English methods' in Amsterdam, the master shipwright at the Rotterdam Admiralty shipyard Paulus van Zwyndrecht had made use of a mathematical design for one of his ships. He continued to do so in later years, and organisational changes in the shipbuilding process leading to a separation of design and building followed.[185] When Blaise Ollivier visited the naval shipyards a decade later, he noted that three different approaches to shipbuilding were current on Dutch Admiralty wharfs: the English method in Amsterdam, traditional (shell-first) methods in Friesland, Zeeland and the Northern Quarter, and the 'new method' of Van Zwyndrecht in Rotterdam.[186] The debate between Amsterdam and Rotterdam shipbuilders of the mid-eighteenth century was not so much concentrated on the question whether or not to use designs as on which method of design was superior. Furthermore, the actual content of the arguments shows that attitudes to the application of advanced mathematics had already changed considerably since the late seventeenth century. Van Yk still strongly argued for experience as the only true way of establishing the proportions of a ship:

> Just as the correct way of erecting columns and fundaments for building a house, even when accepted by all able building masters, still has no other underlying support than only that which finds its utility from experience, and its ornament from custom; in the same way, no one will expect that in speaking of the proportions of ship parts, I will defend them with other reasons, than those that come from experience and custom.[187]

In contrast, in an unpublished manuscript from the late 1750s, Van Zwyndrecht's son Pieter could write about 'the ships that are mathematical machines, and as fishes have water as their element'.[188] Thus,

---

pointen aangaande de scheepsbouw van slands scheepen van oorlog en het geenen daar in is voorgevallen seedert het jaar 1683 tot 1753 incluijs', p. 4.

185 Hoving and Lemmers 2001, p. 77.

186 Hoving and Lemmers 2001, p. 73, and Roberts 1992, p. 318.

187 Van Yk 1697, p. 52.

188 Pieter Paulusz van Zwyndrecht made his career first on a private yard, than the Rotterdam VOC-yard, and finally worked from 1764–83 as master-shipwright at the Rotterdam Admiralty shipyard. His manuscript, 'De groote Nederlandsche scheeps bouw op een proportionaale reegel voor gestelt', is printed as an appendix to Hoving and Lemmers 2001, pp. 181–296. Quotation from page 183.

It is nothing but a very thorough truth, that a master who possesses
knowledge of the laws of nature and the fundamentals of mechanics, will
bring the art of shipbuilding to further perfection, than one that on the
contrary knows nothing about this.[189]

The most common view among advanced Dutch shipbuilders of the second
half of the eighteenth century was one that combined mathematic insights
with experimentation and experience. This idea was put most elegantly by yet
another member of the Van Zwyndrecht dynasty, who was master shipwright
at the Rotterdam Admiralty yard from 1752 to 1764. Commenting on the recent
publication in Dutch of an important French text on shipbuilding mathematics, he wrote that 'the building of Holland's warships is a reflective science and
industrious artistic practice'.[190]

The arguments used by the proponents of such a 'mixed' method were
certainly not irrational. As Hoving and Lemmers explain, the specific natural
properties, cost, and quality of different available pieces of wood meant that a
careful process of 'fitting in' could well prove more efficient in terms of costs
and strength of the ship than blindly following the existing designs.[191] Also, the
low state of development of mathematics and physics made it very hard for
shipbuilders to balance the practical results of their calculations for different
aspects of the performance of their ships. This was the essence of the argument
put forward in 1757 by Udemans, the master shipwright of the Zeeland voc
wharf:

The difficulty of shipbuilding is that one finds contradictory requirements
in a ship; so that in making one improvement and changing this or that
characteristic of a ship, one often creates a larger deficiency on the other
side. The variations of weather and wind also prevent the shipbuilders,
in my opinion, from making a mathematic rule for all those different
requirements; leaving no safer way, than to carefully examine the cause
of the defects in finished ships, and improve those to the best of one's
abilities.[192]

---

189   Hoving and Lemmers 2001, p. 188.
190   Van Zwyndregt 1759, p. 1. The French study was Du Monceau 1759.
191   Hoving and Lemmers 2001, p. 71.
192   Udemans Jr. 1757, pp. 61–2.

Similar thoughts were formulated a quarter of a century later by the master of equipment of the Amsterdam Admiralty Board William May, the son of one of the three original English masters employed by the Admiralty Board in 1727:

> ... [B]ut if one wants to prove the possibility of forming the body of a ship from mathematical rules, that is from curved lines whose equations are known or can be found, then these have to be combined with the unchangeable laws of physics in such a way that in each position of the ships they shall achieve maximum speed. I imagine that computing such a combination would even make the head of a Newton spin.[193]

Though such attitudes may seem like a restatement of the conservatism of earlier years, they must actually be viewed in a more positive light. None of the more advanced masters in Amsterdam and Rotterdam at the end of the eighteenth century rejected mathematics in favour of experience and crafts-manship, as had been done at the start of the century. Their remarks were much more a reflection of the limits of the available knowledge of their days. Significantly, Hoving and Lemmers question the thesis that English and French ships consistently out-sailed Dutch ships.[194]

Changing attitudes towards science and experimentation were not only observable in the area of ship design. Especially the archive of Johan Cornelis van der Hoop, the Amsterdam fiscal advocate of the 1780s and enlightened proponent of state-controlled naval reform, abounds with material on the possible introduction of new techniques. These include discussions on the best and cheapest chemical practices for the protection of the hull, connected to the major innovation of the double copper layer on the outside of the ship;[195] proposals for the introduction of the 'English caboose' and new methods for distilling drinking water;[196] examinations of the chain pump;[197] a new type of

---

193 NA, Archief Admiraliteitscolleges XXXIX, J.C. van der Hoop, no. 11. 'Memorien van de Fransche of andere constructeuren over onse scheepbouw. Reflectien daarop van den equipagie mr May & anderen'.

194 Hoving and Lemmers 2001, pp. 155–6.

195 NA, Archief Admiraliteitscolleges XXXIX, J.C. van der Hoop, no. 14. 'Memorie van de wijze en bevindingen der kopere dubbelingen voorde schepen van oorlog bij het collegie van de Maze', December 1782.

196 NA, Archief Admiraliteitscolleges XXXIX, J.C. van der Hoop, no. 23. 'Nieuwe ijzeren Engelse scheepskombuizen'.

197 NA, Archief Admiraliteitscolleges XXXIX, J.C. van der Hoop, no. 24. 'Brief over kettingpom-pen'.

artillery called the carronade;[198] a new, cost cutting and more durable fashion of fabricating gun-carriages;[199] and many more similar innovations. However, most of these were still product innovations, and even late in the eighteenth century attempts to transform the work process through the application of machines remained almost absent. Furthermore, by the end of the eighteenth century Dutch innovators relied heavily on findings imported from England and France.

Based both on the actual content of the debate between Amsterdam and Rotterdam shipbuilders, and on the evidence of widespread experimentation with new (albeit imported) techniques at the end of the eighteenth century, it seems mistaken to maintain the view that Dutch shipbuilding was fully stagnant after 1700. What is true, however, is that the changes that took place were slow and painstaking. Also, throughout the century there existed extraordinary unevenness in the application of new insights. In general, private shipbuilders were much slower in introducing developed methods of ship design than the larger yards of the Admiralty Board and voc. The latter were more inclined to discuss the performance of their ships in comparison to those of foreign navies and trading companies. But even among the Admiralty Boards sharp differences over the relative merits of various shipbuilding methods, ranging from rule of thumb methods that hardly had changed from the seventeenth century onwards to the integration of sophisticated French and English mathematical methods of ship design, remained unresolved. This unevenness was kept in place by the institutional separation of the five Admiralty Boards, and by the still dominant position of the master shipwrights. A clear indication of the latter is that the Van Zwyndrecht family, who dominated shipbuilding in Rotterdam for a whole century, always kept their ship designs in their own possession.[200]

While it is hard to tell how much of it was simply an expression of the generally prevailing malaise and how much of it was real, the dominant view in public opinion during the late eighteenth century was that even in shipbuilding, once the pride and prowess of the 'Golden Age', the Dutch Republic had now fallen back behind its competitors. Not the absence or presence of Athena's gifts, but social and institutional barriers to their distribution seem to

---

198   NA, Archief Admiraliteitscolleges XXXIX, J.C. van der Hoop, no. 26. 'Stukken over de bruikbaarheid van caronnadekanonstukken'.

199   NA, Archief Admiraliteitscolleges XXXIX, J.C. van der Hoop, no. 27. 'Rapporten over nieuwe rolpaarden'.

200   Hoving and Lemmers 2001, p. 144.

have been the key factor in the loss of momentum in Dutch naval production at a moment when others started making huge strides in innovation. This fed the sense of despair that was well expressed in 1786 by one private shipbuilder in the service of the Amsterdam Admiralty Board: 'That, while thus for some nations twilight has already arrived, and others have already seen the dawn, everything in the Netherlands still remains a dark night'.[201]

Conclusions

Naval shipyards were among the largest, if not the largest, production facilities of the early modern period. Taking care of the building and equipment of entire war fleets, they also were the focus of large-scale supply. Therefore these institutions have drawn the attention of historians interested in the development of bureaucratic management practices, the interplay between states and markets, and the evolution of labour relations. The Dutch Admiralty Boards have been characterised as exceptional for the close relations between naval administrators and local economic elites. The previous chapters have examined these close ties as resulting from structural features of Dutch early capitalism, as well as the institutional make-up of the federal-brokerage state, and have explained how they shaped the use of naval power for the protection of global economic interests. This chapter examined the ways in which the same ties influenced the 'naval economy' at home.

The direct involvement of capitalists in the running of the early modern state has often been seen primarily as a source of corruption, and certainly opportunities for gross forms of self-enrichment abounded in the Dutch Republic. But this chapter has shown that personal favouritism in no way excluded the extensive use of market practices in order to 'rationalise' naval bureaucracy. In many respects, the development of both went hand in hand. Accustomed to the use of commercial means of accounting, pricing and trading, Dutch naval administrators were early in introducing highly advanced forms of standardised bookkeeping in naval administration. Their veritable obsession with calculating, comparing, and orderly management developed well before the 'naval revolution' of the 1650s and 1660s, but the application of these sophisticated techniques came to fruition with the concentration of naval supply and produc-

---

201   NA, Archief Admiraliteitscolleges XXXIX, J.C. van der Hoop, no. 11. G.J. Palthe, 'Memorie, betreffende de bouwing van oorlogschepen, ten dienste van de staten der Zeven Veréénigde Nederlanden', Amsterdam, 1 August 1786.

tion within large centralised shipyards and storehouses. The Amsterdam naval storehouse and shipyard formed the crown on this transformation, continuing to draw admiration from foreign visitors for their efficiency and orderliness well into the eighteenth century. The combination of the commercial mindset of naval bureaucrats, strong state finances, and the ability to draw on a highly developed economic hinterland, translated into a great variety of approaches to the market in order to obtain supplies in ways adapted to the prevailing market conditions in each sector. The most important of these was the widespread use of public tendering, not only for large contracts such as the building of ships or hulls, but also for many smaller acquisitions.

Traditionally, these attitudes have been seen as a result of the Dutch 'Golden Age' of the seventeenth century, while eighteenth-century Admiralty management has been associated with stagnation and nepotism. However, this chapter has shown that at least for Amsterdam and Rotterdam (the most important Admiralty Boards), this approach is false. This can be seen very clearly in the area of labour relations. Far from being lethargic, Admiralty councillors energetically restructured the organisation of work, especially in the face of the financial crisis of the 1730s and 1740s. This chapter has also demonstrated the social significance of this type of 'efficiency', pointing out how the advance of economic rationality went hand in hand with sharp hierarchic and income differentiation between management and the workforce, and the challenging of guild practices pushing shipwrights to become one of the most militant sections of the eighteenth-century Amsterdam labouring classes. Whereas on British shipyards older practices such as the 'right to carry chips' were not eradicated until the nineteenth century, the completeness with which the Amsterdam shipyard was subjected to a 'commodity regime' in which even the smallest bits of waste were considered property of the institution testifies to the thoroughness with which the capitalist attitudes of management were followed through into the minutest details of work relations. Finally, the continued dynamism within those institutions is also apparent from the ways in which scientific progress, especially in mathematics, penetrated the shipbuilding process, although the manufactual basis of production characterising the age of the wooden ship set firm limits to its successful application.

Overall, then, in the eighteenth century naval organisation proved much more dynamic than was long thought. However, there were firm limits to this dynamism as well. The most important of these was that the localism inherent in Dutch economic life and political organisation inhibited the sharing of advantages and innovations between the five Admiralty Boards. The Admiralty Boards of Zeeland and Friesland did not profit from the same access to well-developed markets as the three Holland Admiralty Boards, and never received the same political and financial backing. Even the Rotterdam Admiralty Board had greater difficulties in recruiting skilled workers than that of Amsterdam. Technological and scientific advances were not applied universally, so that Amsterdam, Rotterdam, and Zeeland continued to build warships according to completely different conceptions of drawing and design. Overall, the federal-brokerage state allowed for easy and direct use of local resources, stimulating the interaction between capitalists and the state, but the very success of this interaction at a local level in part became a barrier to the development of similar interaction at the supra-provincial level.

Troop Payments, Military Soliciting, and the World of Finance[*]

The Dutch Republic was not only the dominant power at sea for much of the seventeenth century. It was also a major force on the European continent, a position it preserved well into the eighteenth century. Whereas the previous chapters focused on the political economy of employment of the fleet and the productive systems underpinning the navy, this chapter will look at one of the key economic aspects of warfare on land: military finance. Chapter One examined the emergence of a system in which a large group of financial middlemen, military solicitors, provided short-term credit to allow officers to continue paying their soldiers despite the large arrears of the provincial treasuries. Apart from their role in troop payments, military solicitors also administered many other financial transactions that sustained the army, most importantly providing credit to guarantee continuity in supply. Tracing their activities can shed light on a whole host of aspects of what Fritz Redlich in his classical study termed the *Kompaniewirtschaft* – the small self-contained economy in which the officer rented out his mercenary unit to the state as a private business venture, and in turn took upon himself the responsibility for the upkeep of his troops.[1] Contrary to Redlich's supposition, the independent role of officers, suppliers, and their creditors in the organisation of logistics did not disappear with the integration of the *Kompaniewirtschaft* into larger regimental military structures under state control. In many respects the increase in scale of operations gave captains, contractors, and financiers much more powerful roles in the upkeep of the army. The evolution of soliciting thus again illustrates the persistence of semi-independent 'brokers' in the organisation of warfare. At the same time, army-related expenses and the structures of financial intermediation underpinning them were among the decisive factors in the emergence of international capital markets.

The growth in the size of armies is often viewed as one of the main motors of early modern state formation. As Geoffrey Parker argued: 'It is interesting

---

[*] Part of this chapter previously appeared in Brandon 2011a; the sections on Gebhardt will appear, in somewhat altered form, as Brandon forthcoming.

[1] Redlich 1965, p. 79.

to note that the major waves of administrative reform in Western Europe in the 1530s and 1580s and at the end of the seventeenth century coincided with major phases of increase in army size'.[2] State finance formed a logical transmitter between the changes in the scale of warfare associated with the 'military revolutions' on the one hand, and the rise of fiscal military states on the other. As a result, historians have concentrated heavily on the revenue-raising capacities of the central state, and the reforms that enhanced these capacities.[3] Until recently, the major role of capitalist elites in the process of managing, transferring, and employing these revenues remained understudied. The direct involvement of independent entrepreneurs in areas such as military finance traditionally has been treated as a remnant of earlier forms of state formation, and above all a source of corruption.[4] Usher's *Dictionary of British Military History* (2003) could still define the British regimental agent in the same vein:

> A regimental paymaster employed by the colonel of a regiment. A colonel had complete control of his regiment in the 17th and early 18th centuries and was also responsible for distributing the pay to the troops through his agent. The agent frequently transferred a large amount of the funds to his own pocket by various frauds.[5]

Even in the case of the Dutch Republic, well known for its proficiency in troop payments, military solicitors attracted most attention as likely suspects of large scale embezzlement and as subject for state regulation against fraud.[6]

Recent contributions to the debate, particularly on the eighteenth-century British state, take a very different approach. They emphasise the ways in which the personal networks, private credit, and technical skills of bankers, merchants, and other private investors were central to the success of state reforms.[7]

---

2 Parker 1995, p. 45.

3 Brewer 1988. Among the many more recent contributions, see 't Hart 1993a, Bonney 1995, Lindegren 2000, Glete 2002, and Torres Sánchez 2007.

4 E.g., for England: Clay 1978, pp. 108–10, Nichols 1987, pp. 41–2, for France: Frémont 1906, p. 56.

5 Usher 2003, p. 3.

6 Hardenberg 1858, pp. 81–3, Ten Raa and De Bas 1918, pp. 180–1, Zwitzer 1978. Exceptions are the brief descriptions of soliciting in Zwitzer 1991, pp. 91 ff., and Van Nimwegen 2010, pp. 64–9.

7 Most of these studies are directed at military contracting in general, and treat financial entrepreneurship in this context. E.g., Bannerman 2008, pp. 140 ff., and Knight and Wilcox 2010, pp. 3 ff. Aaron Graham wrote an as yet unpublished PhD on British military finance

While sometimes coated in a highly problematic framework of the supposedly superior efficiency of markets over states, this literature rightly draws attention to the ways in which early modern warfare enhanced rather than diminished the dependence of states on capitalist investors. Indeed, detailed examination of the daily practice of army finance 'on the ground' underlines the mutual dependence of state and capital in this field. Paying the troops did not only require vast sums of money. It demanded that those sums arrived on time, and subsequently were transferred effectively to garrison towns and the frontlines over widely dispersed geographic areas. In order to provide tens of thousands of armed men with the monthly pay necessary to keep them loyal and effective, these financial flows had to be maintained with iron regularity despite the highly erratic flows of government funds. Even those early modern states such as the Dutch Republic that could profit from a relatively well-organised system of taxation were ill-equipped for such a task. Regularly transferring large sums of money – and especially transferring those sums abroad – required a financial infrastructure that in many cases did not exist, or was not easily accessible to the state.[8] Under these circumstances, full reliance on large financiers often proved the only available option. This partly reflects the place of agents and intermediaries in the formative period of capitalist social relations.[9] At a time when stable state institutions were still in the making, the international market for capital and goods was underdeveloped, and communication and exchange were highly insecure, personal networks were indispensable in areas varying from financial transactions and long-distance trade to political administration and the circulation of scientific knowledge. Military solicitors operated in a larger environment in which 'soliciting' was seen as an indispensable function of social and political life.[10]

This chapter will trace the evolution of military soliciting from its disorderly first phase to its much more regulated 'golden age' at the end of the seventeenth and the start of the eighteenth centuries (sections 4.1 and 4.2). It will then examine in detail the careers of two individual military solicitors, whose archives jointly span the crucial period between the start of the Nine Years' War

---

during the War of the Spanish Succession that draws the same conclusions: Graham 2011a. Also see Graham 2011b.

8   As noted by political economist Charles Davenant, in a tract published at the end of the Nine Years' War: Davenant 1698, p. 101.

9   Cf. the earlier cited passage of Marx on the role of intermediaries in the rise of capitalism, Marx 1961b, pp. 772–3. For a recent examination of the forms and functions of agency in early modern Europe, see Cools, Keblusek, and Noldus 2006.

10   On the place of 'soliciting' in Dutch Republican bureaucracy, see Knevel 2001, pp. 167–8.

and the end of the War of the Austrian Succession, enabling a long view on the development of their respective businesses (section 4.3), their daily functioning as intermediaries in paying the troops (section 4.4), and the importance of their personal networks for the execution of this task (section 4.5). The final section looks at the evolution of the system of military soliciting from the end of the War of the Spanish Succession until the final decades of the eighteenth century, a sometimes troubled period in Dutch state finance but also an era of great opportunities for individuals involved in high finance.

4.1   From Disorder to Regulation

The years after the Peace of Westphalia did not see the permanent reduction of the standing army hoped for by large sections of Holland's political and economic elites. The more than half a century up to the Peace of Utrecht of 1713 became one of costly expansion rather than cost-cutting reduction of army size. In this respect, the Dutch Republic simply moved in step with its main competitors. Although exact amounts of troops for this period are notoriously difficult to calculate, the direction of development among Western European states is nonetheless clear. According to one calculation the French army grew from 125,000 in 1648 to 340,000 men during the Nine Years' War.[11] The English army grew from around 40,000 in the pre-Williamite era to an average of 93,000 men during the War of the Spanish Succession, and in the final year of this war the British state had as many as 144,650 men under arms.[12] The Dutch army numbered 60,000 during the last years of the Eighty Years' War, passed the 100,000 mark during the Nine Years' War and almost reached the figure of 120,000 men at the height of the War of the Spanish Succession.[13] Expenses in troop payments rose accordingly. Chart 4.1 shows the monthly costs of soldiers' wages according to the war budget for the Province of Holland, alone responsible for around fifty-eight percent of all troop payments made by the state.[14] Chart 4.2 gives the costs of troop payments as a percentage of the total military budget (excluding the navy). Only in two years – 1715 and 1716 – did troop payments make up less than fifty-five percent of the total military budget.

---

11   Lynn 1995, p. 125.

12   Brewer 1988, p. 31.

13   Zwitzer 1991, pp. 175–6.

14   On the relation of this war budget to state finances in general, see Van Deursen 1976, and for the relations between the finances of the Province of Holland and those of the Dutch Republic, see the introduction to Fritschy and Liesker 2004.

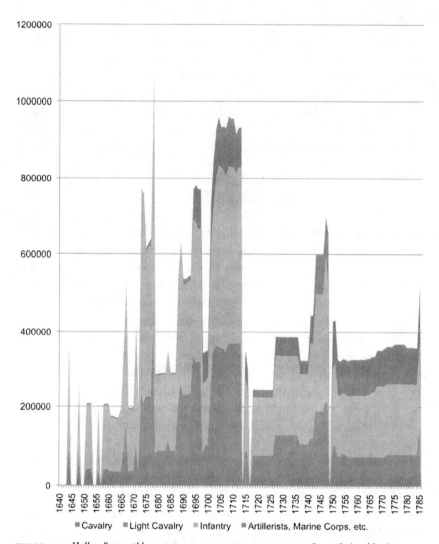

CHART 4.1   *Holland's monthly ex-ante expenses on troop payments, 1644–1785 (guilders)*
SOURCES: NA, ARCHIEF STATEN GENERAAL 1550–1796, NOS. 8054–8,
8060–94, 8096–281. 'ORDINARIS EN EXTRA-ORDINARIS STAAT VAN OORLOG
1644–1785'

For most of the period they comprised over two-thirds of total expenses, rising
to three-quarters or more at times of war. The system of troop payments had to
be adapted to channel this increased pressure. However, the essential feature of
the system as it had emerged from the war against the Spanish Habsburgs – the
independent role of the military solicitor in providing army funds – survived all
attempts at reform.

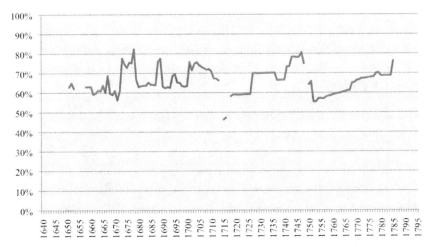

CHART 4.2   *Troop payments as percentage of ex-ante military expenditure, 1644–1785*
SOURCES: NA, ARCHIEF STATEN GENERAAL 1550–1796, NOS. 8054–8,
8060–94, 8096–281. 'ORDINARIS EN EXTRA-ORDINARIS STAAT VAN OORLOG
1644–1785'

As shown in Chapter One, the practice of 'military soliciting' slowly emerged from the various ways in which the state and individual officers dealt with financial emergencies arising in the long drawn-out struggle against the Spanish armies. By the time of the Twelve Years' Truce, making contracts with financial middlemen had become the preferred option to guarantee that troops were paid on time. But the practice of soliciting was still chaotic and state control was limited. From the 1620s onwards military solicitors figured frequently in the resolutions of the Holland Provincial Government. Sometimes general regulation was introduced to make troop payments run more smoothly. This, for example, was the case with the financial protection offered to solicitors who lost part of their investment due to military defeats.[15] But most of the time the members of the Provincial Government solved problems on a case to case basis. By far the most frequent mention of military solicitors occurred under the heading *Justitiële zaken* (judicial affairs) of the resolution indices. For lack of clear guidelines, conflicts between captains and their solicitors over payment, interest rates, or the clearing of debts were settled individually. In the resolutions of the Holland Provincial Government for the period 1624–59 tens of solicitors are mentioned by name, indicating the large number of investors

---

15   NA, Archief van de Gecommitteerde Raden van de Staten van Holland en Westfriesland, no. 3000B. 'Resoluties 1630–1635', fol. 132 vso.

involved in this line of business.[16] Many more resolutions dealt with financial conflicts between officers and private persons who were not solicitors but clearly fulfilled the same functions. Some solicitors surface in the resolutions more than once over a longer period, allowing for conclusions about their staying power. De Bruyne, Van der Mast and Meurskens, three financial agents who were already involved in the soliciting of French and English companies during the first and second decade of the seventeenth century, remained active during the 1630s, and in the case of Van der Mast even as late as 1651. A solicitor named Casembroot first appeared in the resolutions of the States General in 1613, when he handed in a complaint about large arrears suffered by the companies served by him. The name reappeared in connection to other problems in troop payment during the 1620s and 1630s, although this might have been a relative of the first Casembroot.[17] Indeed, there are many examples in which soliciting contracts were handed down from father to son. Also, like in many other businesses in the Republic, widows often continued the soliciting contracts of their deceased husbands.[18]

The resolutions not only prove the success and durability of some businesses, but also the troubles surrounding others. Since no rules existed to prescribe who could become a military solicitor, there also was no real system of control guaranteeing that those who entered the profession possessed the necessary creditworthiness. Frequently, solicitors themselves ran into arrears leaving 'their' captains without the means to pay the troops. This resulted in sharp conflicts and sometimes even in physical confrontation. During the late 1640s the military solicitor Paulus Maes was a frequent visitor of the offices of the Holland Provincial Government. In March 1649 an argument between this solicitor and a soldier from one of the companies that Maes 'served' became so high-pitched that it ended in a fight. According to Maes, this 'old and impotent soldier' had insulted him in the street. To the great dismay of the members of the Provincial Government, Maes had proceeded to hit him in the face 'until blood showed', and what was even worse, he had done so in the offices of one of the ushers of Holland's treasury. The authorities took special exception to the location of the crime. A fight involving a solicitor in one of the offices of the provincial authorities 'could only result in the diminution of Their Highly Esteemed Gentlemen and is incompatible with the respect which

---

16   NA, Archief Staten van Holland, no. 284–288. 'Indices gedrukte resoluties', 1600–68.

17   Van Deursen 1984, p. 82.

18   E.g., in the cases of Bonser and La Mair, two solicitors who were already involved in troop payments during the 1620, and whose widows were still active on the market during the 1640s.

should always be shown at the offices and other premises of the state'. Paulus Maes therefore had to pay a fine of thirty guilders.[19]

The Holland Provincial Government had ample reason to worry about the damage to its reputation that could result from cases such as this. In the period after the 1648 peace, expenditures for the troops had become a highly contested issue, resulting in armed confrontation between stadtholder William II and the city of Amsterdam. As happened so often, the debate on war finances went hand in hand with a debate on the efficiency of state finances in general. Allegations of corruption were flying. In 1652, an anonymous pamphlet argued for stricter examination of the accounts of the receiver general, explicitly directing its attention to the possibilities for fraud in army expenses. The author reserved some special venom for the Province of Holland, 'where by and by, affairs have been handled so horribly and godlessly', accusing the personnel of the office of the receiver general of profiting from trade in payment ordinances.[20] This trade was an essential feature of military soliciting, since ordinances served as guarantees for the loans of the solicitors themselves and were part of a substantial secondary market. The author of the pamphlet described this trade as immoral because it involved state officials in a profit scheme based on their own failure to pay the troops on time, the consequences of which were suffered directly by the ordinary soldiers. The pamphlet suggested that the state should take the monthly payment of the troops directly into its own hands.[21] This suggestion went to the heart of the existing practice, effectively demanding the abolition of military soliciting.

The anonymous pamphlet of 1652 did not stand alone in advocating a greater role for the state in troop payments. Just one year before, a commission of the States of Holland had delivered a report considering the possibilities of a system of 'per capita payment of the militia'. Although the commission concluded that the introduction of a system of direct payment through the central state treasury was not feasible, it spoke highly of the advantages it would entail:

> Per capita payment – if a solid ground for this could be found, and if such would be practicable by the deputies of the government itself – is judged by the commissioners to give a great splendour and respect to the state, and to bind the militia to the same with affection; also to be one of the

---

19   NA, Archief van de Gecommitteerde Raden van de Staten van Holland en Westfriesland, no. 3003. 'Resoluties 1647–1649', 26 March 1649.

20   Anonymous 1652, fol. 3 vso.

21   Anonymous 1652, fol. 3.

surest means to avoid frauds and to enable the country in every respect to clear the accounts of the soldiers, in quantity and quality.[22]

In a wonderfully concise way, this short paragraph formulates the major reasons why modern states from the end of the eighteenth century onwards would favour direct, non-brokerage systems of troop payment: to increase the power of the state, to augment its direct hold over the troops, and to close the existing avenues for fraud at the state's expense. But just as illuminating are the reasons why, according to the committee, centralisation remained unfeasible for the time being.

First, the commissioners re-established the 'incontestable' truth in army payment: 'that in order to maintain a well conditioned militia, the soldiers need short, precise and regulated payment'. However, neither the magistrates in the cities where the troops were garrisoned, nor the deputies of the province, nor deputies of the cities housing the Provincial treasuries, could guarantee such a continuous flow of money. For the group of officials to whom the task of payment was assigned, this would immediately raise the question of where to find credit, and according to the commissioners, without intermediation of solicitors their chances of finding enough money in time were slight. Even if a remedy could be found for the irregularity in state income, the underdeveloped nature of state bureaucracy would pose insurmountable barriers to centralisation. If the task of paying the troops was left to local officials, this would bring back some of the worst problems in the existing system of payment

> considering, that among those ... there are many persons of mean conditions, who will usually seek their own interests from one or another trade, and by this authority [over troop payments] will try to gain some direction over companies and officers ...[23]

The 1651 report clearly shows that in the minds of Dutch policy-makers in the middle of the seventeenth century, troop payments, state access to the credit market, the personal financial capacities of state officials, and the dangers of corruption were closely interrelated problems. In the eyes of the commissioners these problems could not simply be overcome by the introduction of tighter control from above. As an example of the limits of bureaucracy they pointed to

---

22   NA, Archief Staten van Holland, no. 1354 f. 'Consideratien teegen het doen van hoofdelyke betaalinge aande militie', 1651.

23   Ibid.

the King of Spain, 'who despite so much supervision and control over the same payment is being cheated more than anyone'. Similar weaknesses would prevent the introduction of a system of payment through national or provincial envoys, leading the commissioners to the conclusion that 'it was not possible to find a foundation or system by which to regulate per capita payment in such a way that it could be introduced and practiced in good service and orderly fashion'. Attempts to introduce a system of direct payment therefore had to be postponed to the indefinite future. For the time being the report recommended concentrating on fighting the 'frauds and disorders' in the existing system by the introduction of stronger regulation.

Apart from the openly stated reasons of inexpediency, a strong political bias among the commissioners towards solutions that avoided strict state control over troop payment and gave much room to the market certainly played a role in coming to their negative advice. Stadtholder William II's failed attack on Amsterdam and his death soon afterwards had greatly strengthened the anti-centralising wing of the Dutch ruling class, led by the States of Holland. The clash with William II had been directly connected to military expenditures, and the Great Assembly called in the early months of 1651 was dominated by Holland's fight for provincial autonomy, against the reconstitution of the stadtholderate, and for greater provincial control over army finances. The measures taken at the Great Assembly effectively led to devolution of power over the army towards the provincial level, with Holland consolidating its influence most successfully.[24] By strengthening the most commercially-oriented sections of the Dutch ruling class, these reforms also enhanced the partnership between state and private capital which formed the economic basis of brokerage practices. The turn against centralisation in the 1650s thus forms an early example of the close connection between the resistance to increased state control, the provincial particularism that was strongly entrenched in the Dutch political system, and the commercial prosperity that allowed Dutch Republican rulers to rely on the market with much more success than any of their competitors.

After the 1651 report, suggestions to replace the system of military soliciting by a system of direct payment temporarily disappeared from the political agenda. However, important new regulation was introduced, as the commissioners suggested. One of the prime targets was to bar holders of public office from soliciting. These measures were designed to deal with the allegations that financial agency was upheld in order to provide lucrative opportunities for indi-

---

24   Groenveld 1997, pp. 81–2.

viduals within the state apparatus. The charge was certainly not unwarranted. The intermingling of public office and military financial agency had strong antecedents, and went up to the highest regions of administration. Already in the early 1590s receiver general Philip Doubleth had advanced his private money for troop payments.[25] In all likelihood his family continued this lucrative business. In 1659 a younger member of the Doubleth-clan was involved in judicial cases on soliciting that appeared before the Holland Provincial Government.[26] It is not surprising that officials of lower rank tried to get a foothold in this business as well. Given the number of times that decrees had to be repeated and extended prohibiting soliciting by clerks, registrars and public accountants, it seems that separating the worlds of officialdom and financial agency remained an uphill battle well into the eighteenth century.[27]

In 1669 the Provincial Government undertook a serious attempt to clear the Holland Audit Offices of personal involvement in military soliciting. On 5 March it declared that all clerks working for the treasury and the administrative department had to 'effectively and actually quit and let go' of the soliciting of companies.[28] Two days later clerks and accountants were summoned to appear before a commissioner of the States of Holland. Out of twenty-three officials who gave a statement that morning, six were directly involved in troop payments. Clerk of the treasury Harman, auditor Willem Bronsvelt, and clerk Willem Hulshout all 'served' more than one company. Arent and Philips Pijll, both working at the secretary's office, functioned as solicitors for the company of a close relative who was a captain. Accountant of the treasury Bellecherie tried to excuse himself by stating that he did not receive a salary for soliciting the company of count Maurits of Nassau, but 'only was sometimes honoured with an allowance or the like'. Nonetheless, after a stern admonition by his interlocutor, he as well as the others had to promise to resign from soliciting.[29] Despite this apparent strictness, the long-term effect of those measures

---

25   Japikse 1923, p. 159.

26   NA, Archief van de Gecommitteerde Raden van de Staten van Holland en Westfriesland, no. 3009. 'Resoluties 1659', 28 August 1659. On the Doubleth family, see 't Hart 1987 and 't Hart 1993a, pp. 193–4.

27   E.g. NA, Archief van de Gecommitteerde Raden van de Staten van Holland en Westfriesland. 'Resoluties 1729', no. 3079, fol. 56, 9 February 1729, and no. 3085. 'Resoluties 1735', fol. 7–7vso, 8 January 1735.

28   NA, Archief van de Gecommitteerde Raden van de Staten van Holland en Westfriesland. 'Resoluties 1669', no. 3018, 5 March 1669.

29   NA, Archief van de Gecommitteerde Raden van de Staten van Holland en Westfriesland. 'Resoluties 1669', no. 3018, 7 March 1669.

remained limited. In the Dutch Republic, where politics and finance were so intimately interwoven, open or hidden routes between the one and the other could always be found.

4.2   A Golden Age of Military Soliciting

Although the States of Holland did not manage to enforce a strict separation between state officialdom and financial intermediation for the army, in the ensuing years they did intervene to restrict the involvement in military soliciting to more or less professional financiers with strong connections to the capital market. After a brief experiment with a form of state controlled financial intermediation in the early 1670s, military soliciting was re-established on a more solid footing. The four decades of warfare with France that followed created enormous possibilities for military financiers, and those who were able to keep their businesses afloat were able to make fortunes during this period. The increased state dependence on financial intermediaries is an example of how warfare did not automatically lead to nationalisation or centralisation, with states intervening decisively to regulate markets and increasing their influence over society, but could instead strengthen brokerage practices involving reliance on capitalist entrepreneurs.

The joint attack by France, England, and the bishoprics of Munster and Cologne of 1672, one of the gravest military crises in the history of the Republic, at first renewed the cry for a complete reform in the system of troop payments. Growing financial strains seriously affected the ability of the army to put up resistance against the French advance in the south. The weaknesses in army finance were already well known at the time of the fall of Johan de Witt, the leading statesman of the post-1648 period and main opponent of William III. In his final address to the States of Holland, he complained

> that Holland alone has contributed its dues, and Zeeland and Friesland have not furnished the costs of the army; and that posterity will not believe, that such losses can happen in so little time ...[30]

Faced with an army that was unprepared and a country immersed in the political turmoil of the Orangist toppling of the De Witt regime, the French army advanced with great ease to the borders of the Province of Holland,

---

[30]   Hop and Viven 1903, p. 245.

occupying the entire southern half of the Republic. With war at its doorstep and much of the other provinces under French occupation, Holland was forced to take upon itself even more of the financial burden of warfare than the regular 58 percent. Alone, it had to pay for 110 out of 160 companies on horse, and 457 out of 666 companies on foot.[31] In November of that year, with army costs rising to over ƒ9 million, members of the Holland Provincial Government reported a deficit of almost ƒ6 million. It was at this point that they harked back to the 1651 discussions and again proposed to bypass the solicitors as a means to cut back on unnecessary expenses,

> because by doing this, the militia would be encouraged and the solicitors and other secondary costs would be discarded; and the credit of the country would thereby increase, and the enemy would sooner be inclined to conclude peace ...[32]

Stadtholder William III, at that time already firmly in charge of the state, took a personal interest in the organisation of army finances. According to one biographer, since his coming to power it was William III rather than the States General who 'determined all military and naval policy'.[33] In January 1673 he exhorted the States of Holland to take measures for the redemption of the burdens on the war budget, adding that there was 'periculum in mora'.[34]

Heading this call, the members of the Holland Provincial Government took practical steps to alter the structure of army financing. Their main aim was a drastic reduction of the number of solicitors, thereby tightening bureaucratic control over the process of paying the troops. On 28 February 1673 they ordered that all existing companies on the payroll of the Province of Holland would be divided among no more than eight solicitors, determining from above which companies would fall under whom. This meant that each of the eight solicitors among this select group would arrange for the payment of seventy-five to eighty companies. New companies that were to be recruited would be divided among the same group.[35] On 2 March the Holland Provincial Government

---

31   Hop and Viven 1903, p. 250.

32   Hop and Viven 1903, pp. 325–6.

33   Troost 2005, p. 106.

34   Troost 2005, p. 387.

35   NA, Archief van de Gecommitteerde Raden van de Staten van Holland en Westfriesland, no. 3022. 'Resoluties 1673', fol. 156 vso – fol. 161 vso, 28 February 1673. The eight solicitors (number of companies between brackets) were: Johan Dellon (80), David van Hattum (80), Johan van de Heijde (80), Abraham Elsevier (80), Hendrick Winckel (79), Diderick

ordered the receiver general and urban receivers not to give out ordinances to any solicitor except the appointed eight.[36] These measures did not only consist in a drastic reduction in the number of solicitors. They amounted to a whole new system of payment, in which the military solicitors would ultimately be replaced by ten 'directors for the payment of the militia'.[37] The Provincial Government would commission the directors, and the States of Holland would provide them with a sum of f_1 million to be remitted to the troops through direct and per capita payment. The directors would operate in the name of the state, and were to pay only the soldiers whose name was on the muster roll. Thereby, they would bypass the independent role of officers in the system of troop payments and effectively strengthen state control over the make-up of companies. Another innovation was the planned division of the entire army into ten parts of equal strength, each resorting under the responsibility of one of the directors. However, not all features of soliciting were superseded. In case the province remained in arrears, the directors were still expected to pay the troops out of their own means 'or those of their friends', for which they would receive 16 *stuyvers* per hundred guilders every pay month or 6.9 percent interest per year.[38] Affirming the continuity with the old system, the proposal at one point described the new functionaries as 'solicitors or directors'.[39] Nevertheless, if it would have been successful the introduction of this system of payment would have been a real step towards the ideal sketched in the report of 1651.

However, the new scheme did not work out as planned. A strong testimony of this comes from a later generation of solicitors. Arguing against a somewhat similar reform attempt of the early 1720s, they pointed with glee to the failure of 1673:

> [D]espite the authority, power and command with which the general directory was invested ... and above that being assisted with a million guilders from the provincial treasury ... after a few months it ... collapsed out of its own accord ...

---

de Wilde (75), Dirck Arnouts (79) and Willem Bronsfelt (75), the audit officer mentioned in the previous section.

36 NA, Archief van de Gecommitteerde Raden van de Staten van Holland en Westfriesland, no. 3022. 'Resoluties 1673', fol. 162 vso–163, 2 March 1673.

37 Staten Generaal 1682, pp. 171–3.

38 Ibid.

39 Staten Generaal 1682, p. 172.

According to the same testimony, this collapse had created 'such confusions' and financial chaos that the military solicitors who once again replaced the directors after the failure of the new system could only find credit at interest rates of nine to ten percent.[40] The reason for this abysmal failure was simple. Under the immediate pressure of war, the appointed directors proved incapable of providing the necessary funds for the maintenance of the army and the levying of substitute recruits. According to the war budget of 1673, total costs of the companies solicited by the eight directors exceeded one million guilders per pay month.[41] Despite the initial advance to the directors of a million guilders from the general means, frequent recourse had to be taken to emergency payments to the soldiers directly from the provincial treasury. The first time this occurred was only half a year after the introduction of the new system.[42] In January of the next year the order to give out ordinances only to the directors of payment was temporarily withdrawn. This meant that apart from the eight directors, individual solicitors could once again step in as financial agents and creditors to Holland's companies, confirming the statement from the 1720s that reforms did not last more than a couple of months.[43] Around the same time as this unofficial re-entry of a more or less free market for soliciting, allegations of corruption were levelled against one of the appointed directors, Diderick de Wilde. Although the accusation that he had pocketed money destined for the troops was quickly cleared, the rumours further helped to discredit the new system of payment.[44] The failure of the 1673 reform attempt led to a de facto reintroduction of the pre-1673 situation, but in the heated conditions of war and a permanent quest for funds, the situation on the ground became even more chaotic than it had been and interest rates soared. When the members of the Holland Provincial Government tried to deal with this chaos, they had learned their lesson. Instead of a complete reform of the system of army payments, in 1676 they chose to officially restore military soliciting on a much firmer judicial basis. As the 1651 report had predicted, the weakness of state finances, com-

---

40   NA, Archief Staten van Holland, no. 1905. 'Ingekomen stukken 1723', 'Request of the Military
       Solicitors to the States of Holland', 14 April 1723.

41   NA, Archief Staten Generaal, no. 8081. 'Staat van Oorlog 1673'.

42   NA, Archief van de Gecommitteerde Raden van de Staten van Holland en Westfriesland,
       no. 3022. 'Resoluties 1673', fol. 745–745 vso, 6 November 1673.

43   NA, Archief van de Gecommitteerde Raden van de Staten van Holland en Westfriesland,
       no. 3023. 'Resoluties 1674', fol. 22 vso–23, 22 January 1674.

44   NA, Archief van de Gecommitteerde Raden van de Staten van Holland en Westfriesland,
       no. 3023. 'Resoluties 1674', fol. 104 vso–105 vso, 8 March 1674, and fol. 158–160, 13 April
       1674.

bined with the lack of strong bureaucratic structures, had forced the States of Holland back into the arms of private financiers.

The 1672 invasion marked a caesura in Dutch history. A period of four decades of almost continuous warfare started, in which both the Dutch supremacy in world trade and the health of Dutch state finances were seriously threatened. It was a crucial turning point in the development of the Dutch Republic as a great power. But for military financiers the sharpening of international rivalry announced an era of prosperity. The combination of a steep rise in military expenditure and a further institutionalisation of brokerage practices created the conditions for a golden age of soliciting. On 13 March 1676 the Holland Provincial Government accepted a resolution that introduced extensive and precise regulation for financial intermediation in troop payments. The resolution laid the foundation for the system of soliciting as it remained in place for over a century. Referring to the situation that had preceded and followed the 1673 reform attempt, it tried to put an end to 'the excesses and exorbitances that, to the great disservice to the country, are undertaken by some solicitors of companies on horse and on foot'. Among those excesses the resolution listed

> blackmailing and negotiating unbearable interest rates ... as well as too high salaries or rewards enjoyed by aforementioned solicitors for soliciting of ... the ordinances and for managing the affairs of the companies ...

As the main reason, the resolution pointed to the advent of 'different persons of very small means and potential, in large part or entirely ignorant of the practice of soliciting of companies or the handling of money'.[45]

The resolution proposed a number of measures which remained the cornerstones of government control of soliciting. The most important was the reduction of the total number of solicitors to thirty-two 'qualified, well-to-do and capable persons'. Those solicitors had to solemnly swear an oath containing the conditions on which they accepted their commission. The resolution initially limited the interest rate on payments advanced to 6.9 percent annually, an amount that was later reduced to 5.2 percent. It also imposed a maximum on the salary solicitors would receive from the companies they served. Furthermore, solicitors were stipulated to deposit a sum of f5,000, which in case of malpractice would accrue to the provincial treasury. This advance payment

---

45   NA, Archief van de Gecommitteerde Raden van de Staten van Holland en Westfriesland, no. 3026. 'Resoluties 1676', fol. 117 vso–118 vso, 13 March 1676.

primarily served to keep out the 'persons of very small means' mentioned in the 1676 resolution.

Although the 1676 reform increased state control of the practice of soliciting, it also contained considerable benefits for the solicitors themselves. By creating a far clearer legal framework within which they could work, it provided a basis for judicial protection of their interests. This protection was extended in the decades that followed, especially during the War of the Spanish Succession when military solicitors were in a particularly strong position to put demands to the state. A resolution of September 1706 extended the collateral for captains' debts from arms to the company's wagons, horses and equipment.[46] Another resolution from around the same time banned 'Jews and the associates of Jews' from soliciting, thereby allegedly limiting 'outside' competition to the 'indigenous' financiers.[47] In 1711 the Holland Provincial Government resolved that all companies within the same regiment should strive to deal with the same solicitor. They also restricted the freedom of captains to leave their solicitor in favour of another.[48] However, there was still a lot of room for negotiation between captains and their agents. Interest rates, for example, were not simply determined by the maximum rate that was set by the States of Holland, but were negotiated individually. Paulus Gebhardt, the solicitor responsible for the payment of companies from Brandenburg and the Paltz – whose business will be examined in more detail in the coming sections – charged interest rates between 4.8 and 5.2 percent at the start of the Nine Years' War, but lowered these to 4.3 percent at the end of this war.[49] During the War of the Spanish Succession, the pressure was in the opposite direction, and interest rates went up from 4.5 percent to 5.85 percent in 1713. Unable to counter this upward pressure, the States of Holland in 1711 agreed to raise the maximum interest rate to 5.64 percent, but even this higher maximum rate was not respected in practice.[50]

---

46   NA, Archief van de Gecommitteerde Raden van de Staten van Holland en Westfriesland, no. 3056. 'Resoluties 1706', fol. 425, 29 September 1706.

47   NA, Archief van de Gecommitteerde Raden van de Staten van Holland en Westfriesland, no. 3056. 'Resoluties 1706', fol. 471 vso, 22 October 1706. Perhaps this move was also a concession to anti-Semitic aspects of anti-stadtholderly propaganda, which had sometimes been directed towards the large proportion of Sephardic Jews in William III's financial entourage.

48   NA, Archief van de Gecommitteerde Raden van de Staten van Holland en Westfriesland, no. 3061. 'Resoluties 1711', fol. 94, 17 February 1711.

49   NA, Archief Paulus Gebhardt, no. 77. 'Liquidatieboek Interesten 1689–1698'.

50   Fritschy and Liesker 1996, p. 180.

The ability of solicitors to raise interest rates above the legally determined maximum illustrates the strength of their position. The self-consciousness of the new layer of financiers that arose in this way was further bolstered by the notoriously strong bonds between stadtholder William III and the world of finance. A small illustration of the sense of self-importance that could result from these conditions is a court case from 1682, in which the city of Utrecht formally discharged military solicitor Johan Lieftingh and banished him from the town and its surroundings for a drunken rant in a pub. According to several witnesses, the solicitor had shouted:

> That he was on equal terms with the States [of Utrecht]; that he was not in their power; that he did not depend on them, but the States depended on him; that if he wanted to speak to His Highness [stadtholder William III], he could make some of them be fired with infamy; that all the Gentlemen States were thieves – all the while stamping the ground with his feet and using several insolent words and threats ... And around the same time, the defendant had repeatedly told several military men, in speaking of the payment of the militia on the payroll of the States of said Province, that the officers looked at the wrong end for a solution: that they should band together with him and other solicitors, and that together they would go to the Prince His Highness.[51]

The failure of the 1673 attempt at a system of payment controlled by state officials led to a consolidation of brokerage practices rather than their absorption into the (provincial or central) state bureaucracy. But regulation did succeed in limiting access to this line of business, so vital to the preservation of the state, to a small number of financial specialists, replacing the free-for-all that had existed for most of the seventeenth century. In this way, entry to military soliciting gradually became closed off for the likes of the painter Theodoor van der Schuur (1628–1707), who according to an eighteenth-century biographer

> came to the conclusion that Pluto's grains of gold and silver should not be laden in his coffers with shovels but with full ships; for which reason he leaned towards a more profitable profession. He became military solicitor in The Hague, but soon found out that there is truth in the famous saying 'that everything is equally close to anyone, but not equally useful'. His iron

---

51   Gerechte der Stad Utrecht 1682, fol. A2 vso–A3.

coffer fell from dropsy to tuberculosis, his purse collected more wrinkles than the painted face of Petrus, and he almost solicited a place in the hospital for himself, until he was saved by his old friends.[52]

4.3   Two Careers in Military Finance

A very different type of investor became associated with military soliciting after the 1676 reform. Two substantial business archives of such influential war financiers have survived. The first belongs to Paulus Gebhardt, a low-placed functionary who became a large-scale solicitor through the patronage of William III. Gebhardt's business flourished during the Nine Years' War but dwindled shortly after the death of his mighty protector. The second is the archive of Hendrik van Heteren III, whose family had steadily risen through the ranks of the Holland bureaucracy in the course of the seventeenth century. Van Heteren successfully extended his soliciting enterprise during the War of the Spanish Succession and managed to sustain himself as a large-scale financier until his death in 1749. Concentrated on the late seventeenth and first half of the eighteenth century, containing ledgers, individual accounts with captains, and correspondence, these two archives provide an extraordinary wealth of information on the practice of soliciting during its 'golden age'. Furthermore, they shed light on two very different career paths, uniquely highlighting the conditions that determined great success or (partial) failure.

Unfortunately, Gebhardt's career before 1689 remains almost entirely in the shadows. His name, a brother in Frankfurt and his Lutheran faith tell of his German descent. In all likelihood Gebhardt came to the Dutch Republic through a job in the army. In 1674 he appeared before a notary in The Hague as a witness in a conflict between two officers.[53] Two years later he acted as a witness of a financial transaction during the siege of Maastricht. He did so for a captain Dolman, of whom according to the same document he had been secretary, a function he 'presently [fulfilled] with the Lord Count of Nassau'.[54] As company secretary, Gebhardt must have performed his administrative duties close to the actual field of battle. In a testimony about the death of a certain Cyrianus Boderher during the siege of Maastricht, Gebhardt declared 'that above mentioned Boderher was shot in the head in the *aproches* near Maastricht and

---

52   Weyerman 1769, p. 156.

53   The Hague Municipal Archive, Notarieel Archief (HGA – NA), no. 595, fol. 375.

54   HGA – NA, no. 731, fol. 216.

had been dead immediately', and further testified 'that he had seen that above mentioned Boderher had been carried to the grave'.[55]

From this moment on Gebhardt appears frequently in the The Hague's notary archives as 'secretary and auditor' of the regiment of the Guards or Guards Dragoons of William III.[56] In the decade of armed peace between the Peace of Nijmegen of 1678 and the resumption of hostilities after 1688, his tasks seem to have become farther removed from the daily life of the regiment. As a company secretary he was involved in business transactions connected to supply.[57] That this could be a source of serious conflict between him and the officers appears from a request by Gebhardt for disciplinary action against a captain who had insulted him in a conversation with another captain. Reputedly, the captain had told his colleague: 'You have a neat auditor. His name is written on the gallows'.[58]

Luckily for Gebhardt, this seems not to have been the shared opinion among his employers. For a couple of months he even worked at the castle of Doorwerth in the Province of Guelders. William III personally frequented this castle for hunting purposes, and Gebhardt's employment there seems to signal his involvement in increasingly important financial operations.[59] However, his personal wealth at that time must have been modest. During his five month stay at Doorwerth, Gebhardt rented out his house at the west end of the Kalvermarkt in The Hague for a sum of sixty guilders.[60] At a yearly rent of 144 guilders, the possession of this house was not a sign of great riches.[61] Another indication of his modest status was his marriage to Anna Tros, announced during Gebhardt's brief spell at Doorwerth. Despite a certain amount of liberalism in familial relations, marriage and status remained closely intertwined among the higher classes in the Dutch Republic. For entrepreneurs a well chosen marriage

---

55   HGA – NA, no. 462, fol. 260r–260vso.

56   E.g., on 13 October 1678, HGA – NA, no. 655, 741, and on 23 November 1682, HGA – NA, no. 464, fol. 442.

57   E.g., in 1685, he signed a contract for the production of saddlecloths and other equipment in the name of Lieutenant Colonel Eppens. HGA – NA, no. 1008, fol. 210.

58   HGA – NA, no. 1022, fol. 61.

59   William III to William Bentinck, 27 and 30 July 1683, Japikse 1927, pp. 13–14.

60   HGA – NA, no. 464, fol. 442.

61   Comparisons should be made with great care given the differences in real estate prices per city, but Clé Lesger notes rents of $f40$ per year for houses of simple craftsmen in Amsterdam. See: Lesger 1986, pp. 92–3. Bonke 1996, pp. 121ff. gives $f100 – f200$ as an average yearly rent in Rotterdam. However, in the smaller town Enkhuyzen $f210$ already seems to have been a yearly rent of a prosperous household, according to Soltow and Van Zanden 1998, pp. 33–4.

could be a way to strengthen or expand business connections.[62] But Gebhardt's marriage connected him only to lower officialdom. His correspondence shows a strong familial bond with his brother-in-law, the Nijmegen city clerk Barthel Tros, and his sister-in-law Johanna Tros, who married the urban receiver De Jonghste of the same town. A notary act from 1691 also mentions 'the late Harman Tros, by life clerk of the Finance Office of the Nijmegen quarter'.[63] Clearly, these connections indicate that Gebhardt moved in circles of provincial financial officials. However, although having such middle-ranking positions in one of the less influential towns of the Republic might have helped one to become a town notable, they certainly did not provide an easy inroad into the Dutch ruling elite.

Real social advance for Gebhardt came after the start of the Nine Years' War. During or after William III's English expedition Gebhardt entered into the service of Willem van Schuylenburg, treasurer of the Nassau Domain Council and one of the central financial players within the stadtholder's Dutch entourage.[64] At that time Van Schuylenburg was involved in financing the recruitment of troops from Brandenburg, Celle and Wolffenbuttel, Hessen-Kassel and Würtemberg for William's 1688 campaign, transferring some ƒ800,000 from the treasury of receiver general Van Ellemeet to the German allies.[65] After William's ascension to the English throne, these troops became jointly financed by the Dutch and English treasuries. As clerk of Van Schuylenburg, Gebhardt was given the responsibility for the payment of a large number of those companies. From 1689 onwards he fulfilled all the functions of a military solicitor, executing his tasks essentially as an independent business for his own profit. He kept on doing so in the service of Van Schuylenburg until the middle of the 1690s.[66] On 22 March 1695 he acquired permission to act as a solicitor in his own right for the Province of Groningen.[67] Admission as solicitor by the Holland Provincial Government followed a year later.[68] His employment by Willem van Schuylenburg allowed Gebhardt to enter the business of soliciting on a

---

62   Adams 2005, pp. 145 ff.

63   HGA – NA, no. 587, pp. 280–1.

64   Onnekink 2007, p. 88 and p. 101.

65   NA, Archief Raad van State, no. 1903. 'Memorie', October 1688.

66   NA, Archief Paulus Gebhardt, nos. 64 and 65. 'Registers van ontvangsten en uitgaven, bijgehouden door Paulus Gebhardt ten behoeve van Willem van Schuylenburg, "raad en rekenmeester" van Willem III, prins van Oranje 1690–1696'.

67   HGA – NA, no. 672, p. 31.

68   NA, Archief van de Gecommitteerde Raden van de Staten van Holland en Westfriesland, no. 3046. 'Resoluties 1696', 11 May 1696.

grand scale. In 1689 he already served thirty companies.[69] By 1695 the number had grown to ten complete regiments and twenty-three separate companies. In total, Gebhardt had to supply these troops with a yearly pay of almost ƒ1.5 million.[70] Among his clients were most of the Brandenburg regiments, regiments from Brunswick-Lunenburg and Saxen-Gotha.[71] After the 1697 Peace of Rijswijk, the Dutch Republic immediately started to discharge its foreign regiments. The result was a sharp drop in the size of Gebhardt's transactions. By 1699 he only did business with one complete regiment, the infantry regiment under the direction of lieutenant general Ernst Wilhelm von Salisch, and nine individual companies.[72] Of course, his income suffered greatly from this. However, the quick resumption of war seemed to rescue his business for the long term. The Dutch Republic drew up new contracts with German principalities, including Brandenburg-Prussia and the Palatinate.

His strong German connections helped Gebhardt to step in as solicitor, and opportunities seemed great. By January 1703 the size of the payments provided through him already exceeded the monthly average of 1695.[73] But that year disaster struck for Gebhardt, showing the vulnerability of the business of a military solicitor to the vagaries of high politics. The death of William III in the spring of 1702 created serious diplomatic fallout. On 17 May 1702, the King of Prussia stated a claim on William's Dutch inheritance, leading to prolonged conflict with the rather uncooperative States General and William's even more resistant Friesland heirs.[74] The resulting deterioration of relations between the Republic and a number of German allies led to the ending or renegotiation of a large number of troop contracts.[75] Gebhardt was kept out of all new contracts. By 29 July 1703 he had ended his engagement with most of his former clientele, remaining solicitor only for Von Salisch and a small number of

---

69   Based on NA, Archief Paulus Gebhardt, no. 77. 'Liquidatieboek interesten 1689–1698'.

70   NA, Archief Paulus Gebhardt, no. 48. 'Register van maandstaten 1695'.

71   A genealogy of the different regiments is given in Ten Raa 1950, pp. 337 ff.

72   NA, Archief Paulus Gebhardt, no. 51. 'Register van maandstaten 1699', and no. 62. 'Liquidatieboek van maandsoldijen 1699'.

73   NA, Archief Paulus Gebhardt, nos. 54 and 55, 'Registers van maandstaten 1702–1703', no. 67. 'Liquidatieboek van maandsoldijen 1703', and no. 81. 'Stukken betreffende liquidaties met Baron de Rhoo, 1695–1703'.

74   Bruggeman 2007, pp. 205–7.

75   The contract with Lunenburg-Celle was renegotiated on 22 December 1702, with Saxen-Gotha on 7 April 1703 and with Hessen-Kassel on 10 April 1703. NA, Archief Staten van Holland 1572–1795, resp. no. 5134. 'Resoluties 1701', fol. 582–3; no. 5136. 'Resoluties 1703', fol. 216; and fol. 224.

individual companies. Still, it is clear that his fifteen years of close involvement in military soliciting had brought him great financial windfalls. There are many small markers showing that Gebhardt could now maintain the lifestyle of the rich. These include the ample allowance of ƒ610 he paid to his son Hermanus Gebhardt who went to Leiden University, as well as the sum of ƒ6,470 on his account for 1708–9 for the building of a new stable and coach house, a wall around his garden and repairs on one of his several houses.[76] Another small mark of class distinction can be found in a letter from 1713, in which he asked a friend to find him 'some of the lesser people' who could be employed to collect feathers to embellish his harpsichord.[77] Even when he had ceased to be a major war investor for a decade, his past involvement in financing two of the largest and most destructive military confrontations Europe had ever seen had earned him enough to enjoy a life of luxury, leisure and high culture.

The career of Hendrik van Heteren III shows some similarities with that of Gebhardt, but ended very differently. His much stronger embeddedness in Holland's ruling class seems to have provided his business with the necessary staying power to survive major shifts in the political situation. Like Gebhardt, Van Heteren initially came to soliciting through his political connections, although in contrast to Gebhardt these connections stemmed from a long family history in the service of the Dutch state. His father and grandfather (Hendrik I and Hendrik II) had slowly worked themselves up from low-ranking positions as ushers at the offices of the States of Holland and the receiver general to middle-level officialdom.[78] Gradually, Hendrik van Heteren's father had built his network acting as a solicitor (in the general sense) for a number of diplomatic representatives. Both predecessors had engaged in business with the army, but only as a secondary part of their enterprises.[79] Nevertheless this had also brought the family close to the court of William III, a connection that

---

76   NA, Archief Paulus Gebhardt, no. 21. 'Grootboek 1701–1713', pp. 210–12.

77   Paulus Gebhardt to S. Siebert, 25 September 1713, NA, Archief Paulus Gebhardt, no. 39. 'Brievenboek 1713–1714', p. 133.

78   Knevel 2010, pp. 109–10.

79   For Hendrik van Heteren I: NA, Archief Gecommitteerde Raden van Holland en West-friesland, no. 3014. 'Resoluties 1665', 23 June 1665, and for Hendrik van Heteren II: NA, Familiearchief Van Heteren, no. 8. 'Ordonanties'. As officials, both his father and grand-father were also involved in financial transfers for military purposes. E.g., in his function as clerk of the Generalty Audit Office, Hendrik van Heteren II had handled a ƒ120,000 budget for renewing fortifications in the city of Nijmegen in 1688 and 1689. NA, Familiearchief Van Heteren Suplement, no. 16. 'Reeckeninge van Hendrick van Heteren ... als tot de fortificatie wercken der stadt Nimmegen'.

provided crucial support for the career of Hendrik van Heteren III.[80] Merely in his twenties, his father managed to secure him a job at the office of the receiver general in the closing years of the seventeenth century, while the father himself had become increasingly involved in soliciting troop payments.[81] For the young Hendrik III, political functions would soon become subordinate to those he exercised as a financial agent.

It was the War of the Spanish Succession that laid the foundation of Van Heteren's fortune. Following in his father's footsteps, he had already acted as financial agent for a select group of diplomats in the service of the Republic before the start of the war.[82] But the outbreak of hostilities allowed him to expand his clientele in highly profitable directions. Among his newly acquired clients were field marshal Hendrik van Nassau-Ouwerkerk, lieutenant general Tilly, quartermaster general Pieter Mongeij and wagon master general Zuerius.[83] By far the biggest contract he managed to lay his hands on was in the 'soliciting' of oats and hay. Horse-feed was one of the lynchpins of army contracting. Just as wars in the age of the tank thrive on waves of oil, early modern warfare floated on fodder. Contracts for the provisioning of bread and hay were large and had been concentrated into few hands ever since the introduction of a new logistical system focused on central bread magazines during the Franco-Dutch War of 1672–78.[84] This concentration was reflected in the size of financial advances required to guarantee the delivery of oats and hay. Between 1706 and 1711, Van Heteren handled contracts worth the astounding sum of ƒ4 million.[85]

Of course, the end of the War of the Spanish Succession and the ensuing decline of military expenses created a major change in business opportunities for military solicitors. The case of Hendrik van Heteren shows how well-placed financiers could survive such shifts by using a variety of strategies that were common to all early modern merchants and financiers. In the aftermath of

---

80   Wilders 2010, p. 78.

81   NA, Familiearchief Van Heteren Suplement, no. 19. 'Notitie vande Capitalen die den Agent vander Heck vande comijs Van Heteren heeft genegotieert'.

82   NA, Familiearchief Van Heteren, nos. 26 and 32. 'Rekening Gerard Kuijsten', and 'Stukken Christiaan Carel, baron van Lintelo tot de Ehze'.

83   NA, Familiearchief Van Heteren, no. 28. 'Aantekeningen liquidaties'.

84   Van Nimwegen 1995, pp. 20 ff., Van Nimwegen 2010, pp. 366 ff.

85   NA, Familiearchief Van Heteren, no. 118. 'Administratie Zeger Gorisz, etc.'. Van Heteren's archive contains valuable additional sources on conditions for contracting, organization and payment of fodder contracts, particularly NA, Familiearchief Van Heteren Supplement, nos. 77–84.

the War of the Spanish Succession, Van Heteren assertively used his family connections in order to consolidate and expand his business. In 1718 his marriage with Margaretha Lormier, daughter of military solicitor Claudius Lormier, strengthened his financial network.[86] Willem Lormier, brother of Margaretha, had been an associate of Van Heteren since at least 1711, when they jointly handled fodder contracts for the Danish troops.[87] Around the time of the marriage he inherited his father's business, giving him a yearly income of f9,000. After the death of his mother, Willem Lormier likewise inherited the family capital of f80,000, further strengthening the financial base of their partnership.[88] Indirectly, the marriage also connected Van Heteren to Adriaan van der Kaa, married to Margaretha's sister Woutrina Lormier. Like Willem Lormier, Van der Kaa had been involved in fodder contracts with Van Heteren, and from 1724 to 1739 he held the desirable post of designated contractor of the fodder storages.[89] Another family connection that provided Van Heteren with important business opportunities was that with his nephew Leonard Vermeulen, who like Van Heteren came from a family of officials in state finances that had made the transition to soliciting.[90] In the immediate aftermath of the War of the Spanish Succession, Vermeulen had become the agent of Wilhelm van Nassau-Dillenburg, a high-ranking officer in the States army.[91] In 1724 he became solicitor for Wilhelm's brother Christiaan, a position that Hendrik van Heteren took over in 1730 when Leonard Vermeulen died.[92]

Using his family connections was not the only important element of Van Heteren's business strategy. His papers show him actively diversifying his clientele as a financial agent and investor. He took on both military contracts, largely in extension of his previous business as solicitor, and non-military contracts, for example handling the salaries of a number of Dutch diplomatic envoys and

---

86   'Lormier', *De Navorscher*, Vol. LXXXV (1936), pp. 262–3.

87   NA, Familiearchief Van Heteren, no. 124. 'Stukken betreffende een vordering op de Koning van Denemarken'.

88   'Willem Lormier', P.C. Molhuysen and P.J. Blok (eds), *Nieuw Nederlandsch Biografisch Woordenboek.* Vol. I, pp. 1097–8.

89   NA, Familiearchief Van Heteren, nos. 129 and 131. 'Rekeningen aannemers magazijnen van fourage', and 'Liquidaties Adriaan van Kaa, aannemer magazijnen van fourage'.

90   In 1635, a Leonard Vermeulen (perhaps the grandfather of Van Heteren's nephew) was admitted as ordinary clerk in the Generalty Audit Office. NA, Familiearchief Van Heteren, no. 19. 'Akte van admissie Leonard Vermeulen'.

91   NA, Familiearchief Van Heteren, no. 20.

92   NA, Familiearchief Van Heteren, no. 24. 'Minuut rekest Hendrik van Heteren aan Christiaan, vorst van Nassau-Dillenburg'.

putting up loans for the trade with Dutch Suriname.[93] He also solicited contracts for the equipment and maintenance of barrier fortresses. The largest of these was a contract for the deliverance of palisades worth ƒ117,187.[94] Although the size of Van Heteren's individual soliciting contracts declined sharply from their war-time height, the expansion of his businesses into other areas allowed him to maintain his wealth and status. This is shown by, among other things, the possession according to the tax register of 1718 of ƒ7,200 in VOC shares.[95] At his death in 1749, he was able to pass on a large inheritance to his son Adriaan Leonard, appropriately named after his two brothers-in-law who had played such an important role in the continuation of his business. Van Heteren's yearly income around the time of his death was ƒ8,000, and among his possessions were a house with a rental value of ƒ550 per year, a small country estate and a valuable collection of paintings that later became one of the founding collections of the Dutch Rijksmuseum.[96]

Both Gebhardt and Van Heteren started from relatively lowly positions and used the opportunities provided by the Nine Years' War and the War of the Spanish Succession to work themselves up as financial specialists, transferring huge sums of money to the frontlines and making small fortunes in the process. Personal connections mattered greatly for the start and early development of their career. In the case of Gebhardt, these were the connections that he had built up at the frontlines and in the service of treasurer of the princely domains Willem van Schuylenburg. For Van Heteren, they were the family connections that resulted from the employment of his father and grandfather by the States of Holland, as well as their soliciting functions for members of the court of William III. But there were important differences as well. As an outsider to Dutch society, Gebhardt remained much more dependent on his German connections and the patronage of William III. The diplomatic fallout from the death of the Stadtholder-King effectively ended his large-scale involvement in soliciting, although he continued to live well from the spoils of his previous success. Van Heteren was an insider to the ruling elite of Holland, and managed to further strengthen this position in the course of the War

---

93 He did so for the widow and heirs of sugar merchant Jan Coetier, admittedly on a relatively small scale, as is shown by the accounts in NA, Familiearchief Van Heteren Supplement, no. 46. 'Rekeningen suikerplantages'.

94 NA, Familiearchief Van Heteren, no. 113. 'Liquidaties Barthold van Diemen Opgelder'.

95 NA, Familiearchief Van Heteren, no. 9. 'Kwitanties wegens het betalen van de honderdste penning'.

96 'Adriaan Leonard van Heteren', De Navorscher LXXXV, p. 263, and Moes and Van Biema 1909, pp. 144–52 and pp. 190–4.

of the Spanish Succession, resulting in a marriage that connected him to a network of military solicitors. By diversifying his business, he weathered the less favourable financial conditions created by peace, and continued his good fortunes until the end of the 1740s.

4.4   The Daily Affairs of a Financial Middleman

The archives of Gebhardt and Van Heteren do not only provide insights into the overall development of their careers, but also into the daily practice and the problems that had to be overcome by this type of investor. Gebhardt's papers allow for the most detailed examination, since they contain full ledgers over a long period. Most of the observations in this section will thus be based on his accounts, with Van Heteren's papers as an important backdrop.

The size of a military solicitor's business was determined primarily by the number of companies he (or more than occasionally she) served.[97] These companies provided the solicitor with a fixed salary, while the size of advances covering the arrears of the provinces determined the amount of money received in interest. Together, salary and interest payments formed the main sources of income for solicitors. If arrears would become too large, the accumulation of debts by officers would increase the risk of non-payment or even bankruptcy, which could lead to large losses. Handling the personal financial affairs of officers could be an additional task for which solicitors received compensation, although in the case of Gebhardt it seems that he often did not charge more than expenses and saw this side of his activities more as a service to strengthen his personal relations with his clientele. Van Heteren was involved in many similar small, sometimes very personal transactions with his clients, for example selling paintings to the Duke of Marlborough, or assisting in the buying of three pearl necklaces by one of his clients.[98] Following a typical pattern of gift exchange, Van Heteren often asked small personal favours of his clients as well, in this way further strengthening their relations. For example, the secretary of the ambassador of the Dutch Republic in France on his request sent him a large number of commemorative medals, of which Van Heteren was

---

97 The observations in this and the following paragraph are based on Gebhardt's ledgers, NA, Archief Paulus Gebhardt, no. 12–23. 'Grootboeken'.

98 NA, Familiearchief Van Heteren, nos. 31 and 42. 'Liquidatie met Pieter Fariseau' and 'Transacties met diverse andere personen'. It is not clear whether the paintings mentioned here came from Van Heteren's own collection, or whether he merely assisted in their acquisition.

TABLE 4.1   *Gebhardt's expenses on troop payments for a number of selected years*

Year	Amount	Year	Amount
1691	f1,232,599	1703 (Jan.–Jul.)	f 873,562
1695	f1,450,157	1704	f173,036
1699	f212,915	1711	f78,944

SOURCES: NA, ARCHIEF PAULUS GEBHARDT, NOS. 44, 45, 48, 51, 54, 55, 56, 62, 65, 67, 79, 81. 'LIQUIDATIEBOEKEN'

a keen collector.[99] Such favours in early modern business practice frequently formed the necessary grease for maintaining long-term economic relationships built on trust and personal obligations.[100]

The main activities solicitors and their clients engaged in of course remained purely economic. Table 4.1 contains a reconstruction of the size of Gebhardt's advances on troop payments over a number of selected years. The figures show the large size of his financial transactions at the height of his financial success during the 1690s and in the first half of 1703, as well as the sharp drop of business activities in 1699 and 1704. The suddenness of collapse after the first quarter of 1703 is also shown by the amount of money Gebhardt received through letters of exchange between February 1702 and August 1704 (see chart 4.3). The sharp variations between months reflect the irregularity in payment by the Receivers Offices. Nonetheless, the trend is clear. The amount of money Gebhardt received by this means dropped from a monthly average of almost f110,000 from January to March 1703 (with a highpoint of over f140,000 in February 1703 alone) to just over f30,000 in the summer of that year and even less for most of 1704.[101]

The social gains made by Gebhardt and Van Heteren during their involvement in soliciting suggest that they were able to make substantial profits. However, the exact size of their incomes from soliciting remains hard to estimate. One relatively secure source of income from soliciting was the fixed salary that the solicitor received per company. This salary was included on the payroll, and thus in principle determined by the war budget. During the Nine Years'

---

99   NA, Familiearchief Van Heteren, no. 49. 'Liquidatie met Nicolaes Ruysch'.

100   Jonckheere 2008, pp. 162–80.

101   The two peaks in September 1703 and April 1704 were of an accidental nature, consisting of the f32,000 payment of arrears for one of his former regiments and a f25,000 transaction handled for a diplomat in Gebhardt's network.

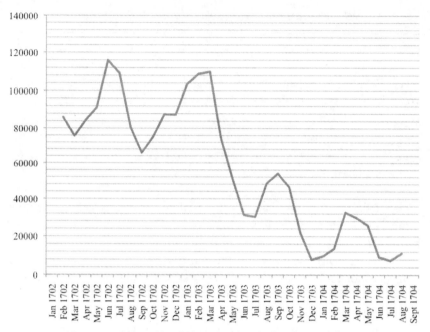

CHART 4.3 *Money received by Gebhardt through letters of exchange, February 1702–August 1704*
(*three monthly moving averages*)
SOURCE: NA, ARCHIEF PAULUS GEBHARDT, NO. 37. 'REGISTER ONTVANGEN
EN VERZONDEN WISSELBRIEVEN'

War, a solicitor's salary was set at twenty-eight guilders per pay month of six
weeks for a cavalry company and twelve guilders for an infantry company.
However, individual solicitors and captains could negotiate substantial discounts or bonuses. An entry in the ledger for 1696 shows the salaries Gebhardt
received from the fifteen companies he solicited for the Province of Groningen. The first two pay months, he received *f*26 for fourteen companies on
horse, and *f*28 for the fifteenth. For the six following full pay months, the
ledgers show a rate of *f*26 for all companies involved. For the last four weeks of
December, comprising the so called 'short month', Gebhardt received another
*f*114 per company, signifying a large financial gratification as part of his standard arrangements. In all, his salary over the year for those fifteen companies
amounted to *f*4,834.[102] Given the total size of his business at this point, including companies in the pay of Holland besides the Friesland companies, it is a safe

---

102   NA, Archief Paulus Gebhardt, no. 16. 'Grootboek 1696', 'Profijt op de Sollicitatie tot Groningen'.

estimate that his total income from salaries must have been at least double this amount. Gebhardt's personal expenses make it quite credible that his income lay within this range. Between 20 January 1694 and 3 April 1695, Gebhardt transferred over f11,500 from his business account to his private account.[103] His private account for the following year notes personal expenses of over f3,000 for the 4.5 months between 15 August 1696 and the end of that year, and over f10,709 for the whole of 1697. For the latter year, his private account includes an income of f3,225 from non-soliciting practices such as investments in obligations. The remaining f7,484 was drawn on his business account.[104] Gebhardt's income must have dropped substantially after 1703. However, even if the eleven infantry companies and four cavalry companies of 1704 paid him nothing more than a regular salary of f12 and f28 per pay month respectively, excluding bonuses and income from interest, this still would have given him an ample yearly salary of over f2,000.

More difficult to calculate than income from salaries is the income Gebhardt drew from interest on advances. The most important source on the size of his outstanding loans is the 'liquidation book of interests' that he kept for the entire period of the Nine Years' War. In this book, he noted the amount of money he advanced per company, the length of arrears, the rate of interest, the amount of interest payments that he subtracted from the payment ordinances in advance (based on an estimation of the length of arrears), and the real sum owed to him by a company after the ordinance had finally been cashed. On this basis, it is possible to calculate the sum received by Gebhardt in interest payments during the Nine Years' War. The interest rates he charged to his companies during this period varied from 4.3 percent to 5.2 percent, and arrears could run up to 2.5 years, although usually they remained around 1.5 years. Over the entire period of the Nine Years' War, Gebhardt received a total of over f314,000 in interest payments. A yearly breakdown is presented in chart 4.4. However, a major part of this sum did not constitute rents accruing to Gebhardt personally, but had to be paid by him to his own creditors. The proportion can be gauged from an – unfortunately exceptional – remark in the ledger of 1696, where Gebhardt calculated that at the closing of the accounts for that year, his own capital invested in his business amounted to f44,083.[105] Based on the figures in his liquidation books, the total sum advanced during the same year can be estimated at around f425,000. This means that of the total sum advanced,

---

103   NA, Archief Paulus Gebhardt, no. 15. 'Grootboek 1694–1696', p. 320.

104   NA, Archief Paulus Gebhardt, no. 16. 'Grootboek 1696', and no. 17. 'Grootboek 1697–Juny 1698', 'mijn particuliere reeckening'.

105   NA, Archief Paulus Gebhardt, no. 16. 'Grootboek 1696', balance.

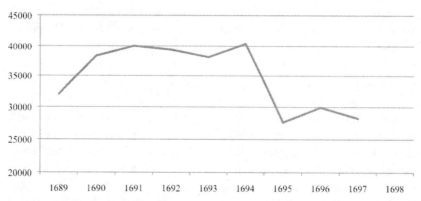

CHART 4.4 *Interest payment received by Gebhardt over advances during the Nine Years' War*
SOURCE: NA, ARCHIEF PAULUS GEBHARDT, NO. 77. 'LIQUIDATIEBOEK
INTERESTEN'

Gebhardt provided only about ten percent out of his own capital, borrowing the rest. His profits thus for a large part depended on the margin between the interest rates he negotiated for himself at the market and the rates he received from the officers to whom he transferred this credit. A register of payment ordinances used by Gebhardt as guarantees for his loans on the capital market in the years 1698–1705 notes the interest rates he paid to his creditors. These fluctuated with the changing market conditions. Between the end of the Nine Years' War and the start of the War of the Spanish Succession, obtaining credit was relatively easy and Gebhardt managed to loan at low rates of between 2.5 and 3.5 percent. At various points he even managed to renegotiate his interest rates after a year, bringing them down in one case from 3 to 2.75 percent, and in July 1700 even from 3 to 2.5 percent. However, similar renegotiations after the outbreak of the War of the Spanish Succession show a shift in interest rates in the opposite direction, with creditors that originally had charged 3 to 3.5 percent now raising their interest rates to 4 percent, and loans in 1702 were mostly concluded at 4.5 to 5, and in one case 5.2 percent.[106] Earlier, it has been shown that Gebhardt himself charged interest rates between 4 and 5.2 percent during the Nine Years' War and between 4.5 and 5.85 percent during the War of the Spanish Succession, leaving a margin that in all probability at most times fell below one percent.

---

106 NA, Archief Paulus Gebhardt, no. 78. 'Register van soldij-ordonnanties, verbonden als panden ter minne, 1698–1705'.

Apart from providing credit for paying the troops, solicitors were involved in many other financial transactions of the companies they served, especially in the settling of supply contracts. For Hendrik van Heteren, during the War of the Spanish Succession this aspect of his business involved a major part of his investments, reaching a total of over $f4$ million in the years 1706–11. Since the terms of the contract gave him the right to a one percent fee on the total amount of money transferred, this must have provided him with the attractive sum of over $f40,000$, not counting the over $f10,000$ guilders he received in compensation for expenses during the same period. His correspondence with Martinus Robijns, one of the main suppliers of oats and hay for the Dutch campaigns in the Southern Netherlands, contains negotiations over deliveries, down payments, and discounts.[107] An account covering the period 1706–8 shows Van Heteren doing business with twenty-four regiments, himself using the financial intermediation of no less than thirty-one other military solicitors located in cities as far apart as Leeuwarden, Groningen, Maastricht, Zwolle, Arnhem, Amsterdam, and The Hague.[108] By maintaining a private network of associates over the entire area of the Republic, private financiers like Van Heteren could counteract the organisational problems created by the federalist structure of Dutch public finances.

Most of the daily practice of solicitors consisted of overcoming the problems connected with transferring large sums of money over long distances. How local differences in economic and political conditions could aggravate the already large difficulty of physically transporting money to war areas is shown by two debates that took place in the States of Holland on 14 July 1689. The first debate highlights the problems involved in international money transfers. Johan Charles van Velthoven, general mint master of the Spanish Netherlands, had filed an official complaint about the negative impact of the influx of large quantities of specie needed to pay the troops fighting on its soil on behalf of the Dutch. The introduction of Dutch coins with a different weight than the coins used in the Southern Netherlands created much confusion with local traders. Van Velthoven proposed to arrange for the transfer of the required sums through letters of exchange enabling payment in local coins, and to split the costs equally between the States of Holland and the Spanish Crown.[109] This arrangement had some real advantages, but depended on the ability of solicitors to find bankers in the Southern Netherlands willing to accept their

---

107   NA, Familiearchief Van Heteren, no. 63. 'Brieven Martinus Robijns'.
108   NA, Familiearchief Van Heteren, no. 118. 'Administratie Zeger Gorisz etc.'
109   NA, Archief Staten van Holland, no. 5121. 'Resoluties 1689', p. 407, resolution of 14 July 1689.

bills. The proposed arrangement between the two states never got off the ground.

A second discussion that took place on the same day concerned difficulties in transferring money across provincial borders within the Dutch Republic itself. At the meeting of the States of Holland, the deputy of Friesland told the story of Aelber Meyert. This messenger of the province had embarked in Leeuwarden with the sum of ƒ43,000 for the payment of the Brandenburg troops on the Friesland payroll, hoping to bring this money to Rotterdam. But after disembarking in Edam, eight men had boarded the ship

> and had cut to pieces the covers and locks of the cases in which the money was kept, and had hauled the skipper to Monickendam where the under bailiff had ordered the unloading of the money which he took into security.

Naturally, the Friesland representative demanded the immediate release of the money and the punishment of those inculpated in its interception. However, the States of Holland decided to start a thorough investigation, first wanting to hear the representatives of Monickendam themselves.[110] Apparently, the outcome of this investigation was not in favour of Friesland. On 1 December 1689 the States of Holland discussed a request by the solicitor of the Prince of Hessen-Kassel (possibly Gebhardt),

> maintaining that it was a necessity for him to receive every six weeks various sums of money from the Province of Utrecht as well as Overijssel for the payment of the troops that his Royal Highness had employed for this state, but that it was impossible for him to accomplish this payment without bringing this money into this province ...

Having been warned that imported specie was seized 'by the officers of the respective cities of this Province', he solemnly requested that he be allowed to bring in coin from Utrecht and Overijssel unhindered.[111]

One of the most important means to alleviate such problems was to have reliable local correspondents, willing and able to assist in money transfers through letters of exchange without charging exorbitant rates. Like most solicitors Gebhardt chose to live in The Hague, because this was the bureaucratic

---

110 NA, Archief Staten van Holland, no. 5121, 'Resoluties 1689', pp. 412–13, 14 July 1689.
111 NA, Archief Staten van Holland, no. 5121, pp. 607–8, 1 December 1689.

centre both of the Province of Holland and of the Dutch Republic, and also the seat of the main bodies for central financial administration.[112] However, at the same time he had to collect money from all of the seven provinces.[113] On top of this he received substantial sums from London for 'subsidy troops' of the English crown. It was impossible for Gebhardt to collect money from all the different parts of the Republic in person. Often the provincial paymasters sent their letters of exchange directly to the places where money had to be dispensed, but this required contacts in the cities in question that were willing to accept those bills. Much of Gebhardt's correspondence was directed at monitoring such transactions between provincial paymasters and his contacts in the garrison towns or cities nearer to the frontlines. Even when the money to pay the troops was available, a lack of reliable intermediaries could lead to delays. In September 1705, the Zeeland provincial receiver Adolph de Groene tried to send Gebhardt a sum of ƒ10,000 divided over two letters of exchange, one of which was addressed to a contact in Arnhem. But, as Gebhardt complained to the officer destined to receive this payment:

> [T]he first is unable to pay until he will have enough money in his cash register, and in Arnhem I do not have any correspondence, and thus it would take too much time to be able to collect this sum ...[114]

The notary archive in The Hague contains numerous cases in which either Gebhardt or one of his contacts refused a letter of exchange that they did not deem trustworthy, creating all sorts of interruptions in the stream of payments.[115]

Things did not fare much better with transactions in cash. Of course, payment of soldiers could not be done in letters of exchange, so solicitors had to dispose of enormous amounts of specie. Given the frequent shortage of mint with higher denomination (guilders and *daelders*), payment could be done in pieces as small as ƒ0.05 or ƒ0.10 (*stuyvers* or *dubbelstuyvers*) or even less (*deniers* or *penningen*). Without the help of counting machines, receiving thou-

---

1 1 2   Knevel 2001, p. 167.

1 1 3   Even the index to Gebhardt's ledger for 1717, which remained empty due to Gebhardt's death early that year, contains entries for the Receivers Offices of the Provinces of Holland (Northern and Southern Quarter), Utrecht, Zeeland, Friesland, and Groningen.

1 1 4   Paulus Gebhardt to Johan Knips, 8 September 1705, NA, Archief Paulus Gebhardt, no. 38. 'Brievenboek 1705–1706', pp. 33–4.

1 1 5   E.g., HGA – NA, no. 680, p. 290, no. 1626, pp. 407–8, and no. 1636, pp. 841–2, all three cases from 1703.

sands of guilders in *dubbelstuyvers* could create serious inconveniences. Such occurred in 1716 between Gebhardt and Marcus Cockeij, one of his principle Amsterdam banking contacts during the later years of his life. With large frequency Gebhardt shipped sums of ƒ10,000 or more to Amsterdam to be put on his account. However, in the summer of that year Cockeij raised some doubts whether the written amounts on his moneybags covered their exact contents. At first Gebhardt tried to avoid the unpleasant consequences of the demand for a recount. In a letter to Cockeij, he assured him that

> there is no person in The Hague who receives his money with greater precaution than I do, but counting all the bags and clearing them in the way as is customary in Amsterdam lies outside my ability or that of anyone else here ...[116]

However, Marcus Cockeij insisted, and a sample recount showed his allegations to have been correct. When Gebhardt again wanted to send Cockeij bags of coins, the latter forced him to demand a count from his supplier, solicitor Van Alphen. Counting four bags of *dubbelstuyvers* cost Van Alphen and his servants a full day, but no irregularities were found. In order to avoid further embarrassment, Gebhardt had to take upon himself the risk of any further shortages.[117] Even though in the end the shortage proved to be not much more than five guilders, the dispute seriously damaged Gebhardt's relations with Marcus Cockeij and Van Alphen.[118]

Not all conflicts however were over such a pittance. The most serious financial threat to a military solicitor was the bankruptcy of one of his debtors. Two of Gebhardt's officers came into financial difficulties of such magnitude that they stopped paying their debts. In both cases this led to judicial procedures. In September 1713 Gebhardt asked a lawyer in Leeuwarden to appeal to the Friesland court about one officer's inability to repay his debts, amounting to a principal of ƒ12,825, a further ƒ2,400 in interest, and a small obligation of ƒ250.[119] He demanded the 'arrest' of his salary and the prohibition of

---

116   Paulus Gebhardt to Marcus Cockeij, 2 September 1716, NA, Archief Paulus Gebhardt, no. 40. 'Brievenboek 1714–1716', p. 211.

117   Paulus Gebhardt to Marcus Cockeij, 28 December 1716, NA, Archief Paulus Gebhardt, no. 40. 'Brievenboek 1714–1716', p. 248.

118   Paulus Gebhardt to Marcus Cockeij, 30 December 1716, NA, Archief Paulus Gebhardt, no. 40. 'Brievenboek 1714–1716', p. 250.

119   Paulus Gebhardt to Johan Werner Valkener, 19 September 1713, NA, Archief Paulus Gebhardt, no. 39. 'Brievenboek 1713–1714'.

selling the company. Such a sale would indeed have been an easy way for the officer to escape his 'extravagantly risen' debts and leave Gebhardt out in the cold.[120] The prohibition was granted, and two years later the court reached a final decision. Gebhardt now was entitled to one-third of the officer's monthly salary.[121] However, he could hardly have been satisfied at this speed of down-payment, and in a letter to his lawyer Valkener he complained that in order for him to retrieve his money, the officer would have to pay him for the rest of his life.[122] A second case proved even more serious, as it involved major general Pritselwitz, who was on the payroll of the Province of Holland. After the end of the War of the Spanish Succession Gebhardt sent many requests to Holland's grand pensionary Heinsius to look into Pritselwitz's affairs. According to Gebhardt, the general had suffered severe financial injustice at the hands of some of his solicitors. As a result, 'a man of high birth, merits, irreproachable behaviour and more than forty years of loyal service [was] forced to consume his own means in the service of this country'.[123] Despite these protests Pritselwitz was forced to auction off f35,000–f40,000 worth of possessions in order to repay his many creditors, including Gebhardt.[124]

A puzzling aspect of early modern credit relations is that the businessmen involved often exhibited the same zeal when prosecuting a debt of a few guilders as when faced with a possible loss of thousands. The very real difficulties in even the smallest transactions bred an almost religious attachment to each guilder on the balance. Perhaps this ardour was only the natural counterbalance to the amoral, if not outright diabolical reputation of the money trade, particularly the use of credit instruments such as paper money and letters of exchange.[125] For Gebhardt at least, gold had achieved a sense of holiness, as he expressed in a letter to his friend Adolph de Groene when the latter was promoted to the position of mint master of the Province of Zeeland:

---

120 Paulus Gebhardt to Johan Werner Valkener, 11 November 1713, NA, Archief Paulus Gebhardt, no. 39. 'Brievenboek 1713–1714', pp. 154–5.

121 Paulus Gebhardt to Issaac Clifford & Carl Const van Putte, 22 June 1715, NA, Archief Paulus Gebhardt, no. 40. 'Brievenboek 1714–1716', pp. 85–6.

122 Paulus Gebhardt to Johan Werner Valkener, 12 November 1715, NA, Archief Paulus Gebhardt, no. 40. 'Brievenboek 1714–1716', p. 140.

123 Paulus Gebhardt to Heinsius, 11 October 1715, in: Veenendaal jr. 1998, pp. 378–9.

124 Paulus Gebhardt to Sambeeck, 17 January 1716, NA, Archief Paulus Gebhardt, no. 40. 'Brievenboek 1714–1716', pp. 156–7.

125 Braudel 1974, p. 358.

[W]ishing that Your Honour will serve this Office ... profiting from those sweet and wholesome lessons that the all-knowing Creator has established for the treatment of minting material and dependent requisites, forming a guide to the procedure that a true Christian has to employ, before he receives the stamp of the image of God on the new creation that alone ... has currency in the land of the living ...[126]

4.5   Networks of Credit and Influence

As the previous section made clear, military solicitors did not operate on their own in providing the money necessary for paying the troops. In fact, they were only the hinges in a wide network of creditors that included state officials, bankers, officers, suppliers, and a whole host of large and small private investors. Whereas research on the revenue raising capacities of fiscal military states has concentrated heavily on taxation and formal structures of long-term state debt, a large part of the outstanding payments of the state always consisted of relatively unregulated forms of short-term credit. Martinus Robijns, Zeger Gorisz and Pieter Pangaert, the forage contractors in the Southern Netherlands for whom Van Heteren functioned as a solicitor, had to wait decades for their payment. Their outstanding bills were turned into obligations, and between December 1719 and March 1727 alone Van Heteren cashed over f150,000 for them in related interest payments.[127] The heirs of steward Johan Hesselt van Dinter only received a payment ordinance for the f7,546 left on military expenses made in 1703 in 1728, and had to beg another seven years for the actual payment, complaining 'that it has caused much bitterness for the deceased steward to have had to wait for his money for such a long time, causing him to fall into great debts that now press on his heirs'.[128] And the heirs of the bread suppliers Josua Castano and Juda Senior Henriquez even had to wait until 1740 before their accounts were (almost entirely) settled.[129]

---

126   Paulus Gebhardt to Adolph de Groene, 3 April 1706, NA, Archief Paulus Gebhardt, no. 38. 'Brievenboek 1705–1706', p. 149.

127   NA, Familiearchief Van Heteren, no. 123. 'Rekeningen Martinus Robijns'. Actual payments on the principle came in small amounts, as is shown by a payment ordinance of 22 June 1719 to cover expenses agreed on by the States General on 7 September 1711. NA, Familiearchief Van Heteren Supplement, no. 60. 'Proces Hof van Holland'.

128   NA, Familiearchief Van Heteren Supplement, no. 63. 'Vordering Johan Hesselt van Dinter'.

129   NA, Familiearchief Van Heteren, no. 127. 'Liquidaties voor leveren brood Paltse troepen'.

Even the closest familial relations could break down under the strain of such financial burdens. This, for example, was the case with the partnership between Van Heteren and Willem Lormier. After more than two decades of waiting for down-payments on the forage contacts that they had jointly solicited, Lormier became impatient with the way in which his brother-in-law divided the payments that did come in. After they fell out with one another, Lormier proceeded to bring his case before the Court of Holland, saying that the way in which Van Heteren prevaricated in re-dividing the payments 'shows clearly by what spirit the defendant is driven', illustrating 'his selfish and money-grabbing inclinations'. Lormier demanded a full return of all the money he had invested in the original partnership plus interest. In turn Van Heteren argued that he had stuck to the terms of the original partnership agreement, and that Lormier should accept discounts on his interest payments in accordance with current practices amongst solicitors. The differences between the two proved too large to solve by simple arbitration, irreparably damaging their personal relations.[130]

Although the last-mentioned case does not disprove the crucial role of trust and personal ties in early modern finance, it does show that even among the closest of partners, trust and friendship were gained or lost on the basis of economic success. Only with very strong creditor networks of their own could military solicitors survive gaps in payment of many years. More than those of Van Heteren, Gebhardt's papers allow for a close examination of the make-up of such creditor networks. Central to his financial connections were a number of very large financiers. The most prominent was Willem van Schuylenburg, who not only acted as Gebhardt's employer and as paymaster to the subsidy troops of the British crown but also provided Gebhardt with large amounts of credit. But Van Schuylenburg's ability to do so was not limitless. There is some evidence that around the middle of the 1690s, the serious financial problems then suffered by the English crown had detrimental effects on Van Schuylenburg's own solvency. In the summer of 1696 he had to try and secure a large loan on the city of Amsterdam in order to avoid 'disorder' among the British subsidy troops. However, this attempt to draw quick credit from the magistrate of Holland's richest city was seriously hindered by the slowness of decision making inherent in the Dutch political system. As Amsterdam regent Jacob Boreel explained to Portland:

> It is a truth, my lord, not assembled pretences or far-fetched excuses, but indeed the result of our form of Government, that to negotiate money

---

130   NA, Familiearchief Van Heteren Supplement, no. 60. 'Proces Hof van Holland'.

from the city ... in the way that is requested, necessitates the consent of the Magistrate, in order to be successful.

Boreel promised to work hard on receiving this consent, but also warned that 'this being dependent on the sentiments of many, I cannot give any guarantees in advance about the result'.[131] In the end, Van Schuylenburg had to resort to others to secure the necessary loans, but this was not without problems. In January 1697 Portland warned the British paymaster in Brussels Richard Hill that he should not expect to receive ready money from Van Schuylenburg:

> ne vous attendez pas que M^rSchuylenburg pourra si tost vous fournir de l'argent, car pui que ces lettres de change ont esté protestées, il a souffert un si grand échec dans son crédit et de si grandes pertes que je crain qu'il aura de la peine à s'en remettre de longtemps.[132]

Although Van Schuylenburg remained one of Gebhardt's principal creditors until the first years of the War of the Spanish Succession, his central place in Gebhardt's financial network was gradually taken over by the Amsterdam bankers George and Isaac Clifford. The choice for Clifford seems logical. At this time Clifford & Co. was gradually establishing itself as one of the major Dutch banking houses.[133] Its prominence was partly due to its strong connections across the Channel. In 1695 George Clifford helped to transfer two million guilders from the Bank of England to the Netherlands for troop payments. A substantial part of this sum went through Gebhardt's account.[134]

Gebhardt's letters form an important source of information on his relations with his bankers. Analysis of his register of outgoing letters show that even after the decline of his business in 1703, Gebhardt wrote to his bankers at least two or three times a week.[135] The content of these letters shows that

---

131   Jacob Boreel to Portland, 16 August 1695, Japikse 1927, p. 402.

132   '[D]o not expect that Mr Schuylenburg could provide you with money soon, for ever since his letters of exchange were protested, he has suffered a large misfortune in his credit and has suffered such large losses that I believe he will have difficulties to pay you for a long time'. Portland to Richard Hill, 5/15 January 1697, Japikse 1927, pp. 226–7. Richard Hill's own position at this time was far from rosy. Jones 1988, pp. 24–5.

133   Jonker and Sluyterman 2000, pp. 94–5.

134   NA, Archief Paulus Gebhardt, no. 16. 'Grootboek 1696', 'Tweede negotiatie met de banck van Londen'.

135   This includes letters to Marcus Cockeij, who was responsible for approximately half of Gebhardt's banking affairs in the final years of his life. Including his letters to Isaac Clifford

Gebhardt not only relied on their credit, but also on their extensive financial networks. For example, in 1715 he asked Isaac Clifford and Carl Constant van der Putte to advise him on arranging his money transfers from Friesland, 'having no acquaintances over there'.[136] His bankers were also crucial in providing information on the oscillations on the Amsterdam market for obligations. The financial distress of the end of the War of the Spanish Succession led to sharp fluctuations which could seriously affect Gebhardt's own investments and those of his clients. Therefore, he repeatedly asked his Amsterdam contacts to keep him closely informed, 'in order to be able to take my measures to provide security'.[137] The separation between The Hague as the administrative centre of the Dutch Republic and Amsterdam as its main financial centre tended to reinforce the need to rely on banking contacts for quick and reliable information.

Apart from his bankers, Gebhardt's largest creditors were merchants in the frontier areas and the major cities of the Southern Netherlands. This could not have been otherwise, since most of the fighting was done in these areas. Cities like the southern garrison town Maastricht became crucial financial nodes in troop payments. The most important of Gebhardt's Maastricht creditors was the merchant Pieter Boomhouwer, who also acted on behalf of other solicitors.[138] Throughout the Nine Years' War Boomhouwer handled sums between ƒ100,000 and ƒ250,000 a year for Gebhardt. Comparable sums were received by the Brussels bankers Gijsbert and Roelof van Biesheuvel at the start of the Nine Years' War. The shifting of the frontlines could have a negative impact on the continuity of relations. In June 1706 Gebhardt restored contact with Cornelis Sneps, a banker from Ghent, which had broken down 'by the fatal coincidences of war'. In the same letter he asked Sneps to assist him in the payment of the regiment of Ernst von Salisch, which at that time had its camp in the environs of Ghent. Sneps was promised an agio of 0.5 percent on all transactions.[139]

    & Carl Constant van der Putte, his letter books contain 105 letters to his bankers for June 1713–January 1714, and 251 letters for July 1714–December 1716. NA, Archief Paulus Gebhardt, nos. 39 and 40. 'Brievenboeken'.

136   Paulus Gebhardt to Isaac Clifford and Carl Constant van der Putte, 22 June 1715, NA, Archief Paulus Gebhardt, no. 39. 'Brievenboek 1713–1714', pp. 85–6.

137   Paulus Gebhardt to Marcus Cockeij, 26 March 1715, NA, Archief Paulus Gebhardt, no. 39. 'Brievenboek 1713–1714', p. 65.

138   NA, Archief van de Gecommitteerde Raden van de Staten van Holland en Westfriesland, no. 3038. 'Resoluties 1688', fol. 288 vso–289, resolution of 26 December 1688.

139   Paulus Gebhardt to Cornelis Sneps, 8 June 1706, NA, Archief Paulus Gebhardt, no. 38. 'Brievenboek 1705–1706', p. 241.

Van Schuylenburg, Clifford & Co. and these merchants and bankers near the
frontlines formed the core of Gebhardt's financial network. But around this
core there was a large group of smaller private creditors who jointly provided
a substantial part of Gebhardt's capital. A register of payment ordinances
put up as guarantees for his loans gives an impression who these creditors
were for the period between May 1698 and February 1705.[140] The forty-eight
persons in this register provided a total of ƒ525,000 in credit. Excluding Willem
van Schuylenburg and Clifford & Co., the total amount came to ƒ300,000,
or an average of approximately ƒ6,500 per creditor. Individual contributions
ranged from a mere ƒ200 by Marie van Duijn, a nanny in the service of Van
Schuylenburg, to ƒ38,000 by Ernst von Salisch, who thus like the traditional
German military entrepreneur provided the credit needed to pay his own
troops as long as the Province of Holland remained in arrears.

Table 4.2 contains the ten largest providers of this type of loan. One of
the notable facts about this list is that exactly half of the top ten creditors
belonged to the political elite of the Dutch Republic. High officials also figured
prominently among the rest of the creditors. These included Portland's secretary Tromer (ƒ8,000), state secretary Van Beaumont (ƒ6,000), and receiver of
the Northern Quarter of Holland Johan de Rhode (ƒ4,000), who was himself
responsible for the payment of ordinances to Gebhardt. The influence of Van
Schuylenburg on Gebhardt's network of creditors might be apparent from the
inclusion of a number of intimates of William III, such as Tromer, and the fact
that Van Schuylenburg's place of residence Delft was well represented in the
top ten. Among the smaller creditors in this register (putting up ƒ5,000 or less)
were quite a number of investors who could be considered part of the middle
classes rather than the upper class. This shows the relatively large section of
society that was involved in the capital market, albeit often on a small scale. The
list includes two shoemakers, a baker, a bookbinder, a female market seller and
a coffee lady from a cafe near The Hague's administrative centre the *Binnen-
hof*. As the latter two suggest the complete male dominance of the top ten is
not entirely representative of the rest of the list, although most women can
be found among the smallest creditors: ten out of a total of 48 creditors were
women, jointly providing a capital of just over ƒ33,000.

The prominent participation of members of the highest government circles
in loans of this type is noteworthy, though not surprising. At this time the use
of ordinances as guarantees for loans was a controversial practice. In 1701 the
States of Holland had to discuss serious problems that had arisen after the

---

140   NA, Archief Paulus Gebhardt, no. 78. 'Register van soldij-ordonnanties'.

TABLE 4.2   *Gebhardt's ten largest creditors, 1698–1705*

Creditor	Function	City	Loan size	Interest paid between May 1698 and Febr. 1705
Willem van Schuylenburg	Council and treasurer of the Domain of William III	Delft	ƒ207,600	ƒ16,809
Ernst von Salisch	Lieutenant general		ƒ38,000	ƒ2,056
Adriaan Bout	Military solicitor	The Hague	ƒ25,000	ƒ1,250
Jan Munter	Councillor of the Court of Holland	Amsterdam	ƒ22,000	ƒ1,200
George and Isaac Clifford	Bankers	Amsterdam	ƒ18,000	ƒ360
Cornelis Spiering	Lord of Spieringshoeck, ex-burgomaster of Delft	Delft	ƒ14,000	–
Johan Kool	Usher of the States of Utrecht	Utrecht	ƒ13,000	ƒ979
Simon van Slingelandt	Secretary of the States of Holland	The Hague	ƒ12,500	ƒ760
Diercquens*	–	–	ƒ12,000	–
Johan Keijser	Wine merchant	Delft	ƒ11,000	ƒ940

* Possibly Jehan Diercquens, a rich Middelburg merchant who lived in Amsterdam.
SOURCE: NA, ARCHIEF PAULUS GEBHARDT, NO. 78. 'REGISTER SOLDIJ-ORDONNANTIES, VERBONDEN ALS PANDEN TER MINNE, MEI 1698–FEBRUARI 1705'

bankruptcy of solicitor Jacob Ferguson. The solicitor had put up a number of ordinances as a guarantee for his loans, which he now was unable to repay. Naturally, his lenders wanted to cash in their ordinances to compensate for their losses. But one of the captains whose ordinances had been used in this way demanded their recall so that he could receive outstanding payments. He even fought his case before the court of Holland. When this became known in Amsterdam and other cities,

> it created such a stir, that not only was it impossible to acquire any new loans, but even those who had already given some capital to the

[solicitors] on interest decided to cancel their loans on the shortest term possible, which not only caused the [solicitors] great embarrassment, but even made it impossible for them to pay the militia ...

The States of Holland decided to exempt ordinances from recall, a decision that weighed heavily against the interests of the captains and strongly in favour of solicitors and their creditors, some of whom might have helped to write the resolution.[141]

A second noticeable feature of Gebhardt's network is that other military solicitors only played a minor role as creditors. As shown earlier, Van Heteren worked actively in partnership with several other military solicitors in handling fodder contracts. Solicitors formed a large part of his overall financial network, and Van Heteren himself functioned as creditor for Middelburg solicitor Abraham de Bruijn and The Hague solicitor IJsbrand van Groenestein, among others.[142] The relative absence of solicitors in Gebhardt's network again affirms his weaker embeddedness in indigenous financial circles, partially explaining his marginalisation shortly after the death of William III. In contrast, Van Heteren's staying power in this difficult line of business certainly stemmed from his embeddedness in Dutch financial circles.

But strong financial networks were not the only connections that mattered for military solicitors. Their prominent role in paying the army arose from the need to bridge the distance between the three spheres of political administration, finance, and the military. Good contacts in all of them increased a solicitor's chances of survival. This point again is underlined by the differences between Gebhardt's and Van Heteren's careers. Military soliciting brought Gebhardt close to the centres of power of the Dutch Republic. But in many respects he remained an outsider. Being of German descent he could not lean on an already established family network, and gradually build his political and business contacts from there. His soliciting practices remained focused on the German companies he had originally acquired. He did not manage to diversify his soliciting practices by getting contracts with other, non-German companies. Instead he opted for a strategy aimed at securing his possessions, investing in oil mills along the Thames, various sorts of obligations, and real estate.[143] His position did give Gebhardt access to some of the leading figures

---

141 NA, Archief Staten van Holland, no. 5134. 'Resoluties 1701', fol. 484, 9 December 1701.

142 NA, Familiearchief Van Heteren, nos. 137 and 138. 'Liquidaties Abraham de Bruijn', and 'Akte van dagvaarding boedelbeschrijving IJsbrand van Groenestein'.

143 NA, Archief Paulus Gebhardt, no. 85. 'Akte van overeenkomst', and Paulus Gebhardt to Marcus Cockeij, 17 July 1714, NA, Archief Paulus Gebhardt, no. 40. 'Brievenboek 1714–1716', p. 3.

in Dutch politics. In May 1700 he handled a number of small personal transactions for Holland's grand pensionary Heinsius.[144] And at the end of his life he rented one of his houses to the secretary of the States General Francois Fagel.[145] The marriage of his daughter Anna Christina to Pieter van Hurck, a lawyer at the Court of Holland, shows no great advance in social status. Although Pieter van Hurck was the son of the secretary of the Court of Holland of the same name and counted among his close relatives a burgomaster of the Holland garrison town Gorinchem and the wife of a burgomaster of Deventer, none of these connections were at such a level that they could counterbalance the negative impact of the death of William III.[146] Finally, even Gebhardt's religious choices separated him from the mainstream of the Dutch elite. His children were all baptised in the Evangelical-Lutheran Church.[147] And at the end of his life he seems to have been drawn closely to a variant of *Collegiant* spiritualism.[148] Though such religious deviation was not an insurmountable barrier to political or social advance – as can be seen from the career of the late seventeenth-century diplomat and committed *Collegiant* Coenraad van Beuningen – it was not particularly helpful either in a society in which adherence to the doctrines of the ruling church was still considered of great importance.[149]

Van Heteren could build on a far larger 'social capital'. Born into a family of officials, he inherited a strong political network. At an early age his father secured him a job at the office of the receiver general, and not long afterwards he obtained a seat in the The Hague city council.[150] Throughout his life Van Heteren continued to fulfil public functions, acting as an administrator for the Reformed Church (the privileged church of the Dutch Republic) and serving on the board of directors of the Leper House.[151] On the board of regents of the latter institution, Van Heteren cooperated with several consecutive secretaries of Holland's Finance Offices and other high officials of the

---

144   NA, Archief Paulus Gebhardt, no. 19. 'Grootboek 1699–1700'.

145   Paulus Gebhardt to Francois Fagel, 1 May 1715, NA, Archief Paulus Gebhardt, no. 40. 'Brievenboek 1714–1716', pp. 74–5.

146   NA, Familiearchief Van Hurck en Barnevelt, no. 11. 'Inventaris van goederen'.

147   Kompagnie 1979, pp. XXVI–XXVII.

148   This can be deducted from the three orders of religious books he placed with his book trader, in Paulus Gebhardt to Jacob Claus, 13 February 1715, 9 May 1716 and 17 August 1716, NA, Archief Paulus Gebhardt, no. 40. 'Brievenboek 1714–1716', resp. p. 52, p. 180, and p. 207, as well as from the exalted religious tone of many of his later letters.

149   On the social position of collegiants and spiritualists, see Roldanus 1938, Chapter VIII.

150   Knevel 2001, pp. 109–10.

151   His administration for the church can be found in NA, Familiearchief Van Heteren, nos. 148–50, that for the Leper House in nos. 151–9.

city and province.[152] In both functions his financial expertise was appreciated: Van Heteren administrated the church collections and controlled the ledgers of the Leper House, and even sometimes advanced money to both institutions for supplies.[153] Almost caricaturing Max Weber's 'protestant ethics', in 1738 Van Heteren took upon himself the task of sharpening the rules of order of the Leper House. He did so with great vigour, proposing to raise the fine for all possible offenses, such as insulting one of the regents – punishable by a six guilders fine to be paid either to the institution or to the insulted regent personally, and in the worst case by a three months expulsion from the house – as well as for insulting other inhabitants of the house, drinking and disorderly behaviour, or bringing in a dog.[154] While thus protecting the lepers from a life of sins and debauchery, Van Heteren strengthened the connections that allowed him to continue his personal advance as a major war investor. In 1749 he died a well-established member of The Hague's urban elite.

4.6   Military Soliciting in the Age of Financialisation

The end of the War of the Spanish Succession opened a period of financial uncertainty as well as new possibilities for financiers. Turmoil arose from the fact that perhaps for the first time in the history of the Dutch Republic real doubts arose over the creditworthiness of the state. In 1715 the accumulated debts of the States General had risen so high that the Treasury of the Generalty was closed and all payments stalled for a nine-month period.[155] Even the Province of Holland ran into arrears of one and a half years. Many of the smaller provinces were financially in far worse shape.[156] The last phase of the War of the Spanish Succession had been a difficult period for those involved in military finances, as was illustrated most poignantly by the collapse of the firm Van der Heyden & Drummond, which had functioned as a clearing house for transactions connected with troop payments between England and the Netherlands.[157] As the conflict between Van Heteren and his brother-in-law shows, military solicitors often struggled for many decades to receive payment for all

---

152   NA, Familiearchief Van Heteren, no. 153. 'Lijst namen regenten leprooshuis'.
153   NA, Familiearchief Van Heteren, nos. 150–1. 'Aantekeningen opbrengsten collecten' and 'Aantekeningen financiën leprooshuis'.
154   NA, Familiearchief Van Heteren, no. 158. 'Uitbreiding reglement van orde'.
155   Aalbers 1980, p. 3.
156   Aalbers 1980, pp. 4–5, and Dormans 1991, p. 82.
157   Hatton 1970, pp. 87–8.

the outstanding bills of the War of the Spanish Succession. The general sense of malaise that surrounded state finances in these years even seeped through in Gebhardt's private correspondence, perhaps strengthened by the ill fortune of his own ventures during the preceding decade. In one of his letters Gebhardt congratulated an in-law with a recent change in the government and finances of Culemborg, a border city that had been sold to the Dutch Republic by a German prince in financial distress. But this congratulation was merely an excuse for a long allegory on the problems of Holland's government and finances:

> With great pleasure I have witnessed the success of Culemborg's united government, and the financial health which is a result of this. Our clockwork in Holland is of an incomparable size, containing a host of dependent wheels to govern so many arms. But ever since our clockmaker [William III?] has died, the arms have gotten out of harmony, and the oil has dried up. The consuming rust is master and nearly makes all hands stop. And although there are those who by the movement of a pendulum[158] want to set to work this clock, it only functions for a couple of minutes, and in this way it is impossible to redress [its defects], unless a wise artist will cleanse it from its rust, oil it, and repair the broken parts.[159]

However, for many others financial turmoil also opened new roads for speculation. The high interest rates at which the state was forced to attract credit, concentration of state obligations in fewer hands, growing opportunities to invest in foreign state debt, and the international *hausse* in speculation connected to the famous South Sea Bubble, all fuelled the 'financialisation' of the Dutch economy.[160] It is noteworthy that some of the main Amsterdam banking houses of the eighteenth century found their origins during or just after the War of the Spanish Succession: Andries Pels and son was founded in 1707, the direct predecessor of Muilman & Sons in 1712, and both Hogguer and Hope & Co. around 1720.[161] The loss of dynamic in important parts of the productive sectors of the Dutch economy from the 1720s onwards increased the weight of foreign investment in Dutch financial portfolios, attracting international fin-

---

158   Pendulum (in Dutch: 'slinger') is probably a pun on the name of Holland's eminent statesman Van Slingelandt, who around this time launched a number of proposals to redress the sorry state of state finances.

159   Paulus Gebhardt to Wagerdus, 11 January 1717, NA, Archief Paulus Gebhardt, no. 41. 'Brievenboek 1717', p. 7.

160   De Vries and Van der Woude 1997, p. 119.

161   Buist 1974, p. 5.

anciers and strengthening the role of the Amsterdam capital market as the
major centre of capital export.[162] This process was aided by the strong integration of the Amsterdam and London capital markets, which had progressed
in a step by step fashion from William III's crossing of the Channel onwards. By
1723 shares of the English chartered joint stock corporations were traded simultaneously on the stock exchanges of Amsterdam and London.[163] This context
helps to explain how in the course of the eighteenth century the activities of
military solicitors became even more strongly concentrated in the hands of
a limited number of financiers with connections on the Amsterdam capital
market. The intermarriage between government and big finance also created
growing concerns over the malicious activities of a new moneyed aristocracy
that put its private interests above those of the nation. Even if this criticism
was not expressed as vociferously in the Netherlands as in Britain, it still con-
stituted one of the major themes in the economic and political debates of the
eighteenth century.[164]

In the decade and a half following the War of the Spanish Succession the
energetic statesman Van Slingelandt tried to break through the financial and
administrative deadlock that the war had created. In his 'Memory of redress of
finances', he concluded

> that the last war, in which the state has made greater efforts than her
> forces allowed for, has deranged the already very troubled finances of the
> Province of Holland and West Friesland to such an extent that the whole
> state is in danger of collapsing at the first unfortunate moment that will
> arise ...[165]

In order to counter this problem he launched a long list of reform proposals
aimed at the fragmented structure of the state apparatus, military command,
and army finances. It was in this context that the States of Holland in 1721
discussed a proposal to erect a Military Office,

> by which, with benefit ... to the Province of Holland and with greater order
> and service to the state, could be paid the ordinary wages of the militia,

---

162   Riley 1980, p. 81.
163   Neal 1990, p. 141.
164   Sturkenboom 2008.
165   'Memorie, dienende om aan te wysen de noodwendigheid van het in practyq brengen van
       het veertiende articul der ordonnancie op de vergadering van Holland', Van Slingelandt
       1784a, pp. 151–2.

the artillerists, the salaries of the generals, colonels, engineers, reformed officers, etc. ... as is done at this time by the respective solicitors ...[166]

The proposal went considerably further than the one of 1673. It anticipated a system of payment run by four directors, assisted by two clerks, as officials of the province. According to the plan:

> The establishment of this office should be backed up by the credit of the Province, which should raise on interest a sum of f5,718,702 ... with which sum could be paid the outstanding wages, salaries, pensions, etc. for one and a half year consecutively, which is approximately the time that the Province is currently in arrears to the militia.[167]

Reflecting the difficult circumstances of the previous decade, the main reason to introduce reforms mentioned in the document was the prevention of 'the mutual bankruptcies' of officers and solicitors that were always 'of great disadvantage to one of the two'. Furthermore, the new system would greatly simplify the business of supply and other financial affairs of the regiments, 'because regiments that have outstanding bills do not have to go to more than one place, while they now often have to trade with four or five solicitors'. Finally, the writers of the report expressed their hope that cutting out the solicitors would enable the state to negotiate lower interest rates on the capital market than were asked under the prevailing system.[168]

However, those arguments depended on a rather rosy take on the financial capacities of the province. In order to liberate themselves from the hold of the solicitors, the provincial authorities had to be willing to pay more in downpayments than they already had to contribute to that year's war budget.[169] This proposal came at a time when financial problems abounded. At f306 million, Holland's debt was hardly reduced from its post-war highpoint. A proposal made in 1720 to clean up the provincial finances had come to nothing.[170] On 14 April 1723 the States of Holland discussed a letter from solicitors protest-

---

166   NA, Archief Staten van Holland, no. 2030. 'Ingekomen stukken, 1720–1728', 'Project tot het oprechten van een Militair Comptoir', no. 30.

167   NA, Archief Staten van Holland, no. 2030. 'Ingekomen stukken, 1720–1728', 'Project tot het oprechten van een Militair Comptoir', no. 30, fol. 1.

168   NA, Archief Staten van Holland, no. 2030. 'Ingekomen stukken, 1720–1728', 'Project tot het oprechten van een Militair Comptoir', no. 30, fol. 3–4.

169   NA, Archief Staten Generaal, no. 8161. 'Staat van Oorlog 1721'.

170   Dormans 1992, p. 81 and p. 85.

ing against the proposed reform. The request, extraordinarily long and signed
by twenty-eight solicitors, took recourse to every argument that one would
expect from a group of influential financiers who saw a threat to an important
source of revenue. The execution of the proposed reform, they alleged, would
be 'of ruinous and unmanageable consequence in relation to their particular
[interest] and [that of] the country in general'. The solicitors then gave a long
elaboration of both points, though dwelling considerably longer on the dreaded
consequences for their private interests. In their opinion the captains, when
asked, would not want to change to a more centralised form of payment, and
the same would go for private creditors. Experience with attempts to raise quick
credit had shown 'that everyone wants to give his money rather to the solicitors
than to the country'. After calling to mind their great contribution to the survival of the Dutch army during the last war, they added the hardly concealed
threat of capital flight, saying that 'many would be easily forced by necessity
to leave the province or their fatherland in order to find their livelihood elsewhere'. They displayed a great sense of drama when describing their sense of
betrayal, explaining that

> it would be the hardest thing in the world that those who have behaved
> themselves as loyal solicitors and subjects, having sacrificed their money
> and credit to the service of the country's militia in the most dangerous
> moment of the heaviest war ever known ... now, when they are only just
> experiencing the effect of a pleasant peace ... [would be] stripped of their
> office ...

After spending more than half of the letter complaining about their own fate,
the request then stated boldly that the execution of the proposal would lead to
disaster. The authors reminded the States of the 'excessive sum of money and
credit that is required, which the country itself, with all due respect, for many
times was unable to furnish', proceeding to argue 'that without the military
solicitors, the militia would have been destroyed'.[171]

This way of putting the argument was a bit too much to stomach even for
a political body as used to the crass promotion of self-interest as the States of
Holland. Two days later, they declined the request on the basis

> that in every way it is transparent that the first [private rather than public
> interest] is the motivation for the solicitors' request, that the loss of profit

---

171   NA, Archief Staten van Holland, no. 157. 'Resoluties 1723', fol. 375. Request of the Military
      Solicitors to the States of Holland, 14 April 1723, and resolution of 14 April 1723.

following the discontinuation of their employment is made to seem a special damage, and even their ruin, using inappropriate expressions to do so ...[172]

On 2 June 1723 the solicitors again requested a chance to present their case concerning the disadvantages of the new system. Prudently focusing solely on the damage it would do the public interest, they achieved considerably more success and the project was shelved.[173] Probably the financial situation of the Province did most of the convincing. All too aware of the dire straits into which the Dutch Republic was now sailing, the regents lacked both the means and the political determination to break out of their dependency on financial middlemen in troop payments.

At least in the Province of Holland, this failure of reforms in the system of troop payments in the early 1720s was not followed by another serious attempt to move beyond the existing practice. The international position of the Dutch Republic helped to create the circumstances for relative stability in military organisation. After the Peace of Utrecht, the Dutch Republic effectively withdrew from armed confrontation on the European mainland. It kept aloof from the War of the Polish Succession (1733–8), and only entered the War of the Austrian Succession (1740–8) in earnest in its final year. But as Olaf van Nimwegen has already shown, this did not lead to a complete neglect of the armed forces. In fact, the period from the 1720s to the late 1740s can best be described as one of armed peace, in which the Dutch Republic maintained a significant army in order to guard its 'barrier' of garrison towns in the Southern Netherlands. When it entered the War of the Austrian Succession, Dutch military organisation was still more or less up to date.[174] This could be ascribed in no small part to the fact that when need arose, Holland could still raise enormous funds to pay for rapid expansion of the armed forces. In 1742 the representatives of the city of Rotterdam countered the arguments of neutralists within the States of Holland with the argument: 'Bad finance no real objection. The money has to come from wherever possible. Never easier to obtain money than for the defence of the country'.[175] Overall, Holland managed to raise ƒ115 million for the war, contributing to a new spring for military soliciting.[176]

---

172   NA, Archief Staten van Holland, no. 157. 'Resoluties 1723', fol. 382.

173   NA, Archief Staten van Holland, no. 157. 'Resoluties 1723', fol. 426.

174   Van Nimwegen 2002, p. 9.

175   Quoted in Van Nimwegen 2002, p. 92.

176   Van Nimwegen 2002, p. 96.

While the relative success of Holland during the War of the Austrian Succession in raising the required funds did prove the elasticity of the existing system of military finance, the long period of parlous state finances did do serious damage to the public image of military solicitors. An anonymous tract, probably written by a captain in the late 1730s, warned officers of the tricks used by military solicitors to muddle their accounts at the captains' expense.[177] The writer complained that 'the general abuses are so widespread, that only few of them are still noted'. As examples of illegal practices he mentioned among others the (prohibited) charging of interest on interest, charging for costs that according to regulation should be carried by the solicitors, and refusal to return interest when solicitors failed to pay in time. All those practices demanded 'careful inspection of a solicitor's account, the method of which is fully unique and [used] nowhere but in the act of soliciting, particularly forming a labyrinth to someone who is not well versed in this subject'.[178] But financial problems did not arise exclusively from the shady dealings of solicitors. Even at times of peace, arrears could reach such proportions that they threatened the financial position of a whole string of suppliers and financiers. Effectively only large-scale solicitors were able to secure themselves against the risks that in these conditions were involved in government contracting, giving them unwarranted influence on the process of public tendering and in some cases even allowing them to place themselves between the state and contractors as the real tendering agents.[179] How far things could get out of hand in the private dealings between captains and solicitors is shown by the case of the captain Rudolf de Salis. This captain, whose company resorted under the Province of Utrecht, turned to the Province of Holland on 24 October 1725. Being under even more serious financial strains than Holland, arrears of the province to De Salis's company had run up to ƒ89,433. This had forced him to indebt himself deeply with a number of solicitors, bankers, suppliers, and other 'good citizens' who now started to demand repayment. In despair De Salis turned to the Province of Holland to guarantee another loan from Holland's solicitors to mollify some of his most obtrusive creditors. 'To rescue him from his labyrinth', he explained, 'he would be helped a great deal if henceforth he could pay to his screaming creditors a sum of twelve thousand guilders'. Two Holland-based solicitors, Heeneman and Vrind, took over De Salis's debt.[180]

---

177   The whole text of this tract is reproduced in Zwitzer 1978, pp. 86–95.

178   Zwitzer 1978, p. 95.

179   NA, Familiearchief Van Heteren Supplement, no. 85. 'Afkondiging Raad van State', 20 May
      1729.

180   NA, Archief van de Gecommitteerde Raden van de Staten van Holland en Westfriesland,

Such debt problems remained rather common, as is shown by a resolution of 24 July 1753 which prohibited solicitors from granting credits to captains and other officers that exceeded the sum of the payment ordinances in their possession.[181]

That De Salis turned towards Holland solicitors when his own province could not provide proper payment is indicative of a wider trend in the second half of the eighteenth century. Reflecting the growing regional imbalances in financial strength, more and more soliciting contracts were concentrated in the hands of Holland investors. At the same time, centralisation of contracts into fewer hands took place within this province as well. The number of new solicitors appointed declined drastically in the course of the eighteenth century. Between 1734 and 1794 fifty-eight new solicitors were officially appointed by the States of Holland. More than half of those new appointments took place in the 1730s and 1740s, with a peak in 1747, when Dutch entry into the War of the Austrian Succession led to the hurried admission of ten new solicitors.[182] In 1753 a resolution limited the maximum number of solicitors employed by the province to twenty-eight. With characteristic caution, rather than firing a number of solicitors, the implementation of this reduction was spread out over a long period by simply refraining from filling the position of solicitors who passed away (mortification).[183] Other provinces tried to cut the number of solicitors in more dramatic ways. Just a year after coming to power, stadtholder William IV introduced a 'Reforming Statute' for the Province of Groningen that, among other clauses for financial redress, ordered:

> All soliciting functions, considered useless services, will be mortified without any of them being filled at a later stage, and payment of the militia will henceforth occur directly from the provincial treasury. The salaries of the solicitors will fall to the benefit of the province, and as much as possible be employed to ensure punctual payment.[184]

---

    no. 3540. 'Documenten tot de resoluties van de Gecommitteerde Raden', January–March 1726, 'Requeste Rudolff De Salis, 24 oct. 1725'.

181   NA, Archief van de Gecommitteerde Raden van de Staten van Holland en Westfriesland, no. 3110. 'Resoluties 1753', fol. 1147, 24 July 1753.

182   NA, Archief Staten van Holland, no. 5775. 'Benoemingen solliciteurs-militair 1731–1794'.

183   NA, Archief van de Gecommitteerde Raden van de Staten van Holland en Westfriesland, no. 3110. 'Resoluties 1753' fol. 1146, 24 July 1753.

184   Quoted in Kok 1788, pp. 662–3.

Since this reform came at a time when the Province of Groningen was completely unable to fulfil its financial obligations towards its troops, in effect this measure did not mean replacement of military soliciting by a state-run system, but forced companies to take recourse to Holland solicitors.

In his study of the army under the Dutch Republic, Zwitzer concludes that by the end of the eighteenth century 'the office of soliciting had become the business of a limited number of persons'. By 1794 only thirty-one military solicitors operated in the whole of the Republic. Of those, fourteen lived and worked in The Hague, five in the Province of Guelders, two in Zeeland, one in Utrecht, five in Friesland, two in Overijssel, one in Groningen, and one in Drenthe. The great majority of companies in all provinces, as well as the foreign troops in the service of the Dutch Republic, were 'served' by a small group of Holland solicitors.[185] Although brokerage practices had survived the eighteenth century, the role of intermediaries in troop payments had shifted from the rather large group of non-specialised or semi-specialised investors of the early seventeenth century to a relatively small group of large-scale professional financiers, half of whom were based in The Hague.

Conclusions

The Dutch system of troop payments through military soliciting showed great resilience. Despite perennial complaints about inefficiency, corruption, the intermingling of public and private interests – standard complaints about private involvement in government finance and contracting throughout early modern Europe – and despite the perceived advantages in terms of costs and control over the troops from a system of 'direct payment' by the state, brokerage practices survived the 1673 and 1721 reform attempts. Military soliciting was only replaced by payment through a small number of state appointed directors in 1795, when a revolution triggered by French arms shook up the whole federal structure of the old Republic. Perhaps the simplest explanation for this persistence is that, like many other areas of federal-brokerage organisation, the system worked remarkably well. Throughout the seventeenth and much of the eighteenth century it allowed the Dutch Republic to mobilise effectively the main factor that underpinned its military strength – large amounts of credit to pay for an army out of all proportion to the size of its population. Military solicitors were indispensible cogs in what Jan Glete has described as 'an impressive

---

185   Zwitzer 1991, pp. 97–8.

fiscal-military machine that raised more resources *per capita* than any other seventeenth-century state and organised these resources into large permanent armed forces of high quality'.[186]

Continuity in army payment resulted from the direct relationship that these solicitors established between the state and the credit market. Handling enormous sums and creating new outlets for financial investment, they functioned as the tubes connecting the two communicating vessels of government debt and early modern capital markets. From the reforms of 1676 onwards soliciting was restricted to a small layer of professional financial entrepreneurs operating through networks of private creditors. The cases of Gebhardt and Van Heteren show how these networks were built and maintained, but also how the vicissitudes of government finance could destroy connections that were seemingly secure. The relatively open political structures of the Dutch Republic allowed for outsiders such as Gebhardt to become involved in major financial contracts, and make considerable money out of this. However, to maintain a soliciting business over many decades required strong embeddedness in the Dutch world of finance, available to Van Heteren but not to Gebhardt.

Van Heteren's career stands out as that of a typical eighteenth-century financial aristocrat. Born into a family of Holland officials and solicitors, he secured himself access to the corridors of power, built a fortune out of the War of the Spanish Succession, actively diversified his investments after the Peace of Utrecht, secured his position by marriage and religious and charitable functions, and remained in business until his death just after the War of the Austrian Succession. The process of concentration of military contracts that started in 1676 continued during Van Heteren's life, ending in the final decades of the eighteenth century in a situation in which most army finances were 'solicited' by only a small group of financiers based primarily in Holland. However, this late process of centralisation was not indicative of the strengthening of the Dutch central state following a transition from brokerage structures to nationalisation. Rather, it signified uneven development within the framework of the federal-brokerage state itself, resulting from the weakening of the financial position of the more peripheral provinces, while Holland financial markets still basked in the afterglow of the 'Golden Age'. It was one more expression of the growing severity of the organisational problems faced by the Dutch state.

---

186   Glete 2002, p. 172.

The Structural Crisis of the Federal-Brokerage State

Intense involvement in war at sea and on land for the Dutch Republic did not usher in a transformation from brokerage practices to nationalisation, but instead strengthened the federal-brokerage character of the state. However, this tendency was reversed in dramatic fashion at the end of the eighteenth century. The crisis of the *ancien régime* was also the crisis of the particular state form that had accompanied the development of Dutch capitalism during the most successful part of its cycle of accumulation. No major area of the organisation of warfare was left untouched by the revolutionary convulsions in which Dutch society was caught. But in contrast to France or Britain, where major attempts at financial and military reform preceded the age of revolutions and revolutionary war, it was the failure to instigate such reforms that radicalised Dutch opposition movements. The current chapter is somewhat different than the three preceding it in that it will not examine the internal functioning of the institutions of the federal-brokerage state, but rather the way in which these institutions became subject to intense debate between reform-minded administrators and radical oppositionists. For readers familiar with the historiography of the late Republic it will not present a substantially new story, but it will provide a re-examination of familiar sources from a new angle: that of the interrelation between the development of the crisis of the old regime and the state form specific to the Dutch Republic. This chapter completes the Gramscian theme introduced at the start of the book, in which the distinct structure of the Dutch state was explained as the outcome of a historic bloc between international merchants and the upper layers of the localised systems of commodity production and exchange, by tracing this structure's eventual dissolution.

Much time has passed since Huizinga could write that historians were 'arrogant' and 'condescending' about the eighteenth century. Few topics in early modern Dutch history have warranted so much attention among contemporary historians as the changes in political discourse during the last decades of the Republic.[1] These contributions show how the second half of the eighteenth century saw a complete reshuffling of the terms of political debate. Long-

---

1 The list is too long to enumerate. Some of the key contributions to the debate are De Wit 1965, Leonard Leeb 1973, Schama 1977, Kossmann 1987a, Kossmann 1987b, Velema 1993, Klein 1995, Van Sas 2004a, Van Sas 2004b, and Velema 2007, from the motto of which Huizinga's quotation is taken.

established concepts such as republicanism, the stadtholderate, federalism, aristocracy, and democracy all became defined, contested, and redefined in radically new ways. In the process the elements of consensus that had bound together conflicting sections of the Dutch ruling class and had formed an ideological basis for compromise on core issues of foreign, military, and economic policy dissipated. Latent contradictions between the seven provinces, between advocates and adversaries of the House of Orange, between regents and the urban lower classes, became focal points of major crises.

Three revolutionary moments marked the last fifty years of the *ancien régime*: the violent restoration of the stadtholderate of 1747, the failed Patriot Revolution of 1785–7, and the Batavian Revolution of 1795–8 that put an end to the old Republic.[2] None of them took place in isolation from international developments. Despite the fact that the eighty years after the Peace of Utrecht saw an almost complete reversal in the proportion of peace and war years compared to the eighty years that preceded it, each major crisis was connected to war. Mirroring the events of 1672, the failure of the stadtholderless regime to prepare effectively for French invasion in 1747 led to the widespread revolts that brought William IV to power. The Seven Years' War between Britain and France (1757–63), in which the Dutch Republic remained neutral, nevertheless brought to light the vulnerability of the Dutch commercial empire to British competition in particular. This led to a sharp shift in political sympathies in which fears of Dutch economic decline became ideologically linked to fierce Anglophobia.[3] The American Revolution inspired opposition against the stadtholderate, and the failure of the Dutch navy in the Fourth Anglo-Dutch War gave opposition its revolutionary edge. Counter-revolution could only be successful because of armed Prussian intervention in 1787, further tying the fate of the old order to international power relations. In 1795 French revolutionary armies gave the tottering regime its final push, sparking a native revolution that surpassed all preceding crises in thoroughness and radicalism.

Focusing on the political process that finally resulted in the dismantling of the federal-brokerage state, this chapter will re-examine the eighteenth-century debates on the Dutch state form. It starts by tracing the development of reform ideologies among sections of the elite directly linked to the state (section 5.1), in order to then investigate the limits of these reform attempts in each of the areas of federal-brokerage organisation examined in the previ-

---

2 For a brief overview of events, see Israel 1998, Chapters 40–4.
3 Van Sas 2003, and Ormrod 2003, pp. 303–5.

ous chapters, as well as the rise of radical challenges outside the state. Section 5.2 examines the arguments for free trade and how they undercut the position of the preceding model of the warring monopoly company, section 5.3 the way in which the divisions between the five Admiralty Boards came to symbolise the defects of the federal state structure, and section 5.4 the debates on the mercenary versus the citizens' army as an important element of the radicalisation of opposition movements between the failed Patriot Revolution of 1785–7 and the Batavian Revolution of 1795. These sections will show that critique of the *ancien régime* and debates on the federal-brokerage state form became connected in complex ways. Rather than a linear transgression from moderate reform to radical renewal, a spectacular 'reversal of positions' took place in which the centralising reformers of the existing state became the conservative defenders of the federal-brokerage state, and the 'restorationist' oppositionists became the radical modernisers of the post-1795 period. The final section traces the fate of the federal-brokerage state after the fall of the Old Republic, and shows how its afterlife came to haunt the promulgators of a new order.

5.1   The Rise and Limits of Reform Agendas

The intensity of the crisis that overtook the Dutch state in the second half of the eighteenth century can only be understood against the background of the end of the Dutch cycle of accumulation. From the early eighteenth century onwards if not earlier it was clear to contemporaries that the economy of the Dutch Republic had lost much of its erstwhile dynamism.[4] The fall from its hegemonic position did not occur in the caricatured version popularised by eighteenth-century oppositionists and long repeated in modern literature, in which the former dominant power in one stroke became an impoverished state ruled by an incompetent aristocratic clique. Previous chapters have shown how the Dutch federal-brokerage state could continue to draw on the immense wealth of the Republic and mobilise it effectively for warfare, even if on a smaller scale than during the seventeenth century.[5] Decline was unevenly divided across the different provinces and over the main sectors of the economy – sharpest in industrial production, only slow to develop in European trade, absent until very late into the eighteenth century in colonial trade and finance, and partly

---

4   Nijenhuis 2002, and Sturkenboom 2008.
5   Also see Fritschy 1988, pp. 61 ff.

compensated by an upturn in commercial agriculture.[6] As late as 1776, no less an authority than Adam Smith could still argue that the Dutch Republic 'in proportion to the extent of the land and the number of its inhabitants, by far the richest country in Europe, has ... the greatest share of the carrying trade of Europe'.[7] Smith described the Republic as 'the only naval power which could endanger the security of England',[8] and ascribed this success to the structure of its state:

> The republican form of government seems to be the principal support of the present grandeur of Holland. The owners of great capitals, the great mercantile families, have generally either some direct share or some indirect influence in the administration of that government.[9]

Of course, Smith's Holland was an ideal type, created for the sake of an argument directed at British society. Here it serves to caution modern observers that the outcome of losing hegemonic status in the capitalist world-system was not the degradation of the Dutch Republic into dismal poverty, but its falling back to a position just behind its most successful European competitors.

Nevertheless, the fallout that this lagging behind produced was real. For one thing, both the urban poor and sections of the middle classes involved in production bore the brunt of economic retardation. This translated both into class anger and defensive corporatist responses against those involved in international trade and finance, who continued to grow richer and – following the fashion of the time – were fond of showing it.[10] And over the long term the decline in military and naval power relative to its competitors did mean the Dutch state became less effective in protecting the overseas trade of its merchant elites, fuelling discontent among leading sections of the ruling class as well.[11] The federal-brokerage state played a particular role in this process. Dutch decline did not produce an absolute loss of dynamism, but rather a severing of the links between the main sectors of the Dutch economy that during the

---

6   De Vries and Van der Woude 1997, pp. 681 ff.

7   Smith 1999a, p. 473.

8   Smith 1999b, pp. 40–1.

9   Smith 1999b, p. 505.

10   On the complex interplay between class and corporatist dynamics of lower-class mobilisations in the Dutch Republic, see Dekker 1982, Prak 1991, and Marc Boone and Maarten Prak 1995, pp. 113 ff.

11   Cf. Chapter Two, section 6.

seventeenth century had evolved in more or less connected rhythms. As has been shown in the previous chapters, far from merchants losing control over the state to 'aristocrats' uninterested in commercial development, the Dutch state remained highly attuned to the interests of capital accumulation. But in the circumstances of the eighteenth century the strong ties of the state to conflicting sections of the merchant elite became a lever for uneven development, rather than for combining the strength of each sector for creating greater international competitiveness. The centrifugal tendencies inherent to the federal-brokerage state-form facilitated the erosion of its underlying historic bloc.

Those at the helm of the Dutch state did not respond passively to the developing crisis. From the early eighteenth century onwards principled agendas for reform were formulated. These started with the writings of Simon van Slingelandt, secretary of the Council of State during the War of the Spanish Succession and its aftermath, and from 1725 to 1737 grand pensionary of Holland. Confronted by the financial crisis that emanated from forty years of warfare with France, and deeply troubled by the unwillingness of many of his fellow regents to take decisive measures to counteract the weakening of the state's international position, he launched a string of proposals for the regeneration of the Republic. His ideas remained of great influence among reformers from within the state as well as challengers from without throughout the eighteenth century. After having circulated widely in manuscript for many decades, a four-volume collection of his memorandums and proposals was eventually printed in 1784–5 as part of the debates between Patriots and Orangists in the aftermath of a new crippling war. It is not hard to see why his observations on the defects of the Dutch state made such an impression two generations after his death. The decline of Dutch military and naval power, the inability to enforce compliance to financial obligations equally in all provinces, and the debilitating effects of federalism for decision-making on urgent matters – themes that had once again become central during the Fourth Anglo-Dutch War – all figured prominently in the writings of this leading statesman of Holland. Already in 1716 Van Slingelandt had argued:

> The inconvenience, in which it [the Dutch Republic] has lapsed because of three heavy wars, especially the last one in which it has made much greater efforts than its powers allowed for, induces anyone who has the slightest understanding of public affairs to judge that a political body can hardly exist that is composed in the manner of that of the United Provinces, consisting of members who in the first place cannot outvote each other, and accordingly cannot or can only very slowly come to a

decision in matters of urgency; who, in the second place, when they have come to a decision, cannot force each other to follow up on the decision that has been taken unanimously; and who in the third place in governing their common affairs are represented by a council [the Council of State], that works without a clear common instruction, without an oath of obligation to the common body [the States General], and without sufficient authority.[12]

Van Slingelandt already pointed out the worrying connection between these institutional defects and the economic problems that the Republic had started to encounter. As he aptly observed, 'a rich household can weather disorders that bring chaos to a poor household'.[13] In order to prevent further collapse, Van Slingelandt counselled special attention to those areas of governance that most clearly determined the power of the Republic: the structure of its finances, the Admiralty Boards, and military command. Van Slingelandt's suggestions for reform concentrated on strengthening the central institutions of the existing state. He proposed to erect a council of government consisting of permanent members without simultaneous duties in provincial government. A finance department, reporting to this council of government, would among other things be made responsible for 'expenditure and control of the nation's fortresses, mustering, and the examining and closing of the army payrolls'.[14] One of the positive effects of this concentration of control would be that the provincial paymasters would lose their influence over the States army, strengthening the position of a captain general – a function tied to the stadtholderate that in both stadtholderless periods remained unfulfilled – that according to Van Slingelandt's plans was to be newly appointed by the state.[15] Similarly, the appointment of an admiral general – the naval equivalent of the captain general – was necessary 'to make the Admiralty Boards, which otherwise have little relation to each other and often even obstruct one another, into one body'.[16]

---

12   'Discours over de defecten in de jeegenwoordige constitutie der regeering van den staat der Vereenigde Nederlanden, en over de middelen van redres' (1716), Van Slingelandt 1784a, pp. 186–7.

13   'Aanwysing van de waare oorsaaken van jeegenwoordig groot verval in de generale regeering van den staat der Vereenigde Nederlanden, en van de noodige Middelen van Redres' (1717), Van Slingelandt 1784b, p. 14.

14   'Discours over de defecten', Van Slingelandt 1784a, pp. 229–31.

15   'Discours over de defecten', Van Slingelandt 1784a, p. 214.

16   'Discours over de defecten', Van Slingelandt 1784a, p. 220.

The sharpness of Van Slingelandt's formulations indicates his growing sense of disquiet with the existing structure of the state. But it is important to note that Van Slingelandt's suggestions were explicitly geared towards 'redress' of shortcomings within the framework of the existing state, not its replacement by an entirely new structure. The innovations he proposed, such as the appointment of a captain general and admiral general during a stadtholderless period, were perceived by him only as variants on old and established practices.[17] In later writings even his modest innovations disappeared in favour of shored up versions of the old system.[18] The proposed agents for his moderate reforms were the ruling regents themselves, and it was to them that he turned his passionate plea,

> to wake up from their current lethargy, that has so much taken the upper hand, that it has to be feared that many will stay in this condition until at one time or another they will be forcefully woken up, to find out that it might be too late to use the remedies that can at present still be employed.[19]

The unwillingness of the regents to heed his call left most of his attempts at reform completely ineffective.[20] As Van Slingelandt predicted, an external shock was needed to shake up the frozen institutional set-up of the Republic. This shock came with the French invasion of 1747. The Orangist revolution that followed shared many of the characteristics of 1672 when William III had successfully appealed to supporters from the middle and lower classes to overthrow the De Witt regime, and had thereafter used popular pressure to reshuffle local government bodies in favour of his own faction. But the events of 1747 also differed in important respects. First, popular anger against the regent regime combined with the dire economic circumstances resulting from industrial decline gave mobilisation from below an independent dynamic that went much farther beyond the intentions of the leaders of the Orangist party. This became apparent in the numerous tax riots, the anti-regent revolt in Amster-

---

17   It certainly goes too far to ascribe to him a 'distinctly modern concept of legislative sovereignty', as is done by Worst 1992, p. 152.

18   'Aanwysing van een korte, en gereede, weg om te koomen tot herstel der vervalle saaken van de Republicq' (1722), Van Slingelandt 1784b, p. 102, where he argues that instead of appointing an admiral general, the States General should merely use their existing powers over the five Admiralty Boards more effectively.

19   'Discours over de defecten', Van Slingelandt 1784a, p. 250.

20   Aalbers 1980, p. 117.

dam, and unrest among Admiralty workers that continued after William IV's ascension to the stadtholderate, pitting the new regime directly against its more revolutionary adherents.[21] Second, the weakening of the provincial elites, including those of Holland, allowed the stadtholder to move towards a more far-reaching concentration of power in his own hands, leading to the acceptance by all Provincial States of a hereditary stadtholderate.[22] Third, the old patronage system, centred upon the stadtholderly court, princely advisors like the Duke of Brunswick, and the 'lieutenant-stadtholders' in each individual province, attained a much more prominent role in the appointment of officials than it had previously had.[23]

The renewed and enlarged power of the stadtholder, combined with the financial problems that the Dutch Republic had to face in the aftermath of the War of the Austrian Succession, stimulated debates on the nature of the state among the stadtholder's followers. In particular, William IV's personal advisor, Bentinck, bombarded him with proposals.[24] These were partly inspired by the 'enlightened monarchism' that at that time was on the rise across Europe. In an important reform plan written in 1749, Bentinck set out what according to him were 'les seuls véritables principes sur lesquels un stadhouder à la tête de cette république devroit se conduire, s'il veut se satisfaire et s'assurer un crédit solide et inébrandable'.[25] Like Van Slingelandt, Bentinck envisioned a centralisation of the state by strengthening its executive branches. But this time the introduction of a number of special departments would issue directly from the stadtholder, furthering the tendencies towards monarchical rule that arose from the introduction of the hereditary stadtholderate. The departments would be bureaucratic rather than representative institutions, guided by the decisions of William IV in all important matters:

> J'entends par département un certain nombre de personnes, chargées de voir et d'examiner tout ce qui arrive et tous les papiers qui entrent et qui ont rapport à telle ou telle sorte d'affaires, d'examiner les retroacta, d'éplucher la matière, et de former un avis, qui, suivant que la chose est plus ou moins importante, doit être portée au Prince ou non. Après

---

21   Rowen 1988, pp. 174–7, and De Jongste 1992, p. 43.

22   Gabriëls 1990, pp. 58–9.

23   Gabriëls 1990, pp. 440 ff.

24   Gabriëls 1990, pp. 169 ff.

25   '[T]he only true principles upon which a stadtholder at the head of this republic should base his conduct, if he wants to satisfy and assure a solid and unshakable credit'. Letter of W. Bentinck to the duke of Brunswick, 4 April 1766, Groen van Prinsterer 1910, p. 1.

quoi ces mêmes personnes doivent avoir le pouvoir d'exécuter ou de faire exécuter ce qui aura été résolu, soit sans, soit avec la décision du Prince.[26]

Bentinck's ideas did not only go farther than Van Slingelandt's because of the decisive role he assigned to the House of Orange, they also went beyond the federal-brokerage model of the state in seeing the central state as the real repository of the interests of the nation, to be shielded from the particularistic pressures of its component parts. This idea was formulated most explicitly when Bentinck described the tasks of the intended department of 'Navy and Commerce':

> Le Prince a dessein d'ériger un Conseil de Commerce. On lui a fourni des idées pour cela. Et certainement, si la chose est bien exécuté et les gens bien choisis, rien au monde ne seroit plus utile ni plus nécessaire. Le Prince verroit alors quel est l'intérêt général de la Nation, à travers des représentations souvent contradictoires des particuliers, des différentes villes et des différentes provinces. Après quoi l'exécution du détail doit selon les formes du gouvernement être l'affaire du Grand-Amiral et des Amirautés respectives (tant qu'elles ne seront pas combines, ce qui seroit très nécessaire).[27]

However, just like in the days of Van Slingelandt, few of Bentinck's suggestions for reform were put into practice.[28] This was not only the result of Wil-

---

26 'With a department I mean a certain number of people who are charged with seeing and examining everything that comes in and who file all the papers and report such and such affairs, examine the retroacta, bind these matters, and form an advise, depending on whether the affairs are more or less important, which must be brought under attention of the Prince and which must not. After this, the same persons must have the power to execute or let execute whatever is decided, either by the Prince or without his active involvement'. Memorandum of W. Bentinck on the organisation of government, 25 March 1749, Groen van Prinsterer 1908, p. 355.

27 'The Prince has the intention to erect a Council of Commerce. Ideas have already been formulated for this. Certainly, if it is well executed and the people are selected well, nothing in the world could be more useful and necessary than this. The Prince will be able to see in this way what are the general interests of the Nation, through the often contradictory representations by individuals, different cities and provinces. After this the execution of details should according to the forms of government be the affair of the Lieutenant-Admiral and the respective Admiralty Boards (as far as they will not be combined, which would be very necessary)'. Groen van Prinsterer 1908, p. 362.

28 Gabriëls 1999, pp. 172–7.

liam IV's weak commitment to change, which despite his turbulent rise to power made him 'neither revolutionary nor reformer', or his early death in 1751 and the minority of age of his heir William V.[29] Their dependency on provincial patronage networks forced the late eighteenth-century stadtholders and their supporters always to compromise with the social groups that formed the very backbone of the federal-brokerage model. Failing to give the state real independence from the main regent families, the late stadtholders instead promoted their own provincial clientele to the point of paralysing the state. This created irreparable rifts with those sections among the regent elite that were marginalised or excluded, while tying the stadtholderate more closely to its local supporters. Because of this dependence the power of the stadtholders remained far from monarchical, let alone absolutist.[30]

Nevertheless, the combination of revolutionary challenges from below and criticism from oppositional regents, the pressure of foreign economic and military competition, and the need to formulate answers to the shortcomings of the existing bureaucratic apparatus did give rise to a substantively new discourse among the supporters of the Orangist regime. Already under William IV this had become apparent in the – once again failed – attempts at tax reform to stimulate Dutch trade.[31] Whereas previously such reforms had always been defended as a return to old traditions – in content if not in form – the famous 1751 *Proposition* for a limited custom-free port system boldly declared the newness of its intentions:

> In this sense ... the plan of redress has to be a novelty, and to make this more apparent, one only has to reflect on the fact that all of Europe, in respect to commerce, has changed completely ... This forces us to adapt our measures, and find solutions that fit our current state and circumstances. For nothing demands such close scrutiny as commerce, that is daily subject to continuous changes, and therefore daily demands new arrangements.[32]

In the decades that followed, renewing the state to create an efficient and rational form of government while avoiding the twin dangers of democracy and revolutionary anarchy became the shared project of leading Orangist thinkers, from the political theorist and historian Adriaan Kluit and the standard bearer

---

29   Rowen 1988, Chapter 9.
30   Brake 1992, p. 84.
31   On the reasons for failure, see Hovy 1966, pp. 610 ff.
32   Van Oranje 1751, pp. 64–5.

of enlightened conservatism Elie Luzac, to the last grand pensionary of Holland Laurens Pieter van de Spiegel. The conservative impulse intersecting their reform-agendas partly stemmed from the rise of revolutionary movements across the Atlantic, and partly from similar movements within the Dutch Republic itself. Especially the oppositional and at times outright revolutionary challenge posed by the Patriot movement of the 1780s forced these leading Orangists to fundamentally rethink their positions. Each in his own way was committed to a 'rationalisation' of the state, and saw it as the only way to prevent imminent collapse.[33] Despite Van de Spiegel's contention 'that the constitution of the United Netherlands is one of the best that a federative Republic can have', his 1783 *Reflections on the defective state of the government of the United Netherlands*, written before his elevation to the position of grand pensionary, acknowledged that 'everyone seems to agree that the defects have now increased to the maximum, and that the Republic can no longer exist on its current footing'.[34] Approximately at the same time, he spelled out the logic of reform as a dam against revolution in a memorandum written for stadtholder William v:

> The constitution of the Republic currently is more vulnerable than ever; the bonds of all direction in government have been loosened, and the people, imbued with thoughts of liberty that it does not distinguish from independence, is ready to shake off a government that has been so incapable of maintaining itself. To leave this urge to its own development is highly dangerous; to counter it is as little advisable. What then remains? Nothing but to take into consideration the nature of the nation, carefully accede and in this way regain trust.[35]

Although still capturing their proposals in the language of restoration, the militant Orangists of the late eighteenth century went much further than earlier reformers in proclaiming the indispensability of an 'eminent head' to supersede the divisions inherent in the federal constitution of the Republic. Wyger Velema has shown how conservatism and anti-egalitarianism underwrote their

---

33   For Elie Luzac: Velema 1993, pp. 182 ff., and for Adriaan Kluit: Stapelbroek, Stamhuis, and Klep 2010.

34   Laurens Pieter van de Spiegel, 'Reflexien over de gebreeken in de gesteldheid der regering van de Vereenigde Nederlanden. September 1783', Vreede 1875, p. 260.

35   Laurens Pieter van de Spiegel, 'Over de tegenwoordige misnoegens tegen den Prins Erfstadhouder' (Tweede memorie ten behoeve van de Stadhouder, 20 januari 1783), Vreede 1875, p. 91.

vision of the stadtholder 'as the protector of the people, the guardian of the common good, the helm and the soul of the state'.[36] The logical conclusion of their theories was, in the words of Van de Spiegel, 'to put the hereditary stadtholderate on solid ground, and to draw an eternal line connecting the authority of the sovereign and the pre-eminence of the Gentlemen stadtholders'.[37]

It is precisely in the Orangist defence of the old order that the erosion of consensus behind the existing state-form taking place in this period is most apparent. In the course of the eighteenth century, the proposals of leading statesmen for tackling the dual problem of economic and military stagnation had shifted from moderate redress, to guarded reform, to a complete reconstitution of the state along centralising lines. But in the practical application of their suggestions they were hindered from two sides. On the one hand, it proved almost impossible to escape the viscosity of federal-brokerage structures without upsetting the entire established order and destroying the support base among the local elites of the stadtholderate itself. On the other hand, both in 1747 and more fundamentally after 1784, the danger of reform from above turning into full-scale revolution from below seemed too real to ignore. In different ways this double dilemma returned in all three areas of federal-brokerage organisation discussed in this book.

5.2   Warring Companies and the Debate over Free Trade

None of the conflicting elite-parties in the late Republic doubted the decisive importance of trade, especially colonial trade, for the future of the state. As late as 1783 the oppositional paper *Post van den Neder-Rhijn* could write that 'except for the truth of the Gospel, it is of nothing so convinced as that this country, that has become great at the same moment as the VOC, will stand or fall with it'.[38] From its foundation in 1602 the VOC had been one of the pillars of the federal-brokerage state. The maintenance of its commercial empire depended on its ability to wield military power on a state-like scale. Its organisational structure paralleled that of the Republic as a whole, in particular the navy. Hundreds of formal, informal, and familial ties connected the enterprise to the state. War had allowed it to strengthen its independent position as a state within the state,

---

36   Velema 2007, p. 135.

37   Van de Spiegel, 'Tegenwoordige misnoegens', Vreede 1875, p. 93.

38   *Post van den Neder-Rhijn*, Vol. IV, no. 193 (3 December 1783), 345. Quoted in Schutte 1974, p. 49.

creating a de facto division of labour in which the Company paid for state protection in European waters while maintaining a free hand in all commercial
and military affairs in Asia. But the second half of the eighteenth century saw
the breakdown of this division of labour under the combined pressure of foreign economic competition, declining profitability of the Asian branch of the
trading empire, and the defeats suffered by the Dutch navy against the English.
Together these forces eroded the company model of trade itself. Many practical suggestions were made for better direction of the Company, but more and
more, these became coupled to proposals for radical change in the relations of
Company and state. Discussion on the future of the Company became tied to
the ideological battles over the regeneration of Dutch commerce and the merits of economic liberalism.

The main lines of debate went in two seemingly opposite directions: on the
one hand increasing state intervention in military affairs in Asia combined with
centralisation of the VOC under more direct bureaucratic control, and on the
other hand the partial admission of free trade. In practice these two trends did
not collide, but were intimately connected. Both arose from the same set of
problems, some of which had already come to light during the 1740s when the
VOC still managed to make substantial profits on its inter-continental trade.[39]
Armed conflicts with Asian rulers, combined with the growing military and
commercial presence of the English and French, led to the decline and eventual
loss of Dutch dominance in India and the Arabian seas.[40] One of the ways
to counter declining incomes for local trading posts of the VOC was to start
engaging in illegal private trade on a larger scale. This was the case with the
Dutch director of Surat Pieter Laurens Phoonsen, who was recalled to Batavia
in 1740 at the charge of setting up a considerable trade in VOC spices for his
own account.[41] However, the VOC governors in Batavia themselves had strong
private interests that partly collided with those of the VOC directors in *patria*.
The extent to which this process undermined the coherence of company power
in Asia is described by Julia Adams as a classical 'principal-agent problem',
exacerbated by the already fragmented political structure of Company control
at home.[42] In this context VOC governor general Van Imhoff suggested the
introduction of limited free trade in 'ante-Asia' (Persia, the Indian coast, Dutch

---

39   Gaastra 2003, p. 148.

40   Winius and Vink 1991, pp. 87 ff.

41   Winius and Vink 1991, p. 94.

42   Adams 1996. The principal-agent problem in economics refers to situations in which
      principals depend on their local agents for profit, but the agents develop an interest of
      their own that is costly to keep in check.

Ceylon). This could have the triple advantage of allowing the VOC to withdraw from unprofitable areas of trade, boosting Batavia's position as Asia's main trading centre by attracting private traders from different nations, and enabling the VOC to levy a tax on existing trade flows that remained off the radar as long as private trade was illegal.[43]

Van Imhoff's suggestions echoed concerns that had been aired within the States General about the VOC's ability to take resolute measures to restore its profits. However, in 1740 the directors of the VOC were still able to brush off attempts by the Dutch state to intervene in what they considered as private affairs, thus forestalling any serious attempt at reform.[44] During the second half of the eighteenth century this balance of forces changed completely. For the first time since the early decades of the seventeenth century the VOC came to depend on the military and financial support of the state. From the War of the Austrian Succession in the 1740s onwards, Britain and France increasingly employed state troops overseas in support of their commercial companies, transforming military confrontations in the colonies into direct extensions of inter-state warfare in Europe. Although the Dutch Republic managed to stay neutral during the Seven Years' War – the first truly global Anglo-French confrontation – the growing presence of rival European armies in Asia began to make itself felt. In 1759 an armed expedition of the VOC to Bengal was routed in a half-hour battle against superior English troops, affirming the strong position of the British East India Company in this part of the Indian subcontinent.[45] The weakness of the VOC vis-à-vis its competitors was shown even more decisively during the Fourth Anglo-Dutch War. In the mid-1760s, VOC forces had managed to defeat the Kingdom of Kandy, strengthening Company rule in Ceylon. But in 1782 the British navy used the circumstances of war to conquer important footholds on the island, and the VOC had to rely on the French navy to arrest its advance.[46] Confronted with this shifting balance of power, the VOC had no choice but to ask for naval assistance from the Dutch state. In December 1782 the States General decided to send six men-of-war to Asia, and after the war the former division of labour in which the VOC was the sole wielder of Dutch military power beyond Cape Hope was not restored. The company's complete dependence on state support during the Fourth Anglo-Dutch War created a situation in which its directors had to accept the transfer of military power to the state and its officials, down to even the minutest details. As Jaap Bruijn

---

43   Steur 1984, p. 45.
44   Steur 1984, p. 42.
45   Winius and Vink 1991, pp. 126 ff.
46   Schrikker 2007, pp. 113–15.

notes, '[t]he instructions for the squadron commander in 1782 were drawn up by the state. Although the company was asked for comment, only minor adjustments were made to the orders'.[47]

Collapsing profits, escalating debts of the Company to the States of Holland and Zeeland, and the changing military role of the state in Asia fundamentally shifted the debate on the relations between the VOC and the state. *Constitutional restoration*, one of the programmatic texts of the Patriot opposition movement, drew attention to the sorry state of Dutch rule in the East and the West:

> The direction of the state, defence, and the entire financial condition there is so dramatic, so bad, so desperate, that the security provided by the recent state support for the VOC can have no other basis than general, radical reform.[48]

From the other side of the political spectrum, grand pensionary Van de Spiegel in 1788 summed up the main lessons drawn from the experience of the past decade:

> Before, the Company did not have to fear wars in which the Republic was involved in Europe, or those of the Company itself against the indigenous population. But today, it has to imagine that its main possessions will be the toy of other powers. Immediately at the outbreak of war they will take into custody our possessions and harbours to make sure that the other party will not profit from them. Such a defenceless and precarious state cannot continue without making the Company despicable in the eyes of Indian rulers, and eventually make it lose its trade. But on the other side, it has to be feared that the finances of the Company will not suffice to carry the burden of the kind of military establishment that her situation requires. This again proves the necessity that the Company and the government of the Republic will be connected more closely.[49]

These were not empty words. Already in 1786 Patriot influence on the States of Holland led to the introduction of a 'Fifth Department', a state agency designed

---

47   Bruijn 2003, p. 116.

48   Anonymous 1785, p. 9.

49   Van de Spiegel, 'Poincten waarop zal moeten gedacht worden in de besognes over de O.I. Comp.', Vreede 1876, pp. 595–6.

to exercise direct control over the VOC directors. The anti-Patriot counter-revolution of 1787 prevented this institution from ever becoming effective, but it is significant that after stadtholderly restoration it was not formally abolished. In 1790 a Holland-Zeeland State Committee was erected to fulfil a similar supervisory task.[50]

That supervision was left to these two provinces rather than a committee consisting of representatives of all seven provinces reflected the fact that they alone provided the enormous loans that kept the Company afloat. It also shows a tacit acknowledgement that the old federal framework no longer provided viable solutions to the challenges that the Republic had to face – an acknowledgement that extended to the federal make-up of the VOC itself. Van de Spiegel argued: 'The Company [in the future] should be characterised as one house of commerce that organises its expeditions from different harbours, but on one single account'.[51] However, the vested interests of the towns in which the chambers were located remained a solid barrier against any attempt at structural reform, and all supervisory institutions that were created foundered on the rocks of local conservatism.[52] Furthermore, the precarious situation in which the state found itself such a short time after the defeat of the Patriots and the outbreak of revolution in France made administrators hesitant to undertake anything that could lead to an implosion of one of its oldest pillars. As four 'plenipotentiaries for the affairs of the VOC' wrote in 1790 to the States General:

> These measures that have to be taken will be subject to insurmountable troubles, when news of the impending or actual collapse of the Company would precede them. Yes, to what surprising and unexpected revolution would such news inevitably lead ... and this at a time, in which a certain tumbling spirit has taken a hold of so many nations and has made them lose their ways.[53]

While the final decade of the Republic did see a rapid transformation of ideas on company-state relations, the integration of Company and state advocated by Van de Spiegel thus for political reasons proved impossible to achieve.

---

50 Dillo 1992, p. 167.

51 Van de Spiegel, 'Idées omtrent de Oost-Indische Compagnie (18 maart 1788)', Vreede 1876, p. 589.

52 Steur 1984, p. 194.

53 G.J.D. van der Does van Noordwyk, J. Rendorp, H. van Straalen, and P.H. van der Wall, 'Rapport wegens de zaaken van de Oost-Indische Compagnie', in Anonymous 1792, p. 24.

A similar situation can be seen in the debates on (partial) liberalisation of East India trade. Even among the Patriots of the early 1780s, generally more inclined to free trade, hardly any writer advocated the complete abolition of the VOC monopoly. Similarly, within the Company itself debates on reform still took place within the parameters set by the existing charter. In his famous 1785 memorandum 'for the benefit of the VOC and the utility of every inhabitant of the commonwealth', VOC director Van der Oudermeulen defended a slimmed-down version of monopoly trade. Repeating suggestions that he already had made in two earlier documents in the 1770s, he argued for 'navigation from port to port in the Indies [to be] handed over to our free citizens, except for some selected products'. He further suggested that unprofitable offices in Asia should be closed, but that the most profitable areas of trade should remain firmly in the hands of the VOC.[54] Without the Company, Van der Oudermeulen argued, all trade of the Dutch Republic would be lost.[55] Not surprisingly, Van der Oudermeulen's limited liberalisation always remained the outer limits of what most VOC directors were willing to contemplate. But the early 1790s did see the rise of a significant minority position within the VOC establishment that argued for a much more far-reaching liberalisation. One of the principal shareholders, Guillelmus Titsingh, wrote a memorandum to convince his colleagues of the advantages of free trade in Asia and between Asia and Europe:

> What liveliness and activity will this freedom of export ... give to all factor-ies, traffics, artisanal production, and retail trade, in this land where every-one knows a way to employ his funds! What liveliness in India's capital [Batavia] that will rise as a great trading city, while today it dwindles because it is ruled by an all-powerful despot [the VOC] which alone wants to master all the profits, and leave nothing to its subjects but the necessity to lie and rob, as grossly as they can, in order to escape from his oppression as soon as possible![56]

Such considerations were taken up positively by the leading VOC official Van Nederburgh, and also underlay proposals for reform by VOC directors Falck, Craayvanger and Scholten.[57] In March 1791 the directors of the Company dis-cussed liberalisation in remarkably favourable terms:

---

54 Van der Oudermeulen, 'Iets dat tot voordeel der deelgenooten van de Oost Indische Compagnie en tot nut van ieder ingezetenen, van dit gemeene best kan strekken', Van Hogendorp 1801, p. 252.

55 Van der Oudermeulen, 'Voordeel', Van Hogendorp 1801, p. 284.

56 [Titsingh] 1791, p. 52.

57 Steur 1984, p. 181 and pp. 185–6.

> That these disadvantages [i.e., the problems of the existing structure of Company trade] could be prevented when commerce could be left to private traders, provided that precautions could be made to prevent that the Company would ever lack such articles that are indispensable for its maintenance ...[58]

In the same year an experiment was made under Company direction allowing private traders to carry certain goods on VOC ships on their own account. All this debating and experimenting did not lead to a real attempt to dismantle the VOC monopoly from within. But they did mean that the revolutionaries of 1795 could fall back on a long line of argument combining trade liberalisation – in part or in full – with centralisation of colonial management under state control.

Developments across the Atlantic also fed into the debates on the place of the VOC within the Dutch state. As was shown in Chapter Two, already in the 1730s the West India Company monopoly had collapsed under the weight of private competition. But the Company did retain a significant role in trade, as well as a typical brokerage-function in colonial management and the organisation of trade protection. During two short periods this dual position seemed to open the way for restoring long-term company profitability. The Seven Years' War (1756–63) and the American War of Independence (1776–80) put Dutch traders in a position to undercut the trade of its major European competitors.[59] But temporary successes had to compete with strong long-term tendencies that undercut the WIC and connected institutions such as the Society of Suriname. The high costs of warfare – especially the brutal expeditions against runaway slaves fighting a determined guerrilla struggle against the planters in Suriname – and the strengthening of regional trading networks outside Company control created strong opposition, mainly concentrated in the Republic itself, against prolonging territorial administration by the Company. The Maroon Wars undoubtedly posed the most fundamental threat to Suriname white rule.[60] Between 1730 and 1770 the number of troops involved in fighting the formerly enslaved increased from 300 to over 3000. For the 1750s, the total cost of warfare was calculated at ƒ3.5 million, excluding ammunition, fortific-

---

58 'Extract uit de resolution', 29 March 1791, Anonymous 1792, p. 138.

59 Den Heijer 1994, p. 186.

60 Famously captured by the eyewitness account of one of the soldiers sent to suppress the revolt of 1772–7, who stated that in 1772 the uprising 'had nearly given the finishing blow' to the colony. Stedman 1972, p. 46. One and half centuries later, these revolts figured prominently in Anton de Kom's hard-hitting indictment of Dutch colonialism, De Kom 1934.

ations and militia costs. This equalled over ten percent of the value of goods exported from the colony.[61] For the years 1770–6 the combined costs of warfare had increased to *f*8 million.[62] The Dutch state, that since 1748 had already provided a regular convoy to Suriname, now also sent troops in large numbers to defend the planter colony. Similar problems for white rule arose in other West Indian possessions, with slave revolts in Berbice in 1763 and Essequibo in 1772, fuelling concerns within the Dutch Republic that commercial societies would be unable to defend Dutch interests overseas.[63] These fears were confirmed by the ease with which the British navy in 1781 conquered St. Eustatius, Saba, St. Maarten, Demerary, Essequibo, and Berbice.[64]

At the same time, extending networks of trade between local elites within the region, especially after the American War of Independence, provided a strong West Indian interest in free trade. Earlier than in the case of the voc, Patriots started to argue against the company structure of commercial organisation itself. In the *Letters of Aristodemus and Sincerus* (1785), a Patriot author argued for the taking over of all West Indian colonies by the Dutch state, including the assumption of full responsibility for defence, the daily governing of the colony, and its judicial system. At the same time, he advocated the destruction of all remnants of the Company monopoly.[65] In 1791, the Orangist States General put this programme into practice. They refused to prolong the wic charter, and bailed out its shareholders by buying their shares at 30 percent of their nominal value, still eight percent above current prices at the Amsterdam stock exchange. Rule over the former wic possessions was brought into the hands of the state through a Committee for the Affairs of the Colonies and Possessions on the Guinean Coast and in America.[66]

Chapter Two showed the contrast between the models of control applied by the wic and the voc, resulting in very different divisions of labour between state, company, and private traders in both areas. During the 1780s and 1790s the growing integration of commercial empires around the globe, as well as the challenges to the model of the Dutch Republican state at home, finally brought the two colonial companies back into the same stream. The debates that accompanied the long trajectory towards the eventual abolition of the voc after the revolution of 1795, connecting (partial) free trade to the need

---

61   Schalkwijk 2011, pp. 210–11.
62   Schalkwijk 2011, p. 216.
63   Goslinga 1985, p. 580.
64   Schutte 1974, p. 54.
65   Schutte 1974, pp. 58–9.
66   Den Heijer 1994, p. 187.

for a strong and interventionist state in full control of its overseas territories, mirrored those leading to the dissolution of the WIC a few years before the revolution. Neither in the West nor in the East did the model of the merchant warrior meet the requirements of the new age. But the connections between East and West, or between free trade and interventionist state, did not become apparent in a single stroke or a straight line. Perhaps the best illustration of this can be found in the person of Guillelmus Titsingh, the writer of the 1791 challenge to the old Company model of trade in the East Indies. Ten years earlier, this same Titsingh in his capacity as representative of Suriname traders had been the driving force behind the fitting out of a private convoy of armed merchant-men to protect the Suriname trade.[67] Thus, as late as the Fourth Anglo-Dutch War, the answer to the failure of the federal-brokerage state to provide protection for its commercial elites could still be a return to the most classical forms of brokerage warfare. Although the ensuing crisis of the Dutch state gave debates on commerce and the state a growing ideological dimension, the main protagonists on either side always remained pragmatists looking for the surest way to secure profits.

5.3   Admiralty Boards at the Centre of the Storm

No section of the federal-brokerage state came under such heavy fire at the end of the eighteenth century as federal naval administration. Chapters Two and Three showed how the five Admiralty Boards tied the global commercial interests of the Dutch ruling class to highly localised spheres of production and political influence. Their strong connections to the leading merchant families stimulated naval administrators to prioritise direct commercial protection over long-term power projection in the make-up and employment of the fleet. The Dutch navy of the eighteenth century was far from passive or lethargic in its execution of this primary task. But the shifting strategic geography of trade inclined Admiralty Boards to concentrate on the specific task of securing long-distance trade, and to rely heavily on the British ally for European power projection. By the time the Anglo-Dutch alliance broke down in the second half of the eighteenth century, the Dutch Republic no longer possessed the kind of navy capable of holding at bay its main European competitors, and the Dutch had lost all vestiges of their former naval supremacy in the Baltic and the Mediterranean. The Fourth Anglo-Dutch War (1780–4) brought this failure into

---

67   Habermehl 1987, pp. 85 ff.

broad daylight. The complete supremacy of the British fleet prevented even the sailing out of regular convoys for the commercial fleet, bringing foreign trade practically to a standstill.

The dismal performance of the Dutch navy further charged the already highly politicised climate. In the eyes of the Patriots of the late 1770s and 1780s, commercial decline, misdirection of the armed forces, and the supposed Anglophilia of the stadtholder all became tied into one big knot. Already in the first year of the war, the Patriot's influential spokesman Joan Derk van den Capellen tot den Poll merged these themes into a single narrative of the historic betrayal of Dutch interests by the House of Orange. In his call to arms *To the People of the Netherlands*, he turned this anger directly on William V:

> You did not want protection at sea, where thousands of defenceless sea-men and treasures that surpass the combined value for the Republic of the three inland provinces Guelders, Utrecht, and Overijssel together ... are being exposed daily to the rapacity and cruelty of your English friends [sic!]. The wailing voices of the merchants, who spoke, prayed, and begged thousands of times for the preservation of the entire fatherland, were scorned by you. The blood of your fellow countrymen – abused, tormen-ted, tortured, killed by your English friends at sea – called for revenge and protection in vain.[68]

In some ways the vitriol directed towards the stadtholder in *To the People of the Netherlands* deflected from a more thoroughgoing critique of the functioning of the navy. Its programme of a fictitious restoration of the 'old constitution' precluded an attack on one of the anchors of the existing federal state form. Nonetheless, at this point a fundamental rethinking of federal naval adminis-tration was already in the offing.

As was the case with the merchant companies, emerging revolutionary discourse was fed by the rise of reform tendencies from within the institutions themselves. In the case of the Admiralty Boards, these went back as far as the discussions on the introduction of a custom-free port system after the Orangist revolution of 1747. The Admiralty Boards came under severe criticism in the text of the 1751 *Proposition*, given their responsibility both for the levying of customs and for the organisation of armed convoys for the merchant fleet. Successive generations of reformers wrestled with the question of how to lower customs that were the main source of income for the navy, while at the same time

---

68   [Van der Capellen tot den Poll] [1781], p. 59.

increasing the size and effectiveness of the Dutch war fleet. One of the most common answers was to look for the source of financial problems of the navy not in the low custom rates, but in the unequal footing on which those were collected by the five Admiralty Boards. Eighteenth-century observers were convinced that especially the Zeeland and Friesland Boards used their ability to under-charge local merchants as a tool to provide 'their own' merchant communities with competitive advantages over those of other provinces. The 1751 *Proposition* singled out this practice as one of the major weaknesses of Dutch trade policy:

> If the same commodities and merchandise pay higher duties in one part of the Republic than in the other, or if some merchants keep on paying them while others because of fraud and evil practices are relieved of this duty, this again can only be of the utmost damage to our commerce.[69]

In the same spirit, a 1754 report of the Generalty Audit Office lambasted the excessive overhead costs of maintaining a separate bureaucracy for the five naval establishments. Many of the 'inutile servants' apparently did not fulfil any other function than 'making an extra man' on the payroll.[70] This, the report argued, was particularly true of the personnel of many of the 'outside offices' for custom collection, the system of offices maintained by the Admiralty Boards outside of their home towns to prevent tax evasion. To show the ineffectiveness of these outside offices – deliberate ineffectiveness, as was at least suggested by the inspectors – the report included a list of forty-two outside offices of the Rotterdam Admiralty Board that collected less customs than they spent on office personnel and maintenance. Most illustrative were those offices like 't Spuy, which brought in thirteen guilders over the course of a year, but spent f1,180 on the clerk, rowers, and administrative costs to collect this meagre sum.[71] Far from seeing this as an incident the writers of the report used it as an example to show the inherent problems of federal administration. Federal naval administration could not function without an overgrowth of costly local administrators:

---

69   Van Oranje 1751, p. 56.

70   NA, Archief J.C. van der Hoop, no. 153. 'Missive van de Generaliteits Reekenkamer', 27 November 1754, p. 10.

71   NA, Archief J.C. van der Hoop, no. 153. 'Missive van de Generaliteits Reekenkamer', 27 November 1754, appendix.

As long as there are five Boards of the Admiralty, and in the Northern
Quarter of Holland two or three shipyards, and as long as there have to be
so many councillors as is required within the old institutional setting –
which can hardly be avoided within the existing constitution of our government – all attempts at administrative reforms will come to little.[72]

The heated debates on fleet augmentation of the 1770s, and then more forcefully during the Fourth Anglo-Dutch War, turned abstract speculations on a
more centralised structure of naval administration into concrete interventions
to change the nature of this institution. Shortly before the outbreak of the war
an official memorandum directly proposed the 'unification of the five Admiralty Boards into one single body'. It contained scathing commentary on the lack
of effectiveness of the existing administrative structure, which pitted the different provinces against each other:

> It is strange that the direction of naval affairs in this Republic is divided
> into various departments and that while they should together form one
> complete or general direction, the separate Boards consider themselves
> as completely alien one from the other, and often think they have con-
> tradictory interests. And for this reason, the direction that should be the
> same in the entire Republic and founded on one unified basis, is practiced
> in a different way by the different Boards, leading to many disputes and
> disagreements to the detriment of the common cause.[73]

The report acknowledged that established interests in the provinces and towns
harbouring the five Admiralty Boards formed a real barrier for realising the proposed unification. Characteristically for most reform attempts from within the
state, rather than challenging the federal principles underlying naval organisation, the document argued that local interests would actually be served best by
unification:

> Since in this way the same provinces far from damaged will be favoured;
> presuming that the shipyards and storehouses will remain in the same
> cities where they are located now. It does not need arguing that the

---

72   NA, Archief J.C. van der Hoop, no. 153. 'Missive van de Generaliteits Reekenkamer', 27 No-
     vember 1754, p. 2.

73   NA, Archief J.C. van der Hoop, no. 153. 'Memorie van eenige Elucidatien op de voorgeslaa-
     gene Poincten van Redres in de Collegien ter Admiraliteit &c &c by resolutie van 1 april
     1778'.

loss of some offices and committees ... cannot be compared with the benefits that the same Provinces would gain because of the building and equipment of a greater number of warships on their respective wharves, by which much money could be made in those provinces. For the unified Navy Board should build on all those shipyards without discrimination.[74]

It is not surprising that after the crushing defeat of the Dutch navy in the Fourth Anglo-Dutch War the arguments about the need for structural reform of naval direction gained new pace. The Patriots' programmatic *Constitutional restoration* suggested the 'reduction of the number of Admiralty Boards' as one of the solutions for the 'affairs of great weight that have to be repaired in our general system of state'.[75] And the Personal Committee for Defence that was instigated by the Patriot-controlled States of Holland in 1785 as one of the two great investigative committees to lay bare the defects of the existing state put much emphasis on the need for unification of the navy. Its final report, which only appeared two years after the defeat of the Patriots in 1787, squarely advocated the integration of the Admiralty Boards into one single department for the navy, and did so without harking back to the Republic's old constitutional forms:

> We are of the opinion that the affairs at sea should be reduced to their first principles – not so much by the erection of a College of Superintendence [a reference to sixteenth century proposals to add an overseeing body to the existing federal navy] ... but by the erection of one single department, or Admiralty Board, located permanently in The Hague close to the high colleges of government, and thus placed directly under the eyes of the same, and in the line of sight of the lord admiral general.[76]

The arguments for this unification put forward by the committee show how far enlightened administrators had moved away from the traditional, federal-brokerage thinking on the nature of state institutions, and how the different strands of criticism underlying debates since the 1750s merged into a single

---

74   NA, Archief J.C. van der Hoop, no. 153. 'Memorie van eenige Elucidatien op de voorgeslaagene Poincten van Redres in de Collegien ter Admiraliteit &c &c by resolutie van 1 april 1778'.

75   Anonymous 1785, iv–v.

76   NA, Archief J.C. van der Hoop, no. 155. 'Memorie, houdende het generaal rapport van de Personeele Commissie van het Defensie-Weezen', p. 23.

narrative of centralisation, rationalisation and national interests. Through the unified Department of Naval Affairs, the state would

> gain control over the collection of customs, which then would no longer be raised by the various towns and provinces on an unequal footing; but to the pleasure of the allied provinces and strengthening of the nation's finance, everywhere be executed on the basis of an equal practice. And in this way, provincial and urban influence will be eliminated also in this area. More than is possible today, it will oversee the interest of all commerce. It will observe the state of all branches of trade from one single point of view. It will search for the causes of the growth of this branch, and the decrease of that, and with more knowledge of affairs propose such measures as the conditions require.[77]

The fact that an official committee could reach such revolutionary conclusions two years after the Orangist restoration of 1787 again confirms the measure to which the federal-brokerage consensus had dissolved among the leading circles within the state itself. Yet this does not mean it went unopposed. In October 1786 the five Admiralty Boards sent a joint letter to the members of the committee that contained an explicit defence of the old structure of federal navy boards with their close ties to the commercial elites:

> It seems to us ... that the interests of commerce, being so closely related to the existence and happiness of the state itself, demand the maintenance of a close connection between this and the nation's power at sea, capable to protect and defend our commerce and navigation against all foreign violence. And therefore, it seems to have been the concern of our forefathers to give the navy of the state a seat in those places where trade flourished most ... In our opinion, this connection would be weakened if all Admiralty Boards would be mortified, and if in their place a single college or council for the Navy would be erected in this city [The Hague]. Such a college, farther removed from its commercial objects and requirements that are now immediately brought at hand and close to the eye, could not so quickly acquaint itself with them, nor be supplied with them at the same speed.[78]

---

77   NA, Archief J.C. van der Hoop, no. 155. 'Memorie, houdende het generaal rapport van de Personeele Commissie van het Defensie-Weezen', p. 29.

78   NA, Archief J.C. van der Hoop, no. 154, 'Missive van heeren gecommitteerden uit de

As this exchange of arguments shows, in the course of the 1780s the very nature of Admiralty direction had become contested. But as in many other areas of state policy, the ideological dividing lines between Patriots and Orangists remained blurred. For many of the federal-minded Patriots local control over Admiralty institutions became a major guarantee against fears of 'Orangist usurpation'. At the same time, enlightened conservatives often envisioned far-reaching centralisation under a stadtholder with royal prerogatives.

In the heated end phase of Patriot mobilisation the very premises of the naval establishments became physical battlegrounds. Appealing to anti-regent sentiments, in the spring of 1787 Orangists started to gather signatures among Amsterdam shipwrights against the Patriot city government.[79] The shipwrights' pub opposite to the entrance of the naval shipyard, appropriately called 'The unfinished ship', became a centre of Orangist agitation.[80] At the same time the Patriots mobilised their supporters within the Free Corps militia and societies against Orangist regents and Admiralty Councillors. At the end of May these tensions erupted in violent clashes in the working-class borough around the naval storehouse, leaving numerous dead and wounded. Seven houses of Patriots and seventeen of Orangists were completely ransacked, including the houses of prominent Orangist regent and Admiralty Board administrator Rendorp.[81] Master of equipment May, together with his wife and children, strategically absented himself from the shipyard to Nieuwendam by boat to hide his complicity in these clashes.[82]

The failure to dislodge the Amsterdam government in this way consolidated the power of the Patriots, starting the series of events that culminated in the arrest of William v's wife Wilhelmina by members of a Patriot Free Corps at Goejanverwellesluis. But a Prussian invasion quickly dispelled the revolutionary illusions of the new government. The restoration of the stadtholderate was celebrated in Amsterdam with a parade of shipwrights at the terrain of the naval shipyard.[83] Restoration did not give an impetus towards thoroughgoing centralisation of the navy under stadtholderly direction. On the contrary, the fact that the Orangist regime could only be saved by foreign arms led to com-

---

respective kollegien ter Admiraliteit aan de Edele Mogende Heeren Gedeputeerden tot de Personele Commissie van het Defensie-Weezen', 5 October 1786, pp. 3–4.

79   Orangist incitement of lower class rebellion, playing on class anger against local regents, was a widespread phenomenon during the Patriot period. De Wit 1974, pp. 30 ff.

80   Anonymous 1787a, Schama 1977, pp. 114–17.

81   Anonymous 1787b, pp. 14–15.

82   NA, Archief Admiraliteitscolleges XXXIX, Van der Hoop, no. 150. 'Getuigenissen'.

83   Deurloo 1971, pp. 63–4.

plete deadlock in the centre of the state. The outbreak of revolution in France further strengthened conservative tendencies at the top of the state.

The thorough reshuffling of political agendas between Patriots and Orangists that followed between the 1787 reaction and the second 1795 revolution can be written as a tale of two administrators. On the one side stood Pieter Paulus, fiscal advocate of the Rotterdam Admiralty Board and leading Patriot, who was ousted from his position in 1788 only to become the radical first president of the National Assembly after the Batavian Revolution.[84] On the other side stood Joan Cornelis van der Hoop, the reform-minded fiscal advocate of the Amsterdam Admiralty Board, confidante of William V and Pieter Laurens van de Spiegel, and organiser of the counterrevolution, who in 1813 was to return as the first minister of the navy under King William I.[85]

Pieter Paulus was a self-made man. The son of a small-town burgomaster, he had started his career in 1772 by writing a youthful eulogy on the stadtholderate at the occasion of the birth of an heir to William V.[86] Even in this work some of Paulus's later ideas were already visible, most clearly in the claim that the monopolisation of Dutch political life by the ruling elites barred entry to the 'middle groups' – to whom Paulus himself of course belonged.[87] Just three years later he made the almost obligatory turn to history by writing a four-volume study of the 'true origins' of the Dutch constitution, moving more explicitly into the confines of oppositionist politics. Promoted to the post of fiscal advocate at the height of Patriot agitation in 1785, he became responsible for investigating the failure of the Dutch fleet at Brest, one of the key events in the story of William V's betrayal of Dutch interests during the recent war. Soon after he became one of the main Patriot spokesmen. But there is little to suggest that he used this position to promote far-reaching reform in the practical management of the institution that he served. His removal from the Admiralty Board was based on an alleged attempt to use the Rotterdam naval shipyard as a centre for the defence against the advancing Prussian troops. Against these charges Paulus argued that he had always loyally fulfilled his obligations to the Union.[88] Only after being ostracised did Pieter Paulus become true to both his apostolic names, in 1793 formulating the doctrine of Batavian liberal egalitarianism by writing its defining text and after 1795 becoming the first

---

84   Vles 2004.

85   Habermehl 2000.

86   Paulus 1772.

87   Schama 1977, p. 94.

88   Anonymous 1788, p. 8.

president of the National Assembly, the organisational rock on which the new state was founded.[89]

Joan Cornelis van der Hoop's career was diametrically opposed to that of Pieter Paulus. Son of a secretary of the Council of State, married to the daughter of the influential Orangist Salomon Dedel, his two brothers a major general in the States army and the treasurer-general of the state, he could hardly have been more integrated into the leading regent families of the late eighteenth century. After a spell as director of the Society of Suriname, he became fiscal advocate of the Amsterdam Admiralty Board in 1781. In his private correspondence he showed a keen interest in structural reform of the Dutch state, as well as a familiarity with the works of Adam Smith. In a 1782 letter to Van der Oudermeulen he inquired after the possibilities of introducing free trade to the East Indies.[90] In facing the challenge of rapid expansion of the war fleet, he favoured far-reaching cooperation between the five Admiralty Boards.[91] And in response to the widespread rumours of betrayal directed against William V he tried to impress on the stadtholder the need for reforms that could take away the real defects behind the failure of the fleet, since

> rejection turns into dissatisfaction and suspicions, if one does not look with calm into the reasons, causes and true motives ... and lets oneself be carried away by phantoms, while the true problem is not grasped.[92]

Writing to Pieter Paulus, who was then an ordinary lawyer and not yet fiscal advocate of the Rotterdam Admiralty Board, he chastised the Patriots for not seeing the causes for naval failure as clearly as William V, and argued that the continued existence of the five separate Admiralty Boards was the prime defect.[93]

For Van der Hoop, however, social conservatism always overshadowed his enthusiasm for rationalisation of the state. When in 1786 Van de Spiegel proposed the formation of a secret party of Orangist loyalists to oppose Patriot

---

89 His 'Republican Catechism' was laid down in Paulus 1793.

90 Van der Hoop to Van der Oudermeulen, 8 February 1782. NA, Archief Admiraliteitscolleges XXXIX, Van der Hoop, no. 54. 'Correspondentie', p. 93.

91 Van der Hoop to grand pensionary Van Bleiswijk, 4 June 1782, NA, Archief Admiraliteitscolleges XXXIX, Van der Hoop, no. 54. 'Correspondentie', p. 216.

92 Van der Hoop to William V, 30 July 1782, NA, Archief Admiraliteitscolleges XXXIX, Van der Hoop, no. 54. 'Correspondentie', p. 251.

93 Van der Hoop to Paulus, 7 December 1782, NA, Archief Admiraliteitscolleges XXXIX, Van der Hoop, no. 55. 'Correspondentie', pp. 30–1.

agitation in Holland, he could fall back on a long period of organisational preparations in which Van der Hoop had played a major role.[94] The logic of their position was summed up in the debates over the erection of a single department for the navy that followed on the heels of the 1787 restoration. A 'Rough draft for the formation of a new government in naval affairs', sent around among leading statesmen in 1791, concluded:

> Indisputably, there are two principal motivations that have to underlie such a plan: unity in government, from which order in execution is born, and unity in maintenance. But when these principal aims cannot be reached, it would be better to keep affairs in their present state, than to displace the old foundations.[95]

Commenting on those two options, William V wrote to Van de Spiegel and Van der Hoop:

> [T]hat to me it would seem very dangerous to reject institutions that are almost as old as the Republic, and that in my opinion it would be better to try to improve the government of the navy and establish equity in the levying of customs, without making such a big change as the abolition of the Admiralty Boards ...[96]

While convinced of the necessity of unification, fear of a further destabilisation of the existing state turned the reformers from within into conservative defenders of the 'ancient constitution'.

5.4   From Citizens' Militias to the Batavian Legion

Debates on the army followed the same by now familiar pattern. Denouncing William V as a 'usurper of power' for his attempts at centralising control over

---

94   Van de Spiegel to Wilhelmina, 24 June 1786, Vreede 1874, p. 452, and the coded correspondence between Van der Hoop and Van de Spiegel on party affairs, e.g., Van der Hoop to Van de Spiegel, 26 September 1783, NA, Archief Admiraliteitscolleges XXXIX, Van der Hoop, no. 55. 'Correspondentie', p. 147.

95   NA, Familiearchief Fagel, no. 1084. 'Ruw ontwerp van het te formeeren bestuur van zee zaaken in 1791, met eenige aanmerkingen.'

96   NA, Familiearchief Fagel, no. 1084. 'Concept advys over de redressen in het bestier der marine'.

the state militia and as betrayer of Dutch interests for his alleged (and real) secret dealings with the English and Prussian crowns, the Patriots continued until the late 1780s to present themselves as defenders of the old constitution. Modelling their plans for the army on Swiss and American examples, they advocated a fictitious 'return' to national defence based on citizens' militias under local supervision. These free corps militias should assist a small, and therefore cheap, mercenary force for purely defensive tasks, while military investment should mainly be directed towards the rebuilding of Dutch naval power. Against this the Orangist party nominally acted as the defender of the ideal of a strong, centralised, well-funded army. The 1789 'Report of the Committee of Defence' even proposed to transfer the payment of troops from the provincial paymasters to the generalty level, and asked the Council of State 'to take the necessary measures by which the payment of the militia can occur in the easiest, best regulated manner'.[97] However, in practice the post-1787 regime was so utterly dependent on the existing federal support base of the state, and the army so infested by the policy of patronage that formed the final refuge of William V's stadtholderate, that any attempt at fundamental reform came to naught.[98] Meanwhile, the French revolution won over the leading section of the former Patriots to a completely new way of thinking about the army as a national force.

Debates on the army throughout the 1770s had been characterised by the sharp antagonism between, on one side, William V, his principal advisor in military and political matters the Duke of Brunswick, and the political representatives of the inland provinces, and, on the other side, the States of Holland led by Amsterdam. While it is a caricature to say that the former favoured the army and the latter the fleet, the two groupings differed fundamentally on the question which of the two should be prioritised. During the second half of the decade the debate became tied to the growing tensions over foreign policy, especially the position to be taken towards Britain as a commercial rival.[99] A strong antipathy towards standing armies as tools of uncontrollable monarchical power against the people, such as existed in British political discourse, did not yet play a great role in these discussions. Both groups based their arguments primarily on conflicting perceptions of the core interests of the Dutch Republic in a new international configuration of power. But the tone of the debates

---

97   NA, Archief Staten Generaal, no. 9258. 'Memorie houdende het generaal rapport van de Personeele Commissie van het Defensie-Weezen met bijlagen, in dato 28 October 1789, ten gevolge van haar Hoog Mogende resolutie van den 4 Meij 1785', fol. 170.

98   Zwitzer 1991, p. 106.

99   Bartstra 1952, especially Chapter 5 and 6.

changed completely with the intensification of Patriot propaganda. Drawing on examples from a distant past such as William II's 1650 attack on Amsterdam, Joan Derk van der Capellen tot den Poll's *To the People of the Netherlands* depicted the controversy over army augmentation as one that immediately touched on the ancient liberties and sovereignty of the people. Claiming that 'there has not been any freedom in Europe, since princes started to maintain standing armies', he went on to depict the consequences in terms that directly linked this danger to all the vices ascribed to William V:

> He who controls the army can do whatever he wants. He can hand over the best part of our commerce, our warships, and our colonies to our enemies. Yes, he can even make himself the Sovereign! The unarmed, defenceless people cannot do anything against this, but have to accept this in tranquillity. Therefore, a people that wants to act sensibly and with care should always make sure it remains the strongest party within the country.[100]

The latter part of his argument led to the rousing call with which Van der Capellen ended his pamphlet: 'All of you, arm yourselves, elect those who have to command you, and proceed in calmness and moderation, like the people of America where not a drop of blood was spilled before the English first strike'.[101] Citizens' armament became one of the cornerstones of Dutch republicanism, an ideal supported by examples from classical antiquity, the American Revolution, and the Swiss federation.[102] From 1782 onwards free corps and societies for the exercise of arms became the organisational centres of Patriot mobilisation, and many thousands of citizens were actively involved in societies with resounding names such as 'Pro Patria et Libertate'.[103]

Despite their rejection of standing armies under princely command, the Patriots did not advocate the replacement of the States army by the citizens' corps, which would leave the Republic without defence in the midst of a period of European military build-up. Van der Capellen himself argued that the Dutch state needed a well-paid force of 36,000 to 40,000 soldiers in times of peace. In the face of war this amount should be doubled.[104] While he presented this as a way to cut back on army expenses, the number of 40,000 soldiers matched

---

100   [Van der Capellen tot den Poll] [1781], p. 19.

101   [Van der Capellen tot den Poll] [1781], p. 76.

102   Klein 1995, pp. 167–76.

103   Israel 1998, p. 1102.

104   [Van der Capellen tot den Poll] [1781], p. 71.

the actual size of the States army at that time, and even after the declaration of war with France in 1793 the strength of the army did not come close to the 72,000–80,000 he proposed.[105] Later Patriot texts such as the influential 1785 *Leiden Draft* also advocated 'the out- and inward defence and security of the country and civil liberty by the armament of the entire nation', but in practice saw the citizens' militias as an auxiliary force for the existing professional army.[106] The Patriots argued for important changes in the structure of the army, such as devolution of military jurisdiction from the stadtholder as captain general to the provinces and towns in which the soldiers were garrisoned, the limitation of the stadtholder's rights of appointment of officers, and the erection of academies for the training of officers.[107] They wanted to stimulate the 'national spirit' of the troops by limiting the number of foreign soldiers and officers serving in the States army. But they equally acknowledged that a professional army in a small country like the Dutch Republic would always depend on recruitment outside national borders.[108]

As could be expected, the Patriots who went through the experience of the French revolution if anything became more committed to the idea of a 'citizenry in arms' as the basis of national defence. But in the short period between 1789 and 1795 they completely redefined the meaning of this phrase. The ardent revolutionary writer Gerrit Paape later argued that by expelling the leading Patriots to France and the Southern Netherlands, 'Orange ... did nothing else but sending them to the polytechnic of Patriotism and revolution'.[109] However, as Joost Rosendaal put it in his major study of Dutch refugees in revolutionary France,

> the French Revolution was not a school in the sense that the Dutch became apprentices of the French. It was a school in which the Dutch and the French jointly passed the revolutionary curriculum, with as sole schoolmaster the dynamics of the revolution.[110]

---

105 Zwitzer puts the total strength of the States army at 41,413 men in 1772 and 58,083 in 1793. Zwitzer 1991, p. 176.

106 [Fijnje and Vreede] 1785, p. 4 and p. 68.

107 Zwitzer 1991, pp. 107 ff., and Janssen 1989, p. 20.

108 Klein 1995, pp. 180–2.

109 Paape [1798], p. 123. The significance of the French experience for the Batavian revolution was the general theme of the first volume of Colenbrander 1905. With important adjustments, it still plays an important role in the literature on the pre-1795 ideological developments. E.g., Frijhoff 1991, Jourdan 2008, pp. 67 ff., and Van den Burg 2007, pp. 26 ff.

110 Rosendaal 2003, p. 454.

It was not merely a school for revolutionary politics that the Dutch refugees attended. It was a school for revolutionary warfare as well, in which the relation between the army, the nation, and the citizenry was fundamentally redefined.[111] The Dutch participated actively in this process. From 1791 onwards the idea of forming a '*légion Batave*' to assist the French armies in the liberation of the Netherlands from the House of Orange and its Prussian-English backers circulated in refugee circles.[112] At the end of May 1792 a delegation of Batavian refugees headed by the later general Daendels spoke about these plans to the French minister of Defence.[113] After complicated political negotiations, the National Assembly agreed in July 1792 to the formation of this unit under the name of Légion Franche Étrangère. This was not a free corps, but a part of the French army that from 1793–5 was at war with the Dutch Republic, consisting of 2812 men and 500 horses under the supervision of a committee of six Dutch refugees.[114] The members of the committee saw themselves as the nucleus of the future government of a liberated Batavian Republic – a view not always shared by their French allies – and started formulating their vision for the future state.[115] In touch with the tenor of the times, and actively encouraged by their revolutionary friends, their plans all hinged on the institution of a republic that was 'one and indivisible'.[116] The 'Acte d'association des amis du rétablissement de la liberté Batave' of 22 October 1792, undersigned, among others, by J.C. de Kock, who was one of the six committee members, and P.A. Dumont-Pigalle, who had been the liaison between the Patriots and the French government, stated as its first aims:

1°. A employer tous les moyens que nous avons, et tous ceux que les circonstances pourront nous offrir, pour abolir dans notre patrie le despotisme stadhoudérien, et repousser tout systême ou tout établissement aristocratique quelconque que l'on pourrait tenter de subsistuer à ce despotisme.

---

111   A process culminating in the unprecedented *levée en masse* of August 1793. Forrest 2003.

112   Rosendaal 2003, p. 311.

113   'Projet de la formation d'une légion Batave', Colenbrander 1905, pp. 35–6.

114   Rosendaal 2003, pp. 316–7.

115   Kubben 2011, p. 162.

116   E.g., by Condorcet in his 'Adresse aux Bataves', Condorcet 1804, p. 343, where he asks: 'Bataves, voulez-vous être libres? que vos sept républiques, confondues dans une seule, n'aient plus qu'une seule volonté, que tous les citoyens aient un égal intérêt à défendre des droits qui soient les mêmes pour tous; alors, vous verrez le peuple fouler aux pieds la honteuse couleur de la servitude pour arborer celle de la liberté'.

2°. Afin de mieux parvenir à ce dernier but, nous nous engageons à employer tous nos efforts pour faire disparaître de notre pays cette diversité de provinces souveraines, cette funeste fédération qui existe entr'elles, et qui a causé tant de maux à la République.

3°. Nous employerons aussi tous nos efforts pour y faire abolir cette disparité de loix, de costumes, de droits et de privilèges locaux, ainsi que toutes corporations quelconques, toutes distinctions, exemptions, prérogatives et privilèges personnels, soit héréditaires ou casuels.

4°. Nous employerons également tous les moyens possibles pour qu'après l'abolition de ces diverses choses nous puissions voir le territoire entier de la République ne plus former qu'un *tout*, distribué en départements, districts, cantons etc., et y voir régner des loix et des droits uniformes et communs à tous; par conséquent la liberté et l'égalité naturelle y être le partage de chaque individu, et notre patrie jouir d'une constitution semblable à celle que la République française va se donner.[117]

By that time, the idea that the Republic should be replaced by a unitary national state had become accepted even by most of the moderate refugees. In a 'Draft Project of the New Form of Government of the Batavian Republic', two leading representatives of the moderates worked out the meaning of the abolition for all major institutions of the state, including the colonial companies, the army, and the navy:

---

117 '1st. To employ all the available means, as well as all of those that circumstances can provide us with, for abolishing stadtholderly despotism in our fatherland, and for removing the entire system or entire aristocratic establishment with which they would attempt to replace this despotism.

2nd. In order to achieve this goal with greater success, we engage ourselves in spending all our efforts to expel from our country this assemblage of sovereign provinces, this disastrous federation that exists between them, and that is the origin of so many woes in the Republic.

3rd. We will also employ all our efforts to abolish that disparity of laws, customs, rights, and local privileges, as well as any corporations, all distinctions, exceptions, prerogatives, and personal privileges, both hereditary and casual.

4th. We will equally employ any means possible to make sure that after the abolition of these diverse points we will be able to see the entire territory of the Republic in no other way than forming one *whole*, distributed in departments, districts, cantons, etc., and to see established there uniform laws and rights for all; by consequence the natural liberty and equality will be shared by each individual, and our fatherland will enjoy a similar constitution to the one that the French Republic will give itself'. 'Acte d'association des amis du rétablissement de la liberté batave', Colenbrander 1905, p. 41.

The Companies of East and West, Society of Suriname, Berbice, and all others ... to be destroyed. The colonies opened up to free trade, members of the union, and represented in the General Assembly by their own deputies.

... All foreign troops, especially Swiss and German regiments, discharged. The army reduced to at most 16,000 men and only for the protection of frontier towns. All citizens and inhabitants, without exception, forced to bear arms to maintain order internally and to counteract foreign violence if necessary.

... All the Admiralty Boards abolished, as well as the outside custom offices that in many places absorb more than they receive in taxes.[118]

The failure of the first French invasion of the Netherlands in 1793, combined with the radicalisation of the French revolution itself, solidified the adherence of Batavian refugees to this new unitary model of the state. On 10 August 1793 a Dutch journalist in Paris translated the reports on the 'Fête de l'Unité et de l'Indivisibilité de la République' and published them for an audience in the Netherlands.[119] That the radical anti-federalist ideas from France had by that time won a following among revolutionaries within the Dutch Republic can be seen from a pamphlet written by Bernardus Bosch, Patriot firebrand and after 1795 one of the leaders of the radical fraction of the Batavian Revolution.[120] This pamphlet, called *Vrijhardt [Free-heart] to the People of the Netherlands on the True Constitution*, apart from arguing for elections by universal male suffrage, forcefully defended the unitary national state. It also contained perhaps the most pointed pre-1795 explanation of why the brokerage-organisation of the Dutch army had to be replaced by that of a national citizens' army:

No longer will fortifications be made in the first year, and flattened or destroyed in the next just to make contractors grow fat ... – no army to show off in *ante-chambres* or in military books – no army to catch rabbits, and what is more – no army that empties the state treasure, and still leaves the officer and soldier poor and desperate ... – no army to oppress society, and make its members into the slaves of an usurper – no military caste will be for sale to the highest bidder, or serve as bait for swindle of corrupt and

---

118 'Schets-project der nieuwe regeeringsform voor de Bataafsche Republiek', Colenbrander 1905, p. 56.

119 Grijzenhout 1989, p. 119.

120 Brandon and Fatah-Black 2011, pp. 8–10.

dishonourable creatures ... – no ordinary man will be forced to eat bread of charity at the cost of a state, that he cannot nor cares not to defend. No, an army of men, of free human beings, defenders of the fatherland, noble, great, and feared only by the enemy; citizens in society, led by few men, but by men worthy to lead and go in front of free human beings, this will be our entire defence.[121]

Bosch' staccato stream of disqualifications bound the old critiques of stadthold-erly usurpation through reliance on a standing army and aristocratic patronage in the appointment of officers to a radically new concept of the national army, bypassing the old language of the restored civic militias. In this sense, his for-mulations form a bridge between the militant federalism of the 1780s and the nationalism of the Batavian Revolution and are representative for the political trajectory of many former Patriots.

In another respect, however, Bosch went considerably further than most of the leading Batavians in exile. His language of naked profiteering through mil-itary contracting and 'swindle' surrounding army regiments, all too familiar from British oppositional discourse at the time, did not constitute an import-ant theme in the arguments of the Batavian exiles in France who prepared the transition to the new Batavian order. This is surprising, since both the high costs of maintaining a standing army and the evils of 'financial oligarchy' did figure in the debates of the 1780s.[122] Furthermore, as has been shown in the previ-ous chapter, the dealings of military solicitors and army contractors had been the subject of critique and reform attempts earlier in the eighteenth century. One possible explanation for this might sound somewhat crudely materialist, but still deserves a mention. The Batavian opposition was far from confined to the poor – on the contrary, substantial lower-class support was only won in the process of the revolution itself. Among the leadership of the exile community were many from extremely well-established regent families. They were connec-ted to the very financial circles that Bosch held responsible for corrupting the army. Daendels, the future general of the Batavian armies, had set up a suc-cessful trading firm while in exile. This firm assisted the French government in the acquisition of 40,000 guns in London. The transaction itself was carried out by Abbema, one of the authors of the 1792 moderate 'draft project' and banker for Daendels' firm.[123] In May 1792, before the French National Assembly agreed

---

121   [Bernardus Bosch] 1793, pp. 18–19.
122   Fritschy 1988a and Fritschy 1988b, p. 93.
123   Rosendaal 2003, pp. 312–13.

to the erection of the Légion Franche Étrangère, leading Batavian refugees had managed to purchase 300,000 livres worth of arms in England.[124] Johan Valckenaer, active participant in the formulation of radical plans for a new constitution, tried to convince the French government that the ousting of the stadtholder would give it access to the strong Dutch credit market, 'la poule aux œufs d'or' for the French Republic.[125] Such activities were hardly conducive for formulating diatribes against the malicious working of high finance, and it seems no coincidence that the development of this part of the critique of the old army structure was left to a radical outside the top circles of Batavian emigration.

There might also have been a second, less self-serving reason why brokerage structures in army finance did not attract the same level of debate as those in colonial warfare and Admiralty management. The previous chapters have shown that not every form of brokerage organisation was equally inimical to the introduction of bureaucratic centralisation. Of the three major areas of brokerage warfare discussed in this book, military soliciting most closely resembled the forms of regulated interaction between state officials and entrepreneurs that characterise modern capitalist states – and came to resemble this more with the concentration of soliciting contracts into the hands of a layer of professional financiers. While both the federal direction over army finances and the independent entrepreneurial role of military officers eventually came to be seen as obsolete by the advocates of state rationalisation, strong connections between the state and capitalist finance per se did not – or at least, not to those whose ambitions were limited to the formation of a more modern form of the bourgeois state.

5.5   The Afterlife of the Federal-Brokerage State

Patriot thinking had come a long way when in January 1795 a revolutionary wave advancing in front of French bayonets destroyed the old regime. Ten years earlier the *Leiden Draft* had still praised the federal and brokerage character of the Dutch state as the surest means to advance the 'common interests' of the nation, defined as 'the protection and advancement of navigation, trade, and manufacture' and the 'maintenance of the Union and protection of its respective forms of government':

---

124   Rosendaal 2003, p. 314.
125   [Valckenaer] 1795, p. 16.

> Each part of society in general governs those affairs that touch on it alone and that others have no business in. These particular societies together from their midst form one body of state, capable of governing the joint interests of an entire province; and these provinces in turn form a general assembly of state, that only occupies itself with the external interests of the entire Union.[126]

In September 1795 representatives of revolutionary clubs, gathered in The Hague for a 'Central Assembly' with the aim of pushing the States General for the convocation of a National Assembly, could write in a completely opposite vein:

> Cannot the cause of all disasters of the Netherlands be found solely in the form of government that exists there? Is not that seven headed monster, that union-ogre, the result of motives of particular self-interest? Is that not the source of confusions? ... Therefore, it is high time that this despicable hole will be filled, to build on the flattened ground a system of state for the Netherlands that affirms the unity and indivisibility of all the various territories of this Republic. One National Assembly, one law founded on the law of nature that guarantees each inhabitant his civil and social relations, those alone are the means that can save the Netherlands.[127]

Eight months after the flight of the stadtholder, institutional realities still lagged far behind the ideas of the more radical fraction of the Batavian Revolution. The revolutionaries inherited the old state form more or less intact, and met with fierce opposition from the old apparatus – as well as from the more conservative elements within their own ranks – in their attempts to put their plans for structural reform into practice. The first years of the new order were dominated by the political struggle between the advocates of a unitary state or 'Unitarians' – in large part overlapping with the more democratic, radical, or, in the eyes of their enemies, 'Jacobin' elements of the revolution – and on the other side the advocates of a settlement closer to the old federal state – largely confined to the moderate elements, and derided by the radicals as 'aristocrats' or 'slimy fellows' (*slijmgasten*). On the national level this conflict became focused on the design of a new constitution. It was heavily influenced by international developments, primarily the trajectory taken by French politics and

---

126   [Fijnje and Vreede] 1785, pp. 9–10.
127   Colenbrander 1906, pp. 493–4.

fears of the return of Orange on the back of an English invasion. On the local level it was intersected by popular mobilisation, often encouraged by the radical Unitarians but paradoxically also closely connected to demands of local autonomy to counteract moderate provincial governments.[128]

Despite these political difficulties, the formal dismantling of key institutions of the federal-brokerage state started soon after the overthrow of the old order. If any proof was needed for the revolutionary nature of the 1795 overturn, it could be found in the speed with which it abolished arrangements that had accompanied the Dutch Republic almost from its birth, and had shown such resilience throughout its existence. Already on 17 February 1795, the States General agreed to the proposal of the Committee for Public Welfare to abolish the existing federal structure of the navy and place at the head of the five former Admiralty Boards a Committee for the Marine, consisting of twenty-one representatives chosen 'from all the provinces, or rather from the entire Republic, without distinction, either three from each province, or so much more or less as is justified by circumstances'. The committee would be assisted in its work by one single fiscal advocate and one secretary. The decree made explicit, that

> the general supervision of all mentioned tasks should rest with the committee *in its entirety*, and the subdivision of work in departments ... according to statute should only be a matter of convenience and order.[129]

Four days earlier, lieutenant admiral Van Kinsbergen and Amsterdam fiscal advocate Van der Hoop had been put under civil arrest.[130]

In colonial policy, likewise, swift measures were taken. Since the WIC had been abolished in 1792 it was not a hard decision for the new provisional government to reorganise colonial administration of the West Indies along national lines. Already in March 1795 the provisional authorities of Holland decided to bring together all former WIC territories under the control of a

---

128   On the general political developments of this period, see Schama 1977, Rosendaal 2005, and Poell 2009. The conflicting and intersecting perceptions of the future of Dutch politics carried by radicals and moderates, Unitarians and Federalists, democrats and aristocrats form the central theme of Van Sas 1989. The impact of French developments on constitutional debates is described in Jourdan 2008. Important studies of the interplay between popular mobilisation on the local level and national developments are Prak 1999, Kuiper 2002, Poell 2004, and Jourdan 2006. For the latter subject, also see Brandon and Fatah-Black 2011.

129   Anonymous 1795, pp. 698–9.

130   Anonymous 1795, p. 671.

Committee for the Affairs of Colonial Possessions on the coast of Guinea and America, whose members were installed by the States General on 9 October of the same year. Debates over the future of the voc lasted longer, partly because they involved an intervention in what still nominally was a private company and therefore touched on the inviolable right of private property that moderates and radicals equally adhered to.[131] Nevertheless, as a Committee for the Affairs of the voc assured the provisional administration of the Province of Holland in June 1795, the 'indescribable weight' of the Company for the common wealth made determined action imperative.[132] On their instigation the Holland administration on 15 September 1795 issued a 'decree for the destruction of the present direction of the voc' that announced the firing of all Company officials and the replacement of the six chambers by a Committee for the Affairs of the East Indian Trade and Possessions modelled after that for the West Indies. Breaking with old practices of equity between the provinces, the committee would consist of twenty-eight persons, twenty of whom should come from Holland as the main guarantor of the Company's huge debts.[133] In December 1795 the States General affirmed the main outline of this decree, de facto nationalising the Company.[134]

The reconstitution of the army on an entirely new basis was viewed by the new regime as a matter of great urgency. Already on 17 February 1795 the States General decided 'that it is of the highest priority that this Assembly directs its attention to the army of the state, as well as the general administration of affairs … that cannot continue on the present footing'.[135] At the start of that month the Finance Committee had already decreed

> as a concession to the military solicitors to order the issuing of pay ordinances according to the old system for the current month, but with the explicit affirmation that this will be for the last time.[136]

Like in all other important areas of reform, a committee was put to work, and on 8 July 1795 its 'Plan for the organisation of the army' was accepted by the States General. In one stroke the plan ended the existence of the independent 'Kompaniewirtschaft' that had survived despite all previous attempts at reform,

---

131   Schutte 1974, p. 107.

132   Provisioneele Representanten van het Volk van Holland 1795b, pp. 3–4.

133   Provisioneele Representanten van het Volk van Holland 1795a, pp. 19–20.

134   Schutte 1974, p. 115.

135   Anonymous 1795, pp. 712–13.

136   Anonymous 1795, p. 576.

ordering that the companies would now belong not to their officers but fully 'to the nation', and 'would be paid out of one and the same generalty pay desk'. Direction over payment was put into the hands of one central agent, assisted by three 'solicitors', who resembled their predecessors only in name.[137] The same month Hendrik van der Burch, Jacobus Tielleman de Schenk, Carel van Hulst and Hendrik Jenny, all inhabitants of The Hague, were appointed at their own request respectively as agent and as solicitors.[138] Problems in the financing of the army, however, continued to haunt the state, and influenced the ensuing debates on the institution of a professional national army.[139]

Out of the flood of committee meetings and proposals of 'Year One of the Batavian Liberty' emerged a coherent view on the role of the national state in managing warfare. In July 1796 the committee for the preparation of a new constitution presented (among others) the following points to the National Assembly:

> That everything belonging to the administration of objects of the outward defence and inward good order of the nation should be put under the special direction of the executive power; and especially
>
> a) The organisation of the national army and armed citizenry, the moving and employment of those – as far as the army is concerned – to wherever is necessary. Further the maintenance of the necessary storehouses and factories that serve those; fortresses and everything that can be used to resist the enemy at times of war.
> b) The administration of affairs concerning armed navigation; the building and equipment of the nation's fleet, for the protection of commerce as well as of the nation's colonies; the direction over the nation's shipyards, iron foundries, sea harbours, coasts, and sea entrances.
> c) The administration of possessions and trade both in East and West India and further coasts, in all matters concerning defence, and in matters of political administration.[140]

Putting those points into effect, however, even more than on practical conditions depended on the political struggle over the fate of the revolution itself. On this terrain, centuries old traditions of localism took their revenge on the

---

137   Zwitzer 1991, p. 96.
138   Provisionele representanten van het volk van Holland 1798, p. 535. Decree of 28 July 1795.
139   Fritschy 1988b, pp. 94–8.
140   De Gou 1975, p. 173.

nationalising revolutionaries. In a recent article on the successive attempts at nationalisation undertaken by the Unitarian leadership, Thomas Poell describes how they came to be pulled between their original democratic intentions and the wish to push through their particular vision of state modernisation in the teeth of local resistance.[141] Their failure to reunite these two strands took shape first in their attempts to break through the hold of federalism by popular mobilisation in the period of 1795–7, then in a series of coups and countercoups that were dressed up in the language of radical democracy but had lost its substance, and finally in their alliance with the French state to modernise from above – laying the basis for the conservative consolidation of the national state of 1813. This process formed the real enigma of the Batavian episode.

The revolution of January 1795 gave an immense impetus to the creation of a new type of state, but did not remove all the remnants of the old order in one clear sweep. Many of the more moderate revolutionaries, fearful of the consequences of a complete unsettling of the *ancien régime*, wanted to leave considerable authority in the hands of the old provincial administrations. They were strengthened by the influx of former Orangist officials into the ranks of the revolution, which gave greater social weight to their party.[142] Against them the leading Unitarians mobilised a motley crew of revolutionary clubs, radically-oriented 'neighbourhood assemblies' that formed the lowest rung of the electoral system, and their supporters among the lower and middle classes. While on the national level conflicts between the two parties concentrated on the institutional make-up of the new state, locally this democratic coalition centred around a classical revolutionary repertoire of cleansing the state of adherents of the old regime, firmer measures against unemployment and other social problems affecting the lower classes, and the extension of the rights of democratic participation.[143] The radical press that had emerged in the wake of January 1795, ranging from the state-minded *De Democraten* (The Democrats) of Gogel and Ockerse to the more rousing *Politieke Blixem* (Political Lightning) to which Bernardus Bosch contributed, served as a vehicle to connect the two processes.[144]

The establishment of a National Assembly in March 1796 did not dampen these contradictions. Rather, it transferred them even more visibly to the level of national politics. At the local level, the revolution seemed to have run into a rut. Revolts in Amsterdam in November 1795 and April 1796 had come to

141   Poell 2009, pp. 319–20.
142   Schama 1977, p. 415.
143   Prak 1999, pp. 246 ff.
144   Jourdan 2008, pp. 415–20.

nothing.[145] In Friesland one of the few radical provincial governments was met with strong opposition, resulting early in 1797 in the Orangist uprising in the village of Kollum, envisioned by the radicals as a Dutch Vendée.[146] The failure of the National Assembly to accept a Unitarist constitution that had been so painstakingly prepared during Year One and Two became the ultimate proof that the revolution did not yet go far enough. Already in May 1796 the radical spokespersons Pieter Vreede, Bernardus Bosch, and Johan Valckenaer – all of whom had been centrally involved in formulating the Unitarist agenda in the pre-revolutionary period – called for popular armament to force the National Assembly into action.[147]

A seemingly innocuous incident that occurred in Leiden in January 1797 can serve to illustrate the reasons for the failure of the democratic coalition to break through the stalemate in national politics.[148] A coalition of well-known local radicals had sent out a call to societies and neighbourhood assemblies throughout the country. In it, they invited them to send delegates to a national meeting of representatives of these rank-and-file organs of Batavian radicalism 'in which the people, as it were, could speak with one voice'. The gathering was to convene in Leiden on the second birthday of the overthrow of the old order.[149] The moderates responded with viperous rage. The provincial authorities of Holland sent representatives to take into custody the originators of the call. An investigation into the lawfulness of this action later concluded, that

> one should be willingly blind if one does not see that this letter has the aim ... to constitute an Assembly that would very soon have rivalled this Assembly [the Provincial authority of Holland], yes, if possible, to take from it the power that has been trusted to it by the people of Holland. And therefore, it can be seen as an attack on the sovereignty of the people of Holland, and one should be an advocate of chaos and anarchy, if one would be able to find salutary intentions behind measures that tend to reverse the established order of affairs and our adopted principles.[150]

---

145   Jourdan 2006, pp. 23–30.
146   Kuiper 2002, pp. 256 ff.
147   Anonymous 1796.
148   The incident is described in more detail in Brandon and Fatah-Black 2011.
149   The text of the invitation was read out in the National Assembly on 16 January 1797. Nationale Vergadering 1797, p. 486.
150   Personeele Commissie 1797, p. 3.

In the National Assembly the leading moderate and future head of the Dutch state under French control Rutger Jan Schimmelpenninck argued that the meeting would even rival the National Assembly.[151] Undoubtedly in part because of these reactions, the arrest of the Leiden radicals briefly became a *cause célèbre* among democrats and Unitarians nationwide. Remarkably enough, however, it became so not primarily as a challenge to the moderates in the provincial governments and the National Assembly, but under the slogan of the defence of local autonomy against the infringement of the provincial arrest team.[152] The leading Unitarians proved as incapable of replacing the old federalist language in which popular mobilisation traditionally was framed, as they were in forging a real national movement to push through their programme against federalist opposition.

The period between the failed Patriot Revolution of 1785–7 and the start of the Batavian Revolution had seen a dramatic reversal in perceptions of the state, in which the restorers of 'the Ancient constitution' of yesteryear were transformed into full-blown Unitarians. The failure of 1795–7 to push through this Unification by revolutionary means set the stage for a second reversal, in which radical democrats became state-rationalisers from above. The main vehicle for this reversal was the 'financial coalition', that came about after radical coups and countercoups did not solve the impasse around the constitution. Leading representatives of moderates and former radicals, primarily Schimmelpenninck and Gogel, worked out a compromise that consisted of major financial reforms at the central level without the threat of popular involvement in politics that had characterised the first years of the revolution.[153] Symbolic for the anti-popular character of the new coalition was its insistence on the abolition of the guilds, an indispensable part of the liberal economic outlook of men like Gogel and for the breaking down of local particularism, but widely perceived as an attack on the living standard of craft workers.[154] Similarly, the introduction of new taxes and of military conscription for the wars fought in collusion with Napoleonic France evoked popular anger. In the first decade of the nineteenth century the pendulum of popular mobilisation swung back towards the old tradition of Orangist populism.[155] Schimmelpenninck and Gogel became the leading statesmen when after 1806 the former Dutch Republic was integrated into the French Empire. Under the aegis of Napoleon

---

151   Nationale Vergadering 1797, p. 520.
152   Brandon and Fatah-Black 2011, pp. 17–9.
153   Poell 2009, pp. 310 ff.
154   Prak 1999, pp. 281–3 and p. 291.
155   Joor 2000.

Bonaparte and his brother Louis Bonaparte, who in 1810 was installed as the first Dutch monarch, they drove through a programme of national modernisation. When they in turn were ousted from power by military defeat, the newly installed Orangist king William I inherited from his enemies the centralised bureaucratic state that his father's regime had been unable to create.

Conclusions

The federal-brokerage character of the Dutch state had been strengthened, not weakened, by warfare in the seventeenth and early eighteenth century. The fundamental character of the state remained intact during the remainder of the eighteenth century, despite grave revolutionary crises in 1747 and 1785–7, and despite the disintegration of the historic bloc underlying the state. Only the Batavian Revolution of 1795 heralded the end of the Old Republic, laying the foundations for the unitary state. The administrative measures taken at lightning speed during Year One of the revolution had been prepared by long debates over state reform in every major area of the organisation of warfare, and in each of the key institutions of the brokerage state. From the days of Van Slingelandt onwards, administrators who wanted to rationalise the existing state apparatus had pointed out the debilitating defects of the federal state structure. By the final decades of the century these defects had become almost generally acknowledged, both by reformers within the state and by Patriot oppositionists. Many plans were formulated to create state control over the colonies, break down trade monopolies that came with the brokerage functions of the commercial companies, unify the five Admiralty Boards into one single Department of the Navy responsible for the protection of merchants and equalising the collection of customs, and bring the army under one unified command and state-centred structure of payment. However, almost every single plan foundered on the inability of central administrators to go against their own support base among the federal elites, as well as their fear of reform spilling over into revolution.

This chapter has shown how the years after the failed Patriot revolution of 1785–7 saw an almost complete reversal of positions on the aims of state reform. While centralisers within the Orangist administration, despite their intentions of bureaucratic rationalisation, clung to the vestiges of the federal-brokerage state to protect the old order, radical revolutionaries dropped their programme of 'reconstitution' of the old republic and became advocates of the unitary state. Clearly reflected in the pages of the radical press that emerged in the course of 1795, the aims of 'democracy' and 'state unification' had been pushed together.

Once the backbone of the old order had been broken by a combination of French revolutionary arms and local uprisings, the old state institutions were easily destroyed. However, replacing them by a functioning centralised state proved much more difficult. The revolutionaries of 1795 faced one of the many ironies of history, expressed in a second reversal of positions that was hardly less dramatic than the first. Failing to achieve the rationalisation of the state that they envisioned from below, the majority of the Unitarian leaders turned towards solutions from above – first revolutionary coups, then reliance on the French army, and eventually bowing to one Bonaparte in France and one in The Hague. To a large extent they were successful in their aims of a renewal of the Dutch state along nationalising lines. The restoration of 1813 left most of their innovations in state management intact, and the old federal-brokerage framework was never to re-emerge. But the institutions they created were neither democratic, nor popular. The revolutionary moment of the national state had died before its birth.

Conclusion

This book followed the development of the Dutch state from its origins in the sixteenth century Dutch Revolt to its structural crisis and eventual collapse in the Batavian Revolution of the final years of the eighteenth century. It has examined the question why in the Dutch Republic brokerage structures, in which independent capitalist investors fulfilled state-like tasks on their own account and for a profit, retained their centrality in the organisation of warfare. It has used this question as a key to a larger riddle: how it was possible that a federal state that parcelled out many of its warring functions, so unlike the dominant image of a great power, could play a central role in the early modern state system for so long. Or, posed from the opposite end, why sustained involvement in warfare did not lead to fundamental transformations in the structure of the state in a direction more similar to the ideal type of centralised, concentrated power associated with the modern nation state. Answers to these questions were based on an investigation of the forms and networks of interaction between the state and capitalists in specific areas of the organisation of warfare, and were arrived at by putting these interactions in their wider institutional contexts.

War is considered the great leveller in state formation. In successive waves of reorganisation early modern rulers introduced and reformed bureaucratic institutions to meet the spiralling costs for the maintenance of large standing armies and navies, the challenges posed by logistics on an increased scale, and the global expansion of the theatres of conflict. All of these tasks required close cooperation between state officials and those social classes in control of society's economic resources. Starting from Charles Tilly's famous dictum that 'war makes states, and states make war', historians have long assumed that the intense military competition of the early modern period inherently favoured the rise of centralised, bureaucratic states that became more and more reliant on impersonal markets to fulfil their martial aims. The ensuing replacement of 'brokerage' structures, in which independent entrepreneurs were responsible for the organisation of violence, by national bureaucracies in which the state took those tasks directly in its own hands, forms a powerful narrative of modernisation. The Dutch Republic of the seventeenth and eighteenth century figures in this narrative either as trailblazer or as false start. The economic success of its seventeenth-century 'Golden Age' allowed this small federal state a short bout as hegemonic power within the emerging capitalist world economy. But once faced with determined competition from successful 'nationalising' states, it allegedly was easily pushed aside, undergoing stagnation and eventually decline.

This book has presented a different story. Without denying the great impact of military conflict on state formation, it has shown that the pressures of warfare did not singularly push competing states onto converging paths. It questions the idea that military conflict in the early modern period by definition favoured national, centralised, and bureaucratic states. It has shown how in the case of the Dutch Republic, federal and brokerage arrangements for the organisation of violence at the heart of the state were strengthened, not weakened, by engagement in European great-power competition. These forms of organisation persisted because of their great success in mobilising the enormous wealth in Dutch society for the production of power. Albeit at a somewhat lower level than during the seventeenth century, brokerage forms of organisation allowed the Dutch Republic to continue functioning as a great power during much of the eighteenth century. The crisis that enveloped the state in its final decades did not stem from any significant failure of brokerage structures to fulfil the specific tasks for which they were designed, and the changing role of the Dutch Republic in the international state system did not flow directly from structural incapacities of the brokerage model of its fiscal-military and naval structures.

Breaking with the teleological overtones of the traditional narrative of state-modernisation, this study has argued that 'brokerage' was not a sharply delineated phase in state-formation that for the more successful states ended somewhere around the year 1700, as was assumed by Tilly and much of the literature on the 'military revolutions', but rather continued to function as one of the solutions to which all early modern rulers continued to resort until well into the eighteenth century, in order to solve their problems in the practical organisation of warfare. The continued reliance on independent capitalist suppliers of the means of violence did not itself make the Dutch Republic exceptional. Most of the recent literature on early modern warfare stresses the limits of eighteenth-century nationalisation even for some of the most 'absolutist' states. State reliance on military entrepreneurship in the eighteenth century was not simply a hangover from a by then superseded phase in bureaucratic development. It remained a central aspect of the organisation of warfare across the board. Differences between states did not arise from their reliance on brokerage forms of organisation per se, but from the manner in which forms of brokerage were integrated into the overall structure of the state. In societies in which capitalist social structures were more marginalised, like Habsburg Spain or Bourbon France, the crown always remained the final arbiter in the employment of entrepreneurs, restraining capitalist development at the same time as relying on it. In societies in which capitalism did attain more developed forms, like the Dutch Republic and England, bureaucrats and capitalists interacted on a much more equal footing.

How and in what proportion market and bureaucracy, impersonal structures and personal networks combined in each case depended not only on material circumstances, but also on the balance of forces inside the state, the historically developed preferences of administrators, and the place of the state in international power-relations. This becomes especially visible when comparing the Northern and Southern Netherlands, geographically close societies that shared common historical antecedents and showed great socio-economic similarities – such as high levels of urbanisation and strong commercial elites – but still developed very different institutional arrangements for the interaction between the state and capitalist entrepreneurs – the state of the Dutch Republic much more market-oriented than its Southern Netherlands counterpart. In the North the Dutch Revolt allowed the newly created Republic to establish itself as an independent centre of capital accumulation. Its successes imbued the Dutch ruling class with exuberant self-confidence and universalising perceptions of the importance of Dutch trade, which were subsequently projected both on the world at large and on the most diverse areas of social organisation within the Republic itself. At the same time, the defeat of the Revolt in the South led to the reconstitution of a state at the mercy of other European powers, prey to invading armies, where wealthy commercial elites for a long time remained the junior partner to state officials close by and far away in negotiating commercial policies, taxation, and the way of organising warfare.

Instead of teleologically envisioning these divergent developments of early modern states as distinct paths towards the national state, it is more helpful to see them as variants on a continuum between market-oriented and state-oriented, localised and nationalised solutions by which European states responded to the challenges of interlocking power struggles and tried to exploit the new possibilities created by the international expansion of markets, finance, labour flows, and production associated with the growth of capitalism as a world-system. Reinterpreting the trajectories of European state formation in this way, the Dutch Republic becomes exceptional not for what it did differently from other states, but primarily for the thoroughness with which it implemented one particular organisational form that was common for all. To capture this defining characteristic – the persistent favour of rulers for institutional arrangements that parcelled out state-like tasks to independent entrepreneurs and divided control over the execution of their tasks among provincial and urban elites – this study has described the Dutch Republic as a 'federal-brokerage state'.

Three areas of interaction between the state and capitalists in the organisation of warfare were singled out for detailed empirical investigation: the joint

activities of Admiralty Boards and commercial companies in the armed protection and expansion of trade; the interaction between Admiralty Boards and
the home economy in the production and provisioning of war fleets; and the
operation of financial intermediaries between provincial treasuries and the
capital market in troop payment. Together, these case studies encompass the
three main strategic terrains of Dutch warfare – the carving out of a commercial empire overseas, great-power struggle in European waters, and the quest
for 'security' on the continental mainland – as well as three key areas of state
investment. They also included three very different types of brokerage organisation. The chartered commercial companies, especially the voc and wic, often
fulfilled warring tasks completely on their own account as extensions of their
commercial activities. Here, organised bodies of merchants themselves bore
full responsibility for the organisation of warfare abroad, strengthening their
position as a 'state within a state' at home. The relations between merchants
and the state in Dutch naval organisation formed an opposite but corollary
pattern, in which the leading merchant houses were directly integrated into
the state through the selection of delegates on the Admiralty Boards. Military
soliciting represented a third category of brokerage organisation, most akin to
modern day sub-contracting. Private financiers retained a semi-independent
role in the execution of state tasks based on the employment of their own funds
and networks, but state regulation strictly determined the contours of their
work. The common element in all three categories was the merger between
the management of state activities and the search for private profit. In each
investigated area, there were strong links between the wish to involve economic
elites directly in the running of the state and the federal nature of bureaucratic institutions that tied administrators to their local constituencies. The
federal and brokerage sides of the Dutch state-form were mutually reinforcing.

Chapter One traced the origins of federal-brokerage arrangements in the
Dutch Revolt and the long war of independence against the Habsburg Empire.
It examined the general features of the federal-brokerage model, and described
the concrete paths of institutional evolution that laid the foundation of federal-
brokerage organisation in the three core areas of investigation. It showed that
the particular institutional form of the state did not emerge according to a
pre-ordained plan. The constitution of the state itself was the result of a long
series of contingencies, triggered by the need to face the emergencies produced
by the long drawn-out struggle against the Habsburg crown, and shaped by
socio-political conflicts inside the rebel camp. The eventual triumph of the
federal-brokerage model around the time of the founding of the Republic in
1588 had not been predictable three decades earlier, and only resulted from

the political defeat of three alternative trajectories – centralisation under the Habsburg monarchy, a closer union between the rebellious provinces and one of Spain's European competitors, or further devolution of political power to the provincial level. The triumph of this model depended on its ability to mobil-ise resources, overcoming the centrifugal tendencies of provincial and urban particularism to meet the direct requirements of military confrontation while preserving forms of local autonomy that allowed the commercial ruling class extraordinary influence over the deployment of power in the course of the war. The erection of institutions for commercial expansion, naval warfare, and troop payments reflecting the general federal-brokerage features of the state likewise took place in an unplanned fashion, through a long series of ad hoc measures heavily influenced by the eternal haggling for influence of the provinces and towns that took the side of the Revolt.

Despite the unplanned nature of its construction, the structure of the state reflected key features of Dutch society. Federal-brokerage arrangements fit well with the highly commercialised nature of the Northern Netherlands. Confident that the state would always keep in mind their interests, the ruling classes were more willing to provide the funds for warfare than their counterparts in other European countries. Mutually beneficial arrangements between the state and capitalist elites greatly increased their range of power at home and abroad. The erection of the VOC and WIC allowed the state to mobilise profit-seeking merchants to help carry the war against the Habsburg crown to the Indies and the Americas, while those merchants in turn could request ample state support for their risky commercial ventures. Strong connections between the Admiralty Boards and merchants facilitated the exchange between custom collection and trade protection, while enabling the navy to fruitfully employ the connections and knowledge of seafaring communities. Military solicitors gave the state easy access to short-term credit with a speed and efficiency that was not obtainable through taxation and long-term state loans, while the willingness of the state to secure their profits stimulated the development of capital markets. The federal build-up of these institutions widened their regional support base by involving local political elites in their management, creating career opportunities and roads of influence for sections of the urban middle classes below the top level of international merchants and large-scale financiers.

Federal-brokerage institutions were more than just executive branches of the state. They also fulfilled a role as islands of political power for conflicting sections of the Dutch ruling class, explaining why throughout the existence of the Republic, urban and provincial representatives clung with so much force to the 'right' to house their own regional chambers of the commercial compan-ies and Admiralty Boards, or to retain a system of troop payments through the provincial treasuries instead of the national state. But for a long time, these islands of interests were able to cooperate remarkably well. Applying a theoretical notion elaborated by Antonio Gramsci, Chapter One explained this success as a function of the ability of the Dutch state to articulate its underlying 'historical bloc'. Its institutions provided a framework for integrating the competing faction networks of ruling-class families, a mechanism for balancing the conflicting interests between Holland and the other provinces, and even a minimum of ideological coherence that allowed the ruling class to overcome its internal struggles by resorting to powerful unifying notions of shared interests. But the manner in which the state fulfilled these functions also came at a price. It consolidated rather than helped to overcome the structural inequalities in political access between sea provinces and inland provinces, between Amsterdam and the other trading towns, between the wealthy international merchant-industrialists and merchant-financiers and the urban small producers. Furthermore, the lower classes always remained excluded from political influence, creating a reservoir of discontent that violently erupted at moments of crisis. These divisions were partially subdued by the positive interplay between overseas commercial expansion and a flowering of the main productive sectors at home that temporarily created a real convergence of interests between wealthy sections of the urban middle classes and large international merchants and financiers, but they were never entirely overcome.

After this general examination of the emergence and structure of the federal-brokerage state in Chapter One, the evolution of each of the core institutions under investigation was traced from the 1650 highpoint of Dutch success to the mid-eighteenth century. Chapter Two focused on the interaction between merchants and the state in the organisation of trade protection. It showed how the naval revolution of the 1650s led to the redefinition of the role of commercial companies, but not to an end to brokerage practices. The direct involvement of merchants in the organisation of warfare was merely cast in new forms. The outcome of this process differed fundamentally for the main geographic areas of trade, depending both on the diverging strategic requirements for each region and the specific configuration of commercial interests. The chapter showed how even before the naval revolution, such differences made themselves felt in the 1644 debates over the introduction of a unified state company for colonial trade. The WIC, heavily dependent on state support and much less secure of its hold over commerce than its East-Indian counterpart, set up an intense political lobby for a merger between the two companies. But the VOC was able to use its strength vis-à-vis the state to brush off any proposals that would harm its independence of action, both in terms of its commercial strategies and its prerogatives for warfare. Following the negotiations between the state and Company directors, the chapter showed how between the First and the Third Anglo-Dutch War, the VOC and the state went from intense cooperation to a systematic division of labour in which the Company managed to retain full independence in Asian warfare and thereby avoid state interference in the Asian branch of its trading activities. For the WIC on the other hand, the undermining of its monopoly position by the growth of private trade tended to force the Company to concentrate even more on its brokerage functions in colonial management and trade protection. Finally, in the European heartlands of trade, inter-state rivalry was so intense that the independence of merchants in organising violence was necesarilly more limited. With the introduction of line-ahead tactics and the start of major building programmes for the erection of purpose built permanent war fleets, the role of European commercial directorates was reduced to that of protection lobbies. Nonetheless, the state navy itself remained closely connected to the commercial elites through the Admiralty Boards, and the commercial directorates contributed to the planning and coordination of convoying operations in very concrete ways. Emphasising the active role of merchants and merchant companies in the formulation of responses to the naval revolution, Chapter Two showed how, contrary to the supposition of older studies of war and trade such as the classic work of Snapper, the gradual replacement of merchant-men by purpose built men-of-war in naval warfare did not lead to a loss of influence that merchant elites could wield collectively over naval employment.

The retention of brokerage relations between merchant elites and the navy during the second half of the seventeenth century defies a simplistic approach to the decline of Dutch naval power in key areas of European trade, in which a partial withdrawal from great-power competitions is seen as the result of a supposed loss of interest in trade by increasingly 'aristocratic' political administrators. Furthermore, an extensive overview of the evolution of naval finances during the 'long eighteenth century' proved that the changes in naval policy were not primarily motivated by a lack of funds. As an alternative to these established views, Chapter Two proposed that the growing conflict between the need to use the navy to gain short-term trading advantages on the one hand, and the prerequisites of power struggles between the major European states involved in securing commercial interests for the long term on the other hand, led to fundamental shifts in the strategic geography of Dutch naval policy. The decisive moment in this process was the conclusion of the Anglo-Dutch naval alliance, allowing Dutch traders to give priority to short-term profits while free-riding on a wave of British naval expansion. The Dutch eighteenth-century navy did not become a navy of the second rate, but was re-designed to fulfil completely different functions than the British and Bourbon fleets. Continuing sensitivity to commercial interests pushed naval administrators to transform their fleet into a lean force destined for long-distance convoying. In the long run, this had disastrous effects for the ability of the Dutch state to withstand direct confrontation with the expanding battle fleets of other European powers, primarily Britain. As a result, these powers started to make substantial inroads into the core areas of Dutch trade. Thus, while the individual Admiralty Boards remained as capable of incorporating the immediate demands of the individual sections of the commercial elites to whom they were tied, these same connections became a barrier to formulating counterstrategies to increased British competition, ultimately damaging the ability of the navy to protect the commercial interests of Dutch capital in general.

Chapter Three investigated similar processes in the relations between the Admiralty Boards and the home economy. It showed how the involvement of leading merchants in the directing bodies of one of the main pillars of the state was an important factor in the success of the Dutch Republic as a global power. The Admiralty Boards were deeply influenced by a commercial logic that seeped down into the minutest details of naval management. The adaptation of commercial methods of accounting for bureaucratic institutions, for which the Dutch Admiralty Boards were worldwide frontrunners, was an important step in the introduction of a specifically capitalist form of rationality in the management of the state. The concentration of the Admiralty economy within large centralised shipyards and storehouses, a product of the naval revolution, made it possible to apply these methods on a large scale. Making use of these methods of administration as well as their strong connections to the market, Admiralty Boards developed highly differentiated systems of supply in which public auctions, sophisticated contracting practices, and systematic control for economic efficiency and costs played important roles. The high degree of commercialisation of Dutch society increased the range of options on which administrators based their strategies in the acquisition of goods. Their personal ties to merchant communities and local politics made sure that Admiralty Boards avoided the rapacious relations between state and suppliers that so often characterised early modern state contracting and which inhibited the possibilities for capital accumulation. Innovations in market practices continued throughout the eighteenth century, countering the image of growing lethargy and corruption in naval management. However, while continuing to stimulate 'rational' practices internally, the local embeddedness of naval institutions tended to prevent similar rationalisation at the supra-regional level. The Zeeland and Friesland Admiralty Boards could never profit from favourable market conditions the way the Amsterdam and Rotterdam Boards did, while the political-commercial advantages to local elites stemming from control over the Admiralty Boards blocked measures to reduce the effects of regional discrepancies, leading to increasing organisational divisions in the course of the eighteenth century.

The same holds true for the evolution of naval production. The example of the Amsterdam naval storehouse and shipyard shows how the successful application of economies of scale could make these state facilities pioneers of capitalist forms of production. More than any other institution in the Netherlands, and perhaps worldwide, the Dutch naval shipyards combined reliance on free labour, strict time management, the successful challenging of established guild practices, and hierarchical control of the work process on the shop floor to reorder the production process. Changes in labour relations were accompanied by product and process innovations, stimulated by a culture of experimentation and the application of scientific knowledge. Again in contrast to strongly entrenched assumptions, the prominent role of naval shipyards in advancing capitalist methods of production continued unabated throughout much of the eighteenth century. In this respect, the 'quiet years' after the War of the Spanish Succession were decades of successful restructuring – a factor that also explains the radicalisation of shipyard workers around this same period. However, just like in supply, large differences between individual Admiralty Boards persisted because of the federal-brokerage structure of naval administration. In shipbuilding the Zeeland, Rotterdam, and Amsterdam Admiralty Boards all preferred their own systems, reflecting the central position of their respective master shipwrights in the production process and the weakness of central bureaucracy. Admiralty Boards competed among themselves for funds and work. The real crisis in naval management that became apparent during the Fourth Anglo-Dutch War was not so much the result of the institutional incapacities of the individual Admiralty Boards as it was of the inability to overcome these inbuilt divisions created by the federal nature of the naval administration.

The Dutch system of army payment examined in Chapter Four again remained based on the role of independent brokers, directed from the provinces rather than The Hague. Cutting out the financial middlemen between provincial treasuries and the troops was seriously contemplated in 1651, 1673, and 1721. But the practical difficulties in implementing a centralised system time and again pushed the state back into the arms of financial intermediaries in tapping the credit markets for funds. How the pressures of war could reaffirm brokerage structures rather than challenge them is particularly clear in the case of the 1673 attempt to hand over troop payments to a small body of directors of payment employed by the state. The inability of these directors to secure the necessary funds on the capital market led to financial chaos at

a precarious moment in the Franco-Dutch war. Instead of facilitating nationalisation, the direct pressures of warfare forced the state in the aftermath of
this failure to introduce regulation that protected the status of military solicitors. This was not a full return to the pre-1673 situation in troop payments. A
rather disorganised form of financial brokerage, in which almost anyone who
could put up the money – qualified or unqualified – could act as a solicitor,
was replaced by a more strictly regulated system in which a small group of
professional financiers attained central roles in all aspects of the 'company economy'. This transition was further favoured by the incipient financialisation of
the Dutch economy, a process signified *inter alia* by the growing role of merchant bankers in backing up soliciting enterprises. The careers of Gebhardt
and Van Heteren showed how the fortune of individual financiers was bound
to the strength of their personal economic and political networks. These networks allowed successful military solicitors to profit from their enterprises on
an immense scale, and later on to diversify their businesses in non-military
directions. While in more centralised and bureaucratic states such as France
and Spain, troop finances hinged on the relations between the crown and a
small number of privileged financiers, creating great dangers for the stability of
state finance, the ability to rely on a large market for credit through the intermediation of the military solicitors meant that Dutch army finances remained
highly stable until the end of the eighteenth century. Individual solicitors did
go bankrupt, but cases of acute collapse of the entire system of army finance
such as occurred among the more centralised and bureaucratic competitors
were largely avoided.

Due to the high level of sophistication of fiscal and financial institutions of
the state in comparison to other areas of bureaucracy, brokerage practices in
troop payments came much closer to 'modern' forms of subcontracting and
market intermediation than the privatised arrangements for colonial warfare
or bourgeois self-rule in naval administration. But even here, in the course
of the eighteenth century the limits of federal-brokerage organisation slowly
started to make themselves felt. When in the course of the eighteenth century
centralisation of military soliciting across provincial borders did take place, this
was not a result of greater unity within the state. It flowed from the growing
role of Holland-based bankers in the world of government finance. As in the
other examples of federal-brokerage organisation, this exacerbated regional
unevenness, focusing financial networks on Amsterdam and The Hague while
leaving political prerogatives firmly in the hands of provincial administration.
And again, as in the other examples, the federal and brokerage aspects of
organisation were mutually reinforcing. The wish of provinces to maintain
control over 'their own' troops, the central position of financiers, and the

independence of officers within the company economy helped to sustain each other, making it more difficult for the state to gain full control over the army.

The concrete institutional developments sketched in Chapters Two to Four thus affirmed the hypotheses formulated in the introduction. In each of the three case studies, not the failure but the continued success of the institutions formed the reason for the perseverance of their federal-brokerage character, even if this overall durability was often combined with internal restructurings. This goes against the grain of much perceived wisdom on the development of the Dutch state from the seventeenth to the eighteenth century. None of the institutions under investigation exhibited clear tendencies towards a loss of internal dynamics, growing inefficiency and corruption, or 'aristocratisation', which could then be held responsible for breaking the connections between the state and the commercial elites. The most notable aspect of their day-to-day functioning was their continued ability to tap into the enormous reserves of wealth that were generated by the spectacular success of Dutch early capitalist development whenever this was necessary. The limits of their success did not arise from a secular disintegration of the bonds between these institutions and the commercial elites. Rather, the organisational forms through which the ruling class managed to consolidate and continue its hold over the state themselves became the long-term barriers to development. By creating islands of influence for the competing sections within this ruling class, the federal-brokerage state tended to emphasise regional and sectional differences and became incapable of counteracting the 'growing apart' of the main branches of the Dutch economy in the late seventeenth and eighteenth century. In the long run, this undercut the basis for Dutch military and naval strength. While individual institutions continued to mobilise resources for specific tasks with great success, the state proved unable to combine these individual areas of success into common strategies to overcome the challenges to Dutch power.

The consequences for the stability of the state became apparent in the crisis of the Dutch *ancien régime*. Chapter Five has shown how the disintegration of the historic bloc that had carried Dutch success forward became articulated in increasingly intense political conflicts over the architecture of the state. Each of the three areas of interaction between state and capital examined in this book became a terrain of struggle. Agendas for centralisation and bureaucratic rationalisation were first developed from within, beginning with Van Slingelandt's proposals for redress in the aftermath of the War of the Spanish Succession, continuing with Bentinck's attempts at reform after the end of the Second Stadtholderless Period in 1747, and culminating in Van de Spiegel's far-reaching plans for a conservative reconstitution of the Republic in the era of democratic revolutions. But an unwillingness to challenge the networks of ruling-class families on which late stadtholderly power increasingly was forced to rely, combined with the real fear that moderate reform might form the prelude to radical revolution, formed insurmountable obstacles to the implementation of their programmes. The successful challenge to the existing state structure therefore had to come from outside. Until the Patriot Revolution of the 1780s, oppositionist discourse was cast in the language of restoration of the Old Republic, making the Patriots passionate defenders of the federal-brokerage model. But the combination of intense Orangist reaction after their 1787 defeat, the visible paralysis of the existing state, and the popularisation of the idea of the unitary state by the French Revolution led to a spectacular reversal of positions. A thorough transformation of all institutions of the federal-brokerage state along nationalising lines became one of the main ingredients of the revolutionary programme. Between 1787 and 1795, radical exiles in France and former Patriots who remained in the Netherlands formulated concrete plans for colonial management, naval administration, and the citizens' army along those lines. However, one of the great ironies of the Batavian Revolution of 1795 was that the eventual success of their proposals did not flow from democratic revolution from below, as envisioned by radical Unitarians before 1795 and during the political struggles of the first years of the revolution, but instead stemmed from the anti-democratic usurpation of this revolution from above.

These considerations make it possible to return to the role of the state in the 'Dutch cycle of accumulation' on the basis of a much more concrete examination of its functioning than that underlying Arrighi's original account. The Dutch Republic was able to gain centre stage in the seventeenth-century world economy not despite, but because of its federal-brokerage structure. The creation of an independent state enabled the foundations of capitalist development that were already in place during the late medieval period to be reproduced and expanded on a far larger geographic grid. Federal-brokerage institutions at one and the same time provided opportunities for the ruling class to use the state as a vehicle for capital accumulation, and allowed the state to maximise its power-producing abilities by employing their economic resources for warfare. Together, these two characteristics made the Dutch state more conducive to capitalist development at home, and more assertive in seeking commercial interests abroad, than any of its competitors. Traditional approaches to Dutch 'rise and decline' supposed that the end of this successful interplay between power and profit was inevitable with the arrival on the European scene of more successful nationalisers such as France and England during the second half of the seventeenth century. But as this study has shown, the Dutch model of development continued to exhibit considerable strength, even if it did not give Dutch capital the competitive edge that it used to have during the first half of the seventeenth century. The internal limits to the success of the federal-brokerage model only became apparent late in the eighteenth century, not because of unambiguous and overall decline, but primarily because of the way in which heavily parcellised state institutions prevented the state as a whole from recombining the still existing sources of strength into renewed long-term strategies to face foreign competition. The bourgeois modernisers of the *ancien régime* only became convinced that the federal-brokerage model no longer sufficed to safeguard the commercial interests of 'the nation' after a long series of failed reform attempts, defeats at the hands of enemies at home and abroad, and their own first-hand experience of the French Revolution and Revolutionary Wars.

As much as the circumstances of its birth, the death of the Dutch federal-brokerage state affirms one of the main theoretical assumptions of this book: that war makes states not through a mechanical process of pressure and response, but through the mediating prism of the institutional relations between the state and ruling classes. State formation during the early modern period did not take the form of a long triumphant march of centralising bureaucracies, carried on the waves of successive changes in the technique of warfare. It consisted of a long series of successive restructurings of state-society relations, characterised by hybrid combinations of bureaucracy and brokerage, administrative experimentation, imitation, and adaptation of highly divergent management models by states interlocked in economic and territorial rivalry. The eventual emergence of the 'modern' bureaucratic state – by no means the simple continuation of any of these forerunners – was intimately connected with the transformations and shifts in the balance of power within the capitalist world-system. Both for its successes and its failures, the Dutch state was thus representative of a long epoch in the development of the relations between state and capital. If the industrial revolution and modern banking, the *levée en masse* and the *Code Napoléon*, nineteenth-century colonialism, *laissez faire* policies, the quality of Prussian boots, along with numerous other factors ultimately conspired in the supersession of independent brokerage as an indispensable building block of the state, the intimate connection between capitalist elites and state power that it helped to establish were carried over in each successive cycle of accumulation. The relevance of this stretches out to our own times. For as long as the second horseman of the apocalypse continues to reap death and profits, the ancestry of the masters of war will be traceable to the meticulous administrators, enterprising merchants, and skilful manipulators of financial flows of the seventeenth and eighteenth century Dutch Republic.

Holland Members of the Amsterdam Admiralty Board

Functions in Local Administration

M	Magistrate
A	Alderman
S	Secretary
B	Burgomaster

Functions in National Administration

CS	Council of State
SG	States General
GAO	Generalty Audit Office
GRG	Generalty Receiver General

Functions in Provincial Administration

PG	Member of Provincial Government
PAO	Provincial Audit Office
AOD	Audit Office of the Domains
RN	Representative of Nobility
CCH	Council Court of Holland
GPH	Grand Pensionary Holland
MG	Mint master General

Name	Year of birth and death	Start of term on Admiralty Board	End of term on Admiralty Board	Represents	Later terms on Admiralty Board	Total years of service on Admiralty Board	Functions in local administration
Fransz, Balthasar	? –?	1586	?	Dordrecht			M
Vinck, Egbert Pietersz	1536–1610	1586	1588	Amsterdam		3	
Cromhout, Barthold Adriaensz	1550–1624	1589	1591	Amsterdam		3	M, A, B
Goedereede, Willem Adriaensz	1537–1599	1589	1589	Rotterdam		1	M, A
Horst, Pieter Claesz van der	?–1604	1589	?	Rotterdam			M, B
Pietersz, Dirck	? –?	1589	1594	Medemblik		6	M
Santen, Heyndrick Dircksz van	?–1608	1589	1591	Delft		3	M, B
Verbrugge, Hendrik Willemsz	?–1604	1590	1595	Gouda		6	M
Florisz, Heinrick	?–1614	1591	1592	Alkmaar		2	M
Hooft, Jan Cornelisz	?–1600	1591	1600	Amsterdam		10	A
Nijenburg, Cornelis Jansz van de	1530–1610	1592	1594	Alkmaar		3	M
Crommendijk, Sijbert Jansz	? –?	1593	1597	Holland		5	

Functions in provincial administration	Functions in national administration	Connection to colonial companies	Other professional or economic ties	Indication of wealth	Sources (in addition to 'repertorium')
			Merchant (herring)		Elias, I: 295, 301, 320, 321, 322
PG	CS, SG		Merchant	His widow bequeaths ƒ435,000	Elias, I: 17, 19, 103, 268, 269, 365
			Merchant (herring), Brewer		Engelbrecht, 38
			Merchant, Tax-farmer		Engelbrecht, 50–51
PG, PAO					
					Bruinvis, Alkmaar
					Elias, I: 50, 149
					Bruinvis, Alkmaar

Name	Year of birth and death	Start of term on Admiralty Board	End of term on Admiralty Board	Represents	Later terms on Admiralty Board	Total years of service on Admiralty Board	Functions in local administration
Vlammenburch, Aert Jacobsz	?–1614	1595	1597	Gouda	1599–1601, 1603–5 and 1607–9	12	M
Aartsz, Willem-Jan	?–?	1597	1601	Schiedam		5	M
Baersdorp, Jan Jansz	?–1608	1597	1600	Leiden		4	M
Schaap, Dirk Cornelisz.	1545–1632	1597	1599	Gouda		3	M
Velaar, Claas Claasz	?–1597	1597	1597	Edam		1	M
Pietersz, Jan	?–?	1598	1606	Edam		9	M
Gael, Laurens Huygensz	ca. 1549–1618	1600	1614	Leiden		15	M
Valckenier, Gillis Jansz	1550–1613	1600	1613	Amsterdam		14	
Poelgeest, Jasper van	?–?	1601	1606	Holland, Nobility		6	
Schoonhoven, Dirck Jacobsz	?–1640	1601	1603	Gouda	1605–7 and 1612–15	10	M
Egmont, Johan van	?–?	1606	1607	Holland, Nobility		2	
Geltsack, Nicolaas Cornelisz	1550–1607	1606	1607	Haarlem		2	M

Functions in provincial administration	Functions in national administration	Connection to colonial companies	Other professional or economic ties	Indication of wealth	Sources (in addition to 'repertorium')
PG					
			Merchant		Elias, I: 12, 409, 411, 413, 414
RN					NNBW, V 523–524
PG					JCBG 1990
RN					

Name	Year of birth and death	Start of term on Admiralty Board	End of term on Admiralty Board	Represents	Later terms on Admiralty Board	Total years of service on Admiralty Board	Functions in local administration
Houttuyn, Claas Claasz	?–1662	1606	1608	Edam	1614–16 and 1642–4	9	M
Soutman, Dierck	? –?	1606	?	Holland, Nobility		?	
Deyman, Frederik Adriaansz	?–1617	1607	1610	Haarlem		4	M
Matenesse, Willem van	? –?	1607	1615	Holland, Nobility		9	
Breed, Jacob Jansz	? –?	1608	1610	Edam	1612–14	6	M
Hart, Jan Hendriksz 't	?–1625	1609	1612	Gouda		4	M
Brasker, Jacob Jacobsz	? –?	1610	1612	Edam		3	M
Schout, Pieter Jacobsz	?–1645	1610	1613	Haarlem	1617–19	7	M, B
Fabricius, Arent Meijndertsz	ca. 1547–1624	1613	1617	Haarlem	1622–4	8	M, A, B
Baersdorp, Jan Jansz van	1565–1614	1614	1614	Leiden		1	M
Overlander, Volckert	1571–1630	1614	1621	Amsterdam		8	M, A, B
Schagen, Albert van	1577–1638	1615	1623	Holland, Nobility		9	
Vroesen, Gerrit Jansz	1555–1630	1615	1618	Gouda		4	M
Dirksz, Pieter	?–1635	1616	1620	Edam		5	M

Functions in provincial administration	Functions in national administration	Connection to colonial companies	Other professional or economic ties	Indication of wealth	Sources (in addition to 'repertorium')
PG, PAO					
RN					
					JCBG 1955, 109
PG					NNBW, VIII 523
PG					
PG			Merchant and ship owner	His widow bequeaths ƒ150,000	Elias, I: 150, 156, 274, 275, 293, 305, 402, 406, 422
RN					

Name	Year of birth and death	Start of term on Admiralty Board	End of term on Admiralty Board	Represents	Later terms on Admiralty Board	Total years of service on Admiralty Board	Functions in local administration
Paedts, Cornelis Pietersz	? –?	1616	1618	Leiden		3	M
Crabeth, Pieter Woutersz	1568–1638	1618	1621	Gouda		4	M
Warmond, Willem van	? –?	1618	1622	Leiden		5	M
Meer, Nicolaas Woutersz van der	ca. 1574–1637	1619	1622	Haarlem		4	M, A, B
Houtcooper, Teunis Jansz	?–1635	1620	1622	Edam	1626–8	6	M
Poppen, Jacob	1576–1624	1621	1621	Amsterdam		1	M, A, B
Raep, Adriaen Pietersz	1556–1647	1621	1625	Amsterdam		5	M, A
Vrije, Jacob Jacobsz de	?–1630	1621	1624	Gouda		4	M
Coedijck, Huig Pietersz	? –?	1622	1625	Leiden		4	M
Trom, Jacob Pietersz	? –?	1622	1624	Edam		3	
Swieten, Adriaen van	?–1623	1623	1623	Holland, Nobility		1	
Cool, Gerard Adriaensz	?–1641	1624	1627	Gouda		4	M
Cornelisz, Frans	?–1642	1624	1626	Edam	1634–6	6	M
Akersloot, Auwel Arisz	1583–1649	1625	1628	Haarlem		4	M
Bas, Pieter Jacobsz	1566–1633	1625	1628	Amsterdam		4	A
Deyman, Pieter Arentsz	1566–1626	1625	1626	Leiden		2	M

Functions in provincial administration	Functions in national administration	Connection to colonial companies	Other professional or economic ties	Indication of wealth	Sources (in addition to 'repertorium')
PG					
PG	SG				JCBG 1975, 59
PG					
		VOC Director	Merchant (Baltic trade)	Bequeaths ƒ920,000	Elias, I: 108, 285–288
			Merchant		Elias, I: 294, 295, 398
	GAO				
RN					
PG					
PG, PAO					
			Merchant (grain)		Elias, I: 85, 244, 249, 275, 386, 442
PG					

Name	Year of birth and death	Start of term on Admiralty Board	End of term on Admiralty Board	Represents	Later terms on Admiralty Board	Total years of service on Admiralty Board	Functions in local administration
Raephorst, Hendrik van	?–1649	1625	1645	Holland, Nobility		21	
Lanschot, Gerard van	1584–1638	1626	1630	Leiden		5	M
Swaenswijck, Andries Laurisz van	?–1643	1627	1630	Gouda		4	M
Meusses, Jacob Pietersz	?–1646	1628	1630	Edam		3	M
Neck, Jacob Cornelisz van	1564–1638	1628	1637	Amsterdam		10	M, A, B
Wildt, Gillis Claasz de	1576–1630	1628	1630	Haarlem		3	M
Bouwensz, Maarten	?–1641	1630	1632	Edam	1638–40	6	M
Nieuwenhoven, Christoffer Dircksz van	?–1632	1630	1632	Leiden		3	M
Steenwijck, Dirck Jansz	?–1633	1630	1633	Gouda		4	M
Veer, Bartholomeus Jansz	?–1642	1630	1634	Haarlem		5	M
Baan, Jacob Jansz	? –?	1632	1634	Edam		3	M
Gallus, Carolus	?–1635	1632	1635	Leiden		4	M
Hogenberch, Govert Aertsz	?–1655	1633	1636	Gouda		4	M
Backer, Cornelis Adriaensz	?–1655	1634	1637	Haarlem	1652–5	8	M
Warmond, Cornelis Adriaensz van	?–1637	1635	1637	Leiden		3	M

Functions in provincial administration	Functions in national administration	Connection to colonial companies	Other professional or economic ties	Indication of wealth	Sources (in addition to 'repertorium')
RN					
	CS				
	CS		Admiral of 1598 East India fleet		Elias, I: 190, 270, 278, 336, 227, 420, 520
					Elias, I: 392
PG					
PAO					
PG					

Name	Year of birth and death	Start of term on Admiralty Board	End of term on Admiralty Board	Represents	Later terms on Admiralty Board	Total years of service on Admiralty Board	Functions in local administration
Ophemert, Joost Jansz	ca. 1578–1636	1636	1636	Gouda		1	M
Teylingen, Jacob van	1583–1640	1636	1640	Gouda		5	M
Westerbaan, Jacob Jansz	?–1645	1636	1638	Edam		3	M
Bicker, Andries	1586–1652	1637	1640	Amsterdam	1650–2	7	M, A, B
Fabricius, Arent	1609–45	1637	1640	Haarlem	1643–5	7	M
Staveren, Adriaan Jansz van	?–?	1637	1641	Leiden		5	M
Hasselaer, Pieter Pietersz	1583–1651	1640	1641	Amsterdam	1643–4	4	M, A, B
Pieterknecht, Jan Pietersz	?–1651	1640	1642	Edam		3	M
Tin, Cornelis van der	?–1648	1640	1643	Haarlem		4	M
Tocht, Cornelis Bouwensz van der	?–1648	1640	1643	Gouda		4	M
Hogeveen, Gerard van	1611–69	1641	1644	Leiden		4	M
Vlaming van Outshoorn, Diederick de	1574–1643	1641	1643	Amsterdam		3	M, A, B
Geelvinck, Jan Cornelisz	1579–1651	1642	1643	Amsterdam		2	M, A, B

Functions in provincial administration	Functions in national administration	Connection to colonial companies	Other professional or economic ties	Indication of wealth	Sources (in addition to 'repertorium')
PG	SG	VOC Director	Merchant (Russia and East India)		Elias, I: 113, 174, 346, 347, 348, 349, 364, 435, 479 / II: 920
PG					
		VOC Director	Receiver Bank of Amsterdam, Merchant		Elias, I: 148, 206, 369, 379, 489
PG			Merchant	In 1631 possessions estimated at ƒ140,000	Elias, I: 228, 233, 279, 352, 424, 431, 506, 530
PG			Merchant, father trades in victuals	In 1631 possessions estimated at ƒ150,000	Elias, I: 108, 228, 279, 352, 353, 354, 360, 431, 435, 440, 482, 498 / II: 584, 626

Name	Year of birth and death	Start of term on Admiralty Board	End of term on Admiralty Board	Represents	Later terms on Admiralty Board	Total years of service on Admiralty Board	Functions in local administration
Lange, Cornelis Cornelisz de	?–1653	1643	1646	Gouda	1653	5	M
Burch, Albert Coenraedtsz.	1593–1647	1644	1647	Amsterdam		4	M, A, B
Keetman, Pieter Claasz	?–1647	1644	1646	Edam		3	M
Vesanevelt, Pieter Andriesz	?–1647	1644	1647	Leiden		4	M
Duyst van Voorhout, Joost	?–1659	1645	1649	Haarlem		5	M
Raephorst, Albertus van	1611–48	1645	1648	Holland, Nobility		4	
Crabeth, Johan Pietersz	?–1652	1646	1649	Gouda	1652–5	5	M
Pols, Pieter Jacobsz	?–1647	1646	1647	Edam		2	M
Goes, Willem	1610–86	1647	1648	Leiden		2	M
Mieusz, Jan	? –?	1647	1650	Edam		4	
Bas, Albert	1598–1650	1648	1650	Amsterdam		3	M, A, B
Swanenburch, Paulus van	1607–74	1648	1652	Leiden		5	M
Cant, Floris	1610–78	1649	1652	Gouda		4	M
Fabricius, Willem	1613–61	1649	1652	Haarlem	1658–61	8	M, A
Liere, Willem van	ca. 1620–54	1649	1654	Holland, Nobility		6	

Functions in provincial administration	Functions in national administration	Connection to colonial companies	Other professional or economic ties	Indication of wealth	Sources (in addition to 'repertorium')
PG	CS		Merchant and diplomat		Elias, I: 327–330, 349, 442, 453, 465
PG					
PAO					
PG	CS, SG				
PG, PAO					
CCH		VOC Director			
		WIC Director, Principal Shareholder WIC	Son of a wealthy Baltic trader, married into merchant families	Bequeaths ƒ180,000	Elias, I: 133, 206, 246, 249, 414 / II: 595
PG	CS, SG				
PG	CS, SG				
					JCBG 1955, 108

Name	Year of birth and death	Start of term on Admiralty Board	End of term on Admiralty Board	Represents	Later terms on Admiralty Board	Total years of service on Admiralty Board	Functions in local administration
Tromp, Jacob Pietersz	?–?	1650	1652	Edam	1654–6	6	M
Leeusveld, Cornelis Jacobsz van	?–1655	1652	1655	Leiden		4	M, A, B
Oetgens van Waveren, Anthony	1585–1658	1652	1653	Amsterdam		2	M, A, B
Taamses, Thijs Heijnsz	?–1679	1652	1654	Edam		3	M
Herberts, Frans Hendricksz	?–1661	1653	1656	Gouda		4	M
Huydekoper, Joan	1599–1661	1653	1654	Amsterdam		2	M, A, B
Witsen, Cornelis	1605–69	1654	1658	Amsterdam		5	M, A, B
Hoef, Floris Pietersz van der	?–1657	1655	1657	Haarlem		3	M, A, B
Warmond, Pieter Joostensz van	?–1655	1655	1655	Leiden		1	M
Wassenaer, Willem van	1619–?	1655	1660	Holland, Nobility		6	
Willigen, Hendrik van	1621–70	1655	1659	Leiden		5	M
Olij, Pieter Muusz	? 1666	1656	1660	Edam		5	M

Functions in provincial administration	Functions in national administration	Connection to colonial companies	Other professional or economic ties	Indication of wealth	Sources (in addition to 'repertorium')
	GAO				
				Bequeaths ƒ24,000	JCBG 1997, 195, 197
PG	SG		Son of a wealthy merchant, married into merchant family	In 1631 possessions estimated at ƒ130,000	Elias, I: 88, 102, 106, 107, 293, 331, 432, 509
PG					
PG	SG				
		VOC Director	Merchant, Diplomat		Elias, I: 84, 93, 97, 146, 309, 311, 384, 389, 390, 482, 519 / II: 763, 764, 869
	SG	WIC Director, Principal Shareholder WIC	Son of wealthy merchant (Moscow)		Elias, I: 167, 272, 437, 440, 545
					JCBG 1955, 110
CCH					
		VOC Director			

Name	Year of birth and death	Start of term on Admiralty Board	End of term on Admiralty Board	Represents	Later terms on Admiralty Board	Total years of service on Admiralty Board	Functions in local administration
Verboom, Jacob Jacobsz	?–1671	1656	1659	Gouda		4	M
Graeff, Andries de	1611–78	1658	1660	Amsterdam		3	M, A, B
Houtman, Aelberts Maartensz	1585–1662	1659	1662	Gouda		4	M
Wittens, Arnold	1616–66	1659	1662	Leiden		4	M
Boetzelaer, Philip Jacob van den	1634–88	1660	1663	Holland, Nobility	1678–86	13	
Outclaes, Pieter Pietersz	?–?	1660	1664	Edam		5	M
Spiegel, Hendrick Dircksz	1598–1667	1660	1663	Amsterdam		4	M, A, B
Fabricius, Gaaf Meyndertsz	?–1666	1661	1664	Haarlem		4	M
Cincq, Gerrit	?–?	1662	1665	Gouda		4	M
Eleman, Johan	1613–69	1662	1664	Leiden		3	M, A, B
Boetzelaer, Carel van den	1635–1708	1663	1678	Holland, Nobility		16	
Vlooswijck, Cornelis van	1601–87	1663	1666	Amsterdam	1672–80	13	M, A, B
Colterman, Gerard	1632–70	1664	1667	Haarlem		4	M, A
Leeuwen, Jan Simonsz van	?–1667	1664	1667	Leiden		4	M

Functions in provincial administration	Functions in national administration	Connection to colonial companies	Other professional or economic ties	Indication of wealth	Sources (in addition to 'repertorium')
AOoD	CS, GAO		Son of wealthy merchant, family moves into nobility	In 1674 possessions estimated at ƒ292,000	Elias, I: 175, 267, 422k 520, 521
PG, RN	CS, SG				NNBW, VIII 153–154
PG					
		VOC Director	Merchant (soap)		Elias, I: 154, 222, 399, 401 / II: 587
PAO					
PG, PAO					NNBW, I 779
AOD, RN	GAO				NNBW, VIII 139–140
		VOC Director	Son of wealthy merchant, married into merchant family		Elias, I: 402, 449, 482, 483, 484
	SG				JCBG 1955, 114

Name	Year of birth and death	Start of term on Admiralty Board	End of term on Admiralty Board	Represents	Later terms on Admiralty Board	Total years of service on Admiralty Board	Functions in local administration
Thoen, Claas Jansz	?–1668	1664	1667	Edam		4	M
Bonser, Jacob	1623–98	1665	1668	Gouda		4	M
Hooft, Henrick	1617–78	1666	1669	Amsterdam		4	M, A, B
Akersloot, Johan	?–1671	1667	1670	Haarlem		4	M, A
Groenendijck, Rippert Johansz van	1604–83	1667	1670	Leiden		4	M
Houttuyn, Jan Theunisz	? –?	1667	1670	Edam		4	
Lange, Cornelis de	1629–82	1668	1671	Gouda		4	M, A, B
Vlaming van Outshoorn, Cornelis de	1613–88	1669	1672	Amsterdam		4	M, A, B
Kerchem, Johan van	?–1670	1670	1670	Leiden		1	M
Schatter, Ysbrant	1622–83	1670	1673	Haarlem		4	M, A, B
Teengs, Jacob Claasz	1632–81	1670	1676	Edam	1679–81	10	M
Dussen, Jacob van der	1631–1701	1671	1695	Gouda		25	M, A, B
Grootveld, Gerrit Leendertsz van	1626–77	1671	1674	Leiden		4	M
Haaswindius, Matthys	1644–79	1673	1676	Haarlem		4	M

Functions in provincial administration	Functions in national administration	Connection to colonial companies	Other professional or economic ties	Indication of wealth	Sources (in addition to 'repertorium')
PAO					
PG					
PG			Son of wealthy merchant, married into merchant family	In 1674 possessions estimated at ƒ340,000	Elias, I: 151, 206, 255, 445, 494, 497, 507 / II: 589, 650, 741
					JCBG 1955, 110
PG					
	CS	WIC Director			De Jong, 355
PG	CS	VOC Director	Son of wealthy merchant	In 1674 possessions estimated at ƒ169,000	Elias, I: 151, 280, 505, 506, 507
PG					JCBG 1955, 115
	GAO				
		VOC Director, WIC Director			De Jong, 342
PG, PAO					
					JCBG 1955, 116

Name	Year of birth and death	Start of term on Admiralty Board	End of term on Admiralty Board	Represents	Later terms on Admiralty Board	Total years of service on Admiralty Board	Functions in local administration
Brouwer, Hendrik	1624–83	1674	1676	Leiden		3	M, A, B
Brouwer, Vincent	?–1705	1676	1679	Edam	1681–8	12	M
Gool, Theodorus	1637–79	1676	1678	Leiden		3	M
Teffelen, Willem van	1618–89	1676	1679	Haarlem		4	M
Marck, Johan van der	1643–94	1678	1680	Leiden		3	M
Backer, Adriaen	1631–93	1679	1684	Haarlem		6	M, B
Bergh, Johan van den	1626–93	1680	1683	Leiden		4	M
Hudde, Johannes	1628–1704	1680	1681	Amsterdam		2	M, A, B
Huydekoper, Joan	1625–1704	1681	1682	Amsterdam		2	M, A, B
Pronk, Claes Hilbrandsz	?–1681	1681	1681	Edam		1	M, B
Corver, Joan	1628–1716	1682	1685	Amsterdam		4	M, A, B
Loreyn, Abraham	?–1685	1684	1685	Haarlem		2	M

Functions in provincial administration	Functions in national administration	Connection to colonial companies	Other professional or economic ties	Indication of wealth	Sources (in addition to 'repertorium')
CS		VOC Director, Principal Shareholder WIC			NNBW, VIII 223–224 / Gaastra, 257
PAO					
			Medic		Prak, 399
		President Suriname Society			JCBG 1955, 113
	SG, GAO				
		VOC Director	Merchant (oxen)	Bequeaths f117,000	Elias, I: 105, 125, 162, 528, 529
		VOC Director	Son of wealthy merchant, married into merchant family		Elias, I: 385, 518 / II: 606, 681, 701, 765, 1014
PG					Bossaers, Annex 2
		VOC Director	Merchant	In 1674 possessions estimated at f419,000	Elias, I: 410, 471, 521, 522, 523 / II: 573, 626, 649, 650

Name	Year of birth and death	Start of term on Admiralty Board	End of term on Admiralty Board	Represents	Later terms on Admiralty Board	Total years of service on Admiralty Board	Functions in local administration
Schrevelius, Theodorus	1643–1704	1684	1686	Leiden		3	M, A, B
Geelvinck, Cornelis	1621–89	1685	1688	Amsterdam		4	M, A, B
Schatter, Mattheus	1625–95	1685	1689	Haarlem		5	M, A, B
Gerard, Isaac	? –?	1686	1689	Leiden		4	M
Liere, Willem van	?–1706	1686	1706	Holland, Nobility		21	
Baan, Claas	?–1700	1688	1694	Edam		7	M, B
Opmeer, Nicolaes	1631–96	1688	1691	Amsterdam		4	M, A, B
Echten, Salomon van	1643–1728	1689	1692	Haarlem		4	M, A, B
Goes van Absmade, Johan	?–1690	1689	1690	Leiden		2	M
Ruisch, Coenraad	1650–1731	1690	1692	Leiden		3	M
Vries, Joan de	1633–1708	1691	1708	Amsterdam		18	M, A, B
Glarges, Anthonie de	1654–1723	1692	1695	Haarlem		4	M, B
Vromans, Jacob	1637–1708	1692	1695	Leiden		4	M, A, B
Pietermaat, Pieter	1659–1707	1694	1707	Edam		14	M

Functions in provincial administration	Functions in national administration	Connection to colonial companies	Other professional or economic ties	Indication of wealth	Sources (in addition to 'repertorium')
	SG			Bequeaths ƒ116,000	Prak, 411
PG			Son of merchant, married into merchant family	In 1674 possessions estimated at ƒ291,000	Elias, I: 160, 175, 353, 355, 378, 476, 481, 485 / II: 624, 641, 1065
PG		WIC Director			JCBG 1955, 111
RN					
PG, PAO					Bossaers, Annex 2
PG		WIC Director	Married into very wealthy family		Elias, I: 356 / II: 571, 572, 639
	GAO				JCBG 1955, 117–118
PG, PAO	SG				
		VOC Director, President Suriname Society	Merchant (Italy)	Bequeaths ƒ200,000	Elias, I: 289, 290, 458, 498, 501 / II: 590
PG	CS				JCBG 1981, 229
PAO					Prak, 419–420
PAO					

Name	Year of birth and death	Start of term on Admiralty Board	End of term on Admiralty Board	Represents	Later terms on Admiralty Board	Total years of service on Admiralty Board	Functions in local administration
Steyn, Johan	1649–1708	1695	1698	Haarlem		4	M, A
Strijen, Hugo van	1646–1710	1695	1698	Gouda		4	M, A, B
Wittens, Cornelis	1646–1709	1695	1698	Leiden		4	M, A, B
Crucius, Karel	1648–1728	1698	1701	Leiden		4	M, A, B
Druyvesteyn, Aernout	1641–98	1698	1698	Haarlem		1	M, A, S, B
Guldewagen, Abraham	1667–1728	1698	1703	Haarlem		6	M, A, B
Immerzeel, Johan van	1643–1702	1698	1702	Gouda		5	M, B
Leyden, Pieter van	1666–1736	1701	1704	Leiden	1707–10 and 1713–16	12	M, A, B
Jongkint, Boudewijn	1655–1713	1702	1706	Gouda	1709–12	9	M, A, B
Boll, Pieter	1661–1719	1703	1706	Haarlem		4	M, A
Alphen, Abraham van	1655–1721	1704	1707	Leiden	1710–13	8	M, B
Craye, Joost	?–1713	1706	1709	Haarlem		4	M
Sommeren van Vrijenes, Pieter van	1635–1714	1706	1719	Gouda		14	M, B
Boetzelaer van Nieuwveen, Jacob Godefroi van	1680–1736	1707	1720	Holland, Nobility		14	
Bost, Claas Harmensz	1651–1709	1708	1709	Edam		2	M

Functions in provincial administration	Functions in national administration	Connection to colonial companies	Other professional or economic ties	Indication of wealth	Sources (in addition to 'repertorium')
					JCBG 1955, 118
		VOC Director			De Jong, 372–373
		VOC Director		Bequeaths f199,000	Prak, 421
PG					Prak, 380
PG	SG				Van der Aa, IV 366
PG					Van der Aa, VII 557
				Bequeaths f32,000	De Jong, 351
					Prak, 396, JCBG 2005
		WIC Director		Bequeaths f16,000	De Jong, 351
					JCBG 1955, 123
		VOC Director		Bequeaths f72,000	Prak, 370
PAO					De Jong, 371, JCBG 1994
PG, RN		VOC Director			NNBW, VIII 150

Name	Year of birth and death	Start of term on Admiralty Board	End of term on Admiralty Board	Represents	Later terms on Admiralty Board	Total years of service on Admiralty Board	Functions in local administration
Munter, Cornelis	1652–1708	1708	1708	Amsterdam		1	M, A, B
Beets, Juriaan	1658–1710	1709	1710	Edam		2	M, B
Fagel, Francois	1674–1718	1709	1712	Haarlem		4	M, A
Pancras, Gerbrand	1658–1716	1709	1710	Amsterdam		2	M, A, B
Haze de Gregorio, Jeronimus de	1651–1725	1710	1711	Amsterdam		2	M, A, B
Wit, Thijs Bastiaansz	1655–1728	1710	1713	Edam		4	M, B
Strijen, Quirijn van	1660–1724	1711	1724	Amsterdam		14	M, A, B
Brandwijk, Gerard van	1673–1725	1712	1714	Gouda		3	M, A, B
Sprang, Jacobus van der	?–1714	1712	1714	Haarlem		3	M
Teengs, Jacob Claasz	1679–1732	1713	1716	Edam		4	M
Lestevenon, Daniel Willem	1681–1754	1714	1717	Gouda		4	M, A, B
Raet, Arent de	1651–1730	1715	1718	Haarlem		4	M
Banchem, Nicolaes van	1658–1729	1716	1720	Leiden		5	M, A, B
Brasker, Jan	1673–1735	1716	1735	Edam		20	M
Abbesteegh, Damianus van	1664–1728	1717	1720	Gouda		4	M, B

Functions in provincial administration	Functions in national administration	Connection to colonial companies	Other professional or economic ties	Indication of wealth	Sources (in addition to 'repertorium')
		WIC Director, President Suriname Society	Son of wealthy merchant		Elias, I: 517, 523 / II: 574, 627, 658, 694, 757, 761
PG					Bossaers, Annex 2
	SG				NNBW, III 387–388
		VOC Director	Merchant (oxen)		Elias, I: 207, 468, 522, 686, 692, 779
PG	CS, SG	VOC Director, WIC Director	Son of very wealthy merchant (Levant)	Bequeaths ƒ3,300,000	Elias, II: 599, 601, 604, 688
PG, PAO					Bossaers, Annex 2
			Married into merchant family		Elias, II: 638, 639, 649, 805
	CS, SG				De Jong, 333
					De Jong, 359
PG		VOC Director			
	GAO		Lawyer		Prak, 373
				Dies in debt	De Jong, 326

Name	Year of birth and death	Start of term on Admiralty Board	End of term on Admiralty Board	Represents	Later terms on Admiralty Board	Total years of service on Admiralty Board	Functions in local administration
Laanen, Samuel van der	1678–1719	1718	1719	Haarlem		2	M
Steyn, Adriaan	1681–1734	1719	1723	Haarlem	1733–4	7	M
Burch, Arent van der	1676–1735	1720	1726	Gouda		7	M, A, B
Does, Baron Steven van der	1700–1732	1720	1732	Holland, Nobility		13	
Gerwen, Abraham van	1663–1727	1720	1723	Leiden		4	M, A, B
Cunaeus, Petrus	1657–1729	1723	1726	Leiden		4	M, A, B
Pauw, Gerard	?–1729	1723	1726	Haarlem		4	M
Trip, Lucas	1666–1734	1724	1732	Amsterdam		9	A, B
Boudens, Gregorius	1667–1732	1726	1732	Gouda		7	M, A, B
Gijs, Pieter	1678–1759	1726	1729	Leiden		4	M, A, B
Waayen, Willem van der	?–1733	1726	1729	Haarlem		4	M, A, B
Hochepied, Jacobus de	1685–1737	1729	1730	Haarlem		2	M, A
Hoogeveen, Gerard Amelis	1691–1746	1729	1730	Leiden		2	M, A, B
Hoogmade, Pieter van	1686–1742	1730	1734	Leiden		5	M, A, B
Sylvius, Cornelis	1687–1738	1730	1736	Haarlem		7	M, A

Functions in provincial administration	Functions in national administration	Connection to colonial companies	Other professional or economic ties	Indication of wealth	Sources (in addition to 'repertorium')
PG					
PG	SG				De Jong, 334
RN				Widow has an income of f10,000 in 1742	NNBW, VI 440
		VOC Director	Lawyer	Bequeaths f133,000	Prak, 386
				Bequeaths f69,000	Prak, 382
			Merchant (Levant)		Elias, II: 554, 558, 821, 834
			Medic		De Jong, 332
				Bequeaths f315,000	Prak, 389
	GAO				JCBG 1955, 125–126
			Bailiff of Kennemerland		JCBG 1955, 126
PG					Prak, 391
			Merchant	Bequeaths f145,000	Prak, 392–393
	SG				JCBG 1955, 125

Name	Year of birth and death	Start of term on Admiralty Board	End of term on Admiralty Board	Represents	Later terms on Admiralty Board	Total years of service on Admiralty Board	Functions in local administration
Crabeth, Reinier	1685–1768	1732	1749	Gouda		18	M, A, B
Munter, Willem	1682–1759	1732	1733	Amsterdam		2	M, A, B
Boetzelaer, Jacob Philip van den	1711–81	1733	1751	Holland, Nobility		19	
Teijlingen, Jan van	1687–1744	1734	1737	Leiden		4	M, A, B
Kroon, Claas	1696–?	1735	1749	Edam		15	M
Deutz, Jacob	1695–1761	1736	1737	Haarlem		2	M, A, B
Akersloot, Paulus	1695–1773	1737	1740	Haarlem		4	M, A, B
Alensoon, Abraham	1687–1758	1737	1740	Leiden	1755–8	8	M, A, B
Dierkens, Willem	1701–1743	1740	1743	Haarlem		4	M, A
Leeuwen, Nicolaes Willem van	1694–1764	1740	1743	Leiden		4	M, A, B
Groeneveld, Jan van	1688–1753	1743	1746	Leiden		4	M, A, B
Steyn, Pieter	1706–72	1743	1746	Haarlem		4	M, A, S, B
Trip, Dirk	1691–1748	1743	1748	Amsterdam		6	A, B
Bije, Nicolaas de	1695–1763	1746	1749	Leiden	1761–3	7	M, A, B

Functions in provincial administration	Functions in national administration	Connection to colonial companies	Other professional or economic ties	Indication of wealth	Sources (in addition to 'repertorium')
		WIC Director	Notary	Bequeaths ƒ84,000	De Jong, 338
			Married into wealthy merchant and banker family	Income in 1742 estimated at ƒ22,000–24,000	Elias, I: 517, 523 / II: 574, 627, 658, 694, 757, 761
PG, RN	CS	VOC Director		Income in 1742 estimated at ƒ10,000	NNBW, VIII 150–151
			Lawyer	Bequeaths ƒ80,000	Prak, 416
PAO					
					Van der Aa, IV 140–141
					JCBG 1955, 126
	CS		Merchant	Bequeaths ƒ16,000	Prak, 370
		VOC Director			JCBG 1955, 128
					Prak, 395
			Medic		Prak, 388
GPH, PG	SG				NNBW, V 817
			Son of wealthy merchant (Levant), married into merchant family	Income in 1742 estimated at ƒ54,000–56,000	Elias, II: 553, 558, 628, 688, 703, 817
	GAO				Prak, 377

Name	Year of birth and death	Start of term on Admiralty Board	End of term on Admiralty Board	Represents	Later terms on Admiralty Board	Total years of service on Admiralty Board	Functions in local administration
Styrum, Anthony van	1679–1756	1746	1748	Haarlem		3	M, A, B
Broek, Pieter van den	ca. 1701–61	1748	1758	Haarlem		11	M, B
Geelvinck, Nicolaas	1706–64	1748	1748	Amsterdam		1	M, A, B
Temminck, Egbert de Vrij	1700–85	1748	1749	Amsterdam		2	M, A, B
Wassenaer, Pieter Baron van	1712–61	1748	1748	Holland, Nobility	1751–61	12	
Boot, Roelof Harmensz	1684–1761	1749	1761	Edam		13	M, B
Buren, Hendrik van	1711–89	1749	1751	Leiden		3	M, A, B
Collen, Ferdinand Ferdinandsz	1708–89	1749	1755	Amsterdam		7	M, A
Quarles, Lodewijk	1719–81	1749	1752	Gouda		4	M, A, B
Leyden, Diderik van	1695–1764	1751	1755	Leiden	1764	6	M, A, B
Hoogwerff, Pieter	1717–62	1752	1755	Gouda		4	M, A
Dieu, Daniel de	1696–1765	1755	1756	Amsterdam	1764–5	4	M, A, B

Functions in provincial administration	Functions in national administration	Connection to colonial companies	Other professional or economic ties	Indication of wealth	Sources (in addition to 'repertorium')
PG					JCBG 1955, 124
PG	CS	WIC Director			Nw 1752, 27
			Married into leading regent and merchant families	Income in 1742 estimated at ƒ14,000–16,000	Elias, I: 523 / II: 659, 683, 688, 706, 727, 822, 825, 827, 838, 865, 924, 943
	CS	VOC Director, WIC Director	Son of merchant, married into merchant family	Income in 1742 estimated at ƒ7,000–8,000 / Bequeaths 289,000	Elias, II: 785, 787, 788, 929
RN					NNBW, II 1534
PG	GAO				Bossaers, Annex 2
PG					Prak, 376
		WIC Director	Married into merchant family	Income in 1742 estimated at ƒ10,000–12,000	Elias, II: 685, 807, 899
PG	SG				De Jong, 366–367
PG					Prak, 397
				Bequeaths ƒ107,000	De Jong, 350
			Married into wealthy merchant family	Income in 1742 estimated at ƒ7,000–8.000 / Bequeaths ƒ70,000	Elias, I: 334 / II: 780, 782, 783

Name	Year of birth and death	Start of term on Admiralty Board	End of term on Admiralty Board	Represents	Later terms on Admiralty Board	Total years of service on Admiralty Board	Functions in local administration
Does, Bruno van der	1715–91	1755	1758	Gouda		4	M, A, B
Hooft, Gerrit	1684–1764	1756	1763	Amsterdam		8	M, A, B
Dam, Christoffel Jan van	1722–98	1758	1761	Haarlem	1788–91	4	M, B
Hoeve, Frederik van der	?–1761	1758	1761	Gouda		4	M, A, B
Hop, Cornelis	1685–1762	1758	1759	Amsterdam	1761–2	4	M, A, B
Sautijn, Willem	1704–89	1758	1759	Leiden		2	M, A
Pla, Jacob	1693–1770	1759	1761	Leiden		3	M, A, B
Bost, Nicolaas Jansz	1706–66	1761	1766	Edam		6	M, B
Dijk, Carel van	1712–80	1761	1764	Haarlem		4	M, A, B
Gronsveld, Bertram Philip Sigismund Albrecht graaf van	1715–72	1761	1772	Holland, Nobility		12	
Mey, Francois de	1726–97	1761	1764	Gouda	1773–6	8	M, A, B
Alphen, Nicolaes van	1716–84	1763	1764	Leiden		2	M, A, B

Functions in provincial administration	Functions in national administration	Connection to colonial companies	Other professional or economic ties	Indication of wealth	Sources (in addition to 'repertorium')
PAO	SG	VOC Director			De Jong, 340–341
		WIC Director, President Suriname Society		Income in 1742 estimated at ƒ24,000–26,000	Elias, I: 440 / II: 590, 591, 820, 822, 825, 827, 865
	CS, GAO				JCBG 1986, 204
	GAO		Brewer	Bequeaths ƒ3,000	De Jong, 348
PG	CS	VOC Director, WIC Director, President Suriname Society	Married into wealthy merchant family	Income in 1742 estimated at ƒ14,000–15,000	Elias, I: 480 / II: 654, 739, 745, 929
					Prak, 410–411
				Bequeaths ƒ99,000	Prak, 406
PG, PAO					Bossaers, Annex 2
PG	CS, SG				JCBG 1955, 130
RN					NNBW, III 504
PG	CS	WIC Director		Bequeaths ƒ230,000	De Jong, 362
		WIC Director	Lawyer	Bequeaths ƒ78,000	Prak, 371

Name	Year of birth and death	Start of term on Admiralty Board	End of term on Admiralty Board	Represents	Later terms on Admiralty Board	Total years of service on Admiralty Board	Functions in local administration
Boudaen, Gualterus Petrus	1704–81	1763	1767	Amsterdam		5	M, A, B
Decker, Willem	1709–80	1764	1767	Gouda	1776–9	8	M, A, B
Heijns, Jacob	1717–84	1764	1767	Leiden	1770–3	8	M, A, B
Testart, Elbert	1712–76	1764	1770	Haarlem		7	M, B
Theengs, Anthonij	1713–96	1766	1770	Edam		5	M
Camerling, Daniel Jan	1715–67	1767	1767	Haarlem		1	M, A
Hooft, Gerrit Gerritsz	1708–80	1767	1770	Amsterdam		4	A, B
Lestevenon, Daniel Willem	1724–98	1767	1773	Gouda	1779–85	14	M, A, B
Meer, Jacob van der	1724–95	1767	1770	Leiden		4	M, A, B
Beeldsnijder, Gerard	1722–1805	1770	1795	Edam		26	M
Deutz, Daniel	1714–75	1770	1775	Amsterdam		6	M, A, B
Valkenburg, Mattheus Willem van	1718–84	1770	1773	Haarlem		4	M, A, B

Functions in provincial administration	Functions in national administration	Connection to colonial companies	Other professional or economic ties	Indication of wealth	Sources (in addition to 'repertorium')
PG		VOC Director	Married into wealthy merchant family (Levant and East India)	Income in 1742 estimated at ƒ16,000–18,000 / Bequeaths ƒ456,000	Elias, II: 800, 802, 804, 940
		VOC Director			De Jong, 339
				Bequeaths ƒ49,000	Prak, 391
PG		VOC Director			Elias, I: 77 / II: 675, 677, 836
PG, PAO	GAO				
PG					JCBG 1955, 132
		VOC Director, President Suriname Society	Married into wealthy regent and merchant families	Income in 1742 estimated at ƒ10,000–12,000 / Bequeaths ƒ838,000	Elias, I: 440 / II: 689, 820, 834
				Bequeaths ƒ75,000	De Jong, 359
					Prak, 402
		President of Berbice Society	Merchant		Elias, II: 635, 790, 836, 837, 914, 929, 940
PG, PAO					JCBG 1955, 130

Name	Year of birth and death	Start of term on Admiralty Board	End of term on Admiralty Board	Represents	Later terms on Admiralty Board	Total years of service on Admiralty Board	Functions in local administration
Huijghens, Willem	1714–86	1771	1772	Amsterdam	1775–80	8	M, A, B
Hompesch, Vincent Gustaaf van	1728–78	1772	1778	Holland, Nobility		7	
Slicher, Anthony	1721–94	1773	1776	Haarlem		4	M, B
Speelman, Cornelis	1722–87	1773	1776	Leiden		4	M, A, B
Clifford, Isaac	ca. 1705–79	1776	1779	Haarlem		4	M, A
Hooft, Hendrick Danielsz	1716–94	1776	1777	Amsterdam	1780–1	4	A, B
Tol, Cornelis van	1730–80	1776	1779	Leiden		4	M, A
Wassenaer, Willem Lodewijk van	1738–87	1778	1780	Holland, Nobility		3	
Koek, Jan Theodorus	1716–1800	1779	1782	Haarlem		4	M, A
Schrevelius, Theodorus	1719–85	1779	1782	Leiden		4	M, A, B
Boetzelaer, Dirk Baron van	1746–1819	1780	1789	Holland, Nobility		10	
Heemskerck, Willem van	1718–84	1781	1784	Amsterdam		4	M, A, B

Functions in provincial administration	Functions in national administration	Connection to colonial companies	Other professional or economic ties	Indication of wealth	Sources (in addition to 'repertorium')
PG		VOC Director, President Suriname Society	Son of banker	Income in 1742 estimated at f7,000–8,000 / Bequeaths f477,000	Elias, II: 594, 736, 842
RN	GAO				
PG, PAO	SG	VOC Director	Merchant (East India)		JCBG 1986, 207, Nw 1782, 25
				Bequeaths f44,000	Prak, 413
			Banker		JCBG 1955, 131
			Merchant (France), Banker, Plantation holder		Elias, I: 376 / II: 726, 728, 885
				Bequeaths f586,000	Prak, 416–417
RN					NNBW, II 1538
					JCBG 1955, 130
PG				Bequeaths f45,000	Prak, 412
RN, MG					NNBW, VIII 144
	CS, SG	VOC Director	Son of Treasurer of William III	Bequeaths f398,000	Elias, I: 77 / II: 696, 795, 901

Name	Year of birth and death	Start of term on Admiralty Board	End of term on Admiralty Board	Represents	Later terms on Admiralty Board	Total years of service on Admiralty Board	Functions in local administration
Huyghens, Joost	1723–1800	1782	1788	Haarlem		7	M
Steen, Jacob Bartram van den	1726–93	1782	1785	Leiden		4	M, A, B
Clifford, Pieter	1712–88	1783	1784	Amsterdam		2	M, A, B
Blijdenberg, Gerard Willem van	?–1820	1785	1794	Gouda		10	M, A, B
Dedel, Willem Gerrit Salomonsz	1734–1801	1785	1787	Amsterdam	1791–3	6	M, A, B
Royen, Jan van	1736–1803	1785	1788	Leiden		4	M, A
Rendorp, Joachim	1728–92	1787	1789	Amsterdam		3	A, B
Leyden, Diderik van	1744–1810	1788	1791	Leiden		4	M, A, B
Bentinck Rhoon, Willem Gustaaf Frederik Graaf van	1762–1835	1789	1795	Holland, Nobility		7	
Huydecoper van Maarseveen, Jan Elias	1738–1808	1789	1791	Amsterdam	1793–4	5	M, A, B

Functions in provincial administration	Functions in national administration	Connection to colonial companies	Other professional or economic ties	Indication of wealth	Sources (in addition to 'repertorium')
PG					JCBG 1986, 179–184 / Gabriels GR, 561
PG				Bequeaths ƒ192,000	Prak, 414
		VOC Director, WIC Director	Banker, married into merchant family	Income in 1742 estimated at ƒ9,000–10,000	Elias, II: 574, 681, 692, 886, 906, 912, 913
					De Jong, 329
			Merchant (France and Atlantic)		Elias, II: 680, 827, 828, 932, 947
		VOC Director			Prak, 410
PG, PAO		President Suriname Society	Brewer		Elias, II: 779, 780, 929, 987, 1019
					Prak, 397–398, JCBG 2005
RN					NNBW, I 303–304
PG		Principal Shareholder VOC, President Suriname Society			Elias, II:829, 918, 947, 1037 / Nw 1794, 62

Name	Year of birth and death	Start of term on Admiralty Board	End of term on Admiralty Board	Represents	Later terms on Admiralty Board	Total years of service on Admiralty Board	Functions in local administration
Kuffeler, Pieter Frederik van	1760–1839	1791	1794	Leiden		4	M
Vermeulen, Pieter	1732–1810	1791	1794	Haarlem		4	M
Burch, Jan Louis van der	1753–1819	1794	1795	Leiden		2	M, A, B
Decker, Francois van Harencarspel	1749–1817	1794	1795	Gouda		2	M, A, B
Lacle, Jean	1738–1802	1794	1795	Haarlem		2	M
Poll, Jan van de	1721–1801	1794	1795	Amsterdam		2	A, B

Functions in provincial administration	Functions in national administration	Connection to colonial companies	Other professional or economic ties	Indication of wealth	Sources (in addition to 'repertorium')
	SG				
PG					Prak, 375–376
			Married into merchant family	Bequeaths ƒ53,000	Elias, II: 776, 836, De Jong, 339–340
		Principal Shareholder VOC	Merchant, Banker		Elias, I: 538 / II: 682, 719, 752, 755, 756, 826, 867, 939, 940, 947, 964, 987, 1066 / Nw 1794, 62

Sources

Only mentioned in table when providing more information than name and functions:

General: Van der Aa 1852–78 / Blok and Molhuysen 1911–37 (NNBW) / De Boer 1914 and De Boer 1915 / Gaastra 1989 / Gabriels 1981 (GR) / Gabriëls 1990 / Hartsinck 1770 / *Jaarboek Centraal Bureau voor Genealogie* (1955, 1975, 1981, 1986, 1990, 1994, 1995, 1997, 2005) (JCBG) / *Naamwyzer, waar in vertoond worden de naamen en woonplaatsen van haar ed. gr. achtb. de heeren regeerders, &c der stad Amsterdam. 1684, 1692, 1733, 1735–1794* (Amsterdam 1684, 1692, 1733, 1735–94) (NW) / 'Repertorium van ambtsdragers en ambtenaren 1428–1861', https://www.historici.nl/resources/repertorium-van-ambtsdragers-en-ambtenaren-1428-1861   accessed 26-11-2014 / Valentyn 1724 / Alkmaar: Bruinvis 1905 / Amsterdam: Elias 1903 and Elias 1905 / Delft: Houtzager, Kunz, Van Leeuwen, Van Noort, and Tienstra 1987 / Dordrecht: Balen 1677 / Enkhuizen and Hoorn: Bossaers 1996 / Gouda: De Jong 1985 / Leiden: Prak 1985 / Rotterdam: Unger 1892 / Engelbrecht 1973

Zeeland Members of the Zeeland Admiralty Board

Functions in Local Administration

M	Magistrate
A	Alderman
Ba	Bailiff
S	Secretary
P	Pensionary
B	Burgomaster

Functions in National Administration

CS	Council of State
SG	States General
GAO	Generalty Audit Office
GRG	Generalty Receiver General

Functions in Provincial Administration

PG	Member of Provincial Government
PAO	Provincial Audit Office
CZV	Council of Zeeuws-Vlaanderen
RGO	Receiver General Overmaze
SSZ	Secretary States Zeeland
GPZ	Grand Pensionary Zeeland

Name	Year of birth and death	Start of term on Admiralty Board	End of term on Admiralty Board	Represents	Later terms on Admiralty Board	Total years of service on Admiralty Board	Functions in local administration
Heyns, Michiel	?–ca. 1613	1584	?	Zeeland			
Pietersz, Jan	? –?	1586	?	Zeeland			
Serooskerke, Jan Florisz van	? –?	1594	1596	Zeeland		3	M
Huyssen, Johan	1566–1634	1597	1634	Goes		38	P
Jacobi, Daniel	?–1606	1597	1606	Zierikzee		10	M, A, S
Malderé, Jacob van	?–1617	1597	1617	Veere		21	Ba
Meyros, Nicolaas Adriaansz	? –?	1597	1605	Middelburg		9	
Polaanen, Eustacen Adriaansz van	?–1600	1597	1600	Vlissingen		4	M
Vosbergen, Caspar van	?–1598	1597	1598	Veere		2	Ba
Zuydtlandt, Joost Marinusz van	?–1614	1597	1614	Tholen		18	A, B
Campe, Jacob	1573–1625	1598	1625	Veere		28	
Oillaerts, Adriaen	1543–1608	1600	1608	Vlissingen		9	S
Tenys, Steven Cornelisz	?–ca. 1630	1605	1630	Middelburg		26	M
Steengracht, Hubert	1565–1618	1606	1618	Zierikzee		13	P, B
Leunissen, Engel	? – 1631	1608	1631	Vlissingen		24	M

Functions in provincial administration	Functions in national administration	Connection to colonial companies	Other professional or economic ties	Indication of wealth	Sources (in addition to 'repertorium')
CZV					
PG					
PG, CZV	SG				Nagtglas, I: 450 / Bijl, Annex III
PG, CZV					Vos, 147–148
PG	SG		Highest Zeeland noble, Diplomat		Nagtglas, II: 120–121
PG					
PG					
PG	SG		Merchant, Investor in reclamations		Nagtglas, II: 894–896
PG	SG				Romeijn, 327–328
PG, CZV					Nagtglas, I: 102
PG	SG				
PG	SG				
PG, CZV					Vos, 315–316
PG					

Name	Year of birth and death	Start of term on Admiralty Board	End of term on Admiralty Board	Represents	Later terms on Admiralty Board	Total years of service on Admiralty Board	Functions in local administration
Tuyl van Serooskerke, Hendrik van	1574–1627	1614	1625	Tholen		12	A, B
Huybert, Eewoud de	1575–1624	1618	1624	Zierikzee		7	M, A, S
Manmaker, Adriaan de	1579–?	1618	1631	Zeeland, Nobility		14	
Cocq, Lieven de	1596–1658	1625	1658	Zierikzee		34	M, A
Vosbergen, Johan van	?–1644	1625	1644	Veere		20	M
Tuyl van Serooskerke, Philibertus	1580–1639	1626	1639	Zierikzee		14	
Palma, Pieter de la	?–1633	1630	1633	Middelburg		4	M
Ingelsen, Appolonius	?–1633	1631	1633	Vlissingen		3	M, S
Knuyt, Jan de	1587–1654	1631	1650	Zeeland, Nobility		20	M, A, B
Moor, Johan de	?–ca. 1644	1633	1644	Vlissingen		12	
Tenys, Cornelis	?–1660	1633	1649	Middelburg	1651–60	27	
Straten, Matthijs Cornelisz van der	?–ca. 1654	1634	1654	Goes		21	M
Tuyl van Serooskerke, Jeronimus	1615–69	1639	1656	Tholen		18	

Functions in provincial administration	Functions in national administration	Connection to colonial companies	Other professional or economic ties	Indication of wealth	Sources (in addition to 'repertorium')
PG	CS			In 1623 possessions estimated at f100,000	Romeijn, 23 en 281
PG					Vos, 242
PG, PAO					Nagtglas, II: 126–127
PG					Vos, 314
PG					
PG					Nagtglas, II: 793
PG					
PG					
PG	GAO		Investor in dike digging and reclamations	One of Zeeland's wealthiest inhabitants, receives a pension of f2,000	Nagtglas, I: 553–555
PG		WIC Director			
PG					
PG					
PG					Romeijn, 281–282

Name	Year of birth and death	Start of term on Admiralty Board	End of term on Admiralty Board	Represents	Later terms on Admiralty Board	Total years of service on Admiralty Board	Functions in local administration
Maecht, Jasper de	? –?	1644	1649	Vlissingen		6	M
Reygersberge, David van	?–1658	1645	1658	Veere		14	M
Guiseling, Johan	?–1653	1649	1653	Vlissingen		5	M
Thibaut, Hendrik	1604–67	1649	1651	Middelburg		3	M, B
Crommon, Marinus van	1629–87	1654	1661	Goes		8	S
Ingels, Casper	?–1679	1654	1679	Vlissingen		26	M, A, B
Vrijberghe, Willem Lievensz van	1624–79	1656	1675	Tholen	1677–9	23	M, P, B
Mauregnolt, Johan de	1607–82	1658	1668	Veere		11	M
Jonge, Job de	1594–1673	1659	1662	Zierikzee		4	M, A, B
Beke, Reynier van der	?–1686	1661	1686	Middelburg		26	
Nisse, Gerard van der	1602–69	1661	1669	Goes		9	M, B
Huybert, Adriaan de	1609–65	1662	1665	Zierikzee		4	M, S, B
Kien, Johan	1618–70	1668	1670	Veere		3	M
Nassau Odijk, Willem Adriaan van	1632–1705	1668	1702	Zeeland, Nobility		35	

Functions in provincial administration	Functions in national administration	Connection to colonial companies	Other professional or economic ties	Indication of wealth	Sources (in addition to 'repertorium')
PG					
PG, PAO					
PG		WIC Director			
PG, CZV		VOC Director, Principal Shareholder WIC	Investor in dike digging and reclamations		Nagtglas, II: 759–761 / Matthaeus, 3
PG	CS, SG				
PG					Bijl, Annex XV
PG					Romeijn, 302–303
PG	SG				
PG	SG			Bequeaths ƒ194,000	Vos, 298–299, 310
PG					
PG	SG				Nagtglas, II: 277 / NNBW
PG					Vos, 385–386
PG	SG				
PG		VOC Director	Owner of various companies of infantry and cavalry		Nagtglas, II: 260–262 / NNBW / Gaastra, 263

Name	Year of birth and death	Start of term on Admiralty Board	End of term on Admiralty Board	Represents	Later terms on Admiralty Board	Total years of service on Admiralty Board	Functions in local administration
Watervliet, Cornelis van	?–1669	1669	1669	Goes		1	M
Westerwijck, Marinus	?–1677	1669	1677	Goes		9	M
Meunincx, Pieter	? –?	1670	1679	Veere		10	M
Pous, Cornelis	1638–94	1673	1676	Zierikzee		4	M, A, B
Vrijberghe, Levinus van	1650–1716	1675	1677	Tholen		3	M, A
Hoffer, Anthony	1638–97	1677	1697	Zierikzee		21	M, A, B
Watervliet, Frederik van	?–1677	1677	1677	Goes		1	M
Nisse, David van der	1644–1705	1678	1705	Goes		28	M, A, B
Bils, Pieter Carel de	1647–1704	1679	1704	Tholen		26	M, A, B
Mauregnolt, Johan de	?–1717	1679	1717	Veere		39	M
Winckelman, Jacob	?–1694	1679	1691	Vlissingen		13	M
Godin, Johan	? –?	1687	1704	Middelburg		18	M
Nachtegael van Gorcum, Jacob	?–1718	1691	1704	Vlissingen		14	M, P, B
Cau, Iman Willem Roelandsz	1663–1734	1698	1734	Zierikzee		37	M, A, B
Meester, Jan	?–1726	1704	1726	Vlissingen		23	M

Functions in provincial administration	Functions in national administration	Connection to colonial companies	Other professional or economic ties	Indication of wealth	Sources (in addition to 'repertorium')
PG					
PG					
PG		VOC Director			Matthaeus, 3
PG				Bequeaths f133,000	Vos, 441–443
PG		Shareholder WIC	Lawyer		Romeijn, 86–87 and 306–307
PG			Large investor in dike digging		Vos, 437–438
PG, PAO					
PG					NNBW, II 996–997
PG		WIC Director	Lawyer		Romeijn, 133–134
PG				In 1720, income estimated at f6,000	
PG		VOC Director			
PG		Family strongly involved in VOC		In 1703, income estimated at f5,000	Bijl, Annex XXII, XXXVIII
PG		VOC Director			Nagtglas, II: 250 / Matthaeus, 5
PG		Family strongly involved in VOC	Supreme deacon of the butchers guild		Vos, 508–510 / Bijl, Annex XXXVIII
PG					

Name	Year of birth and death	Start of term on Admiralty Board	End of term on Admiralty Board	Represents	Later terms on Admiralty Board	Total years of service on Admiralty Board	Functions in local administration
Merct, Jacob van der	?–1710	1704	1710	Middelburg		7	M
Vrijberghe, Johan van	1651–1715	1704	1715	Tholen		12	A, B
Eversdijk, Mattheus	1648–1714	1705	1712	Goes		8	M, A, B
Perre, Joan van de	1663–1730	1710	1730	Middelburg		21	M, A
Nollens, Anthony	?–1745	1712	1745	Goes		34	M
Beaufort, Levinus Ferdinand de	1675–1730	1715	1730	Tholen		16	M, A
Colve, Jacob Lambert	?–1722	1717	1722	Veere		6	M
Nebbens, Francois	?–1742	1722	1742	Veere		21	M
Hoorn, Constantijn Nicolaasz van	1690–1742	1726	1729	Vlissingen		4	M
Hugronje, Jacob Isaacsz	1694–1759	1729	1734	Vlissingen	1746–59	20	M
Turcq, Johan	1686–1748	1730	1748	Tholen		19	A
Versluys, Cornelis	1698–1746	1731	1746	Middelburg		16	M

Functions in provincial administration	Functions in national administration	Connection to colonial companies	Other professional or economic ties	Indication of wealth	Sources (in addition to 'repertorium')
PG		Family strongly involved in WIC	Director Levant trade	In 1703, income estimated at ƒ4,000 / In 1710, income estimated at ƒ5,000	Bijl, Annex XXII, XXIII, XLVIII / Nw 1684, 24
PG, RGO			Lawyer		Romeijn, 301
PG					NNBW, III 371–372
PG				In 1703, income estimated at ƒ2,000 / In 1710, income estimated at ƒ3,000 / In 1720, income estimated at ƒ3,000	Nagtglas, II:373 / Bijl, Annex II, XXII, XXIII, XXIV
PG, PAO					
PG					Romeijn, 329
PG					
PG					
PG		Family strongly involved in VOC			Bijl, Annex XXXVIII
PG		VOC Director			Bijl, Annex XXXVIII
PG					Romeijn, 279
PG				In 1740, income estimated at ƒ2,000	Nagtglas, II: 846 / Bijl, Annex XXVI

Name	Year of birth and death	Start of term on Admiralty Board	End of term on Admiralty Board	Represents	Later terms on Admiralty Board	Total years of service on Admiralty Board	Functions in local administration
Kempe, Adriaan	1695–1759	1734	1759	Zierikzee		26	M, A, B
Pere, Cornelis van	1668–1746	1734	1746	Vlissingen		13	M
Steengracht, Nicolaas	1699–1756	1742	1756	Veere		15	M, A, P, B
Roseveldt, Johan Willem	1713–1791	1746	1791	Goes		46	M
Borssele van der Hooghe, Jan van	1707–64	1747	1764	Zeeland, Nobility		18	M
Reygersberge, Jacob van	1704–62	1747	1762	Middelburg		16	M, A
Vleugels, Jacob	1692–1748	1748	1748	Tholen		1	B
Beaufort, Pieter Bernard de	1713–62	1749	1762	Tholen		14	M
Schorer, Wilhelm	1725–93	1756	1793	Veere		38	M
Dishoeck, Anthony Pieter Ewoutsz van	ca. 1710–67	1759	1767	Vlissingen		9	M, B
Jonge van Campensnieuwland, Bonifacius de	1708–68	1759	1768	Zierikzee		10	M, A, B

Functions in provincial administration	Functions in national administration	Connection to colonial companies	Other professional or economic ties	Indication of wealth	Sources (in addition to 'repertorium')
PG			Supreme deacon of the butchers guild		Vos, 579
PG		Family strongly involved in VOC and WIC			Bijl, Annex XXXVIII, XLVIII
PG, PAO	SG	Principal Shareholder VOC			Nagtglas, II: 697, NNBW, VII 1176 / Bijl, Annex XXXVIII
PG					
PG		VOC Director		In 1740, income estimated at ƒ1,500 / Receives a pension of ƒ10,000	Gabriels, 166–167 / Bijl, Annex XXVI, XXXVIII
PG		VOC Director, Family strongly involved in VOC and WIC		In 1730, income estimated at ƒ1,000 / In 1740, income estimated at ƒ2,000	Nagtglas, II: 487 / Bijl, Annex IV, XXV, XXVI, XXXVIII, XLVIII
PG					Romeijn, 336
PG					Romeijn, 330
PG		Family strongly involved in WIC			Bijl, Annex VII, XLVIII
PG		Family strongly involved in VOC			Bijl, Annex XXXVIII / Nw 1794, 18
PG	SG		Supreme deacon of the skippers guild		Vos, 612–613

Name	Year of birth and death	Start of term on Admiralty Board	End of term on Admiralty Board	Represents	Later terms on Admiralty Board	Total years of service on Admiralty Board	Functions in local administration
Bevers, Galenus Trezel	1725–70	1763	1770	Middelburg		8	M, A
Turcq, Willem Hendrik	1724–87	1763	1787	Tholen		25	A, B
Citters, Wilhelm van	1723–1802	1766	1767	Zeeland, Nobility		2	P
Hugronje, Isaac Phenixz	ca. 1724–76	1767	1776	Vlissingen		10	M
Gelre, Pieter Paul van	1735–1810	1768	1795	Zierikzee		28	M
Perre, Johan Adriaan van de	1738–90	1768	1779	Zeeland, Nobility		12	M, A
Schorer, Johan Gullielmus	ca. 1733–83	1770	1783	Middelburg		14	M, A
Clijver, Evert Jacobsz	? –?	1777	1794	Vlissingen		18	M
Brande, Johan Pieter van den	1734–93	1783	1792	Middelburg		10	M, A, B
Citters, Caspar van	1746–?	1787	1794	Tholen		8	P
Canisius, Willem	1742–1815	1791	1795	Goes		5	M
Huyssen van Kattendijke, Willem Jacob	1758–1826	1793	1794	Middelburg		2	

Functions in provincial administration	Functions in national administration	Connection to colonial companies	Other professional or economic ties	Indication of wealth	Sources (in addition to 'repertorium')
PG					Bijl, Annex X
PG					Romeijn, 279–280
PG, SSZ, GPZ	GRG	Principal Shareholder VOC			Nagtglas, I: 126–127 / Bijl, Annex XXXVIII, XLVIII
PG, PAO		Family strongly involved in VOC			Bijl, Annex XXXVIII
PG			Supreme deacon of the shipwrights guild	Bequeaths ƒ625,000	Vos, 657
PG	SG			Married into one of Zeeland's wealthiest families	Nagtglas, II: 374 / Bijl, Annex II
PG		Family strongly involved in WIC			Bijl, Annex VII, XLVIII
PG					
PG		Family strongly involved in VOC and WIC		One of Zeeland's wealthiest inhabitants	Nagtglas, I: 75 / Bijl, Annex IV, XXXVIII, XLVIII
PG		VOC Director			Bijl, Annex XXXVIII, XLVIII / Nw 1794, 89
PG					
PG					

Name	Year of birth and death	Start of term on Admiralty Board	End of term on Admiralty Board	Represents	Later terms on Admiralty Board	Total years of service on Admiralty Board	Functions in local administration
Loeff, Manta Stephanus van der	1746–1816	1794	1795	Veere		2	M

Functions in provincial administration	Functions in national administration	Connection to colonial companies	Other professional or economic ties	Indication of wealth	Sources (in addition to 'repertorium')

PG

Sources

Only mentioned in table when providing more information than name and functions:

General: 'Repertorium van ambtsdragers en ambtenaren 1428–1861', https://www .historici.nl/resources/repertorium-van-ambtsdragers-en-ambtenaren-1428-1861 (accessed 26-11-2014) / De Boer 1914 and De Boer 1915 / Enthoven 1989 / Gaastra 1989 / Gabriëls 1990 / Hartsinck 1770 / *Jaarboek Centraal Bureau voor Genealogie* (1955, 1975, 1981, 1986, 1990, 1994, 1995, 1997, 2005) (JCBG) / Matthaeus 1759 / *Naamwyzer, waar in vertoond worden de naamen en woonplaatsen van haar ed. gr. achtb. de heeren regeerders, &c der stad Amsterdam. 1684, 1692, 1733, 1735–1794* (Amsterdam 1684, 1692, 1733, 1735–94) (NW) / Nagtglas 1888 and Nagtglas 1893) / Valentyn 1724 / **Amsterdam:** Elias 1903 and Elias 1905 / **Middelburg:** Van der Bijl 1981 / **Tholen:** Romeijn 2001 / **Zierikzee:** De Vos 1931

Income and Expenditure of the Amsterdam Admiralty: Steps from Figures in 'Borderel' to Reconstruction

Step 1: Sum totals of ordinary and extra-ordinary expenditure in 'borderel' checked with totals of individual posts in 'borderel', if difference < ƒ1000: totals of individual posts in 'borderel' taken as guiding, if difference > ƒ1000: checked with individual posts in accounts and corrected accordingly.

Step 2: Totals corrected for posts transported from previous accounts. Ordinary incomes: remainders from previous account subtracted from post 'Diverse respecten' / Extra-ordinary incomes: idem from post 'Andere penningen' / Ordinary expenditures: remainders from previous account subtracted from post 'Verscheidene zaken' / Extra-ordinary expenditures: idem from 'Penningen onder vorige niet begrepen'.

Step 3: Corrected for unpaid subsidies. Subtracted from extra-ordinary incomes, 'subsidies', and post 'unpaid subsidies' in extra-ordinary expenditures removed. From 1715 onwards, only paid subsidies were entered into the accounts.

Step 4: Corrected for double entry of 'Last en veilgeld Amsterdam' (up to 1725) and 'Last en veilgeld VOC' (entire period) (extra-ordinary incomes) in 'Convooien en Licenten Amsterdam' (ordinary incomes) and 'Verscheidene zaken' (ordinary expenditures).

Step 5: Corrected for transfers between ordinary and extra-ordinary accounts (under ordinary incomes and extra-ordinary expenditures).

Step 6: Corrected accounts 1792–5 (on one 'borderel'): inserted yearly averages where individual posts per year could not be inferred.

Step 7: Summarised corrected accounts in general posts, combining ordinary and extra-ordinary incomes and expenditures.

Step 8: Added estimate of income and expenditures 1780, based on summary memoir Van der Hoop plus low estimate custom incomes (ƒ500,000), management costs (ƒ200,000), inland passports (ƒ450,000), and interest and down payment on loans (ƒ35,000).

Sources and Bibliography

Archival Collections

Nationaal Archief, The Hague (NA)
- Admiraliteiten, 1.01.46
- Admiraliteitscolleges XXXI, J. Bisdom 1525–1793, 1.01.47.21
- Admiraliteitscollecties XXXII, Pieter van Bleiswijk 1690–1787, 1.01.47.22
- Admiraliteitscolleges XXXVII, Van der Heim 1591–1786, 1.01.47.27
- Admiraliteitscolleges XXXIX, Van der Hoop 1524–1825, 1.01.47.29
- Admiraliteitscolleges L, Aanwinsten, 1.01.47.39
- De Ruyter, 1633–83, 1.10.72.01
- Directie van de Levantse Handel 1614–1828, 1.03.01
- Directies ter Equipering van Oorlogsschepen 1636–57, 1.03.02
- Familiearchief Fagel, 1.10.29
- Familiearchief Steengracht, 3.20.55
- Familiearchief Van Heteren, 3.20.24
- Familiearchief Van Heteren Supplement, 3.20.88
- Familiearchief Van Hurck en Barnevelt, 3.20.39
- Gecommitteerde Raden van de Staten van Holland en Westfriesland, 3.01.05
- Generaliteitsrekenkamer 1586–1799, 1.01.43
- Lijnbaan in Amsterdam 1712–1892, 1.01.49
- Oude West-Indische Compagnie, 1.05.01.01
- Paulus Gebhardt, 3.01.47
- Raad van State 1581–1795, 1.01.19
- Stadhouderlijke Secretarie 1600–1795, 1.01.50
- Staten Generaal 1431–1796, 1.01.02
- Staten van Holland na 1572, 3.01.04.01
- Van der Hoop, 1.10.42
- VOC, 1602–1811, 1.04.02

Haags Gemeente Archief (HGA)
- Notarieel Archief

Rijksarchief Zeeland, Middelburg (RAZ)
- Rekenkamer C, 508

Stadsarchief Amsterdam (SA)
- Directie van de Moscovische handel, 6
- Directie van de Oostersche handel en reederijen, 78

Universiteit van Amsterdam, Bijzondere Collecties (UB-BC)
- Extracten uit het register van de resolutiën der Staten Generaal en uit de notulen van de Admiraliteit te Amsterdam, alle betr. zeezaken [1671–1780], OF63/985

Printed Sources

Brugmans, H. (ed.) 1897, 'De notulen en munimenten van het College van Commercie te Amsterdam, 1663–1665', *Bijdragen en Mededeelingen van het Historisch Genootschap*, 18: 181–330.

Colenbrander, H.T. 1905, *Gedenkstukken der algemeene geschiedenis van Nederland van 1795 tot 1840*, Volume 1, The Hague: Nijhoff.

———— 1906, *Gedenkstukken der algemeene geschiedenis van Nederland van 1795 tot 1840*, Volume 2, The Hague: Nijhoff.

Colenbrander, H.T., and W.Ph. Coolhaas (eds.) 1919, *Jan Pietersz. Coen. Bescheiden omtrent zijn bedrijf in Indië*, Volume 1, The Hague: Nijhoff.

de Gou, L. (ed.) 1975, *Het plan van constitutie van 1796. Chronologische bewerking van het archief van de eerste constitutiecommissie ingesteld bij decreet van de Nationale Vergadering van 15 maart 1796*, The Hague: Nijhoff.

de Vries, Joh. (ed.) 1958, 'Van de Spiegel's "schets tot een vertoog over de intrinsique en relative magt van de Republijk" (1782)', *Economisch-Historisch Jaarboek*, 27: 81–100.

Fritschy, W., and R. Liesker 2007, *Gewestelijke financiën ten tijde van de Repubiek der Verenigde Nederlanden*, Volume 4: Holland 1572–1795, The Hague: Instituut voor Nederlandse Geschiedenis.

Fruin, Robert (ed.) 1906, *Brieven van Johan de Witt*, Volume 1, The Hague: Nijhoff.

Groen van Prinsterer, G. (ed.) 1908, *Archives ou correspondence inédite de la maison d'Orange-Nassau*, 4th ser., Volume 1, Leiden: Luchtmans.

———— (ed.) 1910, *Archives ou correspondence inédite de la maison d'Orange-Nassau*, 5th ser., Volume 1, Leiden: Luchtmans.

Heeringa, K. (ed.) 1910, *Bronnen tot de geschiedenis van den Levantschen handel*, Volume 1, The Hague: Nijhoff.

———— (ed.) 1917, *Bronnen tot de geschiedenis van den Levantschen handel*, Volume 2, The Hague: Nijhoff.

Hop, Cornelis, and Nicolaas Vivien 1903, *Notulen gehouden ter Staten-Vergadering van Holland (1671–1675)*, edited by N. Japikse, Amsterdam: Müller.

Japikse, N. (ed.) 1917, *Resolutiën der Staten-Generaal van 1576 tot 1609*, old ser., Volume 2, The Hague: Nijhoff.

——— (ed.) 1922, *Resolutiën der Staten-Generaal van 1576 tot 1609*, old ser., Volume 6, The Hague: Nijhoff.

——— (ed.) 1923, *Resolutiën der Staten-Generaal van 1576 tot 1609*, old ser., Volume 7, The Hague: Nijhoff.

——— (ed.) 1926, *Resolutiën der Staten-Generaal van 1576 tot 1609*, old ser., Volume 9, The Hague: Nijhoff.

——— (ed.) 1927, *Correspondentie van Willem III en van Hans Willem Bentinck, eersten graaf van Portland*, Volume 1.1, The Hague: Nijhoff.

——— (ed.) 1930, *Resolutiën der Staten-Generaal van 1576 tot 1609*, old ser., Volume 10, The Hague: Nijhoff.

Kernkamp, G.W. (ed.) 1895, 'Twee memoriën van mr. Gerrit Schaep Pietersz over de regeering van Amsterdam', *Bijdragen en Mededeelingen van het Historisch Genootschap*, 16: 333–71.

Kernkamp, J.H. 1935, 'Twee "niet ter drukpersse bereide" geschriften van Pieter de la Court', *Bijdragen en Mededelingen van het Historisch Genootschap*, 56: 151–214.

Nationale Vergadering 1797, *Dagverhaal der handelingen van de Nationaale Vergadering representeerende het volk van Nederland*, Volume 4, The Hague: Schelle.

Posthumus, N.W. 1943, *Nederlandsche prijsgeschiedenis*, Volume 1, Leiden: Brill.

Rijperman, H.H.P. (ed.) 1950, *Resolutiën der Staten-Generaal van 1576 tot 1609*, old ser., Volume 12, The Hague: Martinus Nijhoff.

——— (ed.) 1957, *Resolutiën der Staten-Generaal van 1576 tot 1609*, old ser., Volume 13, The Hague: Martinus Nijhoff.

——— (ed.) 1970, *Resolutiën der Staten-Generaal van 1576 tot 1609*, old ser., Volume 14, The Hague: Martinus Nijhoff.

Roberts, David H. (ed.) 1992, *18th Century shipbuilding. Remarks on the navies of the English & the Dutch from observations made at their dockyards in 1737 by Blaise Ollivier, master shipwright of the King of France*, Rotherfield: Boudriot.

Provisionele representanten van het volk van Holland 1798, *Decreeten van de provisioneele repraesentanten van het volk van Holland*, Volume 4.1, The Hague: Ter 's Lands Drukkery

Staten Generaal 1682, *Groot placaet-boeck vervattende de placaten, ordonnantien ende edicten van de Hoogh Mogende Heeren Staten Generael der Vereenighde Nederlanden, ende Van de Ed. Groot Mog. Heeren Staten van Hollandt ende West-Vrieslandt etc.* Volume 3, The Hague: Jacobus Scheltus.

——— 1689, *Recueil van alle de placaten, ordonnantien, resolutien, instructien, lysten en waarschouwingen, betreffende de Admiraliteyten, convoyen, licenten en verdere zee-saeken*, Volume 1, The Hague: Paulus Scheltus.

——— 1701, *Recueil van alle de placaten, ordonnantien, resolutien, instructien, lysten en waarschouwingen, betreffende de Admiraliteyten, convoyen, licenten en verdere zee-saeken*, Volume 2, The Hague: Paulus Scheltus.

van Deursen, A.Th. (ed.) 1971, *Resolutiën der Staten Generaal*, new ser., Volume 1, The Hague: Nijhoff.

—— (ed.) 1984, *Resolutiën der Staten Generaal*, new ser., Volume 2, The Hague: Nijhoff.

van Hogendorp, Dirk (ed.) 1801, *Stukken, raakende den tegenwoordigen toestand der Bataafsche bezittingen in Oost-Indie en den handel op dezelve*, The Hague: J.C. Leeuwestyn.

van Rappart, W.A. (ed.) 1978, *Briefwisseling tussen Simon van Slingelandt en Sicco van Goslinga 1697–1731*, The Hague: Instituut voor Nederlandse Geschiedenis.

van Slingelandt, Simon 1784a, *Staatkundige geschriften, opgesteld en nagelaaten door Mr. Simon van Slingelandt*, Volume 1, Amsterdam: Petrus Schouten.

—— 1784b, *Staatkundige geschriften, opgesteld en nagelaaten door Mr. Simon van Slingelandt*, Volume 2, Amsterdam: Petrus Schouten.

Veenendaal Jr., A.J. (ed.) 1998, *De briefwisseling van Anthonie Heinsius 1702–1720*, Volume 13, The Hague: Nijhoff.

Vreede, G.W. (ed.) 1874, *Mr. Laurens Pieter van de Spiegel en zijne tijdgenooten (1737–1800)*, Volume 1, Middelburg: J.C. & W. Altorffer.

—— (ed.) 1875, *Mr. Laurens Pieter van de Spiegel en zijne tijdgenooten (1737–1800)*, Volume 2, Middelburg: J.C. & W. Altorffer.

—— (ed.) 1876, *Mr. Laurens Pieter van de Spiegel en zijne tijdgenooten (1737–1800)*, Volume 3, Middelburg: J.C. & W. Altorffer.

Online Databases and Genealogic Collections

Aa, A.J. van der 1852–78, *Biographisch woordenboek der Nederlanden, bevattende levensbeschrijvingen van zoodanige personen, die zich op eenigerlei wijze in ons vaderland hebben vermaard gemaakt*, Volumes 1–12, Haarlem: Brederode.

Blok, P.J., and P.C. Molhuysen (eds.) 1911–37, *Nieuw Nederlandsch Biografisch Woordenboek*, Volumes 1–10, Leiden: Sijthoff.

Bruijn, J.R., F.S. Gaastra, and I. Schöffer, 'Dutch Asiatic Shipping', online database, https://www.historici.nl/resources/dutch-asiatic-shipping-17th-and-18th-centuries.

De Navorscher. Een middel tot gedachtenwisseling en letterkundig verkeer tusschen allen, die iets weten, iets te vragen hebben of iets kunnen oplossen (1851–1960).

Jaarboek Centraal Bureau voor Genealogie.

Naamwyzer, waar in vertoond worden de naamen en woonplaatsen van haar Ed. Gr. Achtb. De Heeren Regeerders, &c der Stad Amsterdam. 1684, 1692, 1733, 1735–1794 (Amsterdam 1684, 1692, 1733, 1735–94).

Repertorium van ambtsdragers en ambtenaren 1428–1861, https://www.historici.nl/resources/repertorium-van-ambtsdragers-en-ambtenaren-1428-1861.

Zanden, Jan Luiten van, 'Prices and wages and the cost of living in the western part of the Netherlands, 1450–1800', online database: http://www.iisg.nl/hpw/brenv.php.

Pamphlets

Anonymous n.d., *Het ontroerd Holland*, Harderwijk: Willem Brinkink.

Anonymous 1644a, *Aenwysinge datmen van de Oost en West-Indische Compagnien een Compagnie dient te maecken*, The Hague: Jan Veely.

Anonymous 1644b, *Bedenckinge over d'antwoordt der Heeren Bewinthebbers vande Oost-Indische Compagnie*, The Hague: Jan Veely.

Anonymous 1644c, *Claer licht ofte vertooch van 's lants welvaeren aengaende de combinatie vande Oost- ende West-Indische Compagnien*.

Anonymous 1644d, *Consideratie overgelevert by de Heeren Bewinthebberen van de Oost-Indische Compagnie. Aen de Edele Groot-mogende Heeren Staten van Hollant ende West-Vrieslant*, The Hague: Jan Fransen.

Anonymous 1644e, *Ooghen salve tot verlichtinghe, van alle participanten, so vande Oost, ende Westindische Compaignien*, The Hague: Lieven de Lange.

Anonymous 1644f., *Remonstrantie ende consideratien aengaende de Vereeninghe vande Oost ende West-Indische Compagnien ... Door de Gedeputeerde Heeren Bewinthebberen vande Geoctroyeerde West-Indische Compagnie*, The Hague: L. de Langhe.

Anonymous 1644g, *Schaede, die den staet der Vereenichde Nederlanden, en d'inghesetenen van dien, is aenstaende, by de versuymenisse van d'Oost en West-Indische negotie onder een octroy en societeyt te begrijpen*, The Hague: Jan Veely.

Anonymous 1647, *Brasilsche gelt-sack, waer in dat klaerlijck vertoont wort waer dat de participanten van de West Indische Compagnie haer geldt ghebleven is*.

Anonymous 1649, *Remonstrantie, van de hooft-partijcipanten ende geintresseerde vande West-Indische Compagnie aen alle de regenten des vaderlandts*.

Anonymous 1650, *Traicté de la marine, faict, conclu & arresté à la Haye en Hollande, le 17 du mois de Decembre 1650 entre Messire Antoine Brun, Ambassadeur ordinaire du Seigneur Roy d'Espagne d'une, & les Srs Deputez des Seigneurs Estats Generaux des Provinces Unies du Pais-bas d'autre part*, The Hague: Hillebrant van Wouw.

Anonymous 1651, *Antwoort op seker propositie by d'Engelsche gesanten (so sy hun intituleren) den 10/20 Martii 1651, gedaen inde Groote Vergaderinge vande Hoogh Mogende Heeren Staeten Generael der Vereenichde Neder-Landen*, The Hague: Samuel Broun.

Anonymous 1652, *Noodighe aenwysinge tot de uytwerckinge ende krachten, tot de zenuen van oorloge, ende (naest Godt) de behoudenisse van een landt*, Rotterdam: K. Jaspersz.

Anonymous 1653, *Vrymoedighen brief, gheschreven door een liefhebber des vaderlandts*.

Aen de E.Ed. heeren directeuren, tot Amsterdam. Aen haer over-gelevert op vrydagh,
den 25 July 1653.

Anonymous 1664, *The Dutch drawn to the life, in: I. An exact description and character*
of the several provinces of the Netherlands; II. An account of their trade and industry,
etc., London: Tho Johnson.

Anonymous 1675, *Consideratien wegens de commercien ende navigatie in de Oostzee, By*
de tegenwoordige conjuncturen wederom in haer oude vryheyt en fleur te herstellen. By
een liefhebber van 't vaderlandt tot naeder overleg opgegeven.

Anonymous 1748, *Vervolg op de korte schets of dag-verhaal van het tegenwoordige gedrag*
der burgeren van Amsterdam.

Anonymous 1779, *Staat en uitrekening der enorme grove winsten, welke getrokken worden*
door de heeren capiteins, eerste schryvers en doctors, varende op des 's lands scheepen
van oorlog, by het Edel Mogend Collegie ter Admiraliteit, Amsterdam: Dirk Schuur-
man.

Anonymous 1785, *Grondwettige herstelling van Nederlands staatswezen, zo voor het alge-*
meen bondgenootschap, als voor het bestuur van elke byzondere provincie, geschikt om
het voornaam doelwit aan te toonen, waar toe de poogingen van goede regenten en
de requesten van vaderlandlievende burgers moeten strekken, Amsterdam: Johannes
Allart.

Anonymous [1787]a, *De Oost- Wit- en Kattenburger wandelaar. Verhaalende al het ge-*
beurden, zo omtrent de drie voornaamste plaatsen, als ook de gesprekken in het wyn-
huis het Onvolmaakte Schip.

Anonymous [1787]b, *Echte beschryving, van het tumult binnen Amsterdam. En byzonder*
op het eiland Kattenburg, voorgevallen op den 29 May 1787 en eenige volgende dagen,
met de overwinning, Amsterdam.

Anonymous 1788, *Verzameling van stukken betrekkelijk de dimissie van den heer en mr.*
Pieter Paulus. Raad en advocaat-fiscaal van het Ed. Mog. Collegie ter Admiraliteit op
de Maze.

Anonymous 1792, *Staat der Generale Nederlandsche Oost-Indische Compagnie,* Amsterdam: Johannes Allart.

Anonymous 1795, *Nieuwe Nederlandsche Jaarboeken, of vervolg der merkwaardigste ge-*
schiedenissen, die voorgevallen zyn in de zeven provinciën, Bataafsch Braband en
Drenthe, en de buitenlandsche bezittingen, Volume XXX, Amsterdam: J. van den Burgh
en Zoon.

Anonymous 1796, *Voorlichting aan de Grondvergaderingen, indien die moeten raadplee-*
gen over het voorstel ter Nationale Vergadering gedaan, tot uitbreiding van derzelver
magt, Arnhem: Moeleman en Troost etc.

[Bosch, Bernardus] 1793, *Vrijhart aan het volk van Nederland over de waare constitutie.*

[Child, Josiah] 1681, *A treatise wherein is demonstrated, I. That the East-India Trade is*
the most national of all foreign trades, etc., London: Robert Boulter.

[Fijnje, Wybo, and Pieter Vreede] 1785, *Ontwerp, om de Republiek door eene heilzaame vereeniging der belangen van regent en burger, van binnen gelukkig, en van buiten gedugt te maaken*, Leiden: Johan Hendrik Swildens en Leendert Herdingh.

Gerechte der Stad Utrecht 1682, *Sententie, by die vanden Ed. Gerechte der Stad Utrecht, gearresteert jegens mr. Johan Lieftingh, gewesene solliciteur militair*, Utrecht: Jurriaen van Poolsum.

Huygens, Constantijn 1663, *Den herstelden Prins tot Stadt-houder ende Capiteyn Generaal vande Vereenighde Nederlanden, ten dienst ende luyster vande loffelijcke en de wel geformeerde Republijck vande Geunieerde Provincien, &c.*, Amsterdam: Joan. Cyprianus vander Gracht.

Lott, Yeoman, *An account of proposals made for the benefit of His Majesty's naval service*, London: Printed for the author.

Paape, Gerrit [1798], *De onverbloemde geschiedenis van het Bataafsch patriottismus, van deszelfs begin tot op den 12 Junij 1798 toe*, Delft: Roelofswaart.

Parival, L.N.D. 1662, *Ware interest van Holland; Gebouwt op de ruinen van den interest van Holland, onlangs uitgegeven door D.V.H. Toegeeygent aen de dochter van de tijt. Door I.N.D.P.*, Leiden: Jan Princen.

Paulus, Pieter 1772, *Het nut der stadhouderlyke regering, aangetoond by gelegenheid der geboorte van Willem Frederik, prince van Oranje en Nassau, erfstadhouder, capitaingeneraal, en admiraal der Verënigde Nederlanden*, Alkmaar: De weduwe Maagh etc.

Personeele Commissie 1797, *Rapport der Personeele Commissie op het berigt van het Provintiaal Committé enz. mitsgaders het request van P.H. Trap c.s.*, The Hague: 's Lands Drukkery.

Pieter Paulus 1793, *Verhandeling over de vrage: in welken zin kunnen de menschen gezegd worden gelyk te zyn? En welke zyn de regten en pligten, die daaruit voordvloeien?*, Haarlem: C. Plaat.

ΦΙΛΑΛΕΘΙΥΜ, ΙΡΕΝΕΥΜ 1650, *De na-wêen van de vrede, ofte ontdeckinghe, vande kommerlijcke ghelegentheyt onses lieven vaderlandts.*

Provisioneele Representanten van het Volk van Holland 1795a, *Decreet tot de vernietiging van het tegenwoordige bewind der Oost-Indische Compagnie. Gearresteerd by de provisioneele representanten van het volk van Holland, den 15 September 1795*, The Hague: 's Lands Drukkery van Holland.

Provisioneele Representanten van het Volk van Holland 1795b, *Rapport van de gecommitteerden tot de zaaken van de Oostindische Compagnie, aan de provisionele repraesentanten van het volk van Holland. Ingeleverd den 15 Juny 1795* (The Hague 1795).

Rivo Ursino, Galeacco de 1651, *Grondigh bericht, nopende den interest van desen staet, vermidts de doodt van sijn hoogheyt, met het noodtsaeckelijcke redres van dien*, Rotterdam: Jan van Dalen.

Staten Generaal 1637, *Octroy, by de Hooghe Mogende heeren Staten Generael verleent aende West Indische Compagnie, in date den derden Junij 1621. Mette Ampliatien van dien*, etc., The Hague: Weduwe ende erfgenamen van wijlen Hillebrant Jacobssz van Wouw.

Teelinck, Maximiliaen, *Vrymoedige aenspraeck aen sijn hoogheyt de Heere Prince van Oraengjen ... Gestelt tot waerschouwingh en noodige opmerckingh in desen verwerden en kommerlijcken standt van ons lieve vaderlandt* (Middelburg 1650).

[Titsingh, Guillelmus] 1791, *Consideratien van een hoofdparticipant der Generaale Nederlandsche Oostindische Compagnie, bevattende den staat derzelve zoo hier te lande als in de colonien, mitsgaders de voordeelen van een vrije vaart.*

[Valckenaer, Johan] 1795, *Le noeud gordien débrouillé, du solution d'un grand problême politique*, Paris: J.J. Smits et Cie.

van den Vondel, J. 1658, *Zeemagazyn, gebouwt op Kattenburgh t'Amsterdam*, Amsterdam: Abraham de Wees.

[van der Capellen tot den Poll, Joan Derk] [1781], *Aan het volk van Nederland.*

Van Oranje, Willem 1751, *Propositie van syne hoogheid ter vergaderingen van haar Hoog Mogende en haar Edele Groot Mog. gedaan, tot redres en verbeeteringe van den koophandel in de Republicq*, The Hague: Jacobus Scheltus.

Vos, Jan 1653, *Zeekrygh tusschen de staaten der vrye Neederlanden, en het parlement van Engelandt*, Amsterdam: Jacob Lescaille.

Books and Articles

Anonymous 1743, *A description of Holland. Or, the present state of the United Provinces*, 1743 London: J. and P. Knapton

Aalbers, Johan 1980, *De Republiek en de vrede van Europa*, Volume 1, Groningen: Wolters-Noordhoff / Bouma's Boekhuis.

Adams, Julia 1996, 'Principals and agents, colonialists and company men. The decay of colonial control in the Dutch East Indies', *American Sociological Review*, 61, 1: 12–28.

——— 2005, *The familial state: Ruling families and merchant capitalism in early modern Europe*, Ithaca, NY: Cornell University Press.

Adriaenssen, Leo 2007, *Staatsvormend geweld. Overleven aan de frontlinies in de meierij van Den Bosch, 1572–1629*, Tilburg: Stichting Zuidelijk Historisch Contact.

Aerts, Erik, Brigitte Henau, Paul Janssens and Raymond van Uytven (eds.) 1993, *Studia historica oeconomica. Liber amicorum Herman van der Wee*, Leuven: Leuven Universitaire Pers.

Ágoston, Gábor 2009, 'Empires and warfare in east-central Europe, 1550–1750: The Ottoman-Habsburg rivalry and military transformation', in *European warfare, 1350–1750*, edited by Frank Tallett and D.J.B. Trimm, Cambridge: Cambridge University Press.

Aksan, Virginia 2002, 'Breaking the spell of the Baron de Tott: Reframing the question of military reform in the Ottoman Empire, 1760–1830', *The International History Review*, 24, 2: 253–77.

Akveld, L.M. et al. (eds.) 1973, *Vier eeuwen varen. Kapiteins, kapers, kooplieden en geleerden*, Bussum: De Boer

Akveld, Leo, et al. (eds) 2003, *In het kielzog. Maritiem-historische studies aangeboden aan Jaap R. Bruijn bij zijn vertrek als hoogleraar zeegeschiedenis aan de Universiteit Leiden*, Amsterdam: De Bataafse Leeuw.

Allard, Carel 1695, *Nieuwe Hollandse scheeps-bouw, Waar in vertoond word een volmaakt schip, met alle des zelfs uitterlyke deelen* etc., Amsterdam: Carel Allard.

Allen, Kieran 2004, *Max Weber: A critical introduction*, London: Pluto Press.

Anderson, M.S., and Ragnhild Hatton (eds.) 1970, *Studies in diplomatic history: Essays in memory of David Bayne Horn*, London: Archon Books.

Antunes, Cátia 2004, *Globalisation in the early modern period: The economic relationship between Amsterdam and Lisbon, 1640–1705*, Amsterdam: Aksant.

Arrighi, Giovanni 2002 [1994], *The Long Twentieth Century: Money, power, and the origins of our times*, London: Verso.

Asbach, Olaf, and Peter Schröder (eds.) 2010, *War, the State and International Law in Seventeenth-Century Europe*, Farnham/Burlington: Ashgate.

Aston, Trevor (ed.) 1967, *Crisis in Europe 1560–1660*, New York, Anchor Books.

Ashworth, William J. 2003, *Customs and Excise: Trade, production, and consumption in England 1640–1845*, Oxford: Oxford University Press.

Bachman, Van Cleaf 1969, *Peltries or Plantations: The economic policies of the Dutch West India Company in New Netherland 1623–1639*, Baltimore: The Johns Hopkins Press.

Bachrach, A.G.H., J.P. Sigmond and A.J. Veenendaal Jr. (eds.) 1988, *Willem III. De stadhouder-koning en zijn tijd*, Amsterdam: De Bataafsche Leeuw.

Baena, Laura Manzano 2011, *Conflicting Words: The Peace Treaty of Münster (1648) and the political culture of the Dutch Republic and the Spanish monarchy*, Leuven: Leuven University Press.

Balen, Matthys 1677, *Beschryvinge der stad Dordrecht*, Dordrecht: Simon onder de Linde.

Bamford, Paul Walden 1956, *Forests and French Sea Power 1660–1789*, Toronto: University of Toronto Press.

Banaji, Jairus 2010, *Theory as History: Essays on modes of production and exploitation*, Leiden: Brill.

Bannermann, Gordon E. 2008, *Merchants and the Military in Eighteenth-Century Britain*, London: Pimlico.

Bartstra, Han Steffen 1952, *Vlootherstel en legeraugmentatie 1770–1780*, Assen: Van Gorcum.

Baugh, Daniel A. 1994, 'Maritime strength and Atlantic commerce. The uses of "a grand marine empire"', in *An Imperial State at War: Britain from 1689 to 1815*, edited by Lawrence Stone, London: Routledge.

———— 2004, 'Naval power. What gave the British navy superiority?', in *Exceptionalism and Industrialisation: Britain and its European rivals, 1688–1815*, edited by Leandro Prados de la Escosura, Cambridge: Cambridge University Press.

Becht, Harold Edward 1908, *Statistische gegevens betreffende den handelsomzet van de Republiek der Vereenigde Nederlanden gedurende de 17e eeuw (1579–1715)*, The Hague: L.J.C. Boucher.

Bentivoglio, Guido 1983 [1632], *Relatione delle Provincie Unite. Facsimile dell'edizione "elzeviriana" Brusselles 1632*, Florence: Centro editoriale Toscano.

Bentley, Jerry H., and Charles H. Parker (eds.) 2007, *Between the Middle Ages and Modernity: Individual and community in the early modern world*, Lanham, MD: Rowman & Littlefield.

Bijl, A. 1951, *De Nederlandse Convooidienst. De maritieme bescherming van koopvaardij en zeevisserij tegen piraten en oorlogsgevaar in het verleden*, The Hague: Nijhoff.

Bijl, M. 1981, *Idee en Interest. Voorgeschiedenis, verloop en achtergronden van de politieke twisten in Zeeland en vooral in Middelburg tussen 1702 en 1715*, Groningen: Wolters-Noordhoff / Bouma's Boekhuis.

Black, Jeremy 1999, 'War and the World, 1450–2000', *The Journal of Military History*, 63, 3: 669–81.

Blockmans, Wim 1993, 'The Economic Expansion of Holland and Zeeland in the Fourteenth–Sixteenth Centuries', in *Studia historica oeconomica. Liber amicorum Herman van der Wee*, edited by Erik Aerts, Brigitte Henau, Paul Janssens and Raymond van Uytven, Leuven: Leuven Universitaire Pers.

Blok, D.P., et al. (eds.) 1980, *Algemene geschiedenis der Nederlanden*, Volume 9, Haarlem: Fibula-Van Dishoeck.

Blom, Hans W. 1997, 'Oorlog, handel en staatsbelang in het politieke denken rond 1648', in *1648. De vrede van Munster. Handelingen van het herdenkingscongres te Nijmegen en Kleef*, edited by Hugo de Schepper, Hilversum: Verloren.

Blom, J.C.H., and E. Lamberts (eds.) 2006, *Geschiedenis van de Nederlanden*, Baarn: HB Uitgevers.

Blondé, Bruno, Eric Vanhaute and Michèle Galand (eds.) 2001, *Labour and Labour Markets between Town and Countryside (Middle Ages–19th century)*, Turnhout: Brepols.

Blussé, Leonard, and Femme Gaastra (eds.) 1981, *Companies and Trade*, The Hague: Leiden University Press.

Boels, Henk (ed.) 2012, *Overheidsfinanciën tijdens de Republiek en het koninkrijk, 1600–1850*, Hilversum: Verloren.

Böhme, Klaus, Gören Rystad, and Wilhelm Carlgren (eds.) 1994, *In Quest of Trade and Security: The Baltic in power politics 1500–1990*, Volume 1, Lund: Lund University Press.

Bonke, A.J. 1986, 'De oostelijke eilanden. De aanleg van een zeventiende-eeuws indus-triegebied', in *Van VOC tot Werkspoor. Het Amsterdamse industrieterrein Oostenburg*, edited by Werkgroep VOC-Oostenburg, Utrecht: Matrijs.

Bonke, Hans 1996, *De kleyne mast van de Hollandse coopsteden. Stadsontwikkeling in Rotterdam 1572–1795*, Amsterdam: Historisch Seminarium van de Universiteit van Amsterdam.

Bonney, Richard 1995a, 'The Eighteenth Century. II. The struggle for great power status and the end of the old fiscal regime', in *Economic Systems and State Finance*, edited by Richard Bonney, Oxford: Clarendon Press

————— 1995b, *Economic Systems and State Finance*, Oxford: Clarendon Press.

Bontemantel, Hans 1897 [1653–1672], *De regeeringe van Amsterdam. Soo in 't civiel als crimineel en militaire (1653–1672). Volume II*, edited by G.W. Kernkamp, The Hague: Nijhoff.

Boone, Marc, and Maarten Prak 1995, 'Rulers, Patricians and Burghers: The great and the little traditions of urban revolt in the Low Countries', in *A Miracle Mirrored: The Dutch Republic in European Perspective*, edited by Karel Davids and Jan Lucassen, Cambridge: Cambridge University Press.

Bos, Sandra 1998, '*Uyt liefde tot malcander'. Onderlinge hulpverlening binnen de Noord-Nederlandse gilden in internationaal perspectief (1570–1820)*, Amsterdam: IISG.

Bossaers, Katharina Wilhelmina Johanna Maria 1996, '*Van kintsbeen aan ten Staatkunde opgewassen'. Bestuur en bestuurders van het Noorderkwartier in de achttiende eeuw*, unpublished dissertation.

Bowen, H.V., and A. González Enciso (eds.) 2006, *Mobilising Resources for War: Britain and Spain at work during the early modern period*, Pamplona: Ediciones Universidad de Navarra.

Boxer, C.R. 1965, *The Dutch Seaborne Empire, 1600–1800*, London: Hutchinson.

Boxhorn, M.Z. 1674 [1650], *Verbetert en vermeerdert politijck en militair hantboecxken vanden staet der Geunieerde Provintien*, The Hague: Joannes Tongerloo.

Brake, Wayne Ph. te 1992, 'Provincial Histories and National Revolution in the Dutch Republic', in *The Dutch Republic in the Eighteenth Century: Decline, enlightenment, and revolution*, edited by Margaret C. Jacob and Wijnand W. Mijnhardt, Ithaca, NY: Cornell University Press.

Brandon, Pepijn, and Karwan Fatah-Black 2011, '"De Oppermagt des Volks". Radicale democraten in Leiden tussen nationaal ideaal en lokale werkelijkheid (1795–1797)', *Tijdschrift Holland*, 43, 1: 3–23.

Brandon, Pepijn 2011a, 'Finding Solid Ground for Soldiers' Payment: "Military soliciting" as brokerage practice in the Dutch Republic (c. 1600–1795)', in *The Spending of States: Military expenditure during the long eighteenth century. Patterns, organisation, and consequences, 1650–1815*, edited by Stephen Conway and Rafael Torres, Saarbrücken: VDM Verlag.

————— 2011b, 'Marxism and the "Dutch miracle". The Dutch Republic and the transition-debate', *Historical Materialism*, 19, 3: 106–46.

————— forthcoming, 'The Accounts of Solliciteur-Militair Paulus Gebhardt: Finance, profit and troop payments during the Nine Years' War and the War of the Spanish Succession (1689–1713)', in *The Capitalisation of War in the Late Middle Ages and the Early Modern Period*, edited by Matthias Meinhardt and Markus Meumann.

Brandt, Gerard 1687, *Het leven en bedryf van den heere Michiel de Ruiter. Hertog, Ridder, &c. L. Admiraal Generaal van Hollandt en Westvrieslandt*, Amsterdam: Wolfgang, Waasberge, Boom, Van Someren en Goethals.

Braudel, Fernand 1974, *Capitalism and Material Life, 1400–1800*, London: Fontana.

————— 2002 [1979], *Civilization and Capitalism: 15th–18th Century. Volume 3: The perspective of the world*, London: Phoenix Press.

Brenner, Robert P. 2001, 'The Low Countries in the Transition to Capitalism', in *Peasants into Farmers? The Transformation of Rural Economy and Society in the Low Countries (Middle Ages–19th Century) in Light of the Brenner Debate*, edited by Peter Hoppenbrouwers and Jan Luiten van Zanden, Turnhout: Brepols.

————— 2003 [1993], *Merchants and Revolution: Commercial change, political conflict, and London's overseas traders, 1550–1653*, London: Verso.

Brewer, John 1988, *The Sinews of Power: War, money and the English state, 1688–1783*, Cambridge MA: Harvard University Press.

————— 1994, 'The Eighteenth-Century British State: Contexts and issues', in *An Imperial State at War: Britain from 1689 to 1815*, edited by Lawrence Stone, London: Routledge.

Bromley, J.S., and E.H. Kossmann (eds.) 1964, *Britain and the Netherlands. Papers delivered to the Anglo-Dutch Historical Conference 1962*, Volume 2, Groningen: Wolters.

Bromley, J.S. 1987, *Corsairs and Navies 1660–1760*, London: Hambledon.

Bruggeman, Marijke 2007, *Nassau en de macht van Oranje. De strijd van de Friese Nassaus voor erkenning van hun rechten, 1702–1747*, Hilversum: Verloren.

Bruijn, J.R. 1970, *De Admiraliteit van Amsterdam in rustige jaren 1713–1751. Regenten en financiën, schepen en zeevarenden*, Amsterdam/Haarlem: Scheltema & Holkema.

————— 1973, 'Cornelis Schrijver (1687–1768)', in *Vier eeuwen varen. Kapiteins, kapers, kooplieden en geleerden*, edited by L.M. Akveld, Ph.M. Bosscher, J.R. Bruijn, and F.C. van Oosten, Bussum: De Boer.

————— 1993, *The Dutch Navy of the Seventeenth and Eighteenth Centuries*, Columbia, SC: University of South Carolina Press.

————— 1998, *Varend verleden. De Nederlandse oorlogsvloot in de zeventiende en achttiende Eeuw*, Amsterdam: Balans.

————— 2000, 'States and their Navies from the Late Sixteenth to the End of the Eighteenth Centuries', in *War and Competition between States*, edited by Philippe Contamine, Oxford: Clarendon Press.

──── 2003, 'Facing a New World: The Dutch navy goes overseas (c. 1750–c. 1850)', in *Colonial Empires Compared: Britain and the Netherlands, 1750–1850*, edited by Bob Moore and Henk van Nierop, Aldershot/Burlington: Ashgate.

Bruinvis, C.W. 1905, *De regeering van Alkmaar tot 1795*, Alkmaar: s.n.

Bryer, R.A. 1993, 'Double-Entry Bookkeeping and the Birth of Capitalism. Accounting for the Commercial Revolution in Medieval Northern Italy', *Critical Perspectives on Accounting*, 4, 2: 113–40.

Buist, Marten G. 1974, *At spes non fracta. Hope & co. 1770–1815*, The Hague: Martinus Nijhoff.

Burgersdijck, Fransiscus 1644, *Idea oeconomicae et politicae doctrinae*, s.l.: Lugd. Batavorum.

Burke, Peter 1974, *Venice and Amsterdam: A study of seventeenth-century élites*, London: Temple Smith.

Callinicos, Alex, and Justin Rosenberg 2008, 'Uneven and Combined Development: the Social-Relational Substratum of "the International"? An Exchange of Letters', *Cambridge Review of International Affairs*, 21, 1: 77–112.

Callinicos, Alex 2007, 'Does Capitalism Need the State System?', *Cambridge Review of International Affairs*, 20, 4: 533–49.

──── 2009, *Imperialism and Global Political Economy*, Cambridge: Polity.

Carr, William 1744 [1693], *Travels through Flanders, Holland, Germany, Sweden, and Denmark. Containing an account of what is most remarkable in those countries*, Amsterdam: Jacob ter Beek.

Carter, Alice Clare 1971, *The Dutch Republic in Europe in the Seven Years War*, London: Macmillan.

Clay, C.G.A. 1978, *Public Finance and Private Wealth. The Career of Sir Stephen Fox, 1627–1716*, Oxford: Clarendon Press.

Condorcet, A. 1804, 'Adresse aux Bataves', *Oeuvres completes de Condorcet*, Volume 16, Brunswick/Paris: Barbier, Cabanis et Garat.

Contamine, Philippe (ed.) 2000, *War and Competition between States*, Oxford: Clarendon Press.

Conway, Stephen, and Rafael Torres Sánchez (eds.) 2011, *The Spending of States: Military expenditure during the long eighteenth century. Patterns, organisation, and consequences, 1650–1815*, Saarbrücken: VDM Verlag.

Cools, Hans, Marika Keblusek and Badeloch Noldus (eds.) 2006, *Your Humble Servant: Agents in Early Modern Europe*, Hilversum: Verloren.

Cools, Hans, Steven Gunn, and David Grummitt 2007, *War, State, and Society in England and the Netherlands, 1477–1559*, Oxford: Oxford University Press.

Creveld, Martin van 1977, *Supplying War: Logistics from Wallenstein to Patton*, Cambridge: Cambridge University Press.

Dapper, O. 1663, *Historische beschryving der Stadt Amsterdam*, Amsterdam: Jacob van Meurs.

Darby, Graham (ed.) 2001, *The Origins and Development of the Dutch Revolt*, London: Routledge.

Davenant, Charles 1698, *Discourses on the Publick Revenues, and on the Trade of England, &c.* Part 2, London: James Knapton.

Davids, C.A., W. Fritschy and L.A.van der Valk (ed.) 1996, *Kapitaal, ondernemerschap en beleid. Studies over economie en politiek in Nederland, Europa en Azië van 1500 tot heden*, Amsterdam: NEHA.

Davids, Karel, and Leo Noordegraaf (eds.) 1993, *The Dutch Economy in the Golden Age*, Amsterdam: NEHA.

Davids, Karel, and Jan Lucassen (eds.) 1995a, *A Miracle Mirrored: The Dutch Republic in European perspective*, Cambridge: Cambridge University Press.

Davids, K., and others (eds.) 1995b, *De Republiek tussen zee en vasteland. Buitenlandse invloeden op cultuur, economie en politiek in Nederland 1580–1800*, Leuven / Apeldoorn: Garant.

Davids, Karel, and Marjolein 't Hart (eds.) 2011, *De wereld en Nederland. Een sociale en economische geschiedenis van de laatste duizend jaar*, Amsterdam: Boom.

Davids, Karel 2008a, *The Rise and Decline of Dutch Technological Leadership: Technology, economy and culture in the Netherlands, 1350–1800*, Volume 1, Leiden: Brill.

———— 2008b, *The Rise and Decline of Dutch Technological Leadership: Technology, economy and culture in the Netherlands, 1350–1800*, Volume 2, Leiden: Brill.

Davis, Robert C. 1991, *Shipbuilders of the Venetian Arsenal: Workers and workplace in the preindustrial city*, Baltimore: The Johns Hopkins University Press.

———— 1997, 'Venetian Shipbuilders and the Fountain of Wine', *Past & Present*, 156: 55–86.

de Bas, F., and F.J.G. ten Raa 1918, *Het Staatsche Leger 1568–1795*, Volume 4, Breda: Koninklijke Militaire Academie.

de Cauwer, Peter 2008, *Tranen van bloed. Het beleg van 's-Hertogenbosch en de oorlog in de Nederlanden, 1629*, Amsterdam: Amsterdam University Press.

de Feyter, C.A. 1982, *Industrial Policy and Shipbuilding: Changing economic structures in the Low Countries 1600–1800*, Utrecht: HES.

de Groot, Hugo 1614, *Vrye zeevaert ofte bewys van 'trecht dat den Hollanders toecompt over de Indische coophandel*, Leiden: s.n.

de Haas, Madeleine 1982, 'De gebouwen van de Verenigd Oost Indische Compagnie. De scheepswerven en de lijnbanen', in *De Verendigde Oostindische Compagnie in Amsterdam. Verslag van een werkgroep*, edited by F.M. Wieringa, Amsterdam: Universiteit van Amsterdam, Subfaculteit Sociologie/Culturele Antropologie/Niet-Westerse Sociologie.

de Jong, J.J. 1985, *Met goed fatsoen. De elite in een Hollandse stad, Gouda 1700–1780*, Amsterdam: De Bataafsche Leeuw.

de Jong, Michiel 2005, *'Staat van oorlog'. Wapenbedrijf en militaire hervorming in de Republiek der Verenigde Nederlanden, 1585–1621*, Hilversum: Verloren.

de Jonge, J.C. 1858, *Geschiedenis van het Nederlandsche Zeewezen*, Volume 1, Haarlem: Kruseman.

——— 1862, *Geschiedenis van het Nederlandsche Zeewezen*, Volume 4, Haarlem: Kruseman.

de Jongste, Jan A.F., and Augustus J. Veenendaal Jr. (eds.) 2002, *Anthonie Heinsius and the Dutch Republic 1688–1720: Politics, war, and finance*, The Hague: Institute of Netherlands History.

de Jongste, Jan A.F. 1992, 'The Restoration of the Orangist Regime in 1747: The modernity of a "Glorious Revolution"', in *The Dutch Republic in the Eighteenth Century: Decline, enlightenment, and revolution*, edited by Margaret C. Jacob and Wijnand W. Mijnhardt, Ithaca, NY: Cornell University Press.

de Kanter, J. 1795, *Chronijk van Zierikzee*, Zierikzee: Abraham de Vos.

de Kom, Anton 1934, *Wij slaven van Suriname*, Amsterdam: Contact.

de Korte, J.P. 1984, *De jaarlijkse financiële verantwoording in de Verenigde Oostindische Compagnie*, Leiden: Nijhoff.

[de la Court, Pieter] 1702 [1662], *The true interest and political maxims of the Republick of Holland and West-Friesland*, London: S.n.

de Laet, Ioannes 1644, *Historie ofte iaerlijck verhael van de verrichtinghen der Geoctroyeerde West-Indische Compagnie, zedert haer begin tot het eynde van 't jaer sesthienhondert ses-en-dertich*, Leiden: Bonaventuer ende Abraham Elsevier.

de Meer, Sjoerd 1994, *'s Lands zeemagazijn*, Zutphen: Walburg Pers.

de Schepper, Hugo (ed.) 1997, *1648. De vrede van Munster. Handelingen van het herdenkingscongres te Nijmegen en Kleef*, Hilversum: Verloren.

De Schryver, Reginald 2002, 'Warfare in the Spanish Netherlands 1689–1714: Remarks on conquest and sovereignty, occupation and logistics', in *Anthonie Heinsius and the Dutch Republic 1688–1720: Politics, war, and finance*, edited by Jan A.F. de Jongste and Augustus J. Veenendaal Jr., The Hague: Institute of Netherlands History.

de Vries, Annette 2004, *Ingelijst werk. De verbeelding van arbeid en beroep in de vroegmoderne Nederlanden*, Amsterdam: Amsterdam University Press.

de Vries, Jan, and Ad van der Woude 1997, *The First Modern Economy: Success, failure and perseverance of the Dutch economy, 1500–1815*, Cambridge: Cambridge University Press.

de Vries, Jan 1974, *The Dutch Rural Economy in the Golden Age, 1500–1700*, New Haven: Yale University Press.

——— 1978, 'Barges and Capitalism: Passenger transportation in the Dutch economy, 1632–1839', *Afdeling Agrarische Geschiedenis Bijdragen*, 21: 33–398.

——— 2008, *The Industrious Revolution: Consumer behavior and the household economy, 1650 to the present*, Cambridge: Cambridge University Press.

de Vries, Joh. 1959, *De economische achteruitgang der Republiek in de achttiende eeuw*, Amsterdam: Universiteit van Amsterdam.

de Vos, P.D. 1931, *De vroedschap van Zierikzee van de tweede helft der 16de eeuw tot 1795*, Middelburg: Den Boer.

de Wit, C.H.E. 1974, *De strijd tussen aristocratie en democratie in Nederland, 1780–1848. Kritisch onderzoek van een historisch beeld en herwaardering van een periode*, Heerlen: Winants.

────── 1974, *De Nederlandse revolutie van de achttiende eeuw 1780–1787. Oligarchie en proletariaat*, Oirsbeek: Lindelauf.

Dekker, Rudolf 1982, *Holland in beroering. Oproeren in de 17de en 18de eeuw*, Baarn: Ambo.

den Heijer, Henk 1994a, *De geschiedenis van de WIC*, Zutphen: Walburg Pers.

────── 1994b, 'Plannen voor samenvoeging van VOC en WIC', *Tijdschrift voor zeegeschiedenis*, 14, 2: 115–29.

────── 1997, *Goud, ivoor en slaven. Scheepvaart en handel van de Tweede Westindische Compagnie op Afrika, 1674–1740*, Zutphen: Walburg Pers.

────── 2005, *De geoctrooieerde compagnie. De VOC en de WIC als voorlopers van de naamloze vennootschap*, Deventer: Stichting tot Bevordering der Notariële Wetenschap.

Deurloo, A.J. 1971, 'Bijltjes en klouwers. Een bijdrage tot de geschiedenis der Amsterdamse scheepsbouw, in het bijzonder in de tweede helft der achttiende eeuw', *Economisch- en Sociaal-Historisch Jaarboek*, 34: 4–71.

Dickson, P.G.M. 1967, *The Financial Revolution in England: A study in the development of public credit 1688–1756*, London: MacMillan.

Dillo, Ingrid G. 1992, *De nadagen van de Verenigde Oostindische Compagnie 1783–1795. Schepen en zeevarenden*, Amsterdam: De Bataafsche Leeuw.

Dormans, E.H.M. 1991, *Het tekort. Staatsschuld in de tijd der Republiek*, Amsterdam: NEHA.

du Monceau, Duhamel 1759, *Grondbeginselen van den scheepsbouw, of werkdadige verhandeling der scheepstimmerkunst*, Amsterdam/The Hague: Otto van Thol / Gerrit de Groot.

Duffy, Michael, et al. (eds.) 1992, *The New Maritime History of Devon*, Volume 1, London: Conway Maritime Press.

Duits, Henk 1998, 'Ambivalenzen. Vondel und der Frieden von Münster', in *Krieg und Kultur. Die Rezeption von Krieg und Frieden in der Niederländischen Republik und in Deutschen Reich 1568–1648*, edited by Horst Lademacher and Simon Groenveld, Münster etc.: Waxmann.

Dunthorne, Hugh 1986, *The Maritime Powers 1721–1740: A study of Anglo-Dutch relations in the age of Walpole*, New York: Garland.

Elias, Johan E. 1903, *De Vroedschap van Amsterdam 1578–1795*, Volume 1, Haarlem: Loosjes.

────── 1905, *De Vroedschap van Amsterdam 1578–1795*, Volume 2, Haarlem: Loosjes.

────── 1920, *Het voorspel van den Eersten Engelschen Oorlog*, The Hague: Martinus Nijhoff.

———— 1933, *De vlootbouw in Nederland in de eerste helft der 17de eeuw 1596–1655*, Amsterdam: Noord-Hollandsche Uitgeversmaatschappij.

Emmer, P.C. 1981, 'The West India Company, 1621–1791: Dutch or Atlantic', in *Companies and Trade*, edited by Leonard Blussé and Femme Gaastra, The Hague: Leiden University Press.

———— 2000, *De Nederlandse slavenhandel 1500–1850*, Amsterdam: De Arbeiderspers.

Engelbrecht, E.A. 1973, *De Vroedschap van Rotterdam 1572–1795*, Rotterdam: Gemeentelijke Archiefdienst.

Enthoven, V. 1989, '"Veel vertier". De Verenigde Oostindische Compagnie in Zeeland, een economische reus op Walcheren', *Archief. Mededelingen van het Koninklijk Zeeuwsch Genootschap der Wetenschappen*, 49–127.

———— 2002, 'Van steunpilaar tot blok aan het been. De Verenigde Oost-Indische Compagnie en de Unie', in *De Verenigde Oost-Indische Compagnie tussen oorlog en diplomatie*, edited by Gerrit Knaap and Ger Teitler, Leiden: KITLV Uitgeverij.

———— 2003, 'Mars en Mercurius bijeen. De smalle marges van het Nederlandse maritieme veiligheidsbeleid rond 1650', in *In het kielzog. Maritiem-historische studies aangeboden aan Jaap R. Bruijn bij zijn vertrek als hoogleraar zeegeschiedenis aan de Universiteit Leiden*, edited by Leo Akveld et al., Amsterdam: De Bataafse Leeuw.

Epstein, S.R., and Maarten Prak 2008a, 'Introduction', in *Guilds, Innovation, and the European Economy, 1400–1800*, edited by S.R. Epstein and Maarten Prak, Cambridge: Cambridge University Press.

Epstein, S.R., and Maarten Prak (eds.) 2008b, *Guilds, Innovation, and the European Economy, 1400–1800*, Cambridge: Cambridge University Press.

Fatah-Black, Karwan, and Matthias van Rossum 2012, 'Wat is winst? De economische impact van de Nederlandse trans-Atlantische slavenhandel', *Tijdschrift voor Sociale en Economische Geschiedenis*, 9, 1: 3–29.

Félix, Joël, and Frank Tallett 2009, 'The French Experience, 1661–1815', in *The Fiscal-Military State in Eighteenth-Century Europe: Essays in honour of P.G.M. Dickson*, edited by Christopher Storrs, Farnham/Burlington: Ashgate.

Fockema Andreae, S.J. 1961, *De Nederlandse staat onder de Republiek*, Amsterdam: Noord-Hollandsche Uitgevers Maatschappij.

Fokkens, Melchior 1662, *Beschrijvinge der wijdt-vermaarde koop-stadt Amstelredam, van haar eerste beginselen, oude voor-rechten ... en, haar tegenwoordigen standt*, Amsterdam: Abraham en Jan de Wees.

Forrest, Alan 2003, 'La patrie en danger: The French Revolution and the first levée en masse', in *The People in Arms: Military myth and national mobilization since the French Revolution*, edited by Daniel Moran and Arthur Waldron, Cambridge: Cambridge University Press.

Franken, A.M. 1968, 'The General Tendencies and Structural Aspects of the Foreign

Policy and Diplomacy of the Dutch Republic in the Latter Half of the 17th Century',
Acta Historiae Neerlandica, 3: 1–42.

Frémont, P.J.M.R. 1906, *Les payeurs d'armées. Historique du service de la trésorerie et des
postes aux armées (1293–1870)*, Paris: Plon-Nourrit.

Frijhoff, Willem, and Rudof Dekker (eds.) 1991, *Le voyage révolutionnaire. Actes du
colloque franco-néerlandais du bicentenaire de la Révolution française*, Hilversum:
Verloren.

Frijhoff, Willem 1991, 'La société idéale des patriotes bataves', in *Le voyage révolutionnaire. Actes du colloque franco-néerlandais du bicentenaire de la Révolution francaise*,
edited by Willem Frijhoff and Rudolf Dekker, Hilversum: Verloren.

——— 2008, 'Was the Dutch Republic a Calvinist Community? The State, the Confes-
sions, and Culture in the Early Modern Netherlands', in *The Republican Alternative:
The Netherlands and Switzerland compared*, edited by André Holenstein, Thomas
Maissen, and Maarten Prak, Amsterdam: Amsterdam University Press.

Fritschy, W., and R. Liesker 1996, 'Overheidsfinanciën, kapitaalmarkt en "institutionele
context" in Holland en Overijssel tijdens en na de Spaanse Successie-Oorlog', in
*Kapitaal, ondernemerschap en beleid. Studies over economie en politiek in Nederland,
Europa en Azië van 1500 tot heden*, edited by C.A. Davids, W. Fritschy and L.A. van der
Valk, Amsterdam: NEHA.

Fritschy, W., J.K.T. Postma, and J. Roelevink (eds.) 1995, *Doel en middel. Aspecten van
financieel overheidsbeleid in de Nederlanden van de zestiende eeuw tot heden*, Amsterdam: NEHA.

Fritschy, W. 1988a, 'De patriottenbeweging in Nederland. Een verzetsbeweging tegen
een financiële oligarchie?', in *1787. De Nederlandse revolutie?*, edited by Th.S.M. van
der Zee, J.G.M.M. Rosendaal, and P.G.B. Thissen, Amsterdam: De Bataafsche Leeuw.

——— 1988b, *De Patriotten en de financiën van de Bataafse Republiek. Hollands krediet
en de smalle marges voor een nieuw beleid (1795–1801)*, The Hague: Stichting Hollandse
Historische Reeks.

——— 1995, 'Geld en oorlog. Financieel beleid in Holland en Overijssel vergeleken met
Groot-Brittannië en Oostenrijk', in *De Republiek tussen zee en vasteland. Buitenlandse
invloeden op cultuur, economie en politiek in Nederland 1580–1800*, edited by K. Davids
and others, Leuven/Apeldoorn: Garant.

——— 2003, 'A "Financial Revolution" Reconsidered: Public finance in Holland during
the Dutch Revolt, 1568–1648', *The Economic History Review*, New series, 56, 1: 57–89.

Fuks, L. (ed.) 1960, *De zeven provinciën in beroering. Hoofdstukken uit een Jiddische
kroniek over de jaren 1740–1752 van Abraham Chaim Braatbard*, Amsterdam: Meu-
lenhoff.

Gaastra, F.S. 1986, 'Arbeid op Oostenburg. Het personeel van de kamer Amsterdam van
de Verenigde Oostindische Compagnie', in *Van VOC tot Werkspoor. Het Amsterdamse
industrieterrein Oostenburg*, edited by Werkgroep VOC-Oostenburg. Utrecht: Matrijs.

———— 1989, *Bewind en beleid bij de VOC. De financiële en commerciële politiek van de bewindhebbers, 1672–1702*, Zutphen: Walburg Pers.

———— 1994, 'De mythe van de VOC', *Groniek*, 27, 124: 17–33.

———— 2002, '"Sware continuerende lasten en groten ommeslagh". Kosten van de oorlogsvoering van de Verenigde Oost-Indische Compagnie', in *De Verenigde Oost-Indische Compagnie tussen oorlog en diplomatie*, edited by Gerrit Knaap and Ger Teitler, Leiden: KITLV Uitgeverij.

———— 2003, *The Dutch East India Company: Expansion and decline*, Zutphen: Walburg Pers.

Gabriels, A.J.C.M. 1981, '"De Edel Mogende Heeren Gecommitteerde Raaden van de Staaten van Holland en Westvriesland", 1747–1795. Aspecten van een buitencommissie op gewestelijk niveau', *Tijdschrift voor Geschiedenis*, 94, 4: 527–64.

———— 1990, *De heren als dienaren en de dienaar als heer. Het stadhouderlijk stelsel in de tweede helft van de achttiende eeuw*, The Hague: Stichting Hollandse Historische Reeks.

Gawronski, Jerzy 1996, *De equipagie van de Hollandia en de Amsterdam. VOC-bedrijvigheid in 18de-eeuws Amsterdam*, Amsterdam: De Bataafsche Leeuw.

Gelderblom, Oscar, Abe de Jong, and Joost Jonker 2011, 'An Admiralty for Asia: Isaac le Maire and conflicting conceptions about the corporate governance of the VOC', in *The Origins of Shareholder Advocacy*, edited by G.S. Koppell, New York: Palgrave Macmillan.

Gelderblom, Oscar, and Joost Jonker 2011, 'Public Finance and Economic Growth: The case of Holland in the seventeenth century', *The Journal of Economic History*, 71, 1: 1–39.

Gelderblom, Oscar 2009a, 'The Organization of Long-Distance Trade in England and the Dutch Republic, 1550–1650', in *The Political Economy of the Dutch Republic*, edited by Oscar Gelderblom, Farnham/Burlington: Ashgate.

———— (ed.) 2009b, *The Political Economy of the Dutch Republic*, Farnham/Burlington: Ashgate.

Gennaioli, Nicola, and Hans-Joachim Voth 2011, 'State Capacity and Military Conflict', *Barcelona GSE Working Paper Series*, no. 593.

Gerschenkron, Alexander 1962, *Economic Backwardness in Historical Perspective: A Book of Essays*, Cambridge, MA: Harvard University Press.

Gerstenberger, Heide 2007, *Impersonal power: History and Theory of the Bourgeois State*, translated by David Fernbach, Leiden: Brill.

Willem Frijhoff and Maarten Prak (eds.) 2004, *Geschiedenis van Amsterdam*, Volume 2.2, *Zelfbewuste Stadstaat, 1650–1813*, Amsterdam: SUN.

Geyl, P. 1936, *Revolutiedagen te Amsterdam (Augustus – September 1748)*, The Hague: Nijhoff.

Giddens, Anthony 1981, *A Contemporary Critique of Historical Materialism*, Volume 1, *Power, Property and the State*, London: Macmillan.

Glete, Jan 1993, *Navies and Nations: Warships, Navies and State Building in Europe and America, 1500–1860*, Volumes 1–2, Stockholm: Almqvist & Wiksell International.

——— 2002, *War and the State in Early Modern Europe: Spain, the Dutch Republic and Sweden as Fiscal-Military States, 1500–1660*, London: Routledge.

——— 2010, *Swedish Naval Administration, 1521–1721*, Leiden: Brill.

Goossens, Thomas 2012, *Staat, leger en ondernemers in de Oostenrijkse Nederlanden. De centralisering van de militaire organisatie en het beheer van de militaire bevoorradingscontracten*, unpublished dissertation, Vrije Universiteit Brussel.

Goslinga, Cornelis Ch. 1995, *The Dutch in the Caribbean and in the Guianas 1680–1791*, Assen/Maastricht: Van Gorcum.

Graham, Aaron 2011a, *Partisan Politics and the British Fiscal-Military State, 1689–1713*, unpublished dissertation, University of Oxford.

——— 2011b, 'Warfare, Finance and the British Military Entrepreneur, 1705–1713', paper presented at the international conference 'War, the State, and Military Entrepreneurs during the Early-Modern Period', Brussels 1–2 December 2011.

Graswinkel, Dirk 1667, *Nasporinge van het recht van de opperste macht toekomende de Edele Groot Mogende Heeren de Heeren Staten van Holland en Westvriesland*, Rotterdam: Joannes Naeranus.

Grever, John Henry 1973, *The Making of Foreign Policy Decisions in the United Provinces, 1660–1668*, unpublished dissertation, Ann Arbor.

Grijzenhout, Frans 1989, *Feesten voor het vaderland. Patriotse en Bataafse feesten 1780–1806* Zwolle: Waanders.

Groenveld, Simon, Pieter Wagenaar, and Frits van der Meer 2010, 'Pre-Napoleonic Centralization in a Decentralized Polity. The Case of the Dutch Republic', *International Review of Administrative Sciences*, 76, 1: 47–64.

Groenveld, Simon, and Frederik Wagenaar 2011, 'De Republiek der Verenigde Nederlanden. Het 'makelaarskarakter' van het Nederlandse openbaar bestuur (1555–1795)', in *Duizend jaar openbaar bestuur in Nederland. Van patrimoniaal bestuur naar waarborgstaat*, edited by Pieter Wagenaar, Toon Kerkhoff and Mark Rutgers, Bussum: Coutinho.

Groenveld, Simon 1984, *Verlopend getij. De Nederlandse Republiek en de Engelse burgeroorlog 1640–1646*, Dieren: De Bataafsche Leeuw.

——— 1990, *Evidente factiën in den staet. Sociaal-politieke verhoudingen in de 17e-eeuwse Republiek der Verenigde Nederlanden*, Hilversum: Verloren.

——— 1997, 'Unie, religie en militie. Binnenlandse verhoudingen in de Republiek voor en na de Munsterse vrede', in *1648. De vrede van Munster. Handelingen van het herdenkingscongres te Nijmegen en Kleef*, edited by Hugo de Schepper, Hilversum: Verloren.

——— 2009, *Unie – bestand – vrede. Drie fundamentele wetten van de Republiek der Verenigde Nederlanden*, Hilversum: Verloren.

Habermehl, N.D.B. 1987, 'Guillelmus Titsingh. Een invloedrijk Amsterdams koopman uit de tweede helft van de achttiende eeuw (1733–1805)', *Jaarboek Amstelodamum*, 79: 81–124.

Habermehl, Nico 2000, *Joan Cornelis van der Hoop (1742–1825)*. *Marinebestuurder voor stadhouder Willem v en koning Willem I*, Amsterdam: De Bataafsche Leeuw.

Hardenberg, H. 1858, *Overzigt der voornaamste bepalingen betreffende de sterkte, zamenstelling, betaling, verzorging en verpleging van het Nederlandsche leger, sedert den vrede van Utrecht in 1713 tot den tegenwoordigen tijd*, Volume 1, The Hague: Van Cleef.

Harding, Richard 1999, *Seapower and Naval Warfare 1650–1830*, London: UCL Press.

Harding, R., and S. Solbes Ferri (eds.) 2012, *The Contractor State and its Implications (1659–1815)*, Las Palmas de Gran Canaria: Servicio de Publicaciones ULPGC.

Hart, S. 1976, *Geschrift en getal. Een keuze uit de demografisch-, economisch- en sociaal-historische studiën op grond van Amsterdamse en Zaanse archivalia, 1600–1800*, Dordrecht: Historische Vereniging Holland.

Hartsinck, Jan Jacob 1770, *Beschryving van Guiana, of de Wildekust in Zuid-America*, Volume 2, Amsterdam: Gerrit Tielenburg.

Harvey, David 2006a [1982], *The Limits to Capital*, London: Verso.

———— 2006b, 'Notes towards a Theory of Uneven Geographical Development', in *Spaces of Global Capitalism: Towards a theory of uneven geographical development*, London: Verso.

———— 2006c, *Spaces of Global Capitalism: Towards a theory of uneven geographical development*, London: Verso.

Hattendorf, John B. 2002, '"To aid and assist the other": Anglo-Dutch cooperation in coalition warfare at sea, 1689–1714', in *Anthonie Heinsius and the Dutch Republic 1688–1720: Politics, war, and finance*, edited by Jan A.F. de Jongste and Augustus J. Veenendaal Jr., The Hague: Institute of Netherlands History.

Hatton, Ragnhild 1970, 'John Drummond in the War of the Spanish Succession: Merchant turned diplomatic agent', in *Studies in Diplomatic History: Essays in memory of David Bayne Horn*, edited by Ragnhild Hatton and M.S. Anderson, London: Archon Books.

Hibben, C.C. 1983, *Gouda in Revolt: Particularism and pacifism in the Revolt of the Netherlands 1572–1588*, Utrecht: HES.

Hintze, Otto 1927a, 'Der preußische Militär- und Beamtenstaat des 18. Jahrhunderts', in *Historische und Politische Aufsätze*, Volume 1, Berlin: Koops.

———— 1927b, *Historische und Politische Aufsätze*, Volume 1, Berlin: Koops.

Hoare, Quintin, and Geoffrey Nowell Smith (eds.) 1978 [1971], *Selections from the Prison Notebooks of Antonio Gramsci*, New York: International Publishers.

Hobsbawm, E.J. 1967, 'The Crisis of the Seventeenth Century', in *Crisis in Europe 1560–1660*, edited by Trevor Aston, New York, Anchor Books.

Holenstein, André, Thomas Maissen, and Maarten Prak (eds.) 2008, *The Republican*

Alternative: The Netherlands and Switzerland compared, Amsterdam: Amsterdam University Press.

Hoppenbrouwers, Peter, and Jan Luiten van Zanden (eds.) 2001, *Peasants into Farmers? The Transformation of Rural Economy and Society in the Low Countries (Middle Ages–19th Century) in Light of the Brenner Debate*, Turnhout: Brepols.

Hoving, A.J., and A.A. Lemmers 2001, *In tekening gebracht. De achttiende-eeuwse scheepsbouwers en hun ontwerpmethoden. Met daarin opgenomen De groote Nederlandsche scheepsbouw op een proportionaale reegel voor gestelt door Pieter van Zwijndregt Pauluszoon (1757)*, Amsterdam: De Bataafsche Leeuw.

Hovy, Johannes 1966, *Het voorstel van 1751 tot instelling van een beperkt vrijhavenstelsel in de Republiek (propositie tot een gelimiteerd porto-franco)*, Groningen: Wolters.

——— 1980, 'Institutioneel onvermogen in de 18de eeuw', in *Algemene geschiedenis der Nederlanden*, Volume 9, edited by D.P. Blok et al., Haarlem: Fibula-Van Dishoeck.

Houtzager, H.L. et al. 1987, *Delft en de Oostindische Compagnie*, Amsterdam: Rodopi.

Hurtado, Manuel-Reyes García (ed.) 2009, *Ferrol año cero. Una ciudad de la ilustración*, Ferrol: Embora.

Irwin, Douglas A. 1991, 'Mercantilism as Strategic Trade Policy: The Anglo-Dutch rivalry for the East India trade', *Journal of Political Economy*, 99, 6: 1296–1314.

Israel, Jonathan I. 1982, *The Dutch Republic and the Hispanic World 1606–1661*, Oxford: Clarendon Press.

——— 1989, *Dutch Primacy in World Trade, 1585–1740*, Oxford: Clarendon Press.

——— 1991a, 'The Dutch Role in the Glorious Revolution', in *The Anglo-Dutch Moment: Essays on the Glorious Revolution and its world impact*, edited by Jonathan I. Israel, Cambridge: Cambridge University Press.

——— (ed.) 1991b, *The Anglo-Dutch Moment: Essays on the Glorious Revolution and its world impact*, Cambridge: Cambridge University Press.

——— 1998 [1995], *The Dutch Republic: Its rise, greatness, and fall 1477–1806*, Oxford: Clarendon Press.

Jacob, Margaret C., and Wijnand W. Mijnhardt (eds.) 1992, *The Dutch Republic in the Eighteenth Century: Decline, enlightenment, and revolution*, Ithaca, NY: Cornell University Press.

Jacob, Margaret C., and Catherine Secretan (eds.) 2008, *The Self-Perception of Early Modern Capitalists*, New York: Palgrave Macmillan.

Jacobs, Els 2006, *Merchant in Asia: The trade of the Dutch East India Company during the eighteenth century*, Leiden: CNWS Publications.

Janssen, Geert H. 2008, *Princely Power in the Dutch Republic: Patronage and William Frederick of Nassau (1613–64)*, Manchester: Manchester University Press.

Janssen, J.A.M.M. 1989, *Op weg naar Breda. De opleiding van officieren voor het Nederlandse leger tot aan de oprichting van de Koninklijke Militaire Academie in 1828*, The Hague: Sectie Militaire Geschiedenis Landmachtstaf.

Jonckheere, Koenraad 2008, 'The "Solliciteur-Culturel": Some notes on Dutch agents and international trade in art and applied arts', *De Zeventiende Eeuw*, 24, 2: 162–80.

Jones, D.W. 1988, *War and Economy in the Age of William III and Marlborough*, Oxford: Basil Blackwell.

Jones, J.R. (ed.) 1979, *The Restored Monarchy 1660–1688*, London/Basingstoke: Macmillan.

————— 1996, *The Anglo-Dutch Wars of the Seventeenth Century*, London: Longman.

Jonker, Joost, and Keetie Sluyterman 2000, *At Home on the World Markets: Dutch international trading companies from the 16th century until the present*, The Hague: SDU Uitgevers.

Joor, Johan 2000, *De adelaar en het lam. Onrust, opruiing en onwilligheid in Nederland ten tijde van het Koninkrijk Holland en de inlijving bij het Franse Keizerrijk (1806–1813)*, Amsterdam: De Bataafsche Leeuw.

Jourdan, Annie 2006, 'Amsterdam en révolution, 1795–1798. Un Jacobinisme batave?', *Working Papers European Studies Amsterdam*, no. 5.

————— 2008, *La révolution batave entre la France et l'Amérique (1795–1806)*, Rennes: Presses Universitaires de Rennes.

Karaman, Kivanç, and Sevket Pamuk 2010, 'Ottoman State Finances in European Perspective, 1500–1914', *The Journal of Economic History*, 70, 3: 593–629.

Kennedy, Paul 1988, *The Rise and Fall of the Great Powers: Economic change and military conflict from 1500 to 2000*, New York: Random House.

Kirk, Thomas Allison 2005, *Genoa and the Sea: Policy and power in an early modern maritime republic, 1559–1684*, Baltimore: The John Hopkins University Press.

Klein, P.W. 1965, *De Trippen in de 17e eeuw. Een studie over het ondernemersgedrag op de Hollandse stapelmarkt*, Assen: Van Gorcum.

Klein, S.R.E. 1995, *Patriots republikanisme. Politieke cultuur in Nederland (1766–1787)*, Amsterdam: Amsterdam University Press.

Klep, Paul M.M., Koen Stapelbroek, and Ida H. Stamhuis 2010, 'Adriaan Kluit's statistics and the future of the Dutch state from a European perspective', *History of European Ideas*, 36, 2: 217–35.

Knaap, Gerrit, and Ger Teitler (eds.) 2002, *De Verenigde Oost-Indische Compagnie tussen oorlog en diplomatie*, Leiden: KITLV Uitgeverij.

Knevel, Paul 2001, *Het Haagse bureau. Zeventiende-eeuwse ambtenaren tussen staatsbelang en eigenbelang*, Amsterdam: Prometheus/Bakker.

Knight, Roger, and Martin Wilcox 2010, *Sustaining the Fleet 1793–1815: War, the British navy and the contractor state*, Woodbridge, Suffolk: Boydell Press.

Knight, Roger 1999, 'From Impressment to Task Work: Strikes and disruption in the Royal dockyards, 1688–1788', in *History of Work & Labour Relations in the Royal Dockyards*, edited by Kenneth Lunn and Ann Day, London: Mansell.

Kok, Jacobus 1788, *Vaderlandsch woordenboek*, Volume 18, Amsterdam: Johannes Allart.

Kompagnie, J.H. 1979, *Het familiearchief Van Heteren, het archief van de solliciteur-militair Paulus Gebhardt en het archief van de commies van 's Lands Magazijnen te Delft, Dirk van Heemskerk*, The Hague: Rijksarchief in Zuid-Holland.

Koopmans, J.W. 1990, *De Staten van Holland en de Opstand. De ontwikkeling van hun functies en organisatie in de periode 1544–1588*, The Hague: Stichting Hollandse Historische Reeks.

Koppell, G.S. (ed.) 2011, *The Origins of Shareholder Advocacy*, New York: Palgrave Macmillan.

Korteweg, Joke 2006, *Kaperbloed en koopmansgeest. "Legale zeeroof" door de eeuwen heen*, Amsterdam: Balans.

Kossmann, E.H. 1987a, 'Volkssouvereiniteit aan het begin van het Nederlandse *ancien régime*', in *Politieke theorie en geschiedenis. Verspreide opstellen en voordrachten*, Amsterdam: Bakker.

——— 1987b, 'Dutch Republicanism', in *Politieke theorie en geschiedenis. Verspreide opstellen en voordrachten*, Amsterdam: Bakker.

——— 1987c, *Politieke theorie en geschiedenis. Verspreide opstellen en voordrachten*, Amsterdam: Bakker.

Kubben, Raymond 2011, *Regeneration and Hegemony: Franco-Batavian relations in the revolutionary era 1795–1803*, Leiden: Brill.

Kuiper, Jacques 2002, *Een revolutie ontrafeld. Politiek in Friesland 1795–1798*, Franeker: Van Wijnen.

Lachmann, Richard 2002, *Capitalists in Spite of Themselves: Elite conflict and economic transitions in early modern Europe*, Oxford: Oxford University Press.

——— 2003, 'Elite Self-Interest and Economic Decline in Early Modern Europe', *American Sociological Review*, 68, 3: 346–72.

Lademacher, Horst, and Simon Groenveld (eds.) 1998, *Krieg und Kultur. Die Rezeption von Krieg und Frieden in der Niederländischen Republik und in Deutschen Reich 1568–1648*, Münster etc.: Waxmann.

Lane, Frederic C. 1958, 'Economic Consequences of Organized Violence', *The Journal of Economic History*, 18, 4: 401–17.

Leeb, I. Leonard 1973, *The Ideological Origins of the Batavian Revolution: History and politics in the Dutch Republic 1747–1800*, The Hague: Martinus Nijhoff.

Lemmers, Alan 2005, *Van werf tot facilitair complex. 350 jaar marinegeschiedenis op Kattenburg*, The Hague: Nederlands Instituut voor Militaire Historie.

Lemmink, J.Ph.S., and J.S.A.M. van Koningsbrugge (eds.) 1990, *Baltic Affairs: Relations between the Netherlands and North-Eastern Europe 1500–1800*, Nijmegen: INOS.

Lemmink, Jacques Ph.S. 1990, 'Dutch Convoys in the Baltic during the Russo-Swedish War 1741–1743', in *Baltic Affairs: Relations between the Netherlands and North-Eastern Europe 1500–1800*, edited by J.Ph.S. Lemmink and J.S.A.M. van Koningsbrugge, Nijmegen: INOS.

Lesger, Clé, and Leo Noordegraaf (eds.) 1999, *Ondernemers en bestuurders. Economie en politiek in de Noordelijke Nederlanden in de late middeleeuwen en vroegmoderne tijd*, Amsterdam: NEHA.

Lesger, Clé 1986, *Huur en conjunctuur. De woningmarkt in Amsterdam, 1550–1850*, Amsterdam: Historisch Seminarium van de Universiteit van Amsterdam.

———— 1992, 'Lange-termijn processen en de betekenis van politieke factoren in de Nederlandse houthandel ten tijde van de Republiek', *Economisch en Sociaal-Historisch Jaarboek*, 55: 105–42.

———— 1993, 'Intraregional Trade and the Port System in Holland, 1400–1700', in *The Dutch Economy in the Golden Age*, edited by Karel Davids and Leo Noordegraaf, Amsterdam: NEHA.

———— 2006, *The Rise of the Amsterdam Market and Information Exchange: Merchants, commercial expansion and change in the spatial economy of the Low Countries, c. 1550–1630*, Aldershot: Ashgate.

Lindegren, Jan 2000, 'Men, Money, and Means', in *War and Competition between States*, edited by Philippe Contamine, Oxford: Oxford University Press.

Linebaugh, Peter 2006, *The London Hanged: Crime and civil society in the eighteenth century*, London: Verso.

Lis, Catharina, Maarten Prak, Jan Lucassen, and Hugo Soly (eds.) 2006, *Craft Guilds in the Early Modern Low Countries: Work, power and representation*, Aldershot: Ashgate.

Lis, Catherina, and Hugo Soly 1997, 'Different Paths of Development: Capitalism in the Northern and Southern Netherlands during the late middle ages and the early modern period', *Review (Fernand Braudel Center)*, 20, 2: 211–42.

Lis, Catherina, and Hugo Soly 2008, 'Subcontracting in Guild-Based Export Trades, Thirteenth-Eighteenth Centuries', in *Guilds, Innovation, and the European Economy, 1400–1800*, edited by S.R. Epstein and Maarten Prak, Cambridge: Cambridge University Press.

Lourens, Piet, Bert de Munck, and Jan Lucassen 2006, 'The Establishment and Distribution of Craft Guilds in the Low Countries, 1000–1800', in *Craft Guilds in the Early Modern Low Countries: Work, power and representation*, edited by Maarten Prak, Catharina Lis, Jan Lucassen, and Hugo Soly, Aldershot: Ashgate.

Lucassen, Jan, and Erik Jan Zürcher 1998, 'Conscription as Military Labour: The historical context', *International Review of Social History*, 43: 405–19.

Lucassen, Jan 1995, 'Labour and Early Modern Economic Development', in *A Miracle Mirrored: The Dutch Republic in European perspective*, edited by Karel Davids and Jan Lucassen, Cambridge: Cambridge University Press.

———— 2004, 'A Multinational and its Labor Force: The Dutch East India Company, 1595–1795', *International Labor and Working-Class History*, 66: 12–39.

Lunn, Kenneth, and Ann Day (eds.) 1999, *History of Work & Labour Relations in the Royal Dockyards*, London: Mansell.

Lunsford, Virginia 2005, *Piracy and Privateering in the Golden Age Netherlands*, New York: Palgrave Macmillan.

Lynn, John A. 1995, 'Recalculating French Army Growth during the *Grand Siècle*, 1610–1715', in *The Military Revolution Debate: Readings on the military transformation of early modern Europe*, edited by Clifford J. Rogers, Oxford: Westview Press.

Mann, Michael 1986, *The Sources of Social Power*, Volume 1, Cambridge: Cambridge University Press.

———— 1993, *The Sources of Social Power*, Volume 2, Cambridge: Cambridge University Press.

Marx, Karl s.d. [1867], *Capital*, Volume I, Moscow: Progress Publishers.

———— 1953, *Grundrisse der Kritik der politischen Ökonomie (Rohentwurf): 1857–1858*, Berlin: Dietz Verlag.

———— 1961a, 'Kritik des Hegelschen Staatsrechts (§§ 261–313)', in *Marx-Engels Werke*, Volume 1, Berlin: Dietz Verlag.

———— 1961b, *Kapital I. Marx-Engels Werke*, Volume 23, Berlin: Dietz Verlag.

———— 1991 [1894], *Capital*, Volume 3, London: Penguin.

Matthaeus, Christiaan Sigismund 1759, *Kort gevat jaar-boek van de edele Geoctroyeerde Oost-Indische Compagnie der Vereenigde Nederlanden, ter kamer van Zeeland ... Vervattende een naam-lyst van de heeren bewindhebberen der voorsz kamer*, Middelburg: Jan Dane.

McGee, David 1999, 'From Craftsmanship to Draftsmanship: Naval architecture and the three traditions of early modern design', *Technology and Culture*, 40, 2: 209–36.

Meijer, J.F. 1995, 'Voorstellen tot herziening van de heffing van de convooien en licenten in de jaren 1714–1720', in *Doel en middel. Aspecten van financieel overheidsbeleid in de Nederlanden van de zestiende eeuw tot heden*, edited by W. Fritschy, J.K.T. Postma, and J. Roelevink, Amsterdam: NEHA.

Meinhardt, Matthias, and Markus Meumann (eds.) forthcoming, *The Capitalisation of War in the Late Middle Ages and the Early Modern Period*.

Mémain, R. 1936, *Le matériel de la marine de guerre sous Louis XIV. Rochefort, arsenal modèle de Colbert (1666–1690)*, Paris: Librairie Hachette.

Mielants, Eric 2001, 'The Role of Medieval Cities and the Origins of Merchant Capitalism', in *Labour and Labour Markets between Town and Countryside (Middle Ages–19th Century)*, edited by Bruno Blondé, Eric Vanhaute and Michèle Galand, Turnhout: Brepols.

Mitchell, David 2010, *The Thousand Autumns of Jacob de Zoet*, London: Sceptre.

Mokyr, Joel 2002, *The Gifts of Athena: Historical origins of the knowledge economy*, Princeton: Princeton University Press.

———— 2009, *The Enlightened Economy: An economic history of Britain 1700–1850*, New Haven: Yale University Press.

Moore, Bob, and Henk van Nierop (eds.) 2003, *Colonial Empires Compared: Britain and the Netherlands, 1750–1850*, Aldershot/Burlington: Ashgate.

Moran, Daniel, and Arthur Waldron (eds.) 2003, *The People in Arms: Military myth and national mobilization since the French Revolution*, Cambridge: Cambridge University Press.

Mörke, Olaf 1997, 'Stadtholder' oder 'Staetholder'? *Die Funktion des Hauses Oranien und seines Hofes in der politischen Kultur der Republik der Vereinigten Niederlände im 17. Jahrhundert*, Münster/Hamburg: Lit.

Morriss, Roger 1992, 'Industrial Relations at Plymouth Dockyard, 1770–1820', in *The New Maritime History of Devon*, Volume 1, *From Early Times to the Late Eighteenth Century*, edited by Michael Duffy et al., London: Conway Maritime Press.

Mousnier, Roland (ed.) 1985, *Un nouveau Colbert*, Paris: C.D.U.-Sedes.

Müller, Leos 1998, *The Merchant Houses of Stockholm, c. 1640–1800: A comparative study of early-modern entrepreneurial behaviour*, Uppsala: Uppsala University Library.

Murphey, Rhoads 1999, *Ottoman Warfare 1500–1700*, London: UCL Press.

Nagtglas, F. 1888, *Levensberichten van Zeeuwen*, Volume 1, Middelburg: Altorffer.

———— 1893, *Levensberichten van Zeeuwen*, Volume 2, Middelburg: Altorffer.

Neal, Larry 1990, *The Rise of Financial Capitalism: International capital markets in the age of reason*, Cambridge: Cambridge University Press.

Neale, John 1930, 'Elizabeth and the Netherlands 1586–7', *English Historical Review*, 45: 373–96.

Nichols, G.O. 1987, 'Intermediaries and the Development of English Government Borrowing: The case of Sir John James and Major Robert Huntington, 1675–79', *Business History*, 29: 27–46.

Nijenhuis, Ida J.A. 2002, 'Shining Comet, Falling Meteor: Contemporary reflections on the Dutch Republic as a commercial power during the Second Stadholderless Era', in *Anthonie Heinsius and the Dutch Republic 1688–1720: Politics, war, and finance*, edited by Jan A.F. de Jongste and Augustus J. Veenendaal Jr., The Hague: Institute of Netherlands History.

Nimako, Kwame, and Glenn Willemsen 2011, *The Dutch Atlantic: Slavery, abolition and emancipation*, London: Pluto Press.

Noordegraaf, Leo, and Jan Luiten van Zanden 1995, 'Early Modern Economic Growth and the Standard of Living: Did labour benefit from Holland's Golden Age?', in *A Miracle Mirrored: The Dutch Republic in European perspective*, edited by Karel Davids and Jan Lucassen, Cambridge: Cambridge University Press.

Noordegraaf, Leo 2009a, 'Internal Trade and Internal Trade Conflicts in the Northern Netherlands: Autonomy, centralism, and state formation in the pre-industrial era', in *Van vlas naar glas. Aspecten van de sociale en economische geschiedenis van Nederland*, Hilversum: Verloren.

———— 2009b, *Van vlas naar glas. Aspecten van de sociale en economische geschiedenis van Nederland*, Hilversum: Verloren.

North, Douglass C., and Robert Paul Thomas 1973, *The Rise of the Western World: A new economic history*, Cambridge: Cambridge University Press.

North, Douglass C., John Joseph Wallis, and Barry R. Weingast 2009, *Violence and Social Orders: A conceptual framework for interpreting recorded human history*, Cambridge: Cambridge University Press.

O'Brien, Patrick K., and Donald Winch (eds.) 2002, *The Political Economy of British Historical Experience, 1688–1914*, Oxford: Oxford University Press.

O'Brien, Patrick 2000, 'Mercantilism and Imperialism in the Rise and Decline of the Dutch and British Economies 1585–1815', *De Economist*, 148: 469–501.

——— 2002, 'Fiscal Exceptionalism: Great Britain and its European rivals from Civil War to triumph at Trafalgar and Waterloo', in *The Political Economy of British Historical Experience, 1688–1914*, edited by Donald Winch and Patrick K. O'Brien, Oxford: Oxford University Press.

——— 2006, 'Contentions of the Purse between England and its European Rivals from Henry V to George IV: A Conversation with Michael Mann', *Journal of Historical Sociology*, 19, 4: 341–63.

Ogborn, Miles 2007, *Indian Ink. Script and print in the making of the English East India Company*, Chicago: University of Chicago Press.

Onnekink, David, and Gijs Rommelse (eds.) 2011, *Ideology and Foreign Policy in Early Modern Europe (1650–1750)*, Farnham/Burlington: Ashgate.

Onnekink, David 2007, *The Anglo-Dutch Favourite: The career of Hans Willem Bentinck, first Earl of Portland (1649–1709)*, Aldershot: Ashgate.

——— 2011, 'The Ideological Context of the Dutch War', in *Ideology and Foreign Policy in Early Modern Europe (1650–1750)*, edited by David Onnekink and Gijs Rommelse, Farnham/Burlington: Ashgate.

Oosterhoff, F.C. 1988, *Leicester and the Netherlands 1586–1587*, Utrecht: HES.

Opper, Edward 1975, *Dutch East India Company Artisans in the Early Eighteenth Century*, unpublished dissertation, Indiana University.

Ormrod, David 2003, *The Rise of Commercial Empires: England and the Netherlands in the Age of Mercantilism, 1650–1770*, Cambridge: Cambridge University Press.

Otte, Arjan 2004, 'Zeeuwse zeezaken. Een admiraliteit rond de Eerste Engelse Oorlog, 1651–1655', *Tijdschrift voor Zeegeschiedenis*, 23, 2: 142–57.

Oudendijk, Johanna K. 1944, *Johan de Witt en de zeemacht*, Amsterdam: Noord-Hollandsche Uitgevers Maatschappij.

Paesie, Rudolf 2008, *Lorrendrayen op Africa. De illegale goederen- en slavenhandel op West-Afrika tijdens het achttiende-eeuwse handelsmonopolie van de West-Indische Compagnie, 1700–1734*, Amsterdam: De Bataafsche Leeuw.

Palmer, M.A.J. 1997, 'The "Military Revolution" Afloat: The era of the Anglo-Dutch Wars and the transition to modern warfare at sea', *War in History*, 4, 2: 123–49.

Panhuysen, Luc 2009 [2005], *De ware vrijheid. De levens van Johan en Cornelis de Witt*, Amsterdam: Olympus.

Parker, Geoffrey 1970, 'Spain, her Enemies, and the Revolt of the Netherlands 1559–1648', *Past and Present*, 49: 72–95.

———— 1972, *The Army of Flanders on the Spanish road, 1567–1659: The logistics of Spanish victory and defeat in the Low Countries' wars*, Cambridge: Cambridge University Press.

———— 1979, *The Dutch Revolt*, Middlesex: Allen Lane.

———— 1988, *The Military Revolution: Military innovation and the rise of the West, 1500–1800*, Cambridge: Cambridge University Press.

———— 1995, 'The "Military Revolution, 1560–1660" – a Myth?', in *The Military Revolution Debate: Readings on the military transformation of early modern Europe*, edited by Clifford J. Rogers, Oxford: Westview Press.

Parrott, David 2001, *Richelieu's Army: War, government and society in France, 1624–1642*, Cambridge: Cambridge University Press.

———— 2012, *The Business of War: Military enterprise and military revolution in early modern Europe*, Cambridge: Cambridge University Press.

Pocock, J.G. A 1975, *The Machiavellian Moment: Florentine political though and the Atlantic republican tradition*, Princeton: Princeton University Press.

Poelhekke, J.J. 1973a, 'Kanttekeningen bij de pamfletten uit het jaar 1650', in *Geen blijder maer in tachtigh jaer. Verspreide studiën over de crisisperiode 1648–1651*, Zutphen: De Walburg Pers.

———— 1973b, 'Nijmegen, Gelderland en de "Grote Vergadering" van 1651', in *Geen blijder maer in tachtigh jaer. Verspreide studiën over de crisisperiode 1648–1651*, Zutphen: De Walburg Pers

———— 1973c, *Geen blijder maer in tachtigh jaer. Verspreide studiën over de crisisperiode 1648–1651*, Zutphen: De Walburg Pers.

Poell, Thomas 2004, 'Het einde van een tijdperk. De Bataafs-Franse tijd 1795–1813', in *Geschiedenis van Amsterdam*, Volume 2.2, *Zelfbewuste Stadstaat, 1650–1813*, edited by Willem Frijhoff en Maarten Prak, Amsterdam: SUN.

Poell, Thomas 2009, 'Local Particularism Challenged, 1795–1813', in *The Political Economy of the Dutch Republic*, edited by Oscar Gelderblom, Farnham/Burlington: Ashgate.

Pool, Bernard 1966, *Navy Board Contracts 1660–1832: Contract Administration under the Navy Board*, London: s.n.

Poole, Robert 1750, *A Journey from London to France and Holland: Or, the traveller's useful vade mecum*, London: E. Duncombe.

Prados de la Escosura, Leandro 2004, *Exceptionalism and Industrialisation: Britain and its European rivals, 1688–1815*, Cambridge: Cambridge University Press.

Price, J.L. 1994, *Holland and the Dutch Republic in the Seventeenth Century: The politics of particularism*, Oxford: Clarendon Press.

Prokhovnik, Raia 2004, *Spinoza and Republicanism*, Basingstoke: Palgrave Macmillan.

Prak, Maarten, and Jan Luiten van Zanden, 'Tax Morale and Citizenship in the Dutch Republic', in *The Political Economy of the Dutch Republic*, edited by Oscar Gelderblom, Farnham/Burlington: Ashgate.

Prak, M. 1985, *Gezeten burgers. De elite in een Hollandse stad, Leiden 1700–1780*, Amsterdam: De Bataafsche Leeuw.

———— 1991, 'Citizen Radicalism and Democracy in the Dutch Republic: The Patriot Movement of the 1780s', *Theory and Society*, 20, 1: 73–102.

———— 1999, *Republikeinse veelheid, democratische enkelvoud. Sociale verandering in het revolutietijdvlak, 's-Hertogenbosch 1770–1820*, Nijmegen: SUN.

———— 2005, *The Dutch Republic in the Seventeenth Century*, Cambridge: Cambridge University Press.

Pritchard, James S. 1987, *Louis XV's Navy, 1748–1762: A Study of Organization and Administration*, Kingston: McGill-Queens University Press.

Redlich, Fritz 1964, *The German Military Enterpriser and his Work Force: A study in European economic and social history*, Volume 1, Wiesbaden: Steiner.

———— 1965, *The German Military Enterpriser and his Work Force: A study in European economic and social history*, Volume 2, Wiesbaden: Steiner.

Reijn, G. van 1900, 'Schepen op de Admiraliteitswerf gebouwd', *Rotterdams Jaarboekje*, 7: 103–12.

Reinders Folmer-van Prooijen, C. 2000, *Van goederenhandel naar slavenhandel. De Middelburgse Commercie Compagnie 1720–1755*, Middelburg: Koninklijk Zeeuwsch Genootschap der Wetenschappen.

Reinert, Erik S. 2009, 'Emulating Success: Contemporary views of the Dutch economy before 1800', in *The Political Economy of the Dutch Republic*, edited by Oscar Gelderblom, Farnham/Burlington: Ashgate.

Richards, J.F. 1981, 'Mughal State Finance and the Premodern World Economy', *Comparative Studies in Society and History*, 23, 2: 285–308.

Rietbergen, P.J.A.N. 1988, ''s Werelds schouwtoneel. Oorlog, politiek en economie in noord-west Europa ten tijde van Willem III', in *Willem III. De stadhouder-koning en zijn tijd*, edited by A.G.H. Bachrach, J.P. Sigmond and A.J. Veenendaal Jr., Amsterdam: De Bataafsche Leeuw.

———— 1997, 'The Consolidation of the Dutch Overseas Empire: the colonial dimension of the Peace of Munster', in *1648. De vrede van Munster. Handelingen van het herdenkingscongres te Nijmegen en Kleef*, edited by Hugo de Schepper, Hilversum: Verloren.

Riley, James C. 1980, *International Government Finance and the Amsterdam Capital Market 1740–1815*, Cambridge: Cambridge University Press.

Roberts, Michael 1995, 'The Military Revolution in Europe, 1560–1660', in *The Military Revolution Debate: Readings on the Military Transformation of Early Modern Europe*, edited by Clifford J. Rogers, Oxford: Westview Press.

Rodger, N.A.M. 2004, *The Command of the Ocean: A naval history of Britain 1649–1815*, London: Penguin Books.

Rogers, Clifford J. (ed.) 1995, *The Military Revolution Debate: Readings on the military transformation of early modern Europe*, Oxford: Westview Press.

Roldanus, Cornelia W. 1938, *Zeventiende-Eeuwsche Geestesbloei*, Amsterdam: Van Kampen.

Romeijn, A. 2001, *De stadsregering van Tholen (1577-1702). Bestuur en bestuurders van de stad Tholen vanaf de Satisfactieovereenkomst met prins Willem van Oranje in 1577 tot de dood van koning-stadhouder Willem III in 1702*, Giessen: Romeijn.

Romein, Jan 1948a, 'De dialectiek van de vooruitgang. Bijdrage tot het ontwikkelingsbegrip in de geschiedenis', in *Het onvoltooid verleden. Cultuurhistorische studies*, Amsterdam: Querido.

———— 1948b, *Het onvoltooid verleden. Cultuurhistorische studies*, Amsterdam: Querido.

Rommelse, Gijs 2006, *The Second Anglo-Dutch War (1665-1667): Raison d'état, mercantilism and maritime strife*, Hilversum: Verloren.

———— 2010, 'The Role of Mercantilism in Anglo-Dutch Political Relations, 1650-74', *The Economic History Review*, 63, 3: 591-611.

Roodhuyzen-van Breda Vriesman, Thea 2003, 'Onfrisse Friese zaken. Een admiraliteit in opspraak', in *In het kielzog. Maritiem-historische studies aangeboden aan Jaap R. Bruijn bij zijn vertrek als hoogleraar zeegeschiedenis aan de Universiteit Leiden*, edited by Leo Akveld et al., Amsterdam: De Bataafse Leeuw.

Roorda, D.J. 1961, *Partij en factie. De oproeren van 1672 in de steden van Holland and Zeeland. Een krachtmeting tussen partijen en facties*, Groningen: Wolters.

———— 1964, 'The Ruling Classes in Holland in the Seventeenth Century', in *Britain and the Netherlands: Papers delivered to the Anglo-Dutch Historical Conference 1962*, Volume 2, edited by J.S. Bromley and E.H. Kossmann, Groningen: J.B. Wolters.

Rosendaal, J.G.M.M., Th.S.M. van der Zee, and P.G.B. Thissen (eds.) 1988, *1787. De Nederlandse revolutie?*, Amsterdam: De Bataafsche Leeuw.

Rosendaal, Joost 2003, *Bataven! Nederlandse vluchtelingen in Frankrijk 1787-1795*, Nijmegen: Vantilt.

———— 2005, *De Nederlandse Revolutie. Vrijheid, volk en vaderland 1783-1799*, Nijmegen: Vantilt.

Rowen, Herbert 1988, *The Princes of Orange: The stadtholders in the Dutch Republic*, Cambridge: Cambridge University Press.

Rowlands, Guy 2002, *The Dynastic State and the Army under Louis XIV: Royal service and private interest, 1661-1701*, Cambridge: Cambridge University Press.

Roy, Kaushik 2005, 'Military Synthesis in South Asia: Armies, warfare, and Indian society, c. 1740-1849', *The Journal of Military History*, 69, 3: 651-90.

Rule, John 1981, *The Experience of Labour in Eighteenth-Century Industry*, London: Croom Helm.

Scahill, Jeremy 2007, *Blackwater: The rise of the world's most powerful mercenary army*, New York: Nation Books.

Schalkwijk, J. Marten W. 2011, *The Colonial State in the Caribbean: Structural analysis and changing elite networks in Suriname, 1650-1920*, The Hague: Amrit.

Schama, Simon 1977, *Patriots and Liberators: Revolution in the Netherlands 1780–1813*, London: Collins.

——— 1991 [1987], *The Embarrassment of Riches: An interpretation of Dutch culture in the Golden Age*, London: Fontana Press.

Schilling, Heinz 1991, *Civic Calvinism in Northwestern Germany and the Netherlands: Sixteenth to nineteenth centuries*, Ann Arbor: Sixteenth Century Journal Publishers.

Schmidt, J.Th. de (ed.) 1987, *Fiscaliteit in Nederland. 50 jaar belastingmuseum 'Prof. Dr. Van der Poel'*, Zutphen: De Walburg Pers.

Schnurmann, Claudia 2003, '"Wherever profit leads us, to every sea and shore ...": The VOC, the WIC, and Dutch methods of globalization in the seventeenth century', *Renaissance Studies*, 17, 3: 474–93.

Schrikker, Alicia 2007, *Dutch and British Colonial Intervention in Sri Lanka, 1780–1815: Expansion and reform*, Leiden: Brill.

Schutte, Gerrit Jan 1974, *De Nederlandse patriotten en de koloniën. Een onderzoek naar hun denkbeelden en optreden, 1770–1800*, Utrecht: Tjeenk Willink.

Sicking, Louis 2004, *Neptune and the Netherlands: State, Economy, and War at Sea in the Renaissance*, Leiden: Brill.

Silverstein, Ken 2000, *Private Warriors*, London: Verso.

Skocpol, Theda 1979, *States and Social Revolutions: A comparative analysis of France, Russia, and China*, Cambridge: Cambridge University Press.

Smith, Adam 1999a [1776], *The Wealth of Nations*, Volume 1: Book 1–3, London: Penguin.

——— 1999b [1776], *The Wealth of Nations*, Volume 2: Book 4–5, London: Penguin.

Smith, Woodruff D. 1984, 'The Function of Commercial Centers in the Modernization of European Capitalism. Amsterdam as an Information Exchange in the Seventeenth Century', *The Journal of Economic History*, 44, 4: 985–1005.

Snapper, Frits 1959, *Oorlogsinvloeden op de overzeese handel van Holland 1551–1719*, Amsterdam: s.n.

Soll, Jacob 2009a, 'Accounting for Government: Holland and the rise of political economy in seventeenth-century Europe', *Journal of Interdisciplinary History*, 40, 2: 215–38.

——— 2009b, *The Information Master: Jean-Baptiste Colbert's secret state intelligence system*, Ann Arbor: University of Michigan Press.

Soltow, Lee, and Jan Luiten van Zanden 1998, *Income and Wealth Inequality in the Netherlands 16th–20th century*, Amsterdam: Het Spinhuis.

Sombart, Werner 1913, *Krieg und Kapitalismus*, München and Leipzig: Duncker & Humblot.

Staarman, Alfred 1996, 'De VOC en de Staten-Generaal in de Engelse Oorlogen. Een ongemakkelijk bondgenootschap', *Tijdschrift voor Zeegeschiedenis*, 15, 1: 3–24.

Stedman, J.G. 1972 [1799], *Narrative of a Five Years' Expedition Against the Revolted Negroes of Surinam*, Amherst, MA: University of Massachusetts Press.

Steensgaard, Niels 1973, *Carracks, Caravans and Companies: The structural crisis in the European-Asian trade in the early 17th century*, Copenhagen: Studentlitteratur.

Steur, J.J. 1984, *Herstel of ondergang. De voorstellen tot redres van de Verenigde Oost-Indische Compagnie 1740–1795*, Utrecht: HES.

Stevin, Simon 1649, *Verrechting van domeine. Mette contrerolle en ander behouften van-dien*, Leiden: Justus Livius.

———— 2001 [1590], *Het Burgherlick Leven & Anhangh [1590]*, edited by Pim den Boer, Utrecht: Bijleveld.

Stone, Lawrence (ed.) 1994, *An Imperial State at War: Britain from 1689 to 1815*, London: Routledge.

Storrs, Christopher (ed.) 2009, *The Fiscal-Military State in Eighteenth-Century Europe: Essays in honour of P.G.M. Dickson*, Farnham/Burlington: Ashgate.

Strubbe, Benoit 2007, 'Oorlogsscheepsbouw en werven in Zeeland tijdens de Engels-Staatse oorlogen (1650–1674)', unpublished thesis, Ghent University.

Sturkenboom, Dorothee 2008, 'Merchants on the Defensive: National self-images in the Dutch Republic of the late eighteenth century', in *The Self-Perception of Early Modern Capitalists*, edited by Margaret C. Jacob and Catherine Secretan, New York: Palgrave Macmillan.

Swart, Erik 2006, *Krijgsvolk. Militaire professionalisering en het ontstaan van het Staatse leger, 1568–1590*, Amsterdam: Amsterdam University Press.

Swart, K.W. 1994, *Willem van Oranje en de Nederlandse Opstand 1572–1584*, The Hague: SDU Uitgeverij.

Symcox, Geoffrey 1974, *The Crisis of French Sea Power 1688–1697: From the Guerre d'Escadre to the Guerre de Course*, The Hague: Nijhoff.

't Hart, Marjolein C., Joost Jonker, and Jan Luiten van Zanden (eds.) 1997, *A Financial History of the Netherlands*, Cambridge: Cambridge University Press.

't Hart, Marjolein 1987, 'Staatsfinanciën als familiezaak tijdens de Republiek. De ont-vangers-generaal Doublett', in *Fiscaliteit in Nederland. 50 jaar belastingmuseum 'Prof. Dr. Van der Poel'*, edited by J.Th. de Schmidt, Zutphen: De Walburg Pers.

———— 1993a, *The Making of a Bourgeois State: War, politics and finance during the Dutch Revolt*, Manchester: Manchester University Press.

———— 1993b, 'Freedom and Restrictions: State and economy in the Dutch Republic, 1570–1670', in *The Dutch Economy in the Golden Age*, edited by Karel Davids and Leo Noordegraaf, Amsterdam: NEHA.

———— 1997, 'The Merits of a Financial Revolution: Public finance, 1550–1700', in *A Financial History of the Netherlands*, edited by Marjolein 't Hart, Joost Jonker, and Jan Luiten van Zanden, Cambridge: Cambridge University Press.

———— 2000, 'The Impact of the Economy on State Making in Northwestern Europe, Seventeenth and Eighteenth Centuries', *Review (Fernand Braudel Center)*, 23, 2: 209–28.

————— 2011, 'De strijd om de macht: sociaal-politieke ontwikkelingen', in *De wereld en Nederland. Een sociale en economische geschiedenis van de laatste duizend jaar*, edited by Karel Davids and Marjolein 't Hart, Amsterdam: Boom.

————— 2014, *The Dutch wars of independence*, Abingdon/New York: Routledge

Taillenitte, Étienne 1985, 'Colbert et la marine', in *Un nouveau Colbert*, edited by Roland Mousnier, Paris: C.D.U.-Sedes.

Tallett, Frank, and D.J.B. Trimm (eds.) 2009, *European warfare, 1350–1750*, Cambridge: Cambridge University Press

Tallett, Frank 1992, *War and society in early-modern Europe, 1495–1715*, London: Routledge

Teitler, Ger 2002, 'De marine en de Verenigde Oost-Indische Compagnie. Staatse steun voor een benard bedrijf', in *De Verenigde Oost-Indische Compagnie tussen oorlog en diplomatie*, edited by Gerrit Knaap and Ger Teitler, Leiden: KITLV Uitgeverij.

Teschke, Benno 2003, *The Myth of 1648: Class, geopolitics and the making of modern international relations*, London: Verso.

Thompson, I.A.A. 1995, '"Money, Money, and Yet More Money!" Finance, the Fiscal-State, and the Military Revolution: Spain 1500–1650', in *The Military Revolution Debate: Readings on the military transformation of early modern Europe*, edited by Clifford J. Rogers, Oxford: Westview Press.

Tilly, Charles 1975a, 'Reflections on the History of European State-Making', in *The Formation of National States in Western Europe*, edited by Charles Tilly, Princeton: Princeton University Press.

————— (ed.) 1975b, *The Formation of National States in Western Europe*, Princeton: Princeton University Press.

————— 1992, *Coercion, Capital, and European States, AD 990–1992*, Cambridge, MA: Blackwell.

————— 1993, *European Revolutions, 1492–1992*, Cambridge, MA: Blackwell.

Tjaden, Anja 1994, 'The Dutch in the Baltic, 1544–1721', in *In Quest of Trade and Security: The Baltic in power politics 1500–1990*, Volume 1, 1500–1890, edited by Gören Rystad, Klaus Böhme and Wilhelm Carlgren, Lund: Lund University Press.

Temple, William 1673, *Observations upon the United Provinces of the Netherlands*, London: A. Maxwell for Sa. Gellibrand.

ten Raa, F.J.G. 1950, *Het Staatsche leger, 1568–1795*. Volume 7, The Hague: Nijhoff.

Terpstra, H. 1950, *Jacob van Neck. Amsterdams admiraal en regent*, Amsterdam: Van Kampen.

Thomas, Peter 2009, *The Gramscian Moment: Philosophy, Hegemony and Marxism*, Chicago: Haymarket.

Thompson, E.P. 1963, *The Making of the English Working Class*, London: Gollancz.

————— 1991, *Customs in Common*, New York: New Press.

Thurkow, C.T.F. 1945, *De Westfriese Admiraliteit*, Enkhuizen: Fas Frisiae.

Tomlinson, Howard 1979, 'Financial and Administrative Developments in England, 1660–88', in *The Restored Monarchy 1660–1688*, edited by J.R. Jones, London: Macmillan.

Torres Sánchez, Rafael (ed.) 2007, *War, State and Development: Fiscal-military states in the eighteenth century*, Pamplona: Ediciones Universidad de Navarra.

———— 2009, 'La palance de la riqueza. Las repercusiones del arsenal en el crecimiento de Cartagena durante el siglo XVIII', in *Ferrol año cero. Una ciudad de la ilustración*, edited by Manuel-Reyes García Hurtado, Ferrol: Embora.

———— 2012, 'Contractor State and Mercantilism: The Spanish-Navy hemp, rigging and sailcloth supply policy in the second half of the eighteenth century', in *The Contractor State and its Implications: 1659–1815*, edited by Richard Harding and Sergio Solbes Ferri, Las Palmas de Gran Canaria: Servicio de Publicaciones ULPGC.

Tracy, James D. 1985, *A Financial Revolution in the Habsburg Netherlands*: Renten *and* renteniers *in the County of Holland, 1515–1565*, Berkeley: University of California Press.

———— 2001, '"Keeping the Wheels of War Turning": Revenues of the Province of Holland, 1572–1619', in *The Origins and Development of the Dutch Revolt*, edited by Graham Darby, London: Routledge.

Tracy, James D. 2008, *The Founding of the Dutch Republic: War, finance, and politics in Holland 1572–1588*, Oxford: Oxford University Press.

Troost, Wout 2005, *William III, the Stadholder-King: A political biography*, Aldershot: Ashgate.

Trotsky, Leon 2010 [1929], *The Permanent Revolution & Results and Prospects*, Seattle: Pathfinder.

Udemans Jr., Willem 1757, *Korte verhandeling van den Nederlandschen scheepsbouw, zo in theorie, als in practyk, meetkunstig vertoond*, Middelburg/Amsterdam: Midd. en Amst.

Unger, J.H.W. 1892, *De regeering van Rotterdam 1328–1892*, Rotterdam: Van Waesberge.

Unger, Richard W. 1978, *Dutch Shipbuilding before 1800: Ships and Guilds*, Assen/Amsterdam: Van Gorcum.

Usher, George 2003, *Dictionary of British Military History*, London: A&C Black.

Valentyn, Francois 1724, *Oud en nieuw Oost-Indien*, Volume 1, Amsterdam/Dordrecht: Joannes van Braam.

van Aitzema, Lieuwe 1669a, *Saken van Staet en oorlogh, in, ende omtrent de Vereenigde Nederlanden*, Volume 1, *1621 tot 1633*, The Hague: Jan Veely, Johan Tongerloo, Jasper Doll.

———— 1669b, *Saken van Staet en oorlogh, in, ende omtrent de Vereenigde Nederlanden*, Volume 2, *1633 tot 1644*, The Hague: Jan Veely, Johan Tongerloo, Jasper Doll.

———— 1669c, *Saken van Staet en oorlogh, in, ende omtrent de Vereenigde Nederlanden*, Volume 3, *1645 tot 1657*, The Hague: Jan Veely, Johan Tongerloo, Jasper Doll.

van Bavel, Bas 1999, *Transitie en continuïteit. De bezitsverhoudingen en de plattelands-*

economie in het westelijke gedeelte van het Gelderse rivierengebied, ca. 1300–ca. 1570, Hilversum: Verloren.

———— 2010a, *Manors and Markets: Economy and society in the Low Countries, 500–1600*, Oxford: Oxford University Press.

———— 2010b, 'The Medieval Origins of Capitalism in the Netherlands', *Bijdragen en Mededelingen betreffende de Geschiedenis der Nederlanden / The Low Countries Historical Review*, 125, 2–3: 45–80.

van Biema, Eduard, and E.W. Moes 1909, *De Nationale Konst-Gallery en het Koninklijk Museum. Bijdrage tot de geschiedenis van het Rijksmuseum*, Amsterdam: Frederik Muller.

van Brakel, S. 1908, *De Hollandsche handelscompagnieën der zeventiende eeuw. Hun ontstaan – hunne inrichting*, The Hague: Nijhoff.

van Dam, Pieter 1929 [1693–1701], *Beschryvinge van de Oostindische Compagnie*, Volume 1.2, edited by F.W. Stapel, The Hague: Nijhoff.

van den Burg, Martijn Jacob 2007, *Nederland onder Franse invloed. Cultuurtransfer en staatsvorming in de napoleontische tijd, 1799–1813*, s.l.: s.n.

van der Heijden, Manon 2006, *Geldschieters van de stad. Financiële relaties tussen stad, burgers en overheden 1550–1650*, Amsterdam: Bakker.

van der Linden, Marcel 2007, 'The "Law" of Uneven and Combined Development: Some Underdeveloped Thoughts', *Historical Materialism*, 15, 1: 145–65.

———— 2009, 'Charles Tilly's Historical Sociology', *International Review of Social History*, 54: 237–74.

van Deursen, A.Th. 1976, 'Staat van oorlog en generale petitie in de jonge Republiek', *Bijdragen en mededelingen betreffende de geschiedenis der Nederlanden*, 91: 44–55.

———— 2006, 'De Republiek der Zeven Verenigde Nederlanden (1795–1780)', in: *Geschiedenis van de Nederlanden*, edited by J.C.H. Blom and E. Lamberts, Baarn: HB Uitgevers.

van Dijk, H., and D.J. Roorda 1976, 'Social Mobility under the Regents of the Republic', *Acta Historicae Neerlandicae*, 9: 76–102.

van Dillen, J.G. 1970, *Van rijkdom en regenten. Handboek tot de economische en sociale geschiedenis van Nederland tijdens de Republiek*, The Hague: Martinus Nijhoff.

van Goor, Jur 2002, 'De Verenigde Oost-Indische Compagnie in de historiografie. Imperialist en multinational', in *De Verenigde Oost-Indische Compagnie tussen oorlog en diplomatie*, edited by Gerrit Knaap and Ger Teitler, Leiden: KITLV Uitgeverij.

van Ittersum, Martine Julia 2006, *Profit and Principle: Hugo Grotius, natural rights theories and the rise of Dutch power in the East Indies 1595–1615*, Leiden: Brill.

van Kampen, Simon Christiaan 1953, *De Rotterdamse particuliere scheepsbouw in de tijd van de Republiek*, Assen: s.n.

van Kessel, Peter, and Elisja Schulte (eds.) 1997, *Rome / Amsterdam: Two growing cities in seventeenth-century Europe*, Amsterdam: Amsterdam University Press.

van Meer, Johanna Theresia Hubertina 1986, *De Zeeuwse kaapvaart tijdens de Spaanse Successieoorlog*, Middelburg: Koninklijk Zeeuwsch Genootschap der Wetenschappen.

van Nierop, Henk 1997, 'Politics and the People of Amsterdam', in *Rome / Amsterdam: Two growing cities in seventeenth-century Europe*, edited by Peter van Kessel and Elisja Schulte, Amsterdam: Amsterdam University Press.

———— 2001a, 'Alva's Throne: Making sense of the revolt of the Netherlands', in *The Origins and Development of the Dutch Revolt*, edited by Graham Darby, London: Routledge.

———— 2001b, 'The Nobles and the Revolt', in *The Origins and Development of the Dutch Revolt*, edited by Graham Darby, London: Routledge.

———— 2007, 'Corporate Identity and the Revolt in the Towns of Holland', in *Between the Middle Ages and Modernity: Individual and community in the early modern world*, edited by Charles H. Parker and Jerry H. Bentley, Lanham, MA: Rowman & Littlefield.

van Nimwegen, Olaf 1995, *De subsistentie van het leger. Logistiek en strategie van het Geallieerde en met name het Staatse leger tijdens de Spaanse Successieoorlog in de Nederlanden en het Heilige Roomse Rijk (1701–1712)*, Utrecht: De Bataafsche Leeuw.

———— 2002, *De Republiek der Verenigde Nederlanden als grote mogendheid. Buitenlandse politiek en oorlogvoering in de eerste helft van de achttiende eeuw en in het bijzonder tijdens de Oostenrijkse Successieoorlog (1740–1748)*, Amsterdam: De Bataafsche Leeuw.

———— 2010, *The Dutch Army and the Military Revolutions 1588–1688*, Woodbridge: Boydell.

[van Oeveren, Cornelis] [1787], *Levensbeschryving van Cornelis van Oeveren, eertyds wagenmaker, en sedert hellebaardier by het Ed. Mog. Collegie ter Admiraliteit op de Maze, te Rotterdam; ... Uitgegeven naar zyn eigen handschrift*, Rotterdam: J. Hendriksen / J. Bal.

van Rees, O. 1868, *Geschiedenis der staathuishoudkunde in Nederland tot het einde der achttiende eeuw*, Volume 2, Utrecht: Kemink.

van Rossum, Matthias 2011, 'De intra-Aziatische vaart. Schepen, "de Aziatische zeeman" en de ondergang van de voc?', *Tijdschrift voor Sociale en Economische Geschiedenis*, 8, 3: 32–69.

van Sas, N.C.F. 1989, 'Scenario's voor een onvoltooide revolutie, 1795–1798', *Bijdragen en Mededelingen Betreffende de Geschiedenis der Nederlanden*, 104, 4: 622–37.

———— 2003, 'Between the Devil and the Deep Blue Sea: The logic of neutrality', in *Colonical Empires Compared: Britain and the Netherlands, 1750–1850*, edited by Bob Moore and Henk van Nierop, Aldershot/Burlington: Ashgate.

———— 2004a, 'De vaderlandse imperatief. Begripsverandering en politieke conjunctuur, 1763–1813', in *De metamorfose van Nederland. Van oude orde naar moderniteit, 1750–1900*, Amsterdam: Amsterdam University Press.

———— 2004b, 'Talen van het vaderland. Over patriottisme en nationalisme', in *De metamorfose van Nederland. Van oude orde naar moderniteit, 1750–1900*, Amsterdam: Amsterdam University Press.

———— 2004c, *De metamorfose van Nederland. Van oude orde naar moderniteit, 1750– 1900*, Amsterdam: Amsterdam University Press.

van Spaan, Gerard 1738 [1698], *Beschryvinge der Stad Rotterdam, en eenige omleggende dorpen*, Rotterdam: Philippus Losel.

van 't Zand, Laura 1998, 'Gehannes met een admiraalsschip. De bouw van de "Een- dracht" (1652–1654)', *Tijdschrift voor Zeegeschiedenis*, 17, 2: 135–44.

van Tijn, Theo 1992, *De menschelicke societeit. Beschouwingen over staat en maatschap- pij in het zeventiende-eeuwse Holland*, Utrecht: Faculteit der Letteren, Rijksuniversi- teit Utrecht.

van Yk, Cornelis 1697, *De Nederlandsche scheeps-bouw-konst open gestelt*, Delft: A. Voor- stad voor J. ten Hoorn tot Amsterdam.

van Zanden, Jan Luiten 1993, *The Rise and Decline of Holland's Economy: Merchant capitalism and the labour market*, Manchester: Manchester University Press.

———— 2001, 'A Third Road to Capitalism? Proto-Industrialisation and the Moderate Nature of the Late Medieval Crisis in Flanders and Holland, 1350–1550', in *Peasants into Farmers? The Transformation of Rural Economy and Society in the Low Countries (Middle Ages–19th Century) in the Light of the Brenner debate*, edited by Peter Hop- penbrouwers and Jan Luiten van Zanden, Turnhout: Brepols.

van Zwyndregt, L. 1759, *Verhandeling van den Hollandschen scheepsbouw, raakende de verschillende chartres der oorlogschepen*, The Hague: Pieter van Thol.

Veenstra, Wietse 2008, 'Geld is de zenuw van de oorlog. De financiën van de Zeeuwse admiraliteit in de achttiende eeuw (1698–1795)', *Archief. Mededelingen van het Ko- ninklijk Zeeuwsch Genootschap der Wetenschappen*, 91–120.

Velema, Wyger R.E. 1993, *Enlightenment and Conservatism in the Dutch Republic: The political thought of Elie Luzac (1721–1796)*, Assen/Maastricht: Van Gorcum.

———— 2007, *Republicans: Essays on eighteenth-century Dutch political thought*, Leiden: Brill.

Vermeesch, Griet 2006, *Oorlog, steden en staatsvorming. De grenssteden Gorinchem en Doesburg tijdens de geboorte-eeuw van de Republiek (1570–1680)*, Amsterdam: Ams- terdam University Press.

———— 2009, 'War and Garrison Towns in the Dutch Republic: The cases of Gorinchem and Doesburg (c. 1570–c. 1660)', *Urban History*, 36, 1: 3–23.

Vlaeminck, Tom 2005, *Veelzijdige mannen in de haven. Een studie naar de equipagemees- ters binnen de Zeeuwse Admiraliteit tijdens de 18de eeuw*, unpublished thesis, Ghent University.

Vles, E.J. 2004, *Pieter Paulus (1753–1796). Patriot en staatsman*, Amsterdam: De Bataaf- sche Leeuw.

Voorbeijtel Cannenburg, W. 1924, 'De Nederlandsche scheepsbouw in het midden der 18de eeuw', *Jaarverslag Vereeniging Nederlandsch Historisch Scheepvaart Museum*, 76–84.

Voorthuijsen, W.D. 1965, *De Republiek der Verenigde Nederlanden en het mercantilisme*, The Hague: Nijhoff.

Wagenaar, Jan 1765, *Amsterdam in zyne opkomst, aanwas, geschiedenissen, voorregten, koophandel, gebouwen, kerkenstaat, schoolen, schutterye, gilden en regeeringe*, Volume 2, Amsterdam: Isaak Tirion.

Wagenaar, Pieter, Toon Kerkhoff and Mark Rutgers (eds.) 2011, *Duizend jaar openbaar bestuur in Nederland. Van patrimoniaal bestuur naar waarborgstaat*, Bussum: Coutinho.

Wagenaar, Pieter 2012, 'Achttiende-eeuwse overheidsfinanciën. Kleine veranderingen met grote gevolgen', in *Overheidsfinanciën tijdens de Republiek en het koninkrijk, 1600–1850*, edited by Henk Boels, Hilversum: Verloren.

Wallerstein, Immanuel 1974, *The Modern World System*, Volume 1, *Capitalist agriculture and the origins of the European world-economy in the sixteenth century*, New York: Academic Press.

——— 1980, *The Modern World System*, Volume 2, *Mercantilism and the consolidation of the European world-economy, 1600–1750*, New York: Academic Press.

——— 1989, *The Modern World System*, Volume 3, *The second era of great expansion of the capitalist world-economy, 1730–1840s*, San Diego etc.: Academic Press.

——— 2011, *The Modern World System*, Volume 4, *Centrist Liberalism Triumphant*, Berkeley: University of California Press.

Weber, Max 1924, *Abriss der universalen Sozial- und Wirtschafts-Geschichte*, München/ Leipzig: Duncker & Humblot.

——— 1947, *The Theory of Social and Economic Organization*, New York / London: W. Hodge.

Weindl, Andrea 2010, 'Colonial Design in European International Law of the Seventeenth Century', in *War, the State and International Law in Seventeenth-Century Europe*, edited by Olaf Asbach and Peter Schröder, Farnham/Burlington: Ashgate.

Werkgroep VOC-Oostenburg (ed.) 1986, *Van VOC tot Werkspoor. Het Amsterdamse industrieterrein Oostenburg*, Utrecht: Matrijs.

Westera, L.D. 1999, 'De Geschutgieterij in de Republiek', in *Ondernemers en bestuurders. Economie en politiek in de Noordelijke Nederlanden in de late middeleeuwen en vroegmoderne tijd*, edited by Clé Lesger and Leo Noordegraaf, Amsterdam: NEHA.

Weststeijn, Arthur 2010, 'From the Passion of Self-Love to the Virtue of Self-Interest: The republican morals of the brothers De la Court', *European Review of History*, 17, 1: 75–92.

Weyerman, Jakob Campo 1769, *De levens-beschryvingen der Nederlandshce konst-schil-*

ders en konst-schilderessen, Volume 4, The Hague/Dordrecht: De wed. E. Boucquet, H. Scheurleer, F. Boucquet, en J. de Jongh.

Wieringa, F.M. (ed.) 1982, *De Verendigde Oostindische Compagnie in Amsterdam. Verslag van een werkgroep*, Amsterdam: Universiteit van Amsterdam, Subfaculteit Sociologie/Culturele Antropologie/Niet-Westerse Sociologie.

Wilders, Coen 2010, *Dienstbaarheid uit eigenbaat. Regenten in het makelaarsstelsel van stadhouder Willem III tijdens het Utrechts regeringsreglement, 1674–1702*, unpublished dissertation, University of Amsterdam.

Wilson, Eric 2008, *The Savage Republic: De Indis of Hugo Grotius, Republicanism, and Dutch hegemony within the early modern world-system (c. 1600–1619)*, Leiden: Brill.

Wilson, Peter H. 2009, 'Prussia as a Fiscal-Military State, 1640–1806', in *The Fiscal-Military State in Eighteenth-Century Europe: Essays in honour of P.G.M. Dickson*, edited by Christopher Storrs, Farnham/Burlington: Ashgate.

Winius, George D., and Marcus P.M. Vink 1991, *The Merchant-Warrior Pacified: The VOC (the Dutch East India Company) and its Changing Political Economy in India*, Dehli: Oxford University Press.

Witsen, Nicolaes 1671, *Aloude en hedendaegsche scheeps-bouw en bestier*, Amsterdam: Casparus Commelijn; Broer en Jan Appelaer.

Wood, Ellen Meiksins 2002, *The Origins of Capitalism: A Longer View*, London: Verso.

Worst, I.J.H. 1992, 'Constitution, History and Natural Law: An eighteenth-century political debate in the Dutch Republic', in *The Dutch Republic in the Eighteenth Century: Decline, enlightenment, and revolution*, edited by Margaret C. Jacob and Wijnand W. Mijnhardt, Ithaca, NY: Cornell University Press.

Yntema, Richard 2009, 'The Union of Utrecht, Tariff Barriers and the Interprovincial Beer Trade in the Dutch Republic', in *The Political Economy of the Dutch Republic*, edited by Oscar Gelderblom, Farnham/Burlington: Ashgate.

Ypey, Adolf 1789, *De beroerten in de Vereenigde Nederlanden. Van den jaare 1300 tot op den tegenwoordigen tyd*, Volume 11, Amsterdam/Harlingen: Petrus Conradi/V. van der Plaats.

Zambon, Stefano, and Luca Zan 2007, 'Controlling Expenditure, or the Slow Emergence of Costing at the Venice Arsenal, 1586–1633', *Accounting History Review*, 17, 1: 105–28.

Zan, Luca 2004, 'Accounting and Management Discourse in Proto-Industrial Settings: The Venice Arsenal in the turn of the 16th century', *Accounting and Business Research*, 32, 2: 147–75.

Zandvlied, Kees 2006, *De 250 rijksten van de Gouden Eeuw*, Amsterdam: Rijksmusem.

Zuijderduijn, Jaco 2009, *Medieval Capital Markets: Markets for renten, state formation and private investment in Holland (1300–1550)*, Leiden: Brill.

——— 2010, 'The Emergence of Provincial Debt in the County of Holland (Thirteenth-Sixteenth Centuries)', *European Review of Economic History*, 14, 3: 335–59.

Zwitzer, H.L. 1978, 'De controle op de rekeningen van de solliciteurs-militair door de kapiteins in het Staatse Leger. Een handschrift uit de 18e eeuw', *Mededelingen van de Sectie Krijgsgeschiedenis Koninklijke Landmacht*, 1, 1: 75–95.

———— 1991, *'De militie van den staat'. Het leger van de Republiek der Verenigde Nederlanden*, Amsterdam: Van Soeren.

Index